From Leninism to Freedom

From Leninism to Freedom

The Challenges of Democratization

EDITED BY
Margaret Latus Nugent

Westview Press

BOULDER • SAN FRANCISCO • OXFORD

This Westview softcover edition is printed on acid-free paper and bound in library-quality, coated covers that carry the highest rating of the National Association of State Textbook Administrators, in consultation with the Association of American Publishers and the Book Manufacturers' Institute.

Copyright © 1992 by Westview Press, Inc.

Published in 1992 in the United States of America by Westview Press, Inc., 5500 Central Avenue, Boulder, Colorado 80301-2877, and in the United Kingdom by Westview Press, 36 Lonsdale Road, Summertown, Oxford OX2 7EW

Library of Congress Cataloging-in-Publication Data
Nugent, Margaret Latus, 1958–
    From Leninism to freedom : the challenges of democratization /
Margaret Latus Nugent.
        p.   cm.
    Includes bibliographical references and index
    ISBN 0-8133-8524-5
    1. Post-communism.   2. Communist countries—Politics and
government.   3. Democracy—Communist countries.   I. Title.
HX44.5.N84   1992
909'.09717—dc20   92-26060
                                                                                    CIP

Printed and bound in the United States of America

∞   The paper used in this publication meets the requirements
      of the American National Standard for Permanence of Paper
      for Printed Library Materials Z39.48-1984.

10   9   8   7   6   5   4   3   2   1

Contents

Tables and Figures

Tables

Figures

Foreword

Marshall Goldman, one contributor to this volume, suggested that if we had pinched ourselves to take note of the significance of each of the dramatic historical events that has happened in recent years, we would be covered with bruises. Ours is an epoch of freedom sounding the death knell for Leninism.

Recent events have also initiated a growth industry in studies about how these transformations came to pass, whether they will endure, and why scholars of all disciplines generally failed to anticipate the rapid downfall of communism. As this volume was planned in 1990, contributor Peter Toumanoff proposed an analysis of why economic reform was stymied in the USSR, arguing that obstacles to democratic reform would have to be overcome before the economic transformation from Leninism could occur. Accurate though Professor Toumanoff's proposed analysis was, few, including he, anticipated that circumstances would result in the disintegration of the Soviet Union so rapidly that his contribution would require repeated revisions, lest what was in fact foresight appear to be hindsight by the time of publication.

As many scholars rush to understand what they failed even to contemplate, much less predict, this book makes several contributions. It gathers the commissioned and coordinated work of several leading authorities from multiple and diverse disciplines, including history, political science, sociology, economics, and law. Thus, it presents evidence and modes of analysis from many perspectives, though none so specialized as to be inaccessible to the lay reader. Furthermore, because this is not a mere anthology, but has challenged the contributors to respond to each other's arguments, the volume allows readers to appreciate the diversity of opinion that exists on such questions as the causes for what happened and the prospects for the future. While there is a consensus that Leninism has failed, there is no firm agreement about whether and where democracy and a market-oriented economy will ultimately succeed.

But what of China? How can we conclude that communism has collapsed when 1.15 billion of the 1.71 billion people who live in non-free countries in 1992 reside in the People's Republic of China? This critical question explains why our volume encompasses not only the Soviet Union and its former satellites in Eastern Europe, but also the PRC. As the last stronghold of communism, China presents a significant and fitting contrast to the developments sweeping the former Soviet Empire. Thus, many of the authors recognized the need to turn their considerations to the questions, "Why not China?" or "If not now, when?"

The purpose of this book is to stimulate inquiry into important questions about how to facilitate and consolidate transitions from Leninism to market-oriented democracies. Its creation was sponsored by the Bradley Institute for Democracy and Public Values because of our commitment to promote the study, understanding, and practice of democracy and democratic values. We are honored to be able to present the views of so many distinguished authors, noting that these are in fact their views and should not necessarily be considered the positions of the Institute itself. And we are grateful to the Lynde and Harry Bradley Foundation for its generous and ongoing support, which makes this and all the activities of the Bradley Institute for Democracy and Public Values possible.

Thomas E. Hachey, Director
Bradley Institute for Democracy
and Public Values

1

Introduction

Margaret Latus Nugent

The past three years have seen the greatest expansion of freedom in history. Over one-third of the nations on earth, encompassing nearly 30 percent of the earth's population, have consciously decided to radically alter their political systems for more open and democratic forms of government.

-- R. Bruce McColm,
"The Comparative Survey of Freedom: 1992"
in *Freedom Review*, January-February 1992, p. 5.

Democracy is gathering momentum. Nowhere has its impact been more striking than in the triumph of freedom over Leninism in the Soviet bloc. This book was conceived after the false labor pains of democracy in China in 1989 and its birth in Poland, Czechoslovakia, Hungary, and East Germany. Little did we guess how many more dramatic events were to transpire by the date of its completion. From their different perspectives as historians, sociologists, political scientists, and economists, the contributors to this volume do far more than chronicle the transitions to democracy in Eastern Europe and the Soviet Union, contrasting these with the aborted movement toward freedom in China. They offer warnings about the difficulty of consolidating these democratic breakthroughs, provide theoretical analysis of the relationship between democratization and introducing a market-oriented economy, and discuss the importance of the rule of law and of the emergence of civil society in sustaining democracy.

From Andrew Arato through Jeff Weintraub, the authors also turn this volume into an example of the state of the scholarly study of democratic transitions from communism. The one point of agreement from all perspectives is that communism as an alternative social order has failed miserably and is discredited, even though a few faltering strongholds remain. Different views are offered about why the collapse of Leninism was not anticipated by scholars, which historical foundations and social institutions are necessary for the success of transitions to democracy and market-oriented economies, and how to assess the strength of civil society in these emerging democracies.

Perhaps the most significant disputes to which the reader should be alerted concern the definitions of key terms. Initially, we proposed to use the term Leninism to refer to that brand of communism which was characterized by an all-embracing totalitarian state dominated by the Communist party. Others prefer to use the term interchangeably with communism, Stalinism, or simply authoritarianism. Yet, the words are not synonymous for all. Marshall and Merle Goldman refer to Marxism-Leninism in contrast with Stalinism, the latter signifying the move toward a highly centralized economy with great emphasis on heavy industry. In a similar vein, while we prefer to refer to a market-oriented economy as one that favors private ownership, decentralized control, and increased reliance on market forces, some authors refer instead to a pure market or capitalist economy.

Two concepts prove particularly resistive to common understanding -- democracy and civil society -- a fact not unique to this volume. Democracy is seen by Robert Byrnes to be constitutional and representative government, by Jeff Weintraub as a process for collective decision-making about the common good, and by Peter Toumanoff as the participation of all members in political decisions, coupled with the primacy of the rule of law. For Andrzej Korbonski, democratization brings grassroots-motivated political and institutional changes including free and regular elections, pluralism, independent parties, political and economic decentralization, and freedom of expression. In contrast, Kjeld Erik Brødsgaard prefers to speak of double democratization, a term coined by David Held to refer to the expansion of autonomous civil society coupled with the restructuring of state institutions.

Civil society is the concept where the reader should be most attentive to the particular definition of the author. Several authors use the term according to its more common usage in those societies which have thrown off the yoke of Leninism. To them, against the all-embracing totalitarianism of Leninism, civil society is simply all that is *not* the state. In contrast, Jeff Weintraub makes distinctions among the state, civil society, and political society. Andrew Arato's complex definition of civil society differentiates between civil society as a movement versus civil society as an institution or set of institutions. Kjeld Erik Brødsgaard relies upon a conception of civil society that combines consideration of a plurality of autonomous interests outside the state with aspects of civil society that actually penetrate and transform the state. Those seeking theoretical discussions of the concept should pay particular attention to the contributions by Kamenka, Arato, and Brødsgaard, but all should be aware of the differences that exist in the understanding of civil society.

As editor, I wish that with a dictatorial hand I could impose uniformity in the definition of terms and coerce consensus among the authors about how these transitions from Leninism to freedom came to be, which political, economic, and social institutions will sustain them, and what the future will hold. But as pluralism flourishes in the world, so it finds a stronghold in the academic literature about democratization. Thus, I encourage the reader to engage each of the following contributions with a critical eye and discerning mind, seeking for truth that may better emerge through the intellectual interaction of diverse viewpoints than from the apparent consistency of a monograph.

In the following chapter, Marshall and Merle Goldman explore the origins of the crisis of Leninism from two directions. On the one hand, they examine the reasons why communism was apparently partially successful for a time, especially in the USSR and China, and discuss the historical foundations for this success. On the other hand, they note the irony that the seeds of the fall of Leninism were sown in its own practice, such as the economic inadequacies of the command system and the alienation of the repressed populace. In their assessment, Mikhail Gorbachev played the decisive role in the democratic breakthroughs in Eastern Europe and the Soviet Union, an influence that has been lacking in China and that partially explains the PRC's resistance to further reform.

The historical contribution of Robert Byrnes focuses on a case study of the authoritarian tradition in Russia to assess the influence of historical factors on the prospects for successful transitions to democracy there and elsewhere in Eastern Europe. The highly centralized and autocratic regimes dating back to the tenth century, the influence and weaknesses of the Russian Orthodox Church, the ambivalent relationship between various Russian rulers and the West, and the absence of a sense of common values, culture, and traditions are among the factors that inclined the Russian peoples to accept their fate under Leninism. Yet, Byrnes echoes the Goldmans in citing ways in which the achievements of the communist state in the Soviet Union -- and even its dominance of Eastern Europe -- have contributed to the pressures that now impel it towards democracy.

In his philosophical chapter, Jeff Weintraub explicates the tensions between a market-oriented economic system and a democratic political system. He argues that the two are neither inexorably incompatible (as some have previously argued) nor perfectly complementary, as others contend. Because democracy is based on the collective decisions of individual actors, whereas the market features the "invisible hand" which provides automatic regulation for the self-interested actions of individuals, theirs is a marriage not of convenience, but of inconvenience. In his examination of the requirements for democracy, Weintraub also contributes what he terms a "complexification" of the analysis used to discuss the balance between individuals and the state. Relying on the political sociology of Alexis de Tocqueville, he suggests that it may be helpful to distinguish not merely between the state and civil society (with the latter being the residual of all that which is not controlled by the state), but among civil society, political society, and the state. Democracy requires political society as the means by which individuals can make collective decisions to protect against both the centralizing tendency of the state and the danger that the self-interested pursuits of civil society will lose sight of the common welfare.

Political scientist Edward Friedman, while suggesting policies that may assist the consolidation of democracy in those countries that have experienced a breakthrough from Leninism, also cautions that transitions to democracy have never been easy. His analysis complements Robert Byrnes in explaining why the move from Leninism to freedom will be even more difficult than other democratic revolutions have experienced. Democratizing regimes must combat the major obstacles of Leninism: the military and coercive apparatus and the command economy. To overcome these obstacles, he recommends limiting the scope of government by implementing federal structures to adapt to the political geography. Political institutions and compromises must be carefully negotiated with an eye to social equity so as to maintain a consensus of support among diverse peoples. Friedman also warns both democratizing countries and the international community to provide economic aid and to promote fairness in the transition to the market-oriented economies that must accompany political reform, lest the democratic consensus be lost in favor of communalism.

To Friedman's cautions about the political, social, and economic obstacles to consolidating democracy in post-Leninist societies, Elizabeth Clayton adds a detailed exploration of the challenges of moving from a command to a market-oriented economy. She relies heavily upon the concept of a "social contract" to legitimize and support the actions of the new economies as well as those of the transitioning state. The expectations and beliefs of the old Marxist regimes must be overcome in order to foster two fundamental features of the market -- private property and entrepreneurship -- as well as the legal structures necessary to sustain them. She also examines the way the history of Leninism generates particular challenges to reformers who seek to decontrol prices, regulate monopolies, reform banking and currency, and establish equitable public finance systems. Yet, because the resolution of these problems depends upon acceptance of a new, if implicit, social contract, each society will have to craft its own solutions. The technical requirements of a market-oriented economy may be universal, but the ways of institutionalizing them are not.

The role of law is fundamental in reformulating the social contract in Leninist states on the path to democracy. Alice Tay distinguishes the arbitrary and instrumental use of law by Leninist regimes from its role in democratic countries that value the ideal of the rule of law. She explores whether other emerging democracies have the necessary legal traditions to facilitate the transition to a stronger role for law and the judiciary. She also traces promising developments in the status of law, the legal profession, and the judiciary in the USSR and China. Finally, Professor Tay sets the stage for the discussion of the importance of civil society, as she notes the interrelationship of the development of civil society and law and how both must be generated from below rather than orchestrated from above.

Neither democratic revolutions nor consolidated democracies are made solely out of political institutions and economic reforms. They also rest upon civil society -- an elusive concept that is examined in the next two chapters. Eugene Kamenka begins his exploration of the importance of civil society in the revolutions from Leninism to freedom with a discussion of the significance of and factors motivating these transitions. He then traces some developments in the concept of civil society, especially favoring views that see civil society as a complex of factors independent of the state and capable of confronting it. He concludes with an examination of the historical roots and current status of civil society in Russia, China, and Eastern Europe, noting that, while the prospects for civil society are weakest in China, the other countries must also rebuild from the damage done by the totalitarian Leninist state.

Andrew Arato examines two concrete instances of civil society facilitating the transition to democracy as he contrasts the experiences of Poland and Hungary. He traces the evolution from the movement form of civil society, based on Solidarity in Poland and the *samizdat* and other new associations and diverse social movements in Hungary, to the institutionalization of civil society. Illustrating Alice Tay's claim that law reinforces civil society, Arato discusses how a critical issue for Poland was the legalization of Solidarity, whereas in Hungary it was the revision of the law of association. Discussing the role of civil society in consolidating democracy, Arato warns about the danger of subsuming under civil society to political society. Especially in Hungary, he claims that the new political society which was to mediate between the state and civil society not only led to the demobilization of the latter, but to its intentional marginalization. He concludes that only a firmly institutionalized civil society can fully secure freedom in former Leninist societies.

Turning from more theoretical considerations about the transitions from Leninism to freedom, Stephen Szabo's article on Germany is the first of

the case studies on the prospects for consolidating the emerging democracies. In contrast with other nations in Central and Eastern Europe, Szabo
argues that East Germany benefits uniquely from a solid foundation for
a democratic political culture, the inheritance of democratic political
institutions, and the advantage of significant economic aid -- all because
of its reunification with West Germany. Arguing that despite the presence
of neo-Nazi groups these political and economic circumstances will enable
the unified Federal Republic to address "the German question" (how to
sustain a democracy), Szabo concludes with some suggestions about the
political impact the former German Democratic Republic will likely have
on the overall balance of German politics.

Andrzej Korbonski explores the transformations of Czechoslovakia,
Hungary, and Poland through the use of a schema that moves from
"background conditions" (economic difficulties, divisions within the
Communist party, the re-emergence of civil society, and political reforms)
through "changeover conditions" (changes in the Communist party,
government, and economy) to "democratization conditions" (emergence
of pluralism, free elections, freedom of expression, and economic
decentralization). He sees these eleven variables as contributing to the
pace and character of the democratic transitions in these countries, with
the twelfth variable, the attitude of the Soviet Union toward changes in
the members of the bloc, as the necessary but not sufficient condition for
the end of Leninism in these countries in 1989.

In her detailed historical analysis of the movement toward democracy
in Yugoslavia, Barbara Jelavich describes how deep-seated nationalist
tensions have brought the region to economic and political crisis and civil
strife. Yugoslavia presents a case of which Friedman warns, where
communalist drives undermine the prospects for consolidating a democracy, even though many of the republics in Yugoslavia have some historical
foundations in democratic rule. The instability of bitter ethnic conflict,
which found expression in democratic elections and referenda on
independence, turns law into a tool of one regime against another, makes
coordinated economic reform impossible, and obstructs the careful political
balancing act for which Friedman calls.

Economist Peter Toumanoff uses the case of the USSR to present a
model for understanding the interrelationship of economic decentralization
and democratic reform. He argues that there is a synergistic relationship
that most favors marketization and democratization when they go hand
in hand, rather than attempting one without the other. Both the historic
failure of the USSR to achieve economic decentralization in the absence of
democratic reform and its rapid demise once democratic reforms were
embraced support Toumanoff's thesis. Applying this model to the
individual republics of the former USSR, he suggests that those with more
advanced economic development, greater ethnic homogeneity, and smaller

population are the most likely to succeed in consolidating their transformations.

Turning to the greatest country that has so far resisted the wave of democracy, Kjeld Erik Brødsgaard offers a detailed summary of economic and political reforms in China since 1978, followed by their retrenchment in 1979, subsequent reintroduction of reforms in the 1980s, and renewed repression after 1989. He argues that such reforms fostered the development of civil society in two manifestations -- voluntary organizations and associations outside the state, and private enterprises with *guanxi* ties within the state through local party officials. Thus, part of civil society in China actually stems from and penetrates the state. In contrast with civil society in Eastern Europe and the former USSR, the lines between civil society and the state in China are quite blurred. Despite significant reversals in the post-Tiananmen Square era, Brødsgaard still believes that there is a weak but emerging civil society in the People's Republic of China that may be the foundation of a new democracy movement once the leadership changes.

In our conclusion, Su Shaozhi and I summarize the lessons of this volume about the process of the transformation to democracy and market-oriented economies and the obstacles in the path of such successful transitions. We assess the prospects for the eventual consolidation of reform in the former Leninist societies in Eastern Europe and the former USSR. As China appears to be the last major holdout in this recent era of democracy, we examine why it has not yet followed the path of the USSR, yet we predict that, in the long run, its eventual transformation is likely.

2

To Leninism and Back

Marshall I. Goldman
and
Merle Goldman

In retrospect, it is difficult to understand how anyone could have believed that communism or its actualization in Marxism-Leninism would triumph. Even those few who still believe it, such as Fidel Castro and Deng Xiaoping, find it harder and harder to convince others that Marxism-Leninism is the wave of the future. True, China's elderly leaders continue to assert that it will ultimately triumph, but their deeds differ from their words. Whatever they might say about it, the Chinese continue to facilitate the growth of the market, joint ventures and private investment by foreigners as well as private business in both the countryside and urban areas.

Until just before the decade of the 1980s, however, the failings of Marxism-Leninism and the superiority of democracy and the market system were not always that obvious. Even those of us who early on warned that the Soviet Union was in crisis and that the Chinese totalitarian system was intolerable had some occasional doubts. Much as we discounted the barrage of criticisms of our society from Soviet and Chinese propagandists, the United States was vulnerable to criticism. As long as we had to contend with recessions, unemployment, inflation, income inequalities, racism and discrimination of one sort or another, there was still the possibility that there might be a better way.

Occasionally there would be signs that all was not well in the Communist world. Groups of Germans, Hungarians, Czechs and Poles would sometimes tolerate no more and would strike or riot. There was no way of knowing, however, whether this was genuine protest or a CIA or counter-revolutionary plot by a small group of malcontents, as Communist apologists always insisted. Besides, who were we to gloat, with our crime, strikes and periodic riots? Inevitably, protests within the Bloc always seemed to subside, suggesting that, whatever the source of the protest, it was not due to a structural flaw.

Whatever our recurring questions, they were suddenly answered by what can only be called the near simultaneous volcanic eruption in what had been assumed to be the essentially quiescent Marxist-Leninist world. As one Communist country after another in Europe suddenly reconsidered Marxism-Leninism's superiority and, ultimately, its failings, the Western nations were caught by surprise.

Strangely enough it was the Chinese, beginning in the late 1970s, and not the East Europeans who began the unraveling of the Stalinist model of Marxism-Leninism. Their first move was to decollectivize the countryside. Although this bold dismantling of collectivized agriculture, affecting about 80 percent of China's population, met some bureaucratic resistance, it was not aborted by party and state officials. Because of the Cultural Revolution (1966-1976), the bureaucracy was weakened and peasants with the support of local officials took their original plots out of the commune. Because the per-capita production of Chinese peasants had not increased since 1957, instead of stopping this process, the Deng Xiaoping regime encouraged it.

In 1985, the Soviet Union also began to break out of Stalin's swaddling clothes, but unlike China, its break was in the political rather than the economic sphere. The challenge began with the selection of Mikhail Gorbachev as General Secretary in March 1985, but once underway, the movement spread relatively quickly to Eastern Europe. By 1991, virtually every country of Eastern Europe, as well as several of the republics in the Soviet Union, had swept their Communist parties and governments from power.

To Leninism and the Seeds of Its Own Destruction

To understand the reasons for the unraveling of the Communist world, it is necessary to retrace the evolution of the Communist movement. As several observers long ago pointed out, Karl Marx addressed his theory of revolution to the wrong audience.[1] Marx's effort to overthrow the bourgeoisie, give power to the proletariat, end exploitation, and ultimately bring about the withering away of the state was intended to attract the proletarian class in an advanced industrial society. But once industrialization was underway, most workers preferred bettering their economic status rather than their political power. Contrary to what he had anticipated, Marx's ideas seemed much more attractive to intellectuals in the developing world where industrialization had not yet begun or was just beginning than to the proletariat.

Although intended as a prescription for alleviating the abuses of capitalism, newly triumphant Communist leaders and third world leaders took Marxism-Leninism as a recipe for industrialization. Except for capitalism, there appeared to be no other route to economic wealth. In addition, capitalism always seemed to reward the few rather than the many. In any event, the dictatorship of the proletariat or rather the Communist party with its intellectuals, seemed to be the perfect vehicle for mobilizing capital and labor and overseeing the transformation of a backward agrarian country into a modern industrialized society.

Such an approach, however, proved to be very costly. In the capitalist countries, the bourgeoisie had undertaken the difficult work of imposing high savings rates and transforming what had been a relatively relaxed agrarian work force into a disciplined industrial proletariat. Since in Communist countries the capitalists were removed, the Communist parties had to implement industrialization. Because these countries lacked facilitating economic and political institutions such as a middle class with independent incomes, guilds and institutional constraints on unlimited power, however, their "transformations" were accompanied by social, structural and political regimentation and inherent abuses which hindered their economic as well as political modernization.

When Lenin returned to Petrograd from Switzerland in 1917, he understood immediately that if the Marxist concept of communism was to prevail inside the Russian empire, it required some basic readjustment. As was true virtually everywhere that Communist parties came to power, there were few members of the proletarian class involved in the process. As in China, the rural residents in Russia were about eighty percent of the population. In 1913 industrial workers accounted for only fifteen percent of the work force. In 1924, in the aftermath of World War I and War Communism, the proletariat had actually shrunk to only ten percent of the population.[2] In a showdown, there was no way that the proletariat, even if it were joined by intellectuals, could prevail. Faced with no other alternative, Lenin broadened his coalition to include the peasants. Because Marx believed that peasants were incapable of revolution, Lenin was forced to turn Marx upside down, by promising "Bread, Peace and Land." The land was offered as a bribe to the peasants. The Bolsheviks, therefore, gained the support of the peasants and took peasant support away from the peasant-oriented parties such as the Socialists-Revolutionaries. Consequently a large enough percentage of peasants did not oppose the Bolsheviks. As promised, except for a few large farms claimed by the state, the peasants took control over the land they farmed.

This pattern was followed throughout most of the Communist world. Subsequent Communist victories embraced the peasants and provided for the land to be taken from the landlords and divided among the peasants. China was an extreme case. Because of the overwhelming number of peasants and tiny number of workers, Mao Zedong treated the peasants, rather than the workers, as the main force of the revolutionary movement.

Once in power, the new Communist leaderships found themselves constrained not only by the poverty and backwardness of their countries and the hostility of the capitalist world, but also by circumstances of their own making. In the case of the Soviet Union, for example, at first the Bolsheviks were hard pressed to do much more than hold onto power. Faced simultaneously with fighting a civil war at home and fending off external threats from abroad, the Soviet leadership also sought to revive an economy exhausted by all the turmoil. Although Lenin turned to the New Economic Policy (NEP), a mixture of state ownership and private enterprise, Stalin, upon assuming power in the late 1920s, was determined to industrialize the economy as quickly as possible. He sought not only to provide the Soviet people with a more prosperous life, but also to insure that the Soviet Union could withstand foreign aggression and become a major power. This goal necessitated a rapid rate of economic growth, with emphasis on heavy industry, requiring high rates of investment and saving, higher in fact than normally achieved by the Western world. Again, this pattern was to be adopted by almost all subsequent converts to communism. The decision to mount a forced march towards industrialization with its underlying high rate of investment almost inevitably necessitates a smaller investment in consumption. The consumption remainder is even smaller if the leaders also decide that industrialization must be accompanied by a military build-up.

With a majority of the population illiterate and rural and the GNP low, Stalin quickly realized that there was a limited pool of domestic talent available to staff his industrializing society and no readily available sources of capital. Consequently, he went beyond a simple nationalization of the industrial means of production that would have satisfied Marxist-Leninist prerequisites and decided also to impose arbitrary targets for savings and for capital accumulation. To rely only on high interest rates to attract savings would have required too much time and voluntary cooperation. In addition, high rates of growth were almost sure to give rise to higher prices, which would further reduce the effectiveness of interest rates in stimulating capital formation.

Thus as in everything else, Stalin took direct action. He simply ordered that resources be withheld from consumption and diverted to capital formation. Alternatively, when the foreign markets permitted, such goods were used for exports. Construction materials for housing, therefore, were shunted to factory construction. Even though consumption suffered, in the early days when communism was still in its exuberant, idealistic stage, there seemed to be relatively widespread support for such policies. That was also true in China and even Eastern Europe. The support was also a reflection of nationalistic pride. Russia was finally rousing itself and

China, reunited by the Communist party, would finally become "rich and powerful" and stand up to the West; goals it had been searching for since the late nineteenth century. Such chauvinistic assertions even convinced many émigrés, including some who had thought they had left their countries forever, to return home to participate in building their nation as well as socialism. Often the return of the émigrés was supplemented by a number of idealists of other nationalities, who, although less interested in the nationalistic aspects, nonetheless wanted to share in the construction of the great new world promised by Marx, Lenin, and Mao.

Once industrialization had been achieved, it was taken for granted that the accumulated wealth would be used to provide the consumer goods and the housing that had been temporarily sacrificed. Generally, there was little concern that the use of the conventional economic mechanisms of interest rates, prices, profits and markets had been sharply circumscribed. Central planning and planners and a small group of "wise" leaders would handle such matters. Surprisingly, there was little concern about the political impact of such policies. But once Stalin, Mao and other party general secretaries were committed to such an approach, it was inevitable that such leaders would ultimately acquire massive political as well as economic powers. Given their role and the enormous power that evolved from it, even the most balanced of individuals would be unable to restrain himself or prevent the abuses of those around him. Equally important, neither China nor the Soviet Union, nor for that matter most of the other countries of the Communist bloc with the exception of Czechoslovakia, had had much experience with democratic traditions. Czars, kings, and emperors did not concern themselves with checks and balances and neither did the new Communist party secretaries.

If anything, the "new class," as Milovan Djilas called them, were even more powerful than the former czars and emperors because of their control over the economy as well as the political system.[3] For the most part, the pre-Communist regimes limited their control primarily to the political sphere. However, by nationalizing the means of production and subjecting them to central planning, the triumphant Communist leadership took onto themselves control over economic as well as political matters, later extending that control to cultural, intellectual and personal matters. As a result, the rudimentary non-governmental political as well as cultural organizations and activities that began to emerge in the late nineteenth and early twentieth centuries in Russia and China -- the beginnings of civil society -- were eliminated. Not many, therefore, were willing to challenge state decrees, when to do so was likely to mean unemployment, poor housing, lack of medical care and education for one's children, and in many cases imprisonment.

Historically, economic independence has frequently given rise to political assertiveness, pluralism, and even demands for individual independence. Stalin and Mao were determined to prevent that. Thus, by taking control of both political and economic institutions, the Communists made it virtually impossible to challenge their authority effectively. At the same time, the public was asked to make more far reaching sacrifices than they would have accepted voluntarily or than would have been possible with some kind of political and economic feedback. Standard practice in the early days of communism was for the planners to assign overly ambitious production targets to factories. When asked if such impossible plans were feasible, most party "shock" workers would ask to be assigned even higher targets. Few challenged these assertions, even though they knew that the original targets were unrealistic. Seldom would anyone demur, for fear of retribution. One did not want to risk visits from the secret police, loss of privileges, cut-backs in ration allowances, loss of housing, and even a loss of a job.

In their determination to mobilize the country's economic resources as rapidly as possible, Soviet leaders made some serious mistakes. At the time some ideological and even economic justifications were offered for their institutional innovations, if not breakthroughs. Later-day Communist leaders of other countries such as China and North Korea instituted similar practices, even though by the early 1950s they could see that some of them had been ill-suited for themselves as well as the Soviet Union. Either they believed their own propaganda or they believed they could do better. New Communist leaders often acted like highly disciplined marching soldiers who followed blindly those in front of them even though it meant stepping into the same mud puddle. These practices not only meant sacrifices in the present for some distant future, but they also imposed a legacy of resentments and distortions that would live on long after the "reforms" to remedy them were instituted. Such actions may have brought short-term results in the increased production of iron and steel, but as history has shown, these short-term panaceas created long-range political and economic complications, in effect a sort of Faustian bargain that encumbered future growth.

A prime example of such an institutional time bomb was the collectivization of agriculture. Heeding Lenin's call in 1917 to take the land from the landlords, the peasants and recent urban residents eagerly joined in the movement to establish their own farms. The number of farms in the Soviet Union rose from 427,000 in 1917 to 463,000 in 1919.[4] Admittedly, the increase in the number of farms came at the expense of economies of scale that the fewer but larger pre-revolutionary farms were able to generate. This led to a drop in the harvest. In addition, the larger number of small farmers were less interested in marketing their grain than the smaller number of larger farmers. According to the figures used by Stalin, the marketed share of grain fell by about 50 percent.[5] Stalin was using inappropriate data; the harvest and the amount marketed may not have diminished as much as he reported. Nevertheless, with shortages of food appearing in the cities and the state unable to set aside enough grain to export,[6] Stalin believed the peasants were strangling the country. Moreover, Stalin accepted the Marxist view that the peasants as a class tended to be selfish and would rather consume grain themselves than sell it for the greater good of the Soviet state.

Consequently, Stalin endorsed the plan to collectivize Soviet agriculture as the only way to obtain the agricultural surplus needed to finance his industrialization effort. In the late 1920s, he ordered the conversion of private farms into collective farms in order to gain a larger portion of their output for use by the state. The land, livestock and equipment were confiscated by the government. While in theory these farms would be run by the peasants themselves in the form of cooperative farms, in actual fact they were taken over and closely controlled by the state.

The peasants viewed collectivization as an act of betrayal. After all, they had supported Lenin because he had promised them land. He had backtracked a bit during the period of War Communism, but in the NEP period peasants were basically allowed to run their own farms. Beginning with Stalin, however, they once again became enserfed. To most peasants, there was little difference between the power of the chairman of the collective farm and the pre-revolutionary landlord. True, it was the state, not the landlord that claimed the title to the peasants' land, livestock and equipment, but the collective farm chairmen or "Red Landlords" as they came to be called, had as much if not more power over them than the landlords. Moreover, the state assumed powers that went beyond daily work orders. Stalin took away the peasants' freedom of movement. To keep the peasants down on the farm, they were denied internal passports. Without those passports or other special permission, the peasants were unable to travel within their own country.

Under the circumstances it was not surprising that agriculture became known as the Achille's heel of the Soviet economy. For all intents and purposes, the peasants have engaged in a form of passive resistance for over sixty years. A student at Moscow State University in 1977 described what happened to him when, as was the usual practice, he along with other students were assigned to help with the harvest. Because it was a new experience and because he was a hard worker, he set about his assignment with energy and enthusiasm. Before long one of the older peasants pulled him aside and chastised him: "You know you are a strike breaker."

As a result of collectivization and the hostility it engendered toward the state, the Soviet Union transformed itself from one of the world's largest exporters of grain, which it frequently was before the revolution, into the world's largest importer of grain. Despite its failures, virtually every other Communist country would adopt the same strategy. Consequently, most of the new Communist countries (Bulgaria was periodically an exception) found themselves at one time or another confronted with agricultural shortages and the need to import food.   Agricultural collectivization proved to be a political time bomb as well as an economic one.   It not only undermined the regimes' political support from the peasants who felt double-crossed, but also from the urban workers who were to suffer food shortages.

Spiraling Repression

Certainly there was bound to be a day of reckoning for such ill-conceived policies.   Yet the bill was larger than need be because the political and economic environment of the countries which were attracted to the Communist model had not gone through the bourgeois stage which Marx believed was necessary to achieve socialism.   With the exception of Czechoslovakia which was forcibly coerced into the Communist bloc, none of the countries which opted for communism had any substantial experience with capitalist and democratic procedures.   What explains why countries without these procedures were attracted to communism?

Cause and effect become entangled, but one explanation is that democratic societies have a strong independent middle class which finds communism unattractive.   That is not to say that the societies with middle classes are always democracies.   Germany in the 1930s and Argentina in the 1960s and 1970s are good examples of middle class societies which have veered towards fascism.   In each instance, however, fascism became attractive because the middle class found itself threatened by inflation or unemployment.

It can also be argued that democracy is less likely to sprout in a predominantly agrarian and rural society.   Much of the impetus for imposing restraints on the power of the government, which is crucial to democracy, comes from urban residents -- independent professionals, business people and manufacturers, who are more likely to be affected by arbitrary actions of the government.   In an earlier era, some of them organized into guilds, where they learned how to "mobilize" to protect their interests and check the abuses of the central authorities.   Such groups could afford to challenge the state because they were in large part economically independent of the state.   Those who owned their own property and developed their own enterprises and skills to earn a livelihood were less concerned about losing their jobs and more concerned with the individual than the collective.

Conversely, in those countries attracted to communism, in the pre-revolutionary eras, the collective frequently was more important than the individual.   Edward L. Keenan explains this tendency toward the collective in Russia at least, as a natural response to a climactically extreme environment.[7] Living alone in the harsh winters of Russia was dangerous. Therefore, the peasants clustered together in villages and relied on one another for protection against not only nature but also humans. Although Chinese peasants tilled their land as family units, they lived together within the village and worked collectively on irrigation and flood control systems. This was a very different pattern from agriculture in America and some European countries, where the farmers lived on their own homes on their own land. A preference for the collective may explain at least partially the preference for a strong leader, who protects people not only from the extremes of nature, but human invasion and plunder as well. There also seemed to be an extreme fear of chaos and anarchy in these societies, necessitating rigid domestic controls. The fact that the Russians and Chinese tolerated czars and emperors for centuries with remarkably few attempts at revolution until the twentieth century suggests resignation if not outright acceptance of strong central leadership.

A manifestation of this desire for a strong leader is expressed in Fyodor Dostoyevskii's novel *The Brothers Karamazov*. In a sequence commonly referred to as the Grand Inquisitor, the Grand Inquisitor says to Jesus, "We shall persuade them that they will only become free when they renounce their freedom to us and submit to us . . . . Too well they know the value of complete submission! And until they know that, they will be unhappy. No science will give them bread so long as they remain free. In the end they will lay their freedom at our feet and say to us, 'Make us your slaves, but feed us.'"[8] A contemporary explanation of this acceptance of strong state control is provided by Yuri Afanasyev, an historian and more recently a political reformer in the Supreme Soviet. "It was and is very characteristic of Russia to have the people at 'the bottom' harshly subordinated to the people at the 'top,' and for the people generally to be subordinated to the state: such relations were formed back in the twelfth century. The eternal oppression in Russia created a reaction against it of intolerance, aggression and hostility; and it is this oppression and the reaction to it that created cruelty and mass violence. It is true that the policies of the Bolsheviks did not derive from the will of the people, but the people participated in those policies and took part in the mass terror."[9]

This quest for law and order along with the constant fear of chaos naturally led to support for extensive political controls, a strong police presence, and distrust of outsiders, especially fear of invasion by capitalist countries. In response, most Communist countries diverted a disproportionate share of their GNP to military expenditures. Officially, of course, statistics from these countries understated what was being spent. The Soviet authorities, for instance, insisted until the 1980s that they were spending only one percent of their GNP on their military. Gorbachev subsequently acknowledged that the figure was more like seven percent. While Gorbachev's candor was welcome, by the late 1980s it was estimated that the actual figure probably exceeded twenty or even twenty-five percent.[10]

The overemphasis on military expenditures fed into recurring pressure for totalitarian control. Most of the military expenditures necessitated investments of large amounts of capital in a heavy industrial infrastructure. The large proportion of the GNP set aside for military expenditures and heavy industry came at the expense of light industry and consumer goods, provoking a clamor by the consumer-hungry population for more attention to be paid to their immediate needs. After it became increasingly evident by the late 1960s that there would be no imminent improvement in their living conditions, even those who initially supported the heavy industrial approach became increasingly insistent on satisfying everyday needs. Yet, convinced of the correctness of their course, the leaders insisted that all they needed was a little more time to achieve their goals. But the light at the end of the tunnel always seemed to recede.

Recognizing the transition might take longer than originally anticipated, the leaders then tried to curb public pressure. One way was to block out positive news about life in the capitalist world so as to prevent negative comparisons. Most important, because the emerging civil societies of the prerevolutionary periods had been crushed and a legal opposition and free press were nonexistent, no group could openly challenge the leadership's decisions. Once a decision had been made, there was little protest and opportunity for feedback. The fact that the first generation of Communist leadership was still in power in the Soviet Union until 1953 and in China into the early 1990s, often meant the use of extreme measures of suppression. They regarded any challenge as a threat not only to the party, but to themselves personally. After all, they had devoted their whole lives to establishing communism. Therefore, they were less willing to compromise or seek political solutions than their successors. They had achieved power not by seeking consensus and making compromises, but by confrontation and elimination of dissent.

Yet even the most committed revolutionary leaders became more and more motivated by power than by ideology. After a time, especially as the attainment of their goals seemed to slip further and further into the future, something more tangible was required to sustain them. Special stores, housing compounds, resorts and health centers were designed to cater only to this "new class," sometimes called cadres in China and nomenklatura in the Soviet Union. Even though the new class continued to offer lip service to the idea of equality, it was merely rhetoric. Their main concern was holding onto their positions of power and privilege and passing them on to their children.

Fleeting Successes of Communism

Nevertheless, it took some time before the seething resentment engendered by such hypocrisy exploded into protest. Whether due to belief, intimidation or the hope that life would be better than under the obsolete, chaotic old regimes, the majority of the populations of the Soviet Union and the People's Republic of China had genuinely welcomed the new order. Even when those regimes' utopian schemes of collectivization in the Soviet Union in the late 1920s and 1930s and the Great Leap Forward in China in the late 1950s led to the deaths of 20 to 30 million people in their respective countries, the Chinese and Soviet populations continued to support their respective parties and leaders. Government control of the media helped to spread the illusion of well-being. At least superficially it was easy to be misled by all those smiling marchers and dancing children pledging their allegiance. Some of the accomplishments were real. In almost every instance, each Communist regime reduced illiteracy, increased life expectancy, lessened infant mortality and eliminated unemployment. In addition crime, prostitution, and drugs all but disappeared, including from China where such evils had been rampant.

Moreover, in the Soviet Union rates of economic growth of ten percent or more seemed to be setting world records. In 1959 and 1960, Nikita Khrushchev threatened to overtake and surpass American production in a decade or two. Shortly thereafter the Soviet Union began to produce more steel, coal and oil than the United States. In addition, the People's Republic of China in the first decade grew at an impressive five to six percent a year. In many ways the central planning system appeared to be working. The central planners pointed out the superiority of their methods to those of the capitalists who were engaged in wasteful duplication because of the emphasis on economic competition. By contrast, the Communist governments deliberately created monopolies in order to avoid such waste. Almost seventy percent of all the machine tools produced in the Soviet Union, for example, was produced by only one factory. Soviet breakthroughs in space and military technology also dramatically demonstrated the benefits of central planning. In the 1950s the Communist countries were industrializing with record rates of growth that were not only the envy but the concern of the non-Communist world.

Although there were shortcomings in the central planning process from the beginning, it took some time for those inside and outside the Communist world to understand their seriousness. While it was readily acknowledged that there were insufficient consumer goods to satisfy the public, the planners insisted that it was only a temporary inconvenience. By definition, it was assumed that because of the central planning system, change would come more readily to communism than capitalism.

Planners could anticipate major changes in taste and technology and adjust the country's productive capacity accordingly. If they could expand electrical capacity in advance of need, they should be able to do the same with new consumer goods and technologies. By contrast, a number of Western economists lamented their economy's lack of an industrial policy to guide it. But after years of promises with few results, it became clear that central planners were unable to fulfill their promises.

Khrushchev was one of the first to complain about the rigidity of central planners. In an often-quoted comment, he noted that "the production of steel is like a well-traveled road with deep ruts; here even blind horses will not turn off because the wheels of their wagons will break. Similarly some officials have put on steel blinders: they do everything as they were taught in their day. A material appears which is superior to steel and is cheaper, but they keep on shouting, 'Steel, steel!'"[11] Like the horses, the central planners were reluctant to switch lanes from heavy industry to consumer goods. That would mean fundamental restructuring with too many abandoned factories and social disruption with too much unemployment. It was better to produce more steel which nobody used than to close down those factories. Members of the military-industrial complex reacted the same way. For them, there was also a fear of unpreparedness. They did not want to be held responsible for leaving the Soviet Union vulnerable to the United States.

Even though the rigidities of central planning were built into the system from the beginning, they did not become a major concern until the late 1960s and early 1970s. After all, by the more traditional standards of economic growth, such as the amount of steel, the number of machine tools, and the amount of oil production, the Communist world seemed to be doing well. But as the invention of new and more advanced technologies accelerated in the 1970s and 1980s, the central planners were unable to respond quickly and efficiently. They simply could not keep up with the rapid changes in the production processes and in the chemical, computer, electronics and biological industries. At the same time, news about the consumer societies in the West and even in Asia began to penetrate the iron curtain. The new technologies, such as transistors, short-wave radios and television carried those images. Because they could watch West German television, the East Germans saw that no matter how much better off they might be than their Soviet counterparts, they were still far behind their former countrymen in West Germany. The Chinese who watched Hong Kong television concluded the same about their East Asian brethren and even the North Koreans were gaining some awareness of the improving standard of living of their countrymen to the south. Voice of America and the BBC brought information about their societies to the Soviet Union and the other Communist countries. No longer could such news be kept out. The Communist countries which in mid-century seemed to be the ultimate economic winners, by the closing decades had become the economic losers.

An awareness of these events did not occur overnight. Until the Cultural Revolution (1966-1976), there appeared to be widespread support for the Chinese regime. In these countries, the scientists and writers were the first to point out the discrepancies between the propaganda and reality. When the astrophysicist Fang Lizhi, like Andrei Sakharov, discovered that the science he had studied in the lab and books did not correspond with the science prescribed by the state, he began to question other assertions by the state as well. Once aware that the state was not all-knowing or always honest, these scientists, as well as the nonscientific intellectuals, began to speak out and alert others to the party's failings. Given their traditional positions of authority and privilege, the intellectuals attracted followers from other social groups, most of whom came to see how misguided many of the state policies had been, not only in economics, but also on issues of human rights, party dictatorship and militarization.

Eventually even some party leaders came to appreciate the inappropriateness of many of their predecessor's policies. In China, Deng Xiaoping in the 1980s rejected Mao's economic policies and use of terror, though he continued the same Leninist political structure. In the Soviet Union, the Stalinist economic emphasis on heavy industry and collectivization changed much more slowly, but Gorbachev, when he came to power in 1985, gradually tolerated political dissent and ultimately understood the wastefulness of such policies as forcing Sakharov, the country's leading physicist, from his laboratory into exile in Gorky. Although it took Gorbachev almost two years to realize the folly of such policies, in December 1986 he called Sakharov on the phone and invited him to come back to Moscow to work at his laboratory. How could the Soviet Union persecute its best scientists and still expect to compete in the age of high technology? It was a lesson that came gradually to most of the Communist leaderships. China's leaders also sought to join in the technological competition, but with their crackdown on the 1989 Tiananmen demonstration which they regarded as an attack on themselves and the party, they retreated to a Maoist type suppression of political dissent even from scientists.

The Collapse of Communism

The increasing awareness of the outside world and seething discontent with the failings of the Communist system, however, do not themselves explain the suddenness of its collapse. In Eastern Europe after all, the populations of Poland, Hungary and Czechoslovakia had publicly and collectively expressed their discontent earlier, resulting in bloodshed and suppression. Each time Russia, the gendarme of Europe, as Marx described it, took steps to preserve the integrity of socialism. As in the nineteenth century, as long as Russia, now the Soviet Union, stood opposed to revolutionary change in Eastern Europe, there would be no fundamental change in the system.

The big change had to await the rise of a new generation of leaders, specifically Mikhail Gorbachev. Some have argued that it was time for change and that, with or without a Gorbachev, there would have been a breakup of the Communist empire and an accelerating rejection of communism. But such a collapse was not inevitable. Even though the economic performance of the Communist countries continued to suffer relative to the capitalist world, conditions in the early 1980s, before Gorbachev's ascension to power in 1985, were not as desperate as they were to become six years after Gorbachev's reforms. His immediate predecessors, Yuri Andropov and Konstantin Chernenko, had shown little interest in the political reforms that Gorbachev came to espouse. True, Andropov commissioned some studies of the economy, but he took a very hard line approach to political reforms and intensified rather than reduced controls over the economy. Nor was there much interest in reform among any members of the Politburo. For that matter, prior to late 1984, there was little in Gorbachev's record or behavior to suggest any significant commitment to radical reform. Although once in office, Gorbachev began to speak of the need for *glasnost* as well as restructuring or *perestroika*, not until 1987 did his proposals for change differ from the kinds of programs previously offered. For that matter, Gorbachev initially refrained even from using the word "reform."

It was not that Gorbachev was unaware of the need for change. He has described how in December, 1984, he and Eduard Shevardnadze concluded that "it was impossible to live" as they had.[12] Gorbachev acknowledged that both of his grandfathers had been arrested in the Stalinist 1930s and in the process, one-half of his family had starved. In hopes of avoiding the reoccurrence of such tragedies, Gorbachev and Shevardnadze decided on "a simple formula: more democracy, more *glasnost*, more humanity." They both agreed as Gorbachev related that "we want real socialism, because to us the socialist idea is not a threat. I am, for example, a convinced socialist."[13] The context of his speeches and his behavior indicated that Gorbachev believed that the reforms he proposed could be accomplished within the socialist system. He wanted to perfect the system by making needed changes in order to realize its potential. By anticipating change Gorbachev assumed he could continue to maintain control over the process while at the same time improving the life of the Soviet people. A part of this change was to rid the system of the superannuated dogmatic bureaucrats who had come to dominate it and block reforms during the twenty years of Brezhnev's rule.

Gorbachev urged the same reforms for Eastern Europe. After initially supporting the status quo, he moved closer to the Hungarians and Poles, who were more responsive to change than the rest of the bloc. This provoked a particularly fascinating response in the German Democratic Republic, which had always regarded itself as more economically productive than the other members of the Council of Mutual Economic Assistance bloc, including the Soviet Union. Unlike their compliant actions in the pre-Gorbachev era, the East Germans refused to circulate some of the Soviet leader's speeches as well as some Soviet newspapers, especially when they advocated reforms the East German leadership was unwilling to accept. Nevertheless, Gorbachev remained persistent, convinced that the best way to preserve communism in Eastern Europe was to adjust to the needs of the new age, much as he was trying to do in the Soviet Union.

This strategy, however, took a different course in Eastern Europe than Gorbachev had anticipated. Once it became clear that, within the Soviet Union, *glasnost* and democratization were more than just words, most East Europeans also wanted *glasnost* and democratization. Equally important, with such policies the Soviets would be inhibited from interfering in Eastern Europe as they had done in the past. Seizing the moment, the East Europeans began to force out their Communist parties and leaders and ultimately abandoned the Warsaw Pact, demanding the removal of Soviet troops from their soil. By criticizing the failures of communism and attacking the party's interference in day to day operations, the East Europeans were emulating their supposed "big brother."

There was a major difference, however, between communism in Eastern Europe and in the Soviet Union. The Stalinist system of socialism had been imposed on Eastern Europe by outside forces. Therefore, once the process of reform was under way in Eastern Europe, the Stalinist system of socialism was virtually abandoned. To the East Europeans, it was little more than an ideological cover for Soviet imperialism. Just like an avalanche, the pressure from within East Europe to reduce the role of the Communist parties and bring in new, more reform-minded but still Communist leaders was accelerated by pressure from the public at large to push aside the Communist parties and their leaders altogether. By the time Gorbachev fully appreciated the dimensions of what he had set in motion, the only way to halt the process would have been to call out troops. He ultimately decided against such actions for strategic reasons as well as personal compunctions, because he realized they would cost him the support of the West, whose help he needed in transforming his own society. Recognizing that there was no longer anything to fear from the Gorbachev regime, the East Europeans in demonstrations and in elections simply declared that for them communism was no longer relevant.

China: The Exception?

The Chinese took another course. The economic transformation in China began seven years earlier than in the Soviet Union and in many ways moved much further away from the Stalinist economic emphasis on heavy industry, agricultural collectivization and central planning than any of the European Communist countries. By the early 1980s it had already decollectivized the communes and returned to the individual family farms. It began a consumer industry to satisfy the needs of China's 800,000,000 farmers whose incomes had more than doubled in the first half of the 1980s. They had also become involved in joint ventures and in international world trade so that by 1991 the United States had a trade deficit with China of ten billion dollars. It had moved much faster away from the Stalinist economic model because Mao's Cultural Revolution (1966-1976) had literally bankrupted the country economically and politically. Moreover, plagued since the late 1950s by periodic bouts of widespread starvation, political fratricide and ideological utopianism, China was increasingly isolated from the rest of the world. It had fallen behind economically, especially in comparison with its East Asian neighbors. Japan had lost World War II and Taiwan the civil war in 1949, but now they were both becoming significantly richer and more advanced technologically than China.

Therefore, after Mao's death in September 1976, questions as to why this had happened were asked openly. Because the Cultural Revolution had so ravaged the party leadership, in its aftermath the leadership was often unable to respond to such questions and to economic infractions of ideology that in the past would have been suppressed immediately. When peasant families and local officials in the provinces of Anhui and Sichuan began to take their land out of the commune and farm it, the party leadership under Deng Xiaoping did little to stop it. The Deng regime then allowed and even urged the establishment of private and cooperative enterprises in urban as well as rural areas. From 1978 until 1988, particularly as economic growth of about nine percent became real and not just a statistical artifact, Stalinist economic practices all but disappeared. A small number of elderly former revolutionary leaders who still exercised power at the top echelons of power in the party and military, however, still remained committed to some form of central planning. They continued to wield power because, unlike the Soviet Union and Eastern Europe, the Leninist political structure that gives unlimited power to the top party leadership remained intact. The revolutionary elders had not been able to block or even slow the economic reforms because they were implemented so quickly and were pushed by one of their fellow comrades, the paramount leader Deng Xiaoping. In addition, their Chinese countrymen still remembered the entrepreneurial ways of their ancestors and pre-1949 China. Once given permission, they moved swiftly and effectively to resume their entrepreneurial activities

By contrast, the revolutionary elders were able to thwart any political reforms because in this respect they had the support of Deng. Some political reforms were carried out in the localities, such as contested elections for local councils up to the county level. But because they realized that it would mean a dilution of their power, Deng and his revolutionary colleagues refused to allow any changes in the Leninist system of democratic centralism that channeled all power to the top leadership. As a result, the economy virtually exploded at an accelerating rate of growth while a country of over one billion people continued to be ruled by the same party elders who had established the party in the 1920s, made the Long March in the mid-1930s, defeated the Guomindang in a civil war in the 1940s and established the People's Republic in 1949. They regarded any change in the Leninist political structure as a threat to the party, socialism and themselves.

Consequently, to them the spring 1989 Tiananmen demonstration, which demanded reforms of the political system on the Gorbachev model, was a challenge to the cause to which they had devoted their lives. They responded by using their control over the military to suppress the demonstrators with force. Unlike Gorbachev who represented the fifth generation of Soviet party leadership, was a university graduate and was trained as a lawyer, this first generation of professional revolutionaries was unwilling to compromise or allow an end to the party's leading role, which they knew would be an end to their role. Because of their history, power and age, which was still revered even in the People's Republic, they were able to prevent the dismantling of the Leninist structure. But will the next generation of Chinese party leaders be able to wield such power and prestige?

As Marxists, they know that the superstructure no longer corresponds to the substructure. The dynamic private sector of the economy, which by the early 1990s was producing about fifty percent of the GNP and was growing at a rate of more than two or three times the state industrial sector, is bound to overtake the party-controlled sector by the end of the century. Diminishing control over the economy and the increasing democratization of the outside world is bound to weaken the party over time.

Perhaps the most important factor in the inevitable decline of the party is its loss of legitimacy. The Communist party in China may not collapse as suddenly those in the Soviet Union and Eastern Europe. It still has some support in the countryside for having allowed decollectivization. But whereas from the late 1970s through the first half of the 1980s, farmers' incomes more than doubled, thereafter they grew less rapidly. At the same time, the urban population, which has benefitted less from Deng Xiaoping's economic reforms and was affected by the inflation that accompanied the loosening of controls, is becoming increasingly restive. The spring 1989 Tiananmen demonstration was an expression of the urban population's grievances against the party's corruption and inflationary policies as well as its desire for political reform. Although most of the urban population is still tightly controlled by the unit in which they work, which provides housing, medical care and ration coupons, their participation in the demonstration is an indication of the emergence of a degree of independence of the urban population from party authority. One-third of the participants in the demonstration was the "geti hu," the private entrepreneurs, who had emerged in response to Deng's call for small-scale private industry and trade. (The much smaller number of Soviet entrepreneurs similarly supported democracy and Yeltsin's resistance to the August, 1991 coup attempt.) The leaders of the 1989 Tiananmen demonstration were associated with Beijing's first independent social science think tank, the Social and Economic Research Institute, whose directors, Wang Juntao and Chen Ziming, were sentenced to thirteen years in prison, the longest sentences of all the participants. For a short few weeks, workers, intellectuals, journalists and just ordinary citizens set up their own unions, independent of the party and on the model of Solidarity, until they were crushed by the revolutionary elders and the military on June 4, 1989.

Despite its repression, China's civil society that was just beginning to emerge in 1989 is likely to grow when the elders die and no longer control the military. Even before the party's violent crackdown, the party had begun to lose its legitimacy because of the traumas China had suffered in the Cultural Revolution. With the crackdown, it lost its "mandate of heaven," at least with the urban population. In Chinese history, no matter what subsequent leaders may do, it is impossible for the regime to retrieve the "mandate" once it is lost. The party may linger on after the deaths of its revolutionary founders and the economy may continue to grow in the 1990s (in 1991 it grew by seven percent), but the ideology and Leninist political structure have lost their relevance. Like the Confucian state, which lingered on long after it lost its relevance, the Chinese Communist Party may also, but like its predecessor it may slowly fade away.

Since China is ninety-two percent Chinese, it is less likely to disintegrate into ethnic regions as happened in the Soviet Union, but central party control has already been weakened by economic regionalization, particularly the increasing economic pull of the southeast coastal provinces toward the more dynamic market economies of their brethren in Hong

Kong and Taiwan.[14] While this continuing tendency may reduce Beijing's power over the regions, it is unlikly that it will lead to the establishment of independent sovereignties as occurred in the Soviet Union. Rather, it may lead to a diffusion of power to the regions and away from the party or any other central leadership.

Could Communism Have Succeeded?

By the end of the twentieth century, communism, at least as a governing ideology, appears to be dead. Some gross excesses in the capitalist world or the incapacity of the former Communist countries to transform themselves and improve their economies may lead some in the future to want to return to the Leninist model. Maybe in an age with different technologies and different priorities, some form of a more collectivized economy may yet prove to be more attractive, but for now this seems unlikely.

A few still argue that communism would have succeeded if only it had been adopted in the more developed countries of the world, as Marx had originally intended. If so, that would have presumably meant that the process of industrialization would have already been completed. Then there would have been no need for the forced collectivization of agriculture and rapid industrialization with the consequent grief they brought to the Soviet Union, China and Eastern Europe. Perhaps so, but that raises the question of why communism never took hold in the capitalist world in the first place. Most of Western Europe and the United States in the late nineteenth century, with their growing middle classes, burgeoning democracies and ever growing economic prosperity, despite periodic recessions, were not interested in class warfare or economic upheaval. As long as their economic well-being continued to improve, the existing political and economic system seemed to be attractive enough. Moreover, the cultural pluralism and system of checks and balances, even if not perfect, helped prevent excessive abuses of power by their elected officials.

Equally important, Western economic and political systems allowed for evolutionary change and the accommodation of interests and grievances such as the New Deal in the United States and social welfare programs in Western Europe. Such flexibility deflated political and social pressures which, if left unchecked, might have provoked an explosion. In other words, communism was probably never suited for an already industrialized country. Admittedly an industrial country has a large proletariat, but what Marx overlooked was that it also has a large middle class. It is that middle class and the aspirations of the proletariat who seek to join the middle class that caused them to opt for non-Communist solutions, at least as long as there was reasonable economic growth, fulfillment of basic needs and the possibility of some mobility.

Marx had it wrong. Without a prolonged economic crisis in the industrialized world, communism proved to be attractive only to the industrially backward countries, where it gave rise to the abuses we ultimately have come to see. Thus the failure of communism in the modernizing and industrializing countries of the Soviet Union, Eastern Europe and China was more than just a misapplied experiment, it probably was inevitable.

Notes

1. Adam Ulam, "The Historical Role of Marxism and the Soviet System," *World Politics*, October 1955, 20.

2. "Gosudarstvennyi Komitet SSSR po Statistike," *Narodnoe Khoziastvo SSSR, Za 70 Let* (Moscow Publishers); *Financy i Statistika*, 1987, 3, 11, 373.

3. Milovan Djilas, *The New Class: An Analysis of the Communist System* (New York: Praeger, 1957).

4. Lazar Bolin, *A Century of Russian Agriculture* (Cambridge, Harvard University Press, 1970), 135-136.

5. Paul R. Gregory and Robert C. Stuart, *Soviet Economic Structure and Performance* (New York, Harper and Row Publishers, Third Edition, 1986), 108.

6. Gregory and Stuart, 108-110.

7. Edward L. Keenan, "Russian Political Culture," mimeograph, US Department of State, 1722-420-119, July 1976.

8. Fyodor Dostoyevskii, *The Brothers Karamazov* (New York: Random House, The Modern Library, 1950), 299-307.

9. *The New York Review of Books*, January 31, 1991, 38.

10. Conversation with Alexander Yakovlev, former Politburo member, November, 1991.

11. *Pravda*, November 20, 1962, 4.

12. *Pravda*, December 1, 1990, 4.

13. *Pravda*, December 1, 1990, 4.

14. See Ezra Vogel, *One Step Ahead* (Cambridge, MA: Harvard University Press, 1990).

3

Historical Foundations for Democracy in Russia?

Robert F. Byrnes

As the world's experiences with Leninism have demonstrated, a determined, highly-organized political group can seize control of a nation and force its people into an authoritarian system. The same is not true of constitutional and representative governments, for establishing democratic institutions and an open society rests upon a web of beliefs and attitudes that flower only after a difficult and permanent struggle. Establishing a constitutional system based on civil rights is especially difficult when the people must first remove an ancient legacy of authoritarianism as well as the poisonous effects of decades of Leninist rule.

The collapse of communism demonstrates that Marx's deterministic view of history was grossly mistaken. Historical factors did not lead inevitably to communism, nor will they alone determine whether those peoples who have lived under communism will succeed in establishing open governments. Yet the absence of historical foundations for democratic government provides some indication of the troubles that lie ahead. The historical record indicates that Russian foundations for a transition to constitutional and representative government are weaker than those of the peoples in Eastern Europe who suffered under Russian domination and those of other states, such as Spain and Greece, which totalitarian governments have ruled in this century. The Russian case, and that of China as well, demonstrate why the recent resurgence of the age of democratic revolutions that began in the 1770s has had such a belated impact on those two great countries.

This paper examines the historical background of only the Russian peoples of the former USSR. Prospects for the Ukrainians and Belorussians, the peoples of the Baltics and the Caucasus, and those of Central Asia are distinct from those of the Russians because their historical backgrounds and current internal and external situations differ from those of the Russians.

Understanding a foreign culture is difficult because each observer views the world through a set of assumptions and glasses that reflect personal and national experiences and values. Western observers have always found Russia's past and culture baffling because of the nature of the Russian and Soviet systems and because conflicts between the USSR and much of the rest of the world have clouded observers' visions. The rapid changes of every kind sweeping countries the Communists have ruled increase the difficulties for those seeking to reach sensible judgments about developments in the years ahead. Access to somewhat more information than in the past should not blind us to the shallow and uncertain character of our knowledge of Russian society, one that is changing rapidly, or to the elementary level of our understanding of the history upon which that system rests. And looking ahead is far more demanding than determining what has happened.

Briefly, the Russians and many peoples they have ruled have virtually no historical experience, institutions, or understanding upon which to build a democratic society. Russian history has been a continuous one of highly centralized and authoritarian rule under durable institutions that have satisfied national needs as their rulers have defined them. The political culture has been absolutist, without even a revolt for religious freedom to provide a legend for an open and democratic system. Because of the controls on one hand and popular acceptance of them except for occasional violent local revolts on the other hand, the Russian intellectual level was low and political thought sterile, even absent, until the middle of the nineteenth century. Even then, most of the few active citizens showed little interest in or understanding of democratic processes in social relations or political governance. Instead, they advocated utopian arrangements in which a small reactionary or radical elite would provide leadership for believing masses.

The Authoritarian State Tradition

The authoritarian state tradition has been deeply entrenched in Russian history. While the roots lie in Muscovy in the fourteenth and the fifteenth centuries, the Kievan principality founded in the tenth century by merchant warriors from Scandinavia in cooperation with eastern Slavs who had moved into the Kievan area had already established a centralized system. Moreover, as Pechenegs, Cumans and others threatened to cut the thin lifeline of trade that connected Byzantium and Scandinavia, the warrior tradition in Kiev overcame the merchant element. The move northeast to Moscow led ultimately to heavy emphasis upon a centralized system of governance, not just at the political level but throughout a society under constant pressure from nature and from Asia. The grand princes and later the tsars began to consider the people and the land their property, a judgment the people accepted. This tradition grew stronger when Muscovite rulers in the fifteenth century began the long effort to gather the Russian peoples and regain "the Russian land" thirteenth century chroniclers had found at the heart of their national origins. This irredentist process, in part defensive and in part offensive, strengthened the grand prince's power over his family or clan and other potential barons as well. In the process, Muscovy snuffed out the oligarchic systems of Novgorod and Pskov that might have led to an open and democratic society, as such "sham democracies" did in Britain and other societies. In short, Russia did not benefit from feudalism and the other baronial, regional, urban, or church efforts to limit the power of leaders. The center obtained control early and then advanced from commanding heights to assert domination over new areas as it added them.

By the sixteenth century, Russia possessed "an absolute government with an aristocratic administration." Few groups sought to modify this centralized system. For example, the boyar council, which resembled a council of state or the various groupings of *notables* in Western Europe in the sixteenth and seventeenth centuries, did not attempt to acquire authority during the Time of Troubles, when chaos prevailed. Instead, then and in the half century in which the first Romanovs gradually gained full authority, they failed to act as English barons and religious rebels had both acted at that time. They continued to serve meekly because their attitude toward authority and power differed from that of their Western contemporaries. As men who had been conquered, they lacked property of their own and did not develop a corporate sense. They did not establish regional power bases of their own, but were drawn into the center and participated in administration.

The land assembly, or *zemskii sobor*, of these years consisted of servants of the state the tsar selected as advisors because of their official functions. Like the boyar council, they had no desire for power and failed to use the central government's financial difficulties to press for the advantages their Western contemporaries obtained. The land assembly resembled a Communist party congress, rather than a parliament or an estates general. It ratified the ruler's will, rather than helped to shape decisions. Moreover, its years of rejected opportunity for reducing the state's power were also those in which serfdom became a settled feature of Russian society.

In the last third of the unsettled seventeenth century, the type of religious revolt that overthrew or greatly changed religious and political organizations and attitudes toward power in Western Europe instead strengthened the centralized Russian system. Poor in intellect, on the fringes of society, and without an alternative political philosophy, Russia's religious rebels, the Old Believers, failed against the united power of the state and the established church. At about the same time, the Cossacks, the fabled freebooters of the southern steppes, joined Muscovy against Poland and the Poles and accepted state control. The tsar utilized them as military instruments in the same way they used the land assemblies as political tools. The eastward movement through Siberia did not have the effect that the westward movement produced in the Atlantic community, in North America, and throughout Western empires, because Muscovy retained control over these pioneers, as it did over the lands acquired in the West.

The rulers who most dramatically enforced the authoritarian stamp were Peter the Great and Catherine the Great, deliberate and forceful westernizers. Neither understood the intellectual vitality and economic vigor that underlay the achievements of the West, but both sought to borrow the West's weapons, administrative arrangements, and economic instruments to make Russia a European power without changing the political system. Peter concentrated upon increasing economic and military power, extending territory, and making Russia a European state. He smashed institutions and groups that resisted or tried to limit his actions. His stature and dramatic actions enhanced the image of the tsardom's power and enlarged the state's authority.

The guards' regiments that surrounded Peter and symbolized his system then helped block the only eighteenth-century effort to limit Moscow's power, combining with suspicious or jealous nobles to thwart Prince Dmitrii Golitsyn's effort to limit the authority of Anne when she assumed the throne in 1730. This led to Russia's failure to limit central control only four decades after English nobles and armed forces had brought about the Glorious Revolution.

Catherine the Great, a German by origin, began in a weak and illegitimate position, but used inherited instruments and traditions to strengthen the central government's power. She fastened serfdom securely upon the country, corrupted the nobility by turning them away from useful employment in the countryside, and encouraged many to adopt European manners, customs, and even language. This allowed her to use and strengthen Moscow's power in a reign more marked by military conflict than any other.

Modern rulers since Nicholas I have followed the same pattern. Nicholas I not only sent students abroad to acquire the secrets of the West, but established the Third Section, foundation of the KGB, on the model of the French police system. The young men he sent to Berlin brought back the ideas of Hegel, so that the reactionary tsar contributed in several ways to strengthening the authoritarian tradition. Alexander II, the Great Liberator, used the words *glasnost* and *perestroika* in his reform decade.

The controlled intellectual activity then resembled that of the thaw after Stalin's death and the years since 1987. He took six years to abolish serfdom, and then established a system of communes that denied peasants the right to become owners of their land, made recruiting soldiers and collecting taxes easy, and transformed the countryside by 1900 into a base for violent revolution. The *zemstvo* system of local government had such limited responsibilities and tax-raising powers that few *zemstvo* leaders in the next fifty years acquired significant understanding of self-government at the local level before counter-revolution and wars blocked their progress.

Neither Alexander II nor those around him even considered political change. Patching the system by eliminating serfdom, allowing limited local government, and reforming higher education, the courts, and the armed forces served as his reform program. The "constitution" that he considered during his last days and that so alarmed conservatives without impressing liberals or radicals was actually an advisory council of selected men, much like the boyar council. During Alexander II's rule, some intellectuals sought a German *Rechtsstaat*, while a few looked to England and France as political models. However, most Russians interested in change became extreme radicals of the left or right, exalted the state, and sought to seize control of it to carry out their idealistic transformations. In short, Alexander II, like the other westernizers, increased alienations within Russia, stimulated extremist thought, and widened the political gap between Russia and the West. He failed to introduce political revisions at the very time England, France, Germany, Italy, and the Austro-Hungarian Empire were beginning to progress toward constitutional government and freely-elected legislatures. Alexander II and Gorbachev are similar in many ways, except that Gorbachev's reforms escaped his control.

The next two modernizers, Count Witte and Peter Stolypin, followed the same pattern. Witte, an able and tough-minded administrator who rose to high position through the state-owned railroad system, might have become a Carnegie or Rockefeller in another country, but used his talents and ambitions to make Russia an industrial state and to strengthen the autocracy. Even after the Revolution of 1905, he sought to maintain the "Fundamental Law of the Russian Empire." Stolypin, just as able and vigorous in forcing his agricultural program upon the countryside, might have created an independent peasantry through authoritarian means, but his assassination, and war in 1914, ended that possibility.

The return to Moscow and the revised "Orthodoxy, Autocracy, and Nationalism" of Nicholas I under Lenin and Stalin continued and strengthened the autocratic tradition. The centralized Communist state has been more absolute than any of its predecessors, emphasizing control from the center, economic and military strength at whatever cost, an expanded empire, and an ideology and system that prevented independent thought and activity. Even Khrushchev and Gorbachev in their efforts at reform sought to strengthen the state and brought change from the top, as their predecessors had. Until after the failed coup in August, 1991, even Gorbachev sought to preserve the USSR and return to the Leninist tradition.

Internal Causes of Authoritarianism

Historians since Soloviev and Kliuchevskii have blamed the harsh circumstances of the early centuries for the Russian political system and culture.[1] While the circumstances may have been no more dismal than those the first colonists encountered in New England early in the seventeenth century, the northern location, soil, and climate, particularly the precipitation patterns, produced an eternal struggle against poverty and external enemies and stressed authority and order. Above all, the founders of the Kievan principality and Muscovy did not carry English tradition with them: the eastern Slavs were primitive when they arrived in Kiev, and Vikings or Varangians who helped form the Kievan principality were advanced only in terms of administrative and military organization and interest in trade.

Like colonists in North and South America, the early Russians faced unfriendly and unhelpful neighbors, beginning with the Pechenegs and Cumans and continuing with the Tatars or Mongols and the Turks. Pressure from Asia and the steppes increased the emphasis upon order, security, stability, and military rule. Many scholars believe the Mongols strengthened the controlling institutions and tradition enormously during the two and a half centuries in which they ruled much of what is now European Russia. Even if they did not, they isolated Russia when the West expanded, created new wealth and classes, and produced the conditions that led to political change.[2]

The third aspect of this early phase involves what Russian and Soviet historians have called the "ingathering" of the Russian people, or the colonization process others might label imperialism. The Russians for centuries have carried on an endless process of expansion and absorption of other peoples, beginning with the Finns, Mordvinians, and Lithuanians and continuing with the Ukrainians, Belorussians, Jews, Poles, and the peoples of Siberia, the Baltic, the Caucasus, and Central Asia. Russian insistence upon authority over dissatisfied peoples has been a major cause for maintenance of a highly centralized state.

The Grand Prince Vladimir's conversion to Orthodoxy late in the tenth century and Russia's joining the Eastern Orthodox Church also strengthened the absolutist tradition. Russian Orthodox monasteries contributed to the state's expansion, particularly in the northeast in the early years of

Muscovy.   Orthodox Christianity helped to soften and civilize the Russians and other peoples they ruled. It is also responsible for many glories of Russian culture, particularly in architecture, painting, and music, all apolitical until the twentieth century.

However, Russia's acquiring Christianity from Byzantium strengthened the authoritarian tradition. First, in the Byzantine pattern, the Church became part of and strengthened the state, making a heretic a rebel. Russia has never enjoyed religious criticism of the Church or its doctrine or practices from within the hierarchy, the clergy, or the populace itself. The division and conflict between Church and state and among religions that in the West weakened both institutions, spawned independent thought and political theory, and allowed other religious, social, and ultimately political groups to grow between the cracks did not develop in Russia. Russian saints, like most of those in other countries, served their states and societies loyally. But Russia had no Beckets or Thomas Mores or Mindszentys. Its Old Believers were on the fringes of society and were just as absolutist as those who persecuted them.

The Russian Orthodox Church spread elementary knowledge of Christian doctrine and values. The spiritual and moral level of its monks and peasant worshipers may have exceeded that of their Western contemporaries: no one will ever know. But it has lacked intellectual vitality.   Thus, the Church was not an important contributor to the abolition of serfdom in 1861, and Patriarch Filaret even opposed that great action. In more recent times, the Church's role as a defender of human values has been just as undistinguished and even shameful. It condemned oppression and persecution everywhere except in Russia and other countries Communists ruled.

The Church also bears a heavy share of responsibility for the low level of Russian intellectual life. The use of Old Church Slavonic in religious services meant that few Russian clergy learned Greek, Latin, or other languages. They, therefore, lacked the interest and tools to gain access to the treasures of Greece or the West. The absence of other learning and rival religious groups helped produce the same poverty of theology that the absence of conflict between the Church and state and among churches produced in political thought. The first significant Russian theologian was a nineteenth-century layman, so Russia lacked an Aquinas as well as a Reformation.

The predominance of an uneducated and unintellectually inspiring clergy at a time when clergymen in the West were theologians, philosophers, university presidents, administrators, and even leaders of states helped keep the level of intellectual life low. Perhaps the most simple illustration is the Church's failure to found a single institution of higher education beyond its seminaries. On the other hand, the Church, religious orders, and ultimately rival religious groups founded the first Western universities and hundreds of their successor institutions. Religious organizations founded more than three hundred active colleges and universities in the United States. The Soviet Union lacks a single such institution.

Comparing the dates on which the first universities were founded in some other countries struggling to establish democracy in the second half of the twentieth century, such as Spain, Czechoslovakia, Poland, and Hungary, provides an index of Russia's intellectual and political backwardness as well as some insight into prospects for democracy in the years ahead. Thus, Salamanca was founded in 1243, Seville in 1254, Valladolid in 1346, Prague in 1347, Cracow in 1364, and Budapest in 1475. The first Russian university, Moscow, was established in 1755, almost 120 years later than Harvard. As late as 1800, Russia possessed only six universities, and that in Vilnius (1578) was Polish and in Dorpat (1632) virtually German. These six universities had a total of 18,000 students. (One index to the difficulties Romania and Bulgaria face in 1990s is that the first Romanian university was established in Jassy in 1860 and the university of Sofia in 1888.)

In addition, the Russian church received no intellectual or other sustenance from the West. The religious schism in the second half of the seventeenth century deepened and widened the gap between the eastern and Western Churches. Comparing the intellectual qualities of the Church's leaders and, even more, of the Old Believers with the religious reformers of Europe at that time illustrates the Russian intellectual level.

Society and Intellectual Life

Since early modern times, the state has not only dominated Russian society, but has absorbed it, preventing the existence of civil society or spheres of activity outside the structure of the state. The only men of significance in the political system were the tsars, their court, and a growing bureaucracy. The nobility lacked independent political power, the foundations for it, or even the desire for it. They were servants of the tsar. The middle-class was absent because the government exercised a royal monopoly over economic enterprise. Those engaged in trade, manufacturing, and the professions, even education, were state employees. The government and the populace have both been suspicious of entrepreneurs because they were potential rivals to the state and aroused envy in a society that emphasized equality. Moreover, a high percentage of those engaged in the private activities tolerated were Germans, Jews, Poles, Armenians, Old Believers, and others whom the government and people considered non-Russian. They tended to be dependent, did not form corporate groups or guilds as their equivalents in Western and East-

Central Europe did, and did not seek power or influence. Those who were instruments of the crown and those who seemed independent had a weak position in the system, much like that of Jews in medieval Western Europe.

In such a society, political thought naturally did not thrive. Those engaged in rule emphasized practical considerations of order and stability. It is difficult to identify a single philosopher, theologian, or other intellectual who influenced thought within and beyond Russia before the second half of the nineteenth century. Russian writings on justice, legitimacy, and law are as feeble as those in canon law, theology, and political theory and compare badly with achievements in architecture, music, and literature.

Since educated clergymen, nobles, and bureaucrats were servants of a powerful and unchanging state, those who differed tended toward internal exile, as in monasteries, or toward extremes in ideology and rebellion. When educated men began to form small groups or circles in major cities in the nineteenth century, many considered themselves a separate class of intelligentsia, almost a religious order, whose function was to overthrow the state and establish either perfect anarchy or a well-ordered utopia ruled by the most qualified. Intellectual life in the nineteenth century was therefore marked by utopian idealism of the left or right and by a preference for violence to achieve its goals. In short, as Berdiaev and many others have suggested, the Bolsheviks developed from and represented an intellectual tradition that grew from and against the established political system but sought to replace it with an even more absolute state.[3]

Effects of Western Influence

Harsh circumstances and pressures from Asia and the steppes help account for establishment of a strongly centralized state early in Russian history. However, the curious character of Russia's relationships with the more advanced nations of the West in the last three centuries strengthened the autocratic system and traditions, both when relationships were hostile and when they were peaceful. Until the second half of the seventeenth century, the Russian court had absorbed easily the food, clothing, architecture, weapons, and luxuries imported from the West, with no noticeable effect upon the political system or the philosophy sustaining it. However, conflict with the Poles in the seventeenth century over the "western borderlands" and then with Swedes and Germans increased Russian emphasis upon national interest, control, and order. They also brought under Russian rule hundreds of thousands who were not Russians or members of the Russian Orthodox Church. Many Poles and

Baltic Germans served the Russian state loyally, but their presence in the upper levels of the Russian system and that of thousands of others in the sensitive western border areas introduced foreign influence and a double note of tension. Conflict with Poland, Sweden, and German states over these areas and peoples naturally strengthened the state system and the autocratic tradition.

One of the first fateful Western influences upon the political system occurred in the third quarter of the seventeenth century, when Patriarch Nikon and other churchmen sought to reestablish the accuracy of the liturgy, which over centuries had accumulated a number of minor errors. Their use of scholars and translations from newly-acquired territories in the West led to a bitter religious schism that drove many devout members of the Church into rebellion as Old Believers. This process weakened the Church, divided society, and strengthened the state. It also led many Russians, educated and uneducated, to see the West as a source of harmful influence.

Another major contribution relationships with the West made towards strengthening the state rose paradoxically from the autocrats' efforts, from Peter the Great through Gorbachev, to borrow instruments and technologies to narrow the economic and military gap between Russia and the West. These borrowings divided Russia between those few influenced by the West and the great majority, alienated from the artificial and foreign society at the top. They also separated Russia further from the West because the leaders' campaigns to control the infections at the upper levels of society and to force unpopular changes upon the reluctant and hostile population below increased the state's powers. Thus, they made the state ever more absolute and ever less like the more open societies from which Russia had borrowed.

This form of revolution from the top, which produced opposition and counterrevolution from below, continued under even thorough conservatives such as Nicholas I, who himself censored Russia's greatest poet, Alexander II, Witte, and Stolypin. But the ultimate effort to borrow from the West to strengthen Russia came with the Communists, who adapted the Western doctrines of Marx to the autocratic tradition and established a most highly centralized state based on the rule of one infallible party, even one man. The state absorbed society, and the ruling group of party leaders, the *nomenklatura*, the military and organs of repression, and the managers of major industries dominated the state more completely than any early autocrat. They forced their ideology upon the population, went far beyond the royal monopolies of early centuries to control all economic enterprises, transformed the peasants into pre-emancipation serfs, and established control over all aspects of life. After years of Soviet rule, Khrushchev and then Gorbachev sought to soften and civilize, but also to preserve and strengthen the system, while at the same time reducing and even eliminating the gap which separated the Russian economy from that of the West.

The patriarchal state and the controlled society have therefore spiraled downward economically and politically while Western societies, and now societies beyond the West as well, have over the centuries made uneven but gradual progress toward freedoms and prosperity. Russia over the centuries has built a strong state, but not a nation bound by common values, culture, traditions, and institutions. Even in the nineteenth century, Russians lacked a glorious revolution, a legend about transforming new members into equal citizens in an ever more productive society, a national primary educational system, and a common language.

In spite of the pressures and rewards the Soviet government used in the last seventy years to press peoples into a community, neither the Soviet Union nor the Russian Republic constitutes a nation. Contemporary developments indicate that efforts to preserve the Soviet Union complicated and delayed programs to create democracy and a market economy. For many non-Russian nationalities within the former Soviet Union as well as for the Russians themselves, forming their own nation state is a higher priority than democracy. Nationalism has triumphed over communism. Perhaps it will triumph over democracy too, especially because of the magnitude of the interrelated problems these peoples face and the visible hunger for a prosperous life.

Some Comparisons

Peoples in many other societies with strongly centralized political systems are now establishing constitutional and representative governments and achieving prosperity. For example, states on the southern fringes of Europe, Spain and Portugal in the West and Greece and Turkey on the eastern edge, have encountered many handicaps similar to those Russians face but in the past two or three decades have established open and free states.

Spain provides a particularly interesting comparison, because its history until recently resembled that of Russia in some ways. It began the twentieth century as an authoritarian state, remained so until less than two decades ago, and is now a healthy democracy and increasingly prosperous society. Like Russia, Spain is on the fringes of Europe, suffers from poor soil in many areas, and endured centuries of external pressure, invasion, and even occupation. In effect, it has had a national church throughout much of its history, and that church's treatment of critics and religious minorities has often been as severe as that which the Russian state and church have meted out to their dissidents. The Spanish government has often been as centralized and as harsh as Russia's, and a vicious civil war involving foreign interventions marked Spain's history less than sixty years ago.

However, Spanish development in the second half of the twentieth century has been very different from that of Russia, particularly in progress made toward establishing a constitutional system and representative government and Western European standards of living. General Franco, with all his shortcomings, contributed greatly. He did not seek empire and kept Spain out of the Second World War. In the early 1950s, he began to open Spain to Western influences, encouraged the World Bank, UNESCO, and Western foundations to participate in Spanish economic and intellectual development, began rapid expansion and improvement of education, selected and trained Juan Carlos as his successor, and arranged an orderly transition to a more open society.

But other more essential elements have helped account for Spain's successes. It has been open to the oceans and faced intensive competition from France and England throughout much of its history. The Spanish church was never a part of the Spanish state and often collided with the state. In addition, it demonstrated far more interest in education than did the Russian Orthodox Church: the first Spanish university was established more than five hundred years before the first Russian university. Spain benefitted also from possessing strong aristocractic groups and powerful regional authorities, as in Catelonia. Its middle-classes were lively even before exploration and trade in the empire, and they grew substantially in the twentieth century, especially after 1945. In addition, Spain was fortunate in losing all but the last shreds of empire in 1898. Russia's rulers, on the other hand, even after the defeats of 1904-1905 and 1914-1917 and the horrors of 1941-1945 desperately sought to retain and even expand its empire.

In short, for reasons based on historical foundations, abandonment of imperial pretensions, and opening the country to the West after 1950, Spain in the second half of the twentieth century has moved toward an open, free, and prosperous society, a journey the Russian people are trying to begin under circumstances much more difficult than those the Spanish have encountered.

The so-called "northern tier" of states in East-Central Europe, Poland, Hungary, and Czechoslovakia, also compare and contrast in illuminating ways with Russia. They have suffered greatly from harsh circumstances, external pressures, and occupation. Much of their history has reflected their position on the road to Europe from Asia and then between Russians, Turks, and Germans. Their mixtures of religions and nationalities have been even more explosive than those of Russia and the Soviet Union. They are also on the fringes of the West, but are closer than Russia and have been far more open to Western influence. In fact, the peoples of these countries are and have always considered themselves

Europeans, while the Russians have debated since the seventeenth century about the nature and destiny of Russia as a unique society. These states have also benefitted from competition with and emigration from Western states, such as Germany, Sweden, and Italy. They enjoyed feudalism. Serfdom was less rooted and disappeared earlier than in Russia. Many of their clergy were learned, engaged in theological and philosophical inquiries, and contributed to creating a higher national intellectual level and greater awareness of the outside world than did their Russian counterparts. The dates on which their first universities were established provide a simple index of their advantages.

In their years of independence as well as in those under rule by others, these peoples developed strong, well-organized aristocracies, often with substantial regional power bases. Their middle classes also grew, both during periods of rule by foreigners as well as during independence. Since the Reformation, even profoundly Catholic Poland benefitted from competing religions, political groups, and ideologies. In modern times, they have enjoyed extensive periods of independence and self-rule, with quasi-parliamentary government and times in which political parties developed and change came from the bottom, rather than the top. Finally, while it did not appear a blessing at the time, Communist rule sharpened their eagerness to establish democratic systems. For them, communism was doubly illegitimate: it violated their national traditions and was an alien ideology and system foreigners forced upon them. Resistance has therefore been national as well as political, spiritual, economic, and social.

Romania and Bulgaria are also on the fringes of Europe, but have been much less close and have weaker foundations from which to move toward democratic systems. These states suffered from centuries under Ottoman rule. They are basically Orthodox, with the advantages and disadvantages that form of Christianity has brought. Their aristocracies, middle classes, educational systems, intellectual life, economies -- the infrastructure that lies at the foundations of open societies -- have been and remain feeble.

In short, comparing the historical foundations and some of the contemporary factors that affect these societies suggests that Russia's traditions have had a paralyzing effect and that the contemporary effort to move toward democracy must overcome powerful institutions and attitudes as well as a host of complicated, interrelated problems. Poland, Czechoslovakia, and Hungary in particular have much brighter prospects than Russia, even though their problems are also daunting.

A Shaky Foundation for Democracy

Change is constant in every society, even the most highly-controlled, and slow alterations among the country's structural materials have occurred throughout Russian history. However, Russia has always been a conservative society in which most efforts to change have come from the top. The situation in the 1990s differs from earlier ones in that it rests upon the increments left by their failures, and important elemental changes from below have appeared in the last thirty years. These pressures combined with an effort from the top to revive a failed economy to produce an explosive combination. This has placed the country in the center of a continuing revolution which may lead to democracy.

Russia's inherited authoritarian institutions and traditions constitute a serious barrier against moving toward constitutional and democratic government. Russian history has provided virtually no experience in self-rule at any level in government (even local government), economic management, or even education. Russia has no tradition of civic culture, political participation, or compromise. It has been a "believing society," rather than a skeptical one, to use phrases Arnold Toynbee made popular.[4]

Harsh circumstances, Byzantium and the Mongols, pressure from the West, centuries of serfdom, and a political system in which the state has dominated the church have strengthened authoritarian foundations. Russia has not enjoyed an independent aristocracy; an independent, national, popular middle class; a prolonged period of peaceful progress toward democratic governance; a renaissance, reformation, age of exploration, or an era of enlightenment. It has never constituted a nation. Relationships with the outside world have tended to strengthen the authoritarian system and tradition. On this foundation came more than seventy years of Stalinist rule.

But other factors also raise difficulties. The presence of determined defenders of authoritarian rule throughout the bureaucracies of the old political, military, economic, and educational institutions constitutes grave handicaps. Some seek to reestablish the Soviet Union and achieve communism, whatever that is. Much of the weary and confused populace seeks order and regular supplies more than political change. The economy is not only shattered in a society always poor except in things military, but devastated by declining production, broken-down distribution systems, and massive inflation. The society is deeply divided, corrupt, and unstable. The virulent intellectual, social, and economic poisons that the Soviet system inculcated have spread throughout society: pollution is a kind of outer symbol of the inner wretchedness communism has produced. Ethnic quarrels have broken open in the last few years on the fringes of the empire. Maintaining sense and stability in moving ahead is difficult: society is falling apart. And the collapse of an empire creates problems that may resemble those the Weimar Republic faced over the loss of territories that had been German. The difficulties surrounding creation of a new commonwealth may undermine efforts to create an open society.

Those who wish change are not united and many have special priorities of their own. Inexperience with self-management, self-rule, and individual enterprise, low-morale, and appalling ignorance handicap all programs seeking democratic rule. Indeed, Russia is chronologically in the twentieth century, but much of it, urban as well as rural, reflects the eighteenth century or even earlier. Finally, the anatomy of revolution that Taine analyzed 140 years ago suggests that the Soviet Union has just passed 1789 and is in 1791 or 1792 in movement toward change of some kind.[5]

On the other hand, reasons exist for hope. The Leninist system has lost appeal and legitimacy even among most Communists. The party has collapsed, ideology no longer convinces, and no one considers the "heavenly city" possible. The external empire has faded, costly subsidies to other Communist states are ending, and empirical illusions have vanished. The government and people have turned energies inward, and the "enemy without" consists of Samaritans providing assistance. The free speech and free press, multiple parties, and form of parliament elected under arrangements like that in England 160 years ago have given the Russian government legitimacy and popular support no other Russian government has had. Millions now support democracy and participate in active political groups. In short, Gorbachev did far more to destroy the authoritarian system than he planned or wanted. These changes introduced have enabled the Russians to learn far more about their past than they had known and have brought about some of the vast accumulation of failures and evils to public view. They have also increased access to outside information and stimulated development of a spirit of critical inquiry not only about contemporary affairs and the past, but also about future arrangements as well. All these developments promise well.

Russian history is full of paradoxes. For example, Communist achievements contributed substantially to prospects for a more open society. Massive industrialization and urbanization created economic and social bases for advancement toward democracy. The system in theory had no middle classes, because theoretically it lacked an aristocracy and lower classes. However, it trained and gave experience to thousands of professional people and skilled workers whose status resembles that of the middle class in democratic societies, even though they lack thus far its independence. The enormous expansion of education at all levels, particularly of higher education, the emphasis upon science and technology, and the visible chasm between reality and propaganda have produced generations of citizens whose knowledge is superior and whose approach to all issues is different from that of thirty years ago. Even before Gorbachev, slow internal developments had produced subtle social changes and pressures against controls and for more openness and honesty. A country with 18,000,000 graduates from institutions of higher learning faces better prospects for democracy than one with six universities and 18,000 students. Russia now has millions of young men and women who no longer accept being "the revolution's children." The sons and daughters, grandsons and granddaughters, of those who established the Soviet system have turned against it, as most younger generations tend to reject their predecessors' achievements. In a sense, the Soviet system produced the seeds of its own destruction.

In another paradox, Soviet control over Eastern Europe proved a long term blessing to those who seek to establish a democratic system in Russia. The high costs of empire contributed to disintegration of the system. East European peoples proved to be carriers of Western ideas and attitudes, rather than barriers against them. Just as the millions of Poles acquired in the seventeenth and eighteenth centuries proved difficult to absorb and carried infections into Russia, so the East European peoples have acted in the twentieth century. Progress of the northern countries of East-Central Europe towards open societies and economic prosperity will continue to exert a profound influence upon Russia.

Perhaps the most important and least recognized cause of hope is the exposure of the Soviet Union to the outside world at an increasing rate of speed, particularly in the last three decades. Louis XIV three hundred years ago remarked that "nations touch only at the top."[6] Today, that elite is greatly enlarged, as Russia has become an active participant in international politics, economics, and cultural life. This has created a large group in the elite quite well informed about the world, even its languages and cultures, and the ways in which their country measures against others. Their information and attitudes have filtered through the other upper levels down into society. Moreover, the old diplomacy of Louis XIV has vastly expanded, so that academic and scientific exchanges, tours of basketball teams and ballet groups, and trade with many other countries have contributed. As the world has shrunk, jeans and jazz, rock music, and other Western products and symbols have helped dissolve Soviet society as they have Western societies and traditions. Radio and television and the explosion of modern transportation and communication have helped to transform Russian society at the bottom, so that consumer products and the age of information have profoundly affected Eastern Europe and the Soviet Union.

These foreign influences would not have been so significant if the West, including the United States, Japan, and now other countries of Asia and Latin America, had not made such progress toward increasingly democratic societies and high prosperity that even those behind the old iron curtain were impressed. The spiritual and political vitality of Western Europe, the economic recovery of individual countries and the Western area as a whole, the dismantling of Western empires, establishment of the Common

Market and other international institutions, and continued progress towards resolving the eternal economic and social problems modern societies face have all had a profound effect. The progress of countries such as Portugal, Greece, South Korea, many of the Latin American countries, and even South Africa have demonstrated what others have achieved under circumstances as difficult as those Russians face. When the women's liberation movement strikes, as it will, that too will press the Russian people farther toward a more open, equitable, and democratic society.

Russian institutions, experience, and attitudes founded in the distant past but strengthened over centuries continue to exercise enormous influence upon present practices and views. But the age of democratic revolutions that began in the 1770s is enjoying another surge, helped this time by the age of information and modern technology. Indeed, maintaining a dictatorship in an age of supersonic aircraft, billions of pocket computers, and FAX may prove impossible in any state, even the most conservative societies with powerful statist traditions. This time Sisyphus may reach the top and Russia may be able to capture the spirit of the West as well as its artifacts and institutions. Gorbachev may prove different from Alexander II in that he released forces that have swept his party and him away. But the road will remain difficult, as it always has been.

Russian history suggests that Leninism had far stronger roots than did democracy and that those foundations were decisive in the crisis that arose late in the First World War. The historical background remains significant, and together with the many vast interrelated problems that face the Russian people may lead to the reemergence of another form of authoritarianism. Yet, the remarkable surge that has led to establishing a democratic framework in Russia and other states that the Soviet system had ruled may lead to similar changes in the People's Republic of China. The economic revisions introduced there may lead one day to political changes, as the relaxation of political and intellectual controls did in Russia.

But who can tell?

Notes

1. Sergei, M. Soloviev, *Istoriia Rossii s drevneishikh vremen* (Moscow: 1962). Izd-vo sotsial'no-ekonomicheskoi literatury, 15 vols.; and Vasilii O. Kliuchevskii, *Kurs russkoi istorii* (1956-1957) : Nauka, I: 41-64, 69, 308-14; II: 200-219.

2. Charles J. Halperin, *Russia and the Golden Horde: The Mongol Impact on Medieval Russian History* (Bloomington: Indiana, 1985); Donald Ostrowski, "The Mongol Origins of Muscovite Political Institutions," *Slavic Review* (1990): 49, 525-42.

3. Nicholas Berdiaev, *The Origin of Russian Communism* (Ann Arbor: Michigan University Press, 1968).

4. Arnold Toynbee, *A Study of History* (New York: Oxford University Press, 1948), I, 67.

5. Hippolyte Antoine Taine, *Les Origins de la France contemporaine* (Paris: Hachette, 1887-1894) I, i-xii.

6. C. B. Picavet, *La diplomatie francaise au temps de Louis XIV, 1662-1715* (Paris: Alcan, 1930), 29-32.

4

Democracy and the Market: A Marriage of Inconvenience

Jeff Weintraub

It already seems clear that the 1980s will prove in retrospect to have been a landmark decade in the history of democracy, worthy perhaps to be compared to the "age of the democratic revolution" which closed the eighteenth century.[1] They brought to a climax the remarkable wave of democratic openings and transitions that began in the 1970s with the political transformations of Greece, Spain, and Portugal; witnessed the fall or gradual abdication of military regimes across Latin America; produced democratic pressures or even breakthroughs in countries as disparate as the Philippines, Mexico, and South Korea; and culminated in the *annus mirabilis* of 1989, with the general collapse of the neo-Stalinist order in Eastern (or Central and Eastern) Europe, marking the effective bankruptcy of the grand Leninist project which has absorbed so much of the political energy and idealism of the twentieth century.

Nor has the current age of democratic revolution necessarily run its course. If the disintegration of the Soviet Union is followed by the consolidation of political liberty in Russia, the Ukraine, and other fragments of the former Soviet empire; if South Africa, implausibly, manages a successful passage to a multi-racial democratic regime; if there is serious movement toward democracy in China -- then the 1990s may almost overshadow the 1980s.

The hopeful side of this scenario is the continued existence of pressures for democracy and the prospect of new and important democratic openings. Its sobering side is the fact that the long-term *success* of current efforts toward democratization is far from guaranteed. The weakening or collapse of an authoritarian regime is not necessarily the same thing as the successful institutionalization of democracy -- one need only consider the consequences of 1917, or even of 1789. One of the hard lessons of history, as Edward Friedman emphasizes in his contribution to this volume, is that transitions from despotism to democracy are rarely quick or smooth and are often painful, even when they eventually succeed. A few fortunate countries may hope to repeat the extraordinary success story of post-Franco Spain; but in most cases -- and this certainly applies to almost all of the post-Leninist world -- what we are witnessing is only the beginning of a difficult and dangerous drama whose last act cannot be taken for granted.

This is, in short, an historical moment when democracy presents itself with special urgency as both a theoretical problem and a practical challenge. It is therefore appropriate to try to evaluate carefully the theoretical resources available to address the issues involved, and to consider how they can best be brought to bear on current developments. And, on the other hand, this remarkable moment provides an auspicious occasion to reconsider some of the central issues regarding the relationships among democracy, the market, and the state which have been on the theoretical and practical agenda of the modern West, and then of much of the rest of the world, since the early nineteenth century -- the unsettled questions of the political sociology of modernity, to put it Germanically.

The present chapter will attempt to contribute to this double enterprise. It will sketch some elements of an orienting theoretical framework which can provide a guide for approaching, and integrating, certain key issues regarding the problem of democratization. In the process, it will try to convey two larger messages that go beyond the specific topics addressed here.

The first is the need for a considerable degree of refinement, and of what might be called "complexification," in the theoretical paradigms used to address issues of democracy and democratization. Current discussions, as I will try to illustrate, often tend to pose both theoretical and practical alternatives in overly easy and simplistic ways that can be unhelpful at best, misleading at worst.

The second is the need to do justice both to the essential continuity of some of the fundamental issues *and* to the historical particularity of the ways that they currently present themselves. The challenges facing those societies now emerging from under the rubble of the Leninist project are in certain respects unique and unprecedented. The attempt has never before been made to move simultaneously from a state-socialist command economy to a market economy and from post-totalitarian despotism to a democratic regime. But, at the same time, many of the most important underlying issues are not entirely new; they have, in fact, been a source of continuous perplexity since the onset of what Karl Polanyi called the Great Transformation in the West.[2] On the one hand, despite the exasperated sentiment of "no more experiments!" often found in Eastern Europe, those societies are unavoidably engaged in a great leap into the unknown. On the other hand, there is an important sense in which the post-Leninist world, having passed through a gigantic world-historical detour, is now re-encountering the central dilemmas of the great transformation (though not, of course, in *precisely* the same form).

The Present Moment

Let me begin by noting some key features of the intellectual and ideological landscape within which contemporary discourse about democracy takes place, both in the context of academic debate and in the realm of political action. Three elements, taken together, seem to be decisive in defining what is distinctive about the present moment.

The first of these elements is, of course, the unprecedented world-wide power and prestige of the democratic idea. It is worth reminding ourselves how exceptional, even surprising, this situation is. In particular, this is probably the first moment in the twentieth century when the ideal of "democracy" (in some sense that does not actually mean revolutionary dictatorship) has had something like ideological hegemony among intellectuals and political activists in both Europe and the western hemisphere -- and, to a striking though uneven extent, in much of the rest of the world as well. Of course, hegemony does not mean unanimity. But for the moment, at least, almost all the major *principled* alternatives to democracy thrown up by the twentieth century -- Leninism, Stalinism, fascism, authoritarian corporatism -- are discredited or in disarray. (Islamic "fundamentalism," in its different varieties, constitutes the most dramatic exception to this pattern.) How long this situation will last is an open question. But, whatever the outcomes of current efforts toward democratization, the strength and pervasiveness of democratic *aspiration* is one of the grand facts of our time.

The second of these grand facts is that this flowering of democratic aspiration coincides with -- and, indeed, is very often linked to -- a wave of increased enthusiasm, or at least respect, for the magic of the market. This is, again, not at all a localized phenomenon. In Latin America as well as Eastern Europe, if one speaks of "economic reform" this will immediately be understood to mean marketization, just as "political reform" will be taken to refer to democratization--something that would hardly have been true a decade ago.

A third grand fact -- which to some extent brings the previous two together -- is the degree to which, in the last decade of the twentieth century, the societies of Western Europe and North America represent overwhelmingly, for much of the world, the model of successful modernity -- particularly since the collapse of the major *alternative* model of industrial society in Eastern Europe. Over half a century ago Lincoln Steffens captured a very different mood when he said, after a visit to the Soviet Union, that he had seen the future and it *worked*. For most contemporary Eastern Europeans -- and not for them alone -- it is Western society that "works." The contrast with the West played a major role in convincing them that their own societies did *not* work, and the Western model now is a central point of reference guiding their attempts at social reconstruction. The market economy and democracy are two central elements of the package that this model represents.

Modernity and Complexity

I emphasized earlier the need for considerable theoretical "complexification" in many current approaches to the problems of democratization. One reason this theoretical complexification is necessary is that the 'solution' to the dilemmas of modernity worked out (more or less successfully) in the West over the last few centuries is itself much more complex and paradoxical than is often appreciated when it is drawn on to provide a model for the post-Leninist world. Put briefly: The key to the Western 'success' (when it *has* been successful) has *not* involved unleashing a single system of social relationships (e.g., capitalism or democracy) whose principles have subsumed all others, or which necessarily generates or "determines" all the others.[3] Rather, it has involved finding ways to manage and coordinate the ongoing interplay of an *ensemble* of systems which are *potentially* complementary, but which are analytically distinct and potentially in tension, because their central organizing principles are quite different.[4]

This pattern is exemplified dramatically in the relationship between *democracy* and the *market economy*. I will argue for the irreducible complexity of this relationship, try to elucidate the reasons for this complexity, and explore some of its implications for the problems of democratization. To summarize: The essential verdict, in light of historical experience from 1789 to 1989, is that democracy and the market economy are potentially compatible and even (for the foreseeable future) inescapably complementary, but *also* in necessary and permanent tension. This is a possible and necessary marriage, but an inherently difficult one. We might go so far as to call it a marriage of inconvenience.

Some Preliminary Clarifications

Before proceeding, I should offer some indication of what I mean in speaking of "democracy" and the "market economy." These are two complex and contested notions, for which rapid definitions will be of only limited help; but some initial clarification may be useful.

By "democracy" I mean self-government -- or, to put it more technically, a system of ongoing collective self-determination. This implies that, to a significant degree, (1) consequential collective outcomes are subject to discussion and conscious decision; (2) the decision-making process is, in one way or another, ultimately controlled by the people affected by those outcomes; (3) those people are treated as being, in principle, fundamentally equal in political rights. As an essential definition, I admit I find it hard to improve on Abraham Lincoln's formulation: "government of the people, by the people, for the people." Of course, any actual democratic system will achieve this objective only to a greater or lesser degree.

Centuries of historical experience have suggested a set of basic institutional requirements for a democratic regime, which can be touched on here only selectively and schematically. In a community of any size and complexity, democratic government must include a representative system in which power-holders are ultimately accountable to popular election. Representative government, in turn, requires a party system in which parties compete for a mandate and governing parties can lose. Furthermore, a democratic system can work only if individuals are effectively guaranteed certain rights under law, not least those which allow them to speak and organize freely. Such a situation requires the existence of a form of state based on the rule of law, in which the legal system is administered by an independent judiciary who can secure the rights of individuals against the abuses of power-holders, or even against the transient will of democratic majorities.[5] It requires, that is, what the Germans call a *Rechtsstaat*. A *Rechtsstaat* is not necessarily a democratic regime; but a democratic regime is necessarily, among other things, a *Rechtsstaat* (to settle by fiat, for the moment, a subject of centuries of debate).

Representative government need not necessarily be democratic, since it may involve the extension of political rights to only a small fraction of the population. Only a representative regime with an inclusive electorate is properly termed a democracy. Even where there is formally a democratic electorate, a sizable portion of it may be effectively unable to exercise political power, whether because of economic dependence, inability to organize, intimidation, or other reasons. The result will be one of those oligarchic pseudo-representative regimes all too familiar from Latin American history -- which tend to collapse in the event of serious social conflicts. Finally, the elected government must itself be capable of exercising effective power; where actual power is monopolized by other actors -- e.g., an uncontrolled army -- democracy is, again, nominal rather than genuine.

There is a good deal more to be said about the nature and requirements of democracy -- and some of it will be said later in this chapter -- but the foregoing should be enough to establish the basic contours of the concept.

With the market economy I will be even more brusque. A market is a system of relationships based on the exchange of commodities for gain. A market economy is an economic system in which the market is the *predominant* mechanism coordinating production and distribution (in no socio-economic system has it ever been the *exclusive* mechanism). This entails, not only that most social production be exchanged as commodities on the market, but also that the means of production and labor be effectively treated as commodities. The commoditization of labor means in practice that large-scale, coordinated production is carried out primarily by means of wage labor.

The significance of the wage-labor relationship is that the individual productive enterprise is a command system, with inequality of power between workers on the one hand and capitalists and/or managers on the other. It is possible in principle to imagine an economy in which overall coordination was achieved by the market but specific enterprises were not based on wage labor -- in which they were organized, for example, as democratic cooperatives. One would then have a market economy, but not a capitalist one. However, it is hard to see such arrangements as the wave of the forseeable future; and, at all events, as long as different enterprises are coordinated by the market, this change would not affect most of the dynamics of the market system on which my discussion will focus.

It is important to emphasize that capitalist economies can be organized in a variety of ways and -- even more important -- can be articulated in very different ways with other social institutions. Sweden, the United States, and Guatemala are all societies with capitalist economies; but it would be hard to maintain seriously that identifying the three as "capitalist societies" told us everything important we wanted to know about them.

A Marriage of Inconvenience

One of the central questions posed for Western social thought by the interplay of the French and industrial revolutions (one which is again becoming a burning issue in the post-Leninist world) may sound surprising to some readers at this moment: Is democracy compatible with the capitalist market economy? It is easy to forget how genuinely uncertain the answer appeared before 1945. The answer provided by history seems to be "yes," but it is important to consider the weight and cogency of the qualifications. A variety of figures -- ranging from Karl

Marx and Karl Polanyi to Augusto Pinochet -- have answered "no" for quite intellectually respectable reasons; and it is worth bearing in mind that European history from the nineteenth century through the 1940s provided a good deal of evidence to render this verdict plausible.

The terms of the question, however, have been decisively changed by two crucial developments since World War II. The first is the consolidation of stable representative regimes based on a mass franchise throughout Western Europe -- an astonishing achievement in light of previous history, which people are now inclined to take too much for granted. This suggests that democracy and the market economy can cohabit. And the second is the accumulation of evidence that no one has come up with an adequate, let alone superior, alternative to capitalism as a way of organizing a modern economy -- certainly not one which holds out more auspicious prospects for democracy. Marx's vision of socialism and the "actually existing socialism" of Leninism and Stalinism differ in quite drastic ways. But, for both, the transcendence of the market is at the heart of socialism; and it is precisely the idea that this goal is practicable and desirable that has ceased to be credible.

Much of the theoretical debate and political conflict of the last two centuries has been colored by the widespread belief -- which took a variety of forms -- that a fundamental alternative to the market economy existed and could be readily put into practice. The general collapse of faith that such an alternative is available is thus a world-historical event of the first magnitude. It eliminates any easy way out of confronting the dilemmas involved in the relationship between democracy and the market economy.

These dilemmas are real, however, and continue to exist. It has always been clear that we can have capitalism without democracy. But the contrary now seems unlikely (and is certainly undemonstrated). At this point in history, any serious consideration of democracy must take it as a premise that, if democracy is to exist, it will have to be in co-existence with some version of the capitalist market economy (and, over the long run, probably only in co-existence with a fairly healthy market economy). But it is unwarranted to leap to the conclusion, often expressed in the easy use of the phrase "democratic capitalism," that the relationship between a capitalist socio-economic system and a democratic regime is straightforward and unproblematic. In fact, they remain two quite different systems, with a permanent potential for disharmony; and this is not accidental, since (among other reasons) their organizing principles are in profound tension.

To state this contrast somewhat ideal-typically: In the market, collective outcomes emerge from the relatively spontaneous operation of impersonal forces, the systemic "discipline" of the "invisible hand." And this impersonal constraint is not an incidental feature of the market system, but is inseparable from what is potentially *valuable* about the market. In the individual capitalist enterprise (as in the administrative dimension of the modern state), coordination is enforced by authority from above, and increasingly by what Alfred Chandler calls the "visible hand"[6] of bureaucratically administered formal organization. But the central premise of democracy is that collective outcomes are subject, in some important degree, to the conscious consideration and collective decision of the people affected.[7]

The two systems may be compatible in practice -- even, under the right conditions, mutually supportive -- but they remain analytically distinct; each runs according to a different inner logic and generates a different theoretical problem. The *laissez-faire* utopia of the fully self-regulating market is no more equivalent to democracy than is the "mono-organizational" utopia (to use Rigby's apt phrase) of post-Stalinist state socialism.[8] Thus, attempts to collapse democracy theoretically into the market (often the import of analyses deriving from utilitarian liberalism, which currently go under the name of "rational choice") are fundamentally misconceived and misleading.

Nor is this distinction important only at the level of formal abstraction. It has important practical implications, which are likely to manifest themselves with particular urgency precisely when the attempt is made to move simultaneously toward *both* democracy and the market economy. The heart of the tension between them is obvious but profound (Polanyi's account remains the most penetrating): (1) The essence, and the marvel, of the market is that it is a (more or less) spontaneously self-regulating *system* of interdependence, which is coordinated by the impersonal *constraint* it exercises over the actors in the system.[9] It is not the case that any interference with the "magic of the market" is necessarily destabilizing; but it *is* the case that there is a limit to how much blockage and interference the market system can withstand before starting to short-circuit and malfunction. On the other hand, (2) the dynamics of the market system (which Schumpeter, who loved capitalism, called a "continuous gale of creative destruction"[10]) are inherently disruptive both to the interests of particular groups and to the more general fabric of cultural continuity, so that they provide continual inducements for interference in the form of collective action and state intervention. And democratic empowerment (where it is genuine and not merely formal) gives an ever-wider range of social groups the means (as well as the right) to act politically so as defend themselves against the unhampered operation of the market and to try to influence collective outcomes to their own advantage.

Therefore, the two systems can coexist only if democracy is willing to be (to a degree yet to be determined) "self-limiting" with respect to the autonomous dynamics of the market. And this will require, among other things, a cultural framework which includes at least a minimal acceptance of market-oriented values and activities, and also a basic acceptance of the need to defer to the market's impersonal discipline. In the long run, maintaining this coexistence probably also requires some minimum rate of economic growth, as well as the buffering effects of various non-market phenomena: policies which are able to contain or offset the market's most socially disruptive effects without short-circuiting the system; enough underlying social solidarity to keep conflicts from getting out of hand; and so on. Otherwise, what results is economic decline at best, and, at worst, escalating crisis and social conflict and, eventually, some form of political authoritarianism (or worse) when the going gets rough.

This sort of deference is necessary to maintain the health of the *market*. But, from the point of view of democracy, this deference cannot amount to abdication. Democracy may be able to coexist with the market, but it cannot be expected to surrender entirely to the logic of a fully self-regulating market. This is not only utopian from a practical point of view; it would also mean giving up any possibility of democratic control over the course of social life, which would make it suicidal rather than self-limiting. Democracy also requires a *different*, and partly conflicting, set of practices, assumptions, and values from those of the market, since it is organized around processes of collective decision-making, collective action, and collective self-determination. In so far as democracy is genuine rather than purely nominal, individuals and groups have the potential power to call collective outcomes into question, and will therefore have to be convinced (more or less) of the *fairness* of collective outcomes through a process of discussion and negotiation. As Friedrich Hayek brings out with particular clarity and forthrightness, these processes and concerns are incompatible in principle with the central logic of the market system.[11] This is a tension that can be managed but not eliminated.

For most of the last several centuries, as I noted earlier, it has been widely believed that there is a way out of these dilemmas based on abolishing, transcending, or sharply restricting the market economy. This belief has yielded two key positions: (1) Democracy can be made possible, and rendered genuine, by eliminating the market economy and replacing it with socialism. (This is the standpoint of various forms of democratic socialism, including Polanyi's -- and, with some special features, of Marx's socialism.) (2) One of the *advantages* of eliminating democracy is precisely that it makes possible the abolition (or drastic curtailment) of the market economy in favor of some form of command arrangement. (This is the standpoint of Leninism and Stalinism, and also of the "magic anti-capitalism" of fascism, as well as various less extreme tendencies. In the twentieth century, the supposedly "left-wing" and "right-wing" strands here have often come together in some forms of "dependency theory" and contemporary "anti-imperialism.")

However, the essential foundation for all these positions is the premise that there exists a superior, and readily available, alternative to the market economy. Therefore, the intellectual collapse of this premise has been devastating in its impact. There are some who see the results leading to the demise, not only of Leninism, but of socialism more generally. This outcome seems to me unlikely; but it is certainly true that, for the forseeable future, no credible socialism can conceive itself in terms of the abolition of the market.

There is, of course, a third possible response to the tension between democracy and the market: the Chilean or South Korean route of combining a capitalist socio-economic system with an authoritarian regime. The Chilean example is a particularly pure case of using the terroristic power of a despotic regime to break the population's resistance to the self-regulating market. While the economic consequences of despotic regimes are generally disastrous, it is clear that in certain cases the authoritarian/market strategy has yielded genuine results in terms of economic development. But the successes of this model are hardly cheering for those committed to democracy; they have been more likely to encourage, for example, those Chinese "reformers" who hope to escape economic stagnation while avoiding any concessions to democracy.[12] But in recent years this model has also lost some of its aura of prestige and inevitability. The case for this strategy relies too much on assumptions about the inherent impossibility of stable democratic regimes which now appear to be overdrawn. And it is clear that this strategy eventually generates important socio-political contradictions of its own, including, if it is economically successful, increasing demands for democracy, as Peter Toumanoff argues in a later chapter.

In short, we can have capitalism without democracy but not, it appears, democracy without capitalism; and a recognition of this fact must form the starting-point for any serious thinking about democracy and democratization in our era. *But*, at the same time, the combination of democracy with capitalism requires living with a permanent tension. The relationship seems to be at once inextricably interdependent and inescapably contradictory, and it will be necessary to recognize its irreducible ambivalence.

Political Society, Civil Society, and the State

Thus far the discussion has focused primarily on the requirements of the market economy. But what are the requirements of democracy, and how are they affected by the impact of the market economy?

One necessary step toward elucidating this relationship is a complexification in the theory of democracy itself. In this respect, I would propose a reformulation and refinement of one of the most significant conceptual distinctions in modern social and political analysis, one which has become ubiquitous in recent discussions, including those in this volume: the distinction between civil society and the state. The concept of "civil society" has a long and checkered history in Western thought, in the course of which it has been given a range of different and even contradictory meanings.[13] With the sudden and sweeping increase in the popularity of this notion during the last decade or so--in both scholarly and political circles -- it has become increasingly hazy and ambiguous. (The main common denominator is that almost everyone now agrees that, whatever it is, "civil society" is a Good Thing -- as opposed to, say, Marx, who wanted to abolish it.)

This is not the place to survey the different usages or enter into the relevant controversies. Let me simply say that the valid intuition behind the fascination with "civil society" is the recognition that democracy is not simply a matter of how the state is organized, but has to do above all with the *relationship* between state and society. One basic requirement of democracy is that members of the society have the capacity to organize in order to exert control over the state, and this in turn requires the existence of a sphere of activities and institutions independent of the control of state power. However, the usual dichotomous distinction between state and civil society, in which "civil society" often tends to serve as a more or less undifferentiated residual category, is both inadequate and misleading for addressing the relevant issues.

Lessons from Tocqueville

One element in building up a more effective theory of democracy should be a conceptual framework that distinguishes analytically between the *state* (in the sense of the more or less centralized apparatus of domination and administration), civil society (the modern sphere of individualistic relations centered above all on the market and private life), and *political society* (the sphere of collective action, conflict, and cooperation which mediates between the two), so as to be able to trace their interplay and interpenetration in a systematic and historically specific way.[14] In making this suggestion, I draw in particular on my understanding of Tocqueville's political sociology, which he intended to be a sociology of liberty -- that is, one whose central problem was the possibility and social conditions of liberty in the modern world. Tocqueville's decisive contribution lies in his insistence that genuine democratic self-government must rest on more than legal mechanisms and formal political institutions, though these are of course indispensable. It requires, in addition, the existence and vitality of a wider political community supported by a political culture of citizenship -- which, as we will see, is a rather special and delicate thing.[15]

One point of terminological clarification before proceeding: We can avoid some common confusions by reminding ourselves of the ways that Tocqueville uses some of the key terms involved, beginning with "democracy" itself. Although Tocqueville's terminology is not absolutely consistent here, he generally uses "democracy" to mean, not a particular kind of political regime, but rather a certain kind of social order -- that is, one based on fundamental equality and individualism. The term he generally uses to denote a regime based on self-government and collective decision-making is *political liberty*. A system of political liberty may be based on a restricted franchise, like England's in the eighteenth and nineteenth century; or it might come to incorporate (more or less) the whole adult population. In the latter case, political liberty becomes democratic and can be called, as a shorthand, democratic liberty. But a "democratic" social order is also compatible with a distinctively democratic *despotism* (of which the former People's Democracies would be good examples). Following common usage, I will often speak of democracy where Tocqueville would say democratic *liberty*, but it is worth keeping Tocqueville's conceptual vocabulary in mind.

Tocqueville's starting point is the decay of those forms of organic community and independent authority which, in a more traditional society, serve to limit and counterbalance state power. The kind of "aristocratic" liberty that they supported, rooted in tradition and a spirit of resistance, is not viable under modern conditions. The *political* liberty possible in a democratic age is different in form and requires a new theory ("a new science of politics").

Tocqueville is often misinterpreted as either a nostalgic conservative aristocrat or a liberal exponent of a purely "negative" liberty. In fact, Tocqueville's "new science of politics" centers on a theory of political community developed within the framework of what I call the republican virtue tradition,[16] a theory which focuses on the interaction between political institutions and political culture. What I mean by the republican virtue tradition is that broad current of modern Western social thought oriented above all to the idea of *citizenship*.

Now, citizenship is not a word to be used lightly. The defining mark of democratic citizenship, in any strong sense of the term, is the capacity of individuals to enter, directly or indirectly, into a process of collective decision-making and collective self-determination, involving the conscious consideration and resolution of public issues. This process may be mediated through a variety of institutional mechanisms. But its effective operation requires a certain degree of active and responsible participation in a decision-making *community* based on fundamental equality and maintained by fundamental solidarity and the exercise of what used to be called republican virtue.[17] The practice of citizenship thus requires a distinctive ethos, and involves a distinctive set of skills and orientations, different from those pertaining to, for example, the market or bureaucratic administration.

As I indicated above, the key to Tocqueville's position is that he does not draw his crucial distinction between the state and civil society but instead distinguishes -- at times implicitly, sometimes explicitly -- among the state, civil society, and *political society*.[18] Political society is the whole realm of activities oriented toward voluntary concerted action, conscious solidarity, and the discussion and collective resolution of public issues. As an analytical category it cuts across the more obvious division between governmental and non-governmental, excluding much administration and including -- to give some well-known examples -- local self-government, voluntary associations, trial by jury, some aspects of religion, and so on.

The heart of Tocqueville's approach is precisely that he analyzes political society as a *system*, as a distinctive sphere of social life with its own special dynamics and requirements. For example, the self-governing township analyzed in *Democracy in America* is only one of a range of democratic "secondary" or "intermediate" powers based on the active participation of citizens as equals in collective decision-making (as opposed to the "secondary" powers of aristocratic society, which rest on tradition and dependent ties). The guiding insight here is that political liberty is about the exercise of *power* -- meaning not simply power over others but, more fundamentally, the capacity to get things done) -- and that political power is constituted by the ability to act in concert. The moral isolation of individuals, on the contrary, makes them not autonomous, but weak and powerless.

Such "secondary" powers serve two, mutually reinforcing, functions in a system of democratic liberty: (1) They serve as centers of resistance against, and as socially workable *alternatives* to, centralized or arbitrary power. And (2) the experience of participating in the exercise of political liberty is a crucial element in the formation and "practical political education" of *citizens* -- that is, it contributes to the process through which individuals (and groups) develop the values, skills, and commitments (i.e., the "mores") which render them willing and able to make political liberty *work*. And these "secondary powers" can do this, of course, only if they form elements in a larger national polity in which political liberty is institutionalized and exercised.

What defines a democratic political society is this active interplay of power and culture, and not any fixed or invariant set of institutions or organizations. In some societies, for example, we can see the labor movement as a crucial element in political society (to use an example about which Tocqueville might have been ambivalent) -- and in other contexts it may simply consist of some narrowly defensive organizations in civil society. The political significance of voluntary associations (even, frequently, those without explicitly "political" aims) is that they serve as a series of points of *mediation* between civil society and political society, and contribute to the political education of citizens.[19] Parties can also play this role, of course -- but not necessarily. And Tocqueville famously saw religion as, in a sense, the most important political institution in America -- *not* because it had any direct influence over government, but because of the (rather subtle) role it played in forming the political culture of citizenship.

The mores of citizenship -- or, as Tocqueville also puts it, the spirit of the *citizen* -- require a delicate, and in some ways difficult, balance of two complementary elements. On the one hand, the citizen must be active and assertive (as well as competent) in insisting on his participation in the collective exercise of political power, both to advance his own interests and beliefs and to resist arbitrary or illegitimate power; on the other hand, the spirit of the citizen requires a willingness and capacity for *self*-discipline and self-restraint which grows out of a sense of responsibility for the collective results of his actions. And this combination of activism and responsibility rests, in turn, on a sense of fundamental *solidarity* with other citizens, and of commitment to the political community and to the regime of political liberty itself.

By contrast, the spirit of the *subject* combines habitual political passivity with, from time to time, periodic outbursts of riot or disorder in moments of outrage or of the weakening of authority. What marks both sides of the spirit of the subject, Tocqueville emphasizes, is the absence of any sense of responsibility for the management of social affairs -- which are someone else's concern. Of course, rulers would like subjects to be responsible and self-disciplined as well as passively obedient (this attitude has certainly not passed from the historical scene). But it is futile (certainly in a democratic age) to expect people to develop a sense of responsibility unless they are also accustomed to having power -- not just formally, but in terms of the experience of actually participating in its exercise. The reader will recall Acton's famous aphorism that absolute power corrupts absolutely; Tocqueville would certainly agree, but he would add that the absence of political power -- of the active *exercise* of political power -- can *also* be corrupting.

Tocqueville's analysis of political liberty is of course mirrored by a penetrating, though hostile, analysis of the modern centralized state. The centralized bureaucratic state is potentially quite threatening to political society, Tocqueville emphasizes, not only in terms of direct repression, but also because the pervasiveness of centralized administration chokes off the sources of political life at their source and smothers political society. If participation in political liberty is part of a process of political education which helps generate the spirit of the citizen, then we can say that the experience of subordination to bureaucratic despotism furthers a kind of political mis-education which strengthens the spirit of the subject. Thus, even if a despotic regime is overthrown, its legacy will help to insure that, after an interlude of instability, it will be replaced by another despotic regime.

But the threat posed by the state is only one side of Tocqueville's analysis. Tocqueville argues that civil society can *also* pose a threat to political society. This is because the central tendency of modern civil society -- if left to itself -- is precisely to isolate individuals, to disrupt ties of community, and to encourage a single-minded focus on purely private concerns -- above all, on making money. That is, the mores of the market are not the mores of citizenship. If these atomizing tendencies of civil society are not *counterbalanced* by an active political society based on democratic citizenship -- as they were, he believed, in the America of the 1830s -- then they will help produce a society incapable of political community and self-determination, in which the despotism of a cen-tralized bureaucratic state will be irresistible. In an important sense, it will also be indispensable, since society will have lost the capacity to run itself. Historically, a despotic centralized state and a privatized civil society actually reinforce each other in various ways; the danger, from the point of view of political liberty, is that political society will be squeezed out between them.

Tocqueville's picture of the relationship between state and society in the modern world is thus dominated by two polar alternatives: In the first, society is both active and cohesive, capable of self-organization and of both resisting and controlling state power. In the second, society is an inert and passive mass of isolated individuals (or small intimate circles) dominated by a centralized state that surmounts it like a foreign body. And both these situations are, to a certain extent, self-reinforcing.

Tocqueville and Transitions from Leninism

It is clear that these themes have a strong and immediate resonance with the key issues thrown up by the experience of Leninist state-socialist regimes. In particular, one might well say that a whole generation of Eastern European critical intellectuals (beginning in Poland and Hungary) went -- quite unconsciously -- through a process of painfully rediscovering Tocqueville's problematic. However, they did so under the formula -- which I have been arguing is in some ways quite misleading -- of "civil society against the state." Since this line of thought helped stimulate the revival of concern with "civil society" in the West over the last few decades, and was then re-imported into the political and intellectual debates of other state-socialist societies (among others), it is now of far more than merely Eastern European relevance.

While one aspect of (say) the Hegelian approach is the failure to focus sufficiently on the distinction between *the state* and political society, in many current usages certain key issues are obscured by collapsing *civil society* and political society. Let me give one concrete example of the distinction: In both Hungary and Poland the state increasingly lost its grip on society during the last decades of the post-Stalinist regime. But the Hungarian pattern centered on the gradual building up of *civil society*, based on the growth of the "second economy" and the leaching-away of social energies into privatization (as Elemér Hankiss once put it, what was emerging was not simply a "second economy" but a "second society"[20]). This was partly the result of a deliberate Kadarist strategy of finding an Eastern European mode of coexistence between the state and civil society, based on the effective suppression of political society -- but it was a strategy that went awry. Poland, however, saw the dramatic eruption (though not, in the short run, the successful institutionalization) of *political society*, based on conscious collective action, social self-organization, and (of course) active solidarity. The dynamics, as well as the long-term effects, of these two processes are very different.[21] It is therefore important to have a conceptual vocabulary which brings out sharply, rather than blurring, the key analytical distinctions. And this requires marking off political society as a distinctive and coherent (though complex) object of analysis.[22]

Tocqueville's sociology of political liberty can therefore offer us especially valuable guidance in approaching some of the challenges and dilemmas of post-Leninist democratization, both because of the conceptual resources it provides and because of the orienting moral commitment that informs them. Let me sum up some particularly crucial lessons that are highlighted by Tocqueville's perspective.

While "anti-politics" -- to quote a resonant East European phrase -- represented a significant and often honorable form of resistance to the despotism of the party-state, the construction of a democratic alternative requires something else: a "counter-politics" of genuine citizenship. As we have seen, "politics" and the political realm should not simply be identified with the state. As Tocqueville observes in *The Old Regime*, when the absolutist state had reached its apogee, political life reached its nadir. And observers of state-socialist regimes have noted over and over that the attempt at total state control of society, which supposedly "politicizes" everything, actually leads in the long run to massive de-politicization and privatization, in the sense of a profound cynicism and disillusionment about public life and an emotional retreat to the world of intimate relations and personal ties. This was, in many cases, a healthy reaction to a mendacious and ritualized pseudo-public life, but it is not a healthy basis for a democratic polity. What is now required is precisely the re-politicization of social life -- but in a democratic rather than a totalitarian way. In this respect, civil society (in the strict sense) can serve either as a complement *or* as an alternative to the vitality of political society. In order to consolidate a democratic order, *both* have to be rebuilt.

It is thus important to be reminded of the crucial significance of the political culture of citizenship for the maintenance of political liberty. This realization drives home the dangers inherent in some current strategies of all-out marketization that disregard or even undermine the distinctive, and in some respects, countervailing, requirements of reconstructing political society. As Andrew Arato notes in his chapter for this volume, now that the governments of post-Leninist societies are in place and have to grapple with the overwhelming problems of social reconstruction, there is a dangerous temptation to believe that politics should be the business of political elites and trained technocrats, and that between elections ordinary people should go back to private life. This temptation is particularly strong because of the enormous social pain that marketization will necessarily cause; the response is to conclude that it will be best for the masses to be demobilized while the bitter medicine is administered. However, this is likely to be a false realism. If the pain continues, short-run passivity and political withdrawal -- something which has already become noticeable in several East-Central European countries -- could turn rapidly into support for demagogic and anti-democratic movements able to mobilize a politics of helpless rage. On the other hand, if one wants to appeal to a sense of social responsibility and cooperation, one is more likely to get it from a population who think of themselves as active citizens. And they are more likely to think of themselves in this way if it accords with their actual experience.

This point suggests a final, indispensable lesson. It is not airy idealism but hard realism to say that democracy rests in the end on virtue, on the capacities and commitments of its citizens. And, as Tocqueville insists, the spirit of the citizen necessary to maintain democracy must embody a commitment which goes beyond narrow self-interest or the *purely* instrumental use of political institutions. Underlying the conflicts and disagreements of political life, there must be some fundamental civic commitment, some aspiration for democratic liberty for its own sake, some sense of common membership and shared responsibility which cannot be reduced to the moral logic of the market. As Tocqueville's mentor Montesquieu puts it in *The Spirit of the Laws*, in a formulation which strikes me as especially topical in connection with current efforts at democratization: "In [democracies] alone the government is entrusted to each citizen. Now, a government is like everything else: to preserve it we must love it."[23] This admonition is especially compelling at a moment when political liberty must not simply be maintained but be *created*, and created in circumstances of dislocation and economic crisis that will put civic commitments and capacities to the most demanding test.

Democracy as a Permanent Challenge

To those engaged in the difficult struggle for democratization in the rest of the world, Western societies are likely to stand out as spectacular success stories. And there is good reason for this. The argument that democracy in the West has been simply a sham, whether advanced from the standpoint of Marxism or elite theory or deconstruction, is wrong and pernicious. Democracy has been, to a greater or lesser extent, a genuine achievement of a number of (mostly but not exclusively Western) societies; and this degree of success is not part of the "superstructure" of modern society, but part of what defines modernity itself. But it would be equally misleading to assume that "democracy" in the West is an accomplished fact, which can simply be taken over as a model (by other societies) and comfortably enjoyed (by those of us here). Rather, it should be seen as an ongoing *project* which is still only partly accomplished and permanently precarious. In that respect, Western societies and post-Leninist societies are now -- for all their differences -- in the same boat.

Notes

1. I borrow this phrase from R.R. Palmer, *The Age of the Democratic Revolution: A Political History of Europe and America, 1760-1800*, 2 vols. (Princeton: Princeton University Press, 1959, 1964).

2. Karl Polanyi, *The Great Transformation: The Political and Economic Origins of Our Time* (Boston, Beacon Press, 1957; originally published in 1944).

3. Thus, few phrases have been more misleading than "capitalist society" when it is taken to mean, not that a capitalist socio-economic system is *a* crucial defining characteristic of "modern society," but that it is *the* defining feature.

4. This is not simply an argument about the "structural differentiation" of modern societies -- at least, as that idea is often conceived. The term "differentiation" is often used to convey the image of "subsystems" that are separated but harmoniously coordinated or mutually indifferent. I want to stress the potential for *tension* between certain of these systems.

5. For a more extended discussion of the rule of law and its importance, see Alice Erh-Soon Tay's chapter in this volume.

6. Alfred D. Chandler, Jr., *The Visible Hand: The Managerial Revolution in American Business* (Cambridge: Harvard University Press, 1977).

7. The conceptual discussion in this section is extracted in part from the argument of my forthcoming book, *Freedom and Community: The Republican Virtue Tradition and the Sociology of Liberty* (University of California Press), where the ideas are developed more fully.

8. T.H. Rigby, "Stalinism and the Mono-Organizational Society," in Robert Tucker, ed., *Stalinism: Essays in Historical Interpretation* (New York: Norton, 1977).

9. Thus, one of Smith's most prominent and sophisticated current disciples, the Hungarian economist Janos Kornai, speaks of the existence of a "hard budget constraint" on individual firms as the decisive reason for the superiority of capitalist over state-socialist economies. Janos Kornai, *The Economics of Shortage*, 2 vols. (Amsterdam: North Holland, 1980).

10. Joseph Schumpeter, *Capitalism, Socialism, and Democracy* (New York: Harper Torchbooks, 1942).

11. These arguments are developed in a number of his works, but see particularly *The Constitution of Liberty* (Chicago: University of Chicago Press, 1960) and *Law, Legislation, and Liberty*, 3 vols. (Chicago: University of Chicago Press, 1973, 1976, 1980). For Hayek, liberty is tied to the "spontaneous order" of the market, which is incompatible in principle with attempts at conscious control over collective outcomes. The health of the market thus requires rather drastic restrictions on the scope of democratic decision-making. In the second volume of the latter work (*The Mirage of Social Justice*), Hayek argues that it is not only illegitimate but, strictly speaking, meaningless to question the "fairness" or "unfairness" of market outcomes, as long as everyone has played by the rules.

12. As Kjeld Erik Brødsgaard notes in his contribution to this volume, this attempt "to combine political authoritarianism with economic liberalism" is rather laughably called "socialism with Chinese characteristics."

13. Some of the basic references are provided by Eugene Kamenka and Kjeld Erik Brødsgaard in their chapters.

14. For a more comprehensive treatment of the logic of modern societies, I think it is important to distinguish civil society analytically, not only from the more "public" realm of political society, but also from the more "private" or "personal" realm of the family and other intimate relationships. (For more details, see my paper on "The Theory and Politics of the Public/Private Distinction," noted below.) But I also think the conceptual scheme advanced here is at least a useful first step in the direction of analytical complexification.

15. My discussion here is drawn, again, from my larger argument in *Freedom and Community*. The organizing conceptual framework is laid out primarily in chs. I-II. The direct examination of Tocqueville is primarily in ch. VII. Elements of my argument here are also to be found in two unpublished papers (which have, however, circulated in the public domain): "Tocqueville's Conception of Political Society" (Unpublished paper, U. of California at San Diego, 1986) and "The Theory and Politics of the Public/Private Distinction" (Paper presented at the 1990 annual meeting of the American Political Science Association).

16. What I have termed the republican virtue tradition overlaps to some degree with what other scholars have studied under the rubrics of "classical republicanism" and "civic humanism." But I came on it from a different direction and have construed it somewhat differently (in ways I cannot elaborate fully here), so it will be clearer for me to stick to my own terminology.

17. In Tocqueville's terminology, usually "public spirit," "public virtues," or the "spirit of citizenship." These are pervasive themes in both *Democracy in America* (originally published in 1835 & 1840) and *The Old Regime and the French Revolution* (originally published in 1856).

18. See, e.g., Alexis de Tocqueville, *The Old Regime and the French Revolution* (Garden City, Doubleday, 1955), 223.

19. Many of the kinds of groups that Tocqueville calls "voluntary associations" would now be termed "social movements."

20. Elemér Hankiss, "The 'Second Society': Is There an Alternative Social Model Emerging in Contemporary Hungary?" *Social Research* 55:1 (Summer 1988).

21. This point is taken up, and applied to the Polish case, by Z.A. Pelczynski in "Solidarity and 'The Rebirth of Civil Society' in Poland" (included in John Keane, ed., *Civil Society and the State*, Guilford, Verso, 1988); see, in particular, note 14. It is now clear that the Hungarian 'solution' was less stable, and the eruption of political society in Poland less transitory, than many people once believed.

22. For two useful efforts to utilize conceptions of "political society" similar to the one being advanced here, in very different contexts, see Grzegorz Ekiert, "Democratisation Processes in East Central Europe: A Theoretical Reconceptualization" (*British Journal of Political Science* 21:3 [1991], 285-313) and Carlos Forment, "The Formation of Political Society in Spanish America: The Mexican Case, 1700-1830" (Unpublished dissertation, Harvard University, 1990). (In neither case, of course, is the author's conceptual framework precisely the same as my own.) Alfred Stepan has independently developed his own tripartite distinction among state, civil society, and political society (introduced in *Rethinking Military Politics: Brazil and the Southern Cone* [Princeton: Princeton University Press, 1988]). To avoid confusion, it is worth noting that his formulation and mine are different in key respects, and highlight somewhat different concerns. Stepan's notion of "political society" is more narrowly conceived than the one to which I want to call attention. What Stepan tends to mean by "political society" is primarily the world of professional political elites -- what Colombians call the "país político," or the French and Italians call the "political class" -- and the institutions through which they operate. This is an extremely important element of a democratic political society, in the sense discussed in this chapter, but only one element.

23. Montesquieu, *The Spirit of the Laws*, tr. Thomas Nugent (New York, Hafner, 1949; originally published in 1748), Book IV, Ch. 5, 34 (translation slightly amended).

5

Consolidating Democratic Breakthroughs in Leninist States

Edward Friedman

When the Berlin Wall fell and democracy danced on the rubble of crumbling tyranny, ecstasy was tempered by the knowledge that a breakthrough in the confining bonds of despotism does not automatically guarantee a successful consolidation of democracy. When the walls of tyranny tumble, forces surface from beneath the smelly heap whose resultant foul winds are not friendly to freedom. Wise voices warn that a nasty fate may still await the celebrants who have triumphed over the inhuman Leninist party-state. They decry "a nationalism that readily slides into an exclusive, aggressive, xenophobic chauvinism. . .drawing on the most backward and reactionary interpretations of religion."[1] Emerging from the garbage of Leninism, a "social Pandora's box. . .a Hobbesian *bellum omnium contra omnes* of ethnic, corporatist, nationalist, etc., interests,"[2] can spread "some of the most sordid aspects of traditional culture,"[3] motivating "a populace so ignorant that the main alternative to communism itself seems to be. . .vicious bigotry."[4] These latent, divisive responses to the brutally divisive rule of Leninism include the delegitimation of the prior nationalism of Leninist anti-imperialism and, consequently, a need for a new national identity, even for the dominant ethnic group.[5] This nationalist need may complicate the building of a democracy, may make the democratization of a Leninist system more complex than the democratization of many other kinds of dictatorships.

The Difficult Political Geography of Democratization

How then should a polity craft a democracy so that it will become institutionalized such that the gains from consolidating political freedom out of Leninist dictatorship last through the generations? The late twentieth century emergence of democracy in Latin America has led to an insightful, universal and political approach to the crafting of democracies.[6] Based on the notion that democracy can be politically crafted, a profound study has suggested that democracy can even be engineered in as seemingly unlikely political soil as that of a much-divided South Africa.[7] The continuation of India's struggle to devise political institutions and social policies to keep its democracy viable[8] and new attention to the fledgling democracies of most of the post-Leninist world (Ethiopia, Mongolia, Nicaragua, Cambodia, Angola, Poland, Hungary, Czechoslovakia, et al.) provide rich data for drawing policy lessons on how to analyze and solve political problems in order to consolidate democracy in the post-Leninist world.[9]

Yet, some of the conclusions from a political and universal approach to crafting democracy are less than cheering. From whatever despotic origins come a democratic people, the harsh truth is that simple and safe evolutions from despotism to democracy are most rare. So frequently were democracies superseded by some other political form in ancient Greece, that democracy seemed but a moment in a continuous cycle. In contrast, in the age of modern nation states, democracies have been frequently institutionalized for centuries such that they often seem a uniquely stable form of politics. However daunting is the task of democratization, the outcome is well worth the effort.

When the provinces of the Netherlands first united in the sixteenth century, the beginning of an age of modern nation states, the alliance between Catholics and Protestants, and between South and North, would not hold, eventually unleashing more years of wanton slaughter, civil war and chaos before the would-be Dutch republic split and the North formed the United Provinces of the Netherlands. When the democratic Netherlands "became the first in the history of modern Europe to retain power and found a durable regime,"[10] it did so only after many false starts, much bloodshed and destruction, and a permanent surrender of the region most opposed to democracy. It took quite a while before a political consensus could be formed that could hold and deal with issues that had to be dealt with. While democratic openings may be frequent, consolidations of democracy are rare. One secret of successfully consolidating democracy, already apparent with the Netherlands, is limiting the scope of government. That is, by reserving a large role for societal, non-political spheres, the burden of responsibility, and therefore the potential blame of democratic government are reduced.

The vicissitudes of democratization in the Netherlands were not unique. The 13 American colonies, that in 1781 won their independence from Great Britain, drew up Articles of Confederation that did not achieve the advantages of union, that failed to hold the 13 constituent parts together in a shared quest for freedom and prosperity. After much trauma and loss, a new Constitution was implemented in 1789 aimed at perfecting the union. But, as with the first construction of a United Netherlands, the regional political compromises of conflicting political identities involved in crafting a consensus in support of the new Constitution augured eventual bloodshed and potential national disintegration.

The Constitution of the American nation included the legalization of slavery, a form of domination absolutely incompatible with liberty or democracy. The Constitution, a flawed pact with the devil, carried fiendish fuel for a fiery Civil War that, almost a century after independence, ended slavery at a cost in lives greater than all other American wars, past and subsequent. Generalizing from the Dutch and American experiences suggests that consolidating a democratic breakthrough is a long-term, multi-stage, complex and potentially explosive political task.[11] Post-Leninist democratization may prove more formidable. As will be explicated below, the regional and communalist forces that must be conciliated in the wake of a Leninist opening to democracy tend to be uniquely obdurate.

Still, the original Dutch and American political compromises that made possible the constitutional compact embody general lessons. All the compacting units had to be persuaded that there was a fairness in how power was apportioned between center and regions, between bigger and smaller states. There is a craftable political geography at the base of democratization. Going back to ancient Athens, political divisions for choosing representatives had to be carefully drawn to make most likely an outcome that would keep the polity united but not dominated by a predictable special interest.[12] Since all potentially democratic states have their own histories, regional divisions, economic interests and communal divisions, these political rules have to be devised to suit each nation state to keep the compact viable and flexible so as to meet changing conditions. While reality puts a limit on what can be theorized at a general level about democratization, no state, no matter how much it fools itself about being homogeneous, can avoid the nettlesome task of forging a geographical compact for choosing representatives to avoid experiential unjustness that would lead some major entity to find its interests irreconcilable to the democratic pact.

Even early democratic consolidation, the 1688 limited constitutional republic in Britain, confronted obdurate obstacles of political geography that left a festering, conquered Ireland to haunt the dreamers of permanent peaceful progress in a liberal democracy. Time and again history reveals that succeeding in democratic consolidation after a popular, legitimate democratic opening is far from guaranteed.

German Weimar democracy failed. So did the February 1917 democratic revolution in Russia. And why the 1789 liberal breakthrough in France

could not be consolidated for almost a century bedeviled many generations of the French. The ubiquitous failure of democratic breakthroughs
in Latin America led analysts of that region to see the swing to democracy
from dictatorship and then back as an historically given, deeply driven,
almost permanent, feature of politics. It seemed impossible to consolidate
democracy.

In Asia, China's 1911 republican breakthrough to democracy was lost
in less than two years. Similarly, Japan's 1920s Showa era opening to
democracy was soon harshly clamped closed by military dictatorship. The
1961 popular democratic revolution in Korea was also swiftly reversed by
a military coup. Liberal democratic African regimes established at
independence from European colonial rule had a similar sad, short life.
Democratic openings could not be consolidated.[13] The post-Leninist
problems of legitimating a new nationalism and conciliating regional
communalisms make the usually difficult consolidations yet more
problematical.

In every region of the world, in Europe, the Americas, Africa, and Asia,
democratic openings were not peacefully, easily and immediately
consolidated. American political science is replete with attempts to
explain why it is so difficult to consolidate democracy. Studies of
revolution, such as Crane Brinton's conservative classic, *Anatomy of
Revolution*, find that revolutions cannot consolidate an initial liberal
republican state form but must move on to a radical terror.[14] The
approach to democratization from the perspective of political crafting,
cited above, instead would ask what was wrong in the French political
pacts of 1789 or 1792 or Russia's of February 1917 that facilitated the
demise of those democratic republics. Political scientists try to draw
meaning from past democratic failures so that political wisdom can
overcome rooted political obstacles that would otherwise obstruct
democratization. As Western political philosophy distinguishes between
the roles of *fortuna* and *virtu*, so the role of political knowledge is to
expand the force of *virtu*, that is to learn better how to craft democratic
systems that will not be fated to fail because of contingent, social
inheritances of geographical divisions and communal differences among
diverse peoples and interests.

The Challenge of Leninism to Democratization

Most of post-World War II American social theory, however, has found
that *fortuna* tends to be decisive, that the social inheritance is stronger than
the will and wisdom of democratization. The dominant hypothesis has
been that stable democracy requires a democratic civic culture and a
society dominated by urban middle classes, neither of which purported

democratic preconditions have been attained in most of the world. Hence the policy advice of post-World War Two American political science hastened to favor supporting so-called military modernizers over a supposedly impossible democratic project. Department of State Policy Planning Director George Kennan noted in 1948,

"We should cease to talk about. . .human rights. . .and democratization. . . . [W]e should not hesitate before police repression by the local government. This is not shameful since the Communists are essentially traitors. . . . It is better to have a strong regime in power than a liberal government if it is indulgent and relaxed and penetrated by Communists."[15]

Along these lines, in his famous study, *Political Order in Changing Societies*, Samuel Huntington, writing in 1968, offered an explanation of why the "attempt to establish some sort of liberal, democratic constitutional state" "frequently" fails and the democrats

are swept from power. Their failure stems. . .from their inability to deal with. . .political mobilization. . . . [T]hey lack the drive and ruthlessness [requiring concentration of power] to stop the mobilization of new groups. . . . [T]hey lack the radicalism to lead it. . . . [T]he liberals are brushed away either by counter revolutionaries who perform the first or by more extreme revolutionaries who perform the second.[16]

Nothing in Huntington, with his stress on mobilization and ruthlessness, gives hope for a broad expansion of democracy. Almost nothing in the political science of democratic crafting builds on Huntington's hypotheses. His perspective seems a product of the assumptions of a short historical moment. Beyond Cold War rationalization of policy preferences, and beyond not being able to imagine that a democratic pact can be created for almost any society,[17] Huntington's basic social science error lies in his theoretical premise, the presupposition of modernization theorists (which includes analysts with very different political orientations such as Barrington Moore and Theda Skocpol)[18] that all political systems must undergo a once and for all painful transformation to a state system dubbed modern. The evanescent nature of what is thought of as the modern world is, in actuality, more a permanent social crisis of change out-pacing consciousness, than a problem with a solution definable as "political order," as Huntington wrongly had it.[19] Democracy's superiority includes its ability to be open to the conflicts of continuous change and to adapt flexibly. Because those who choose a communalist alternative to the uncertainties of democratization do so out of fear of the openness of democracy in a post-Leninist world, democracy should be crafted so that it can grapple with this modern dilemma of permanent change that threatens communalist identities.

Post-Leninist Obstacles to Democratization

Still, whatever the flaws in his analysis, Huntington called attention to the historical difficulty of consolidating liberal democratic breakthroughs, and a major institutional cause of that difficulty, a recalcitrant military. Post-Leninist democratizers also must confront this difficulty. The works on crafting democracy cited above offer precise suggestions for taming the anti-democratic tendencies of powerful military institutions.

In addition, consolidating a democratic breakthrough from a Leninist dictatorship may be particularly difficult.[20] First, the usual obstacles are unusually strong. The coercive apparatuses usually include vicious, politically loyal, army-like security forces that have so much blood on their hands that they may well fight against an opening to democracy. In addition, the pervasiveness of the Leninist secret police apparatus and the complicity of so many with it means that to reveal the truth and to do justice in a democratizing era may threaten so many as to add greatly to the recalcitrants who will try to reverse the democratic breakthrough. To decrease the likelihood of success for the anti-democratic forces, democrats should study the lessons detailed in the Wechsler book, cited above, on forgiving even torturers, while exposing the truth of the worst criminals, as a way of decreasing any future likelihood of a reversion to a brutal Leninist police state. Caution and mercy are needed to decrease the numbers opposed to democracy. Since breakthroughs to democracy are lost more often than they are consolidated, democratizers should act prudently to preclude worst case reversals.

The 1989-90 breakthroughs to democracy are but initial steps in a prolonged political struggle. Openings to democracy in Leninist systems were nastily and swiftly slammed shut before 1989-90. That history contains a warning for the future. The great 1956 democratic Hungarian revolution was crushed at its birth by the Soviet Union. The 1967-68 democratic opening in Czechoslovakia to "socialism with a human face" was quickly repressed by Soviet-led Warsaw Pact forces. The democratic opening won in 1980 by Solidarity in Poland suffered a cruel defeat a couple of years later when a Polish martial law regime imposed itself. Democratic forces in the early Bolshevik Party were readily quashed by the secret police. Mao easily sent off to forced labor people who sought democracy in response to his 1956-1957 liberalization campaign that invited people to point out flaws in the system. Even in 1991 the militaries in Romania and China both seem to have sealed off democratic openings. In Mongolia, democratic leaders feared a military re-imposition of Leninist dictatorship. Whereas some people contend that with Moscow no longer opposing democratization, that process will be smooth sailing, in fact, the complexities of the struggle to consolidate a democratic opening in a Leninist state are not mere matters of whether or not a people was or was not included in the Soviet orbit.[21] The same complex processes are at work in Russia as in Hungary, in Mongolia, China and Yugoslavia as in Czechoslovakia. Internal forces are decisive. And even beyond the potential opposition of those in the institutions of coercion and of those who are complicitous, there are many people who prefer a different kind of dictatorship to democracy.

For clues to the yet more painful problems for democratizers wrought by Leninism, more attention should be given to Yugoslavia. Already in 1953, it specifically committed itself to negating Stalinism and institution-alizing decentralist political reforms. Yugoslavia should not be treated as distinct from all other Leninist countries because of ethno-nationalist features supposedly peculiar to Yugoslavia. Perhaps the mainstream social science proposition explicated so lucidly by Huntington, that Leninist political institutions have to be successful, has long led, mislead-ingly, to treating Leninist failures as anomalies. The persistence of anti-democratic forces in Yugoslavia, rather, may, in crucial ways, be paradig-matic. Yugoslavia is the Leninist polity that has for the longest time pursued policies of agricultural decollectivization, world market openness (including lots of travel to democratic West Europe), and great economic reforms in order to construct a competitive, modern economy. Yet 40 years of such seemingly enlightened, anti-Stalinist policies did not consolidate democracy. All actual democratic breakthroughs were quickly suppressed. The causes are not peculiar to Yugoslavia.

To the large extent that Leninism is a conservative militarist chauvinism (anti-imperialism), its beneficiaries could, in a post-Leninist era, ally with conservative communalists who also experience freedom as foreign pollution. One serious problem in post-Leninist democratization is that Leninist rule can engender a new, tough nationalism tied to a dominant ethnic group, the old military and the secret police and then identify its opposition to liberty or individualism or the secular with a national project of unity, size, prestige, order and keeping out foreign ways depicted as subverters of all that is good and healthy in the historical heritage. Understanding Leninist states as similar to traditional or feudal ones may help explain similar proclivities when the old system breaks down, tendencies toward order through "populist, usually military, dictator-ship."[22] The vicissitudes of post-Leninist democratic consolidation resemble France in the century after the Bastille fell, a century in which cries for military order often won out over constitutional liberty. Clearly, the general difficulties of democratization when compounded by the peculiarly difficult consequences of Leninism suggest that consolidating an original breakthrough from Leninism to democracy is no simple matter.

All the wise economic reforms, starting in 1958, that brought the people in Hungary, as in Yugoslavia -- and, after 1978, in post-Mao China -- great economic progress, not only do not automatically evolve into democracy, but, in fact, add to those who feel a stake in the political system and who therefore oppose democratization. But, at the same time, the reforms also actually further delegitimate the ruling group, thus increasing the likelihood of a bloody clash between recalcitrant polar forces, when democratic consolidation, in contrast, requires a broad middling consensus. This perceived intensifying of all the divisive forces in the society makes it seem to many that only a dictatorship can keep the nation from disintegrating. With a renewed central ethnic nationalism legitimate, and with chaos the seeming alternative, many prefer the superficial security of communalist dictatorship to the untried risks of democracy. Coercion, charisma, cooptation, fear of chaos, and chauvinism may, in sum, permit the old ruling group to hang on to power, but at the price of a political paralysis and a further poisoning of group reconciliation. Chaos and division may seem the price of abandoning Leninist despotism for a democratic experiment, such that extreme nationalistic despotism seems a preferable option to many.

The problem and promise of democracy will therefore be most attractive if it offers a loose confederation with negotiated equities that hold the prospect of a continuing yet more just nation avoiding worst case outcomes. Democrats will do best if they can enter the political fray with a means to meet the demands of communities and social equity. The problem for democrats is how to get this message out and how to make it persuasive. This issue of democratic union or bloody alternatives (civil war, cruel repression, communalist strife) is central because the first moves away from Leninism tend to intensify many of the evils of the system that foster loyalties other than the democratic kind.

Leninist reforms make worse societal cuts and sores, turning them into life-threatening wounds because, fearing cleansing open air, Leninists cover up the splitting sores, guaranteeing that, beneath the surface, not only does no healing occur, but that poisonous scapegoating and political mistrust become ever more presuppositional to politics, making it painfully difficult to build broad coalitions based on a shared national identity that could permit a swift and peaceful evolution into, and consolidation of, democracy.[23] To the extent that Leninist states foster tough chauvinistic militaries, state/society polarization, and powerful and conflicting, yet ultimate, sub-national communalist identities, Leninism obstructs a consolidation of democracy that

> requires a disenchantment with central authority in general, an army too weak or demoralized to impose its will on society, and a broad alliance between elites and popular groups in defense of individual [and communal] freedoms[24]

To consolidate a democratic opening in a post-Leninist world therefore requires dealing with a national and nationalist legitimation crisis in a peculiarly sharp and explosive form, perhaps worse than is the case in a transition from other kinds of tyrannies. The intensity of this difficulty occurs because Leninist states not only freeze prior regional, ethnic and religious divisions, but also because Leninism worsens the communalist contradiction because all groups are kept to a territory and frozen into place -- no market, mobility, individualism, no growth of cross cutting cleavages to cushion primordial conflict. All communities are made to feel the victim of the dominant group, while the dominant group blames all others. The result is a pervasive, poisoned pattern of "nation blaming nation."[25] An elite from the dominant community can then appeal to renewed chauvinism to maintain national unity. The smaller groups, in opposition to the central community, tend to reflect populist nationalisms.

A problem for crafting democracy in a post-Leninist order is whether to accept division or bring peoples (many? all?) together in a federation. Usually the task of the democratizers will be easier if they do not seem the enemies of popular patriotism. Some new glue must replace the desiccated and deadly bond of chauvinistic Leninist anti-imperialism. This requires legitimating a new national identity and establishing political institutions that will both support that new, national center and also seem fair to all the diverse regional communities. It is not easy.

Hence the relation between center and region is crucial to potential stability. Political compromise and civil freedoms are required to guarantee cultural authenticities. The democracy's lines and rules should build in incentives to trans-communalist coalitions.

But the political center in an economically reformist but still Leninist political system that is based on a command economy with powerful central ministries and money-losing state enterprises can only offer minor concessions to federalism. The center remains self-interestedly economically irrational. Regions therefore lack any large incentive to compromise with a reforming Leninist center that still holds on to the central ministries and heavy industry enterprises of a politico-economic formation that fears devolution, market and democracy as death. That old Leninist system is based on pricing and distribution that hurt the regions. The burdensome Leninist command economy is also a political machine of incompetents. Its costly, oppressive institutions are overstaffed, parasitic, massively polluting, extraordinarily wasteful and mammoth. No area or community outside of that privileged, useless economy wishes to see its hard earned money go to taxes to support the devouring dinosaur of the outmoded Leninist center. A new stability based on compromise and coalition is unlikely if all divisions of the tax take seem inherently arbitrary and illegitimate. The center must concede, an imperative that can seem to threaten national unity. The contradictions are explosive. The economi-

cally illegitimate can seem politically legitimate. Two potential forces --
national disintegration and an unaccountable and thievingly heavy, outmoded central economy -- are in absolute conflict.. That makes consolidating democracy in a post-Leninist world peculiarly difficult because early
reform strengthens local power, undercuts the center's tax take, and makes
the struggle over regional or federal power seem all or nothing,[26]
whereas democracy requires a broad compromise consensus.   Post-
Leninist forces tend to run counter to the imperatives of compromise and
consensus.   Thus a section of the Leninist old guard, especially if it
experiences itself as chauvinistic, can act with military and secret police
hard-liners, presenting themselves as the only alternative to disintegration
and chaos. The regions or communities in opposition to the tyrannical,
parasitical center may then feel compelled to opt for disunion. These
forces of polarization greatly complicate post-Leninist democratization.

The Inevitability of the Democratic Option

The same general tendencies apply in China as elsewhere. The crisis
of dictatorship or disunion as seeming political alternatives surfaces after
the original Leninist anti-imperialist leaders disappear and as time erodes
popular illusions about the possibility of a reforming socialism resolving
historically deep conflicts that are intensified by the politics of Leninism.
Given the particularities of ruling group or chronological moment, one
cannot predict how long illusions last that Leninism can be a basis for a
new stable compromise. Eventually the old rulers will split. But given
the power of anti-democratic alternatives, reformers and democratic
stability will do best if the democrats can ally with opposition moderates
swiftly to craft a consensual democracy. Given regional and communalist
divisions, as well as nationalist passions, plus outrage at earlier Leninist
inhumanities, such a coalition of compromise and consensus is not
guaranteed. It is not easy. It has a higher likelihood the more it succeeds
in some post-Leninist system, the more it seems a legitimate and
successful post-Leninist option. Clearly an alternative to dictatorship and
disunion should be so welcome that the democratic path can seem
imperative, the only salvation of nation, equity and ordered progress.

Yet every place has its peculiarities. The old guard in Beijing wins time
and political latitude because it has delivered the economic goods.
Chinese openness to the world economy benefits from China's economic
geography, its proximity to the world's most dynamic economic region.
Decollectivization is a success in China because of the survival of the
peasant household whose economic actions cause speedy rural development. Finally, the traditionalism of the Chinese regime seems legitimate
to many because Mao's prior locking up of villagers in the countryside for

a generation has allowed regime fundamentalists, in a post-Mao reform and mobility era, to appeal both to proto-fascist rural dwellers anxious over rapid change, experienced as foreign and individualistic, and to urban status anxiety, based on fear of an influx of lower paid rural workers. These Chinese particularities can perpetuate chauvinist Leninism in China. Still, Leninism in China, too, is threatened by eventual limits on growth inherent in the system. The system itself inevitably gets experienced popularly as an illegitimate, selfish and private realm that stands in opposition to popular needs. The Leninist system creates similar delegitimating forces in China, Cuba or Czechoslovakia.

All the usual questions of consolidating democracy apply then to each and all -- with the added caveat of the need to confront the peculiar issues of Leninist democratization: nationalist legitimation, regional disintegration and ending the burdens of a command economy. Still, in general, when the first generation of rulers is gone, with an acknowledged need for market-oriented world openness, some group within the regime seems likely one day to try to build bridges to the broad, moderate voice of the excluded citizenry so as to peripheralize both anti-democratic recalcitrants within the old order and also vengeful oppositionists seeking justice for innumerable, extraordinary crimes. The imperative of making democracy succeed is almost inevitably going to appear on the political agenda. Consequently, it is worthwhile, even for democratic opponents in a still Leninist state, to begin to contemplate how they would consolidate a democratic breakthrough, how they would quell the fears of those who could be attracted to alternatives to democracy.

Surely it will help make the transition more peaceful and stable if it is clear that democrats can, after a democratic opening, craft institutions that truly consolidate the breakthrough. How does one de-fang the secret services, reduce and professionalize the military, turn the nomenklatura apparatus into a meritocratic civil service, etc? The literature on crafting democracy already addresses all of these questions. Whatever the particulars, in general, the answer is, by crafting a political framework of reconciliation that protects diversity, promotes consensus and civilizes conflict. An early attempt to figure out solutions to the problem of consolidation permits democratizers to appear more in command of the forces to be grappled with, permits them to appeal to latent nationalisms and to soothe those anxious over potential chaos. The democratic alternative can be made into a political imperative.

An Economic Pact for Social Equity

But those goals are not easily achieved in a post-Leninist world. With debt and budget crises compounded by the wasteful, parasitic, weighty command economy, there is little money to buy off -- or buy in -- so many groups. And swift solutions may be needed to hold the nation together, since Leninism's nasty inheritance leaves little popular faith in half measures, given the mistrust and hate of angry and long-suffering communalist groupings that have run out of patience and trust. Given the need to persuade so many that they will not be economically or communally destroyed, it is no solution to suggest that the market is all the answer needed, although, at the same time, no solution is possible until market-oriented dynamics are basic to the system. Ways must be devised compatible with a market orientation that also seem equitable to numerous outraged communities. That need requires an economically active state center. While the literature on crafting democracy already addresses equity, including matters of making the civil service open and professional, it tends to abjure the requirements of state action in the economic realm.

Each nation, of course, must resolve equity problems within its peculiar set of conflicting social forces. There is, however, a major danger of heeding the conventional wisdom that tends to come from generalizing from the transition to democracy in Latin America and other regions where American intervention seems divisive. This is because Latin Americanists, explainers of anti-Yankee sentiment to the people of the USA, tend to see the United States only as a problem in building democracy because ties to the Yankees may easily discredit one's nationalism in Latin America. Actually, the United States and other democracies can have a large influence in helping fledgling democracies consolidate political freedom, especially in the economic realm.[27]

Latin Americanists, however, tend to be ignorant of Leninist realities. Not understanding the pervasive corruption and economic irrationality of the Leninist apparatus, seeing their own region's murderous right wing military dictatorships as the worst evil, a Latin Americanist wrongly comments that "the prospects for democratization look better in the post-socialist nations than in military dominated dictatorships. . .[because the former] have a better bedrock of professional public institutions upon which to build than with authoritarian regimes which have been corrupted by personalism and parasitism."[28] In addition, Di Palma contends that, in comparison to Latin America, where American power could still disrupt the fledgling democratic effort, East European peoples, in post-Leninist systems, are fortunate because Russia simply got out of the way and allowed the people's democratic urges to rise and win -- surely not a description of Gorbachev's actions toward Honecker. More importantly, this analysis misses both the economic pact needed to consolidate a fledgling democracy and the great impact international economic aid can have in making that economic pact work. International help matters, as democrats in post-Leninist democracies deeply appreciate.

Democrats in Russia and East Europe have consequently been contributing to the democratic cause in Tibet. It is worth generalizing from these post-Leninist tendencies of international cooperation and social equity.

The writings of Gillespie, Di Palma and other students of democratization in Latin America and Southern Europe insufficiently appreciate the major points made in this essay about the extraordinary obstacles to democratization in post-Leninist or reforming Leninist systems. They do not see the daunting nature of economic reform. In addition, given the centrality of world market competitiveness to expanding wealth since World War II, the peculiar weakness of the Leninist system in this regard makes it less likely that internally generated resources will, in a post-Leninist era, swiftly be sufficient to meet the pent-up demands of various sub-national communities. If the economy contracts, all communities can experience themselves as victims. Therefore, the fledgling democracy seeks foreign aid on almost any terms. That weakness can make the fragile democracy seem a dependent traitor to the patriotic cause. This weak, post-Leninist political economy entering the world market is profoundly threatened by seeming dependence on the near-by hegemon (Germany for Poland, Japan for North Korea or China), a matter that further complicates the democratizers' need and attempt to win nationalist legitimation, because the economics of survival could also seem a politics of losing the nationalist mantle.[29]

An issue that cries out for more attention in any analysis seeking ways to make it more likely that an opening to democracy will lead to a true consolidation of democracy in post-Leninist states, an issue over-looked in the present literature on democratic crafting, is that of the international economic realm, including finance, trade and production. In the post-Bretton Woods world, democratization would be greatly facilitated -- and the likelihood of vengeful chauvinistic backlash lessened -- if international economic institutions and richer nations had ways of providing an economic package to facilitate and cushion the related, traumatic economic transitions concomitant to the political transition. These costly and painful economic transitions are not necessarily required or traumatic in transitions from non-Leninist despotisms to democracy. The fragile post-Leninist democracy is less likely to shatter if it can seem a new center fair to all communities, if it can preclude an all-out war of region against region that strengthens communalist identities as orders of exclusive meaning that increase the forces tending toward group hatred, non-reconciliation and even civil war.[30]

In this area of reconciliation, the conventional wisdom, premised on non-Leninist experience, about the political institutions facilitating a successful transition from despotism to democracy slights the importance of creating a shared economic interest in the democratic process. Analysts of democratization in non-Leninist states tend to see consolidation as a building of a broad coalition, a matter of conciliation and ending fears of worst case treatment by the new state so that there is a shrinkage and peripheralization of anti-democratic recalcitrants among both elites and opposition. In addition, the state is less likely to be a target of outrage if it is able to surrender much of the economic burden to private arenas. This means weakening the state and sharing power. For such purposes a parliamentary system with proportional representation is promoted as superior because it helps prevent a winner-take-all outcome that might overly concentrate the fruits of victory and thus undermine the ties holding various suspicious groups in the fragile democratic coalition. There is obvious wisdom in this general approach.

But a post-Leninist state, as part of democratization, needs to legitimate a new nationalism and prove that all now will be treated fairly. It needs to guarantee an equity pact among regions and communities. These needs may make superior a presidential system with a program agenda that includes a social equity pact. Because of the profoundly alienating experience during the age of Leninism of inordinate unfairness to all groups, the tendency of those generalizing from Latin America and Southern Europe to focus singularly on the importance of fair rules of one central political game and to decry as dangerous the seeking of *any* particular socio-economic outcome misses the imperative, in a post-Leninist world, in trying to consolidate a democratic polity, of re-establishing the notion that the system is equitable to various regions and peoples, that there are numerous political games at work, and that they have to be coordinated from one political entity. The new polity must engineer an institutional consensus with a weaker political center in many realms, yet strong in the realm of economic coordination, as is the European Economic Community.

To maintain stability and build legitimacy in post-Leninist democratization, it may be worth learning from the examples of social equity in post-World War Two Japan, South Korea and Taiwan in knitting together a common national enterprise in which the state center began as quite illegitimate to most people, as in the post-Leninist world. Unfortunately, the conventional wisdom, with its focus on the lessons of Latin America and Southern Europe, has tended, misleadingly, to treat East Asia as an anomaly or miracle.[31] Without an East Asian style legitimately interventionist state in the realm of socio-economic justice and coordination, the tendencies of reforming Leninist states to intensify regionalism can be multiplied by immediate losses of groups and regions from sudden marketization and competitive criteria that can short circuit any attempt to institutionalize an experience of fairness in the political networks of democracy.

Growth without equity can keep a regime illegitimate. This has been the experience of South Korea, since the mid 1960s the world's most rapidly developing nation. Yet its political center enjoys little popular legitimacy for, among other reasons, caring for rich cronies while ordinary people were told to tighten their belts, for having changed the rules of entrance to schools, and for not having made entrance to the civil service sufficiently competitive by exam. A legitimate central economic capacity is needed to act to make the overall pattern of benefits seem fair and equitable. Consequently, to enhance the likelihood of successfully consolidating a post-Leninist democracy, mere privatization and market-ization will not do. A balance must be created between state intervention for growth and equity and central state disentanglement in so many other realms, so that the central government is not the target of all economic frustrations and so that local groups can be assured their most sacred interests will be protected.

Conclusion

Atul Kohli, in *Democracy and Its Discontents*, finds that an inability to achieve this balance is a major cause of disintegrative tendencies in India, a state that long tried to combine features of both political democracy and a closed, Leninist-style command economy in a nation divided by numerous communalist identities threatening national disintegration.[32] Kohli concludes that facilitating stable national parties to run the state increases national identity, as party and political programs help maintain a precarious balance and can prevent disintegration, and even consolidate democracy. This means that in crafting the original breakthrough to democracy, it is worth worrying over how to avoid a proliferation of parties that will preclude a needed national consensus.

In sum, the failure of democratization is usefully seen as a political failure, as an inability of political elites and democratic challengers to concern themselves with, imagine and build institutions, rules, expecta-tions, coalitions and balances suitable to consolidating an original breakthrough. Guidelines for consolidating post-Leninist democracies cannot simply repeat the lessons of Latin America. Lessons from democratic struggles in South Korea and India seem far more relevant. Most relevant are the struggles of democrats in reform Leninist regimes. These already manifest the issues and changes described above. They highlight the imperatives of political reconciliation, communalist confeder-ation and social equity.

The political problematic of democratization is never easy. Leninism makes it particularly difficult. But because the problem is political, a realm of action open to creative human intervention, there should be political solutions to get past the obstacles to consolidating democracy in post-Leninist states. This essay sketches and summarizes hopeful political crafting that constructs political bridges to get by these obstacles and to enhance the likelihood of success in consolidating democracy.

Notes

1. Ralph Miliband, "What Comes After Marxist Regimes?" in Ralph Miliband, et. al., eds., *Communist Regimes. The Aftermath* (London: Merlin Press, 1991), 324.

2. *Telos*, No. 81, 148.

3. Harry Harding, *China's Second Revolution* (Washington: Brookings Institution, 1987), 29.

4. Letter, Sunday *New York Times Magazine*, February 25, 1990, 10.

5. See Edward Friedman, "Ethnic Identity and the Denationalization and Democratization of Leninist States," in M. Crawford Young, ed., *Rethinking Ethnicity And Its Impact*, University of Wisconsin Press, forthcoming. People who think China uniquely resistant to democratization because its Leninism had nationalist legitimacy ignore national Leninism in Albania, Mongolia, Yugoslavia, Soviet Russia, Ethiopia, Mozambique, Angola, and even Czechoslovakia and East Germany. Those who see East Europe's democratization as a simple nationalist response to Russian colonialism ignore potent sub-national divisiveness (e.g., Czechs versus Slovaks). In fact, the cruel contradictions of Leninist dynamics impel decentralist and democratic forces and struggles everywhere in the Leninist world.

6. Giuseppe Di Palma, *To Craft Democracies* (Berkeley: University of California Press, 1991).

7. Donald L. Horowitz, *A Democratic South Africa: Constitutional Engineering in a Divided Society* (Berkeley: University of California Press, 1991).

8. Atul Kohli, *Democracy and Its Discontents* (Cambridge: Cambridge University Press, 1991).

9. The rich literature on the democratization of formerly Leninist states grows larger by the day. A good place to begin is the work on Poland by shrewd analysts such as Adam Michnik, Roman Laba and David Ost.

10. Perez Zagorin, *Rebels and Rulers 1500-1660*, Volume II (New York: Cambridge University Press, 1982), 127.

11. Barrington Moore, Jr., *Social Origins of Dictatorship and Democracy* (Boston: Beacon, 1966) contends that the American democratic revolution should be conceived as including the Civil War because without the defeat of feudal-like, military-oriented, old-fashioned plantation owners, the anti-democratic forces in the United States could have precluded the consolidation of a successfully industrializing democratic polity.

12. For an introduction to political crafters in democratic Athens, see the following books and their sources: M. I. Finley, *Politics in the Ancient World* (Cambridge: Cambridge University Press, 1983); Eli Sagan, *The Honey and the Hemlock* (New York: Basic Books, 1991).

13. An exception is Botswana. See John Holm and Patrick Molutsi, eds., *Democracy in Botswana* (Athens: Ohio University Press, 1989).

14. Brinton, *Anatomy of Revolution* (New York: Vintage, 1957).

15. Cited in Lawrence Weschler, *A Miracle, A Universe: Settling Accounts With Torturers* (New York: Penguin, 1990), 115, 116.

16. Huntington, *Political Order in Changing Societies* (New Haven: Yale University Press, 1968), 268, 269.

17. Democracies persist not only in Botswana, but also in Hindu India, Buddhist Sri Lanka, Shinto Japan, Jewish Israel, Catholic Latin America, and the animist South Seas, and have begun in Confucian, Lamaist and Islamic nations.

18. Skocpol, *States and Social Revolution* (New York: Cambridge University Press, 1979).

19. For a discussion of the inappropriateness of Leninism to post mass production led technologies, see Friedman, "Permanent Technological Revolution and the Vicissitudes of China's Path to Democratizing Leninism," in Richard Baum, ed., *Democracy and Reform in China and Their Enemies* (New York: Routledge, 1991).

20. See Friedman, "Theorizing the Democratization of China's Leninist State," in Arif Dirlik and Maurice Meisner, eds., *Marxism and the Chinese Experience* (Armonk: Sharpe, 1989), 171-189.

21. In contrast, Su Shaozhi, in this volume, finds the distinction between imposed and indigenous Leninism to be decisive.

22. Jack Goldstone, *Revolution and Rebellion in the Early Modern World* (Berkeley: University of California Press, 1991), 499.

23. For a shrewd analysis of democratization in these terms, see Di Palma, *To Craft Democracies*.

24. Goldstone, *Revolution and Rebellion*, 480.

25. Sonja Licht, "Pluralism or Nationalism," *East European Reporter*, reprinted in *CADDY Bulletin*, No. 65 (June 1991), 20.

26. This essay will not discuss the economic issues associated with dismantling the rigid command economy since so much good work already exists on that.

27. See Barbara Stallings and Robert Kaufman, eds., *Debt and Democracy in Latin America* (Boulder: Westview Press, 1989).

28. Charles Gillespie, "Di Palma on Democratization," *San Francisco Review of Books* (Spring 1991), 36. Informed people would know that Kiev, in the Czarist era, suffered pogroms against Jews, but usually only specialists would know that a rich Jewish culture in Kiev of around 200 synagogues continued and was reduced to one only in the Leninist era of thorough-going repression.

29. In China, because the conservative reformers so fear opening to the democratic world, an over-reliance on Japan--seen as not caring about human rights--could lose the surviving patriotic credentials of the Leninist remnant. See Friedman, "The Foreign Policy of the Li Peng Group," *Asian Outlook*. 26.4 (May-June 1991).

30. Actually, as suggested earlier, the political coalition consolidating democracy can involve compromises that inadvertently, yet rigidly, institutionalize certain rules to the exclusion of certain people, and thus increase the likelihood of future implosions of the democracy, if changes are not made. No rules of the game, however democratic, can be considered finally appropriate or fair.

31. Edward Friedman, "Democratization: Generalizing the East Asian Experience," in Friedman, ed., *The Politics of Democratization*, forthcoming.

32. Atul Kohli, *Democracy and Its Discontents*.

6

Implementing a Market-Oriented Economy

Elizabeth Clayton

The previous chapter highlighted the difficulties of consolidating democratic breakthroughs in Leninist states. This chapter examines the challenges involved in establishing and maintaining a market-oriented economy. Many of these challenges are not simple problems easily addressed by economic theory. Rather, they require the establishment of an implicit if not an explicit "social contract" to replace the expectations citizens had in the Leninist societies.[1] By "social contract" I mean an understanding of the values to be sought in the reformed economy and the role of the state in promoting these values. Thus, how each new post-Leninist society facilitates and sustains a market will depend largely upon the new non-socialist social contract that evolves between citizenry and government.

The implementation of a market-oriented economy in a reforming Leninist society is hindered by confrontation between the new social contract and the previous social contract based on Marxist theory and Leninist practice. To oversimplify, the old social contract emphasized an economic equality and a faith in a scientifically controlled economy. In its dogma, it fostered distrust of private property and disdain for wealth. It raised expectations for job security and fixed prices, and it implied a guarantee of affluence in desirable consumer goods and services. The social contract increasingly was unfulfilled. Eventually it disintegrated; in its place has risen a new and often innocent faith in the market economy, with dogma yet to be determined. This is the focus of the first part of this paper, where I will discuss how beliefs and expectations affect the creation

of two fundamental features of a market-oriented economy -- entrepreneurship and private property -- and the legal infrastructure necessary to
sustain these features.

The remainder of the chapter focuses on macroeconomic policies that
sustain market economies, including price decontrol, the elimination or
regulation of monopoly, banking and currency reform, and public finance.
Observation will demonstrate that a reforming economic system, like all
others, faces discontinuities and voids that make a transformation to a
perfectly competitive market economy impossible. Such a transformation
would also be ill-advised, however, for market economies everywhere rely
on state intervention, subsidies, and investment. The goal is, therefore,
not a pure market economy, but a productive market-oriented economy
to replace the static, socialist planned economy.[2]

Establishing a Market Economy

Two features are essential to the functioning of a market-oriented
economy, but introducing them to former Leninist societies is problematic.

Entrepreneurship

One of the foundations of a market-oriented economy is entrepreneurship, the arduous trial of new and risky products and processes. This
breaks a pattern of stagnation, where growth was a mechanical replication
of the past, but it also introduces new risks and insecurities. Reformers,
if they are to succeed, must explore new ideas and means. The atmosphere of risk-taking and experimentation that accompanies entrepreneurial behavior is one hallmark of successful reform. Yet, social and
economic barriers may curtail this vital process. At the broadest level,
society's reform-minded decisionmakers must be willing to reward
entrepreneurial change; at a narrower level, the recently-socialist elite must
embrace society's commitment and bring it to realization by coalescing
pockets of support and removing serious barriers, such as laws against
speculation.

In general, official policies to promote entrepreneurship are inadequate.
For example, patent protection creates and preserves royalties for the
inventor and rewards entrepreneurship in products (technology). Yet, in
the Soviet Union, a patent-user rewards an inventor only in a first use,
and not in subsequent uses, which discourages investments in products
with high risk, high cost, and long-term payoff.

Encouraging entrepreneurship in its broadest sense, including both
technological and societal change, is essential to make proposed reforms
a reality. In a study of Soviet agricultural reform, Butterfield asked why

organizations with a reform mandate with attractive legal, psychological, and economic incentives would refuse to change.[3] He concluded that the farm managers were fearful, skeptical, and hedging their bets. Their attitude was reasonable in the socialist environment, especially when the managers were under-qualified, deferential, and suspicious (perhaps justifiably). The result, however, was that reforms often failed because the environment failed to promote an entrepreneurial ability to grasp an opportunity and to provide clear and unambiguous incentives.

Contrary to what some observers claim, entrepreneurship abounds in socialist systems. Sometimes, such entrepreneurship has rewarded the entrepreneur but has not satisfied social needs. Other socialist entrepreneurship, invested in grey or black market activities, in fact serves the population but in law is only marginally tolerated. Thus a buyer's distrust of market activities, fostered by the social contract's expectation of low and stable prices, accompanies a seller's risk of being charged with official corruption. Another aspect of socialist entrepreneurship is seen in those who grease the wheels of the planning system. The expediters (*tolkachi*) who speed from supplier to supplier arranging barters, and the consumers who devote their resources to friendship networks that supply goods by reciprocity are entrepreneurs-in-action in the distribution system.

An example of entrepreneurship, the process of marketing in recently socialist countries presents an extraordinary opportunity for growth. Under Marxist socialism, marketing activity had low status, low investment, and low activity. Marketers were not organized politically to press the state for quite legitimate marketing needs such as roads and other transportation. Furthermore, marketing did not attract the bureaucratic entrepreneurs who were found in production. In contrast, the production ministries, despite the inertia of hierarchy, were better organized to press their needs and had the competitive advantage in ideology that favored material production and despised middlemen.

The Marxist cultural predisposition against marketing is further reinforced by public opposition to the accumulation of wealth. Socialist institutions by and large have sought to equalize income, which discourages entrepreneurship. This distrust of affluence will be hard to uproot, especially in the countryside. As van Atta attests, the collective farm -- despite its economic flaws -- is a symbol of security and an engine of equity that farmers are loathe to relinquish.[4] Surveys of the population affirm this opposition to wealth accumulation.[5]

The devaluation of the marketing process in Leninist states has resulted in a gap between the needs of consumers and the supply of consumer goods. Even without the infrastructure to facilitate marketing and despite the risk of raising the ire of the public as well as the authorities, entrepreneurs did emerge to fill this gap -- so essential and profitable was the need for marketing services. To facilitate marketing entrepreneurship, however, post-Leninist states will need both social and economic encouragement. If these societies seek reform to enhance growth, they must revise their social contract to accommodate wealth accumulation and to augment the state's role to provide the infrastructure that private processes cannot support, such as roads and transportation.

Private Ownership

Those wary of private ownership ask why a government should defend the ownership of one person at the expense of the rest of society. The economic answer is that the protection of one person's rights will generally benefit society as a whole because private ownership performs useful functions in a market economy. Coupled with entrepreneurship and a desire to make profits, a private owner will respond to what consumers want, in contrast to a planner who will plan what the consumer should have. Private ownership of capital and land will encourage entrepreneurs to find more efficient uses than planners did and to shift from less to more productive activities. Labor in planned economies has always been owned privately in this sense of supply, but labor demand has been centrally planned and would, in a market economy, respond to entrepreneurial decisionmaking.

Private ownership, as analyzed by Wigmore,[6] also complements entrepreneurship when the entrepreneurs are legitimately rewarded for risking what they own and claiming rightfully the residual profits as a reward for the risk-taking. Private ownership can also facilitate financial transactions, e.g., when buying a bond is a reward less for risk-taking than for supplying capital or postponing consumption. Finally, private ownership can provide citizens with a means of providing themselves with financial security, be it for leisure or future goods.

In a modern economy with large-scale industry and accumulations of capital, ownership ordinarily is split from control. In market-oriented economies, private owners delegate control to professional managers, yet retain rights to oversee the performance and effectiveness of the managers. Curiously, the socialist economies ordinarily also separated ownership (by the state) from control (by the managers). What they lacked, however, was an owner's single-minded, profit-seeking oversight of managers. They also lacked the information that private decisions in the market make public. Socialist planners never found economic dynamism because they could not easily tell where and why to transfer resources. Private owners, with all their flaws, can learn easily and act quickly on information from market processes.

Private ownership, however, requires much supporting infrastructure. First needed are the means of describing a property: the titles to land and equipment plus the social understanding and trust that pieces of paper can represent items of much greater value. Second, the means of transferring ownership, usually without physical movement of the tangibles, must be established in exchanges, bourses, and markets. Finally, the rules of ownership and its transfer must be lawfully established and fairly implemented, with security and good faith.

Once the former Leninist societies overcome the ideological barrier to accepting private ownership, experience has demonstrated that many practical ethical questions need to be answered. The first decisions concern restitution to former owners: Can they be identified and located? Can heirs inherit a claim? Should they receive the same property, equivalent property, or cash compensation? The second set of decisions concern the new owners: Must they use the property they buy, or even live in the nation where it is located? Can society at large participate in private ownership? Should some assets like roads or schools remain in public hands at any level? Finally, there are decisions about the mode of transfer from the state to private hands: Should the state use public auctions, vouchers to some people or all, or even giveaways?

Economic theory cannot answer these questions because it is ordinarily indifferent to persons and transactions processes. People rarely share the disinterest and will quickly oppose privatization they perceive as unjust. Yet the ultimate answers to these practical questions depend on considerations of individual and collective ethics. In a sense, they depend on the evolving social contract.

The experiences of emerging democracies have been diverse in addressing these issues of privatizing property. Even once a process of privatization has been sanctioned, different approaches have been used. Underlying the acceptance of any such processes must be a sense of legitimacy in the evolving social contract of the society. Some countries such as Czechoslovakia have embraced foreign ownership in order to attract financial and managerial resources. Others such as Poland have espoused a voucher system that distributes shares to the adult population and aggregates these claims into mutual funds. Thus, the population receives income; the mutual funds provide managerial oversight and represent the shareholders. Accompanying this system, however, Polish privatization at the factory level has been castigated as "kleptocracy" because socialist managers and workers acquired public property without compensation.

Legal Infrastructure

Both entrepreneurship and private ownership are buttressed by the strength of law, both formal and informal. As Alice Tay examines in the next chapter, after 1917, socialist systems developed law peculiar to the new societies that they envisaged. The newest post-Leninist societies similarly must transform the role of law and reach out to other legal systems or back to pre-socialist experience to find appropriate models for their legal systems.

During the search for the legal structure to meet the needs of a particular market economy, several legal structures may compete for power and influence. These may go back to different antecedents of formal law -- such as Islamic law or Roman law -- and they may rely on the informal law drawn from local culture as well. Furthermore, a wellspring of informal law may rise up to exert its own countervailing influence. For example, both formal law from old Russia and Marxist ideology lie behind the widespread opposition to wealth accumulation and private land ownership. Professor Tay provides a detailed analysis of the transformation of law that needs to occur in Leninist societies. My main points are that no one legal system will satisfy all economies and that culture, ethics, and history will inevitably shape what is finally chosen as a new social contract is articulated through law. I also wish to focus specifically on some issues that law must resolve in evolving market-oriented economies.

The benefit of a legal system for a market economy is to provide a predictable infrastructure that reduces the costs of transactions. It provides a stable environment in which to structure voluntary exchange. Two functional areas of law -- property and contracts -- are critical for a market economy. In property law, the legal system defines who can own property, how it is to be transferred between owners, and what are the appropriate uses for a class of property. Similarly, contract law sets up a framework for facilitating transfers.

In creating a legal structure for a market-oriented economy, three issues have become especially prominent. First is the definition of an owner. Can foreigners or absentee landlords be permitted? Must a would-be owner demonstrate an ability to work the property and care for it? Must an owner have certain personal characteristics, such as a religious background or no past party membership? Deciding these issues involves both formal and informal law, in the sense of a social contract, and each evolving Soviet and East European economy has vacillated on these issues.

A second issue of some consequence is what kind of ownership organization can be permitted. Here the right to hire labor has taken on particular significance. Family-owned enterprises that hire no labor seem to bother no one, except that the privatization experience in agriculture of the People's Republic of China indicates that women and children may lose rights and protection that had been guaranteed by central controls. Cooperative organizations have inherited some status from the socialism, but their conservative nature rarely encourages entrepreneurship. Finally, large units with the financial need for joint ownership have drawn the most fascination and criticism. Their need for wealth accumulation, which often is proscribed by both law and culture, can bring in foreign owners who wish to exert control and introduce change. Their many employees, who desire the security of strong labor law, can lessen the firm's value to investors. So far, each post-Leninist system -- fancying a "foreign investment" that is free of demands from investors -- is gradually making its own accommodation to the reality it faces.

Under socialist law, a contract system transferred property by specifying the buyer, the seller, and the terms of the transaction. In many ways, that process was indistinguishable from the transactions internal to a large corporation. In a market economy, contract law makes these same decisions, but handles the transactions outside the enterprise and allows the buyer and seller -- once they have been legally defined -- to negotiate the terms of the transactions.

The evolution of contract law must accompany changes in the law regarding property in post-Leninist societies. Consider the previously mentioned example of "privatization from below," the *de facto* private appropriation of socialist firms without any compensation to the state. Whether such actions should be viewed as theft depends in part on the existing legal system and in part on the prevailing social contract. On one hand, contract law in most Western traditions would presume that the new owners need to compensate former owners at the time of the transfer, but it also assumes that the property has value, when it may in fact have none. It is a theft of something without value. On the other hand, some formal socialist contract law may have supported the new owners' rights as workers to transfer state property to themselves, in the same sense that Western law occasionally preserves squatters' rights. The laws that encourage workers' cooperatives, for example, may establish rights to ownership from below. As for how such privatizing actions relate to the social contract, many citizens might consider the taking to be legitimate because the socialist economy had failed to use the property efficiently and fairly. Then, public dissatisfaction with the command system competes with other values in the emerging socialist social contract, such as the distrust of private property and wealth accumulation. The main point to be gained is that one legal system and its presumptions, particularly when they incorporate the obscurities from the social contract, are not effortlessly transferred to another legal system.

Sustaining a Market Economy

This section explores some considerations for sustaining a market oriented economy in a transitioning state.

Prices

Implementing a market economy requires change not only in the household and workplace, where entrepreneurship, private property and the legal structure directly affect outcomes, but in the macroeconomy where indirect policies can wield equal power. The first area of concern involves prices. Administered prices, which have long hampered socialist change because they cannot keep up with technology and because they reflect costs, and not consumer desire, have influenced the Leninist social contract and created inordinate expectations for stability and subsidy. In the labor market, socialist workers have come to expect full employment and stable wages. In product markets, socialist consumers expect full shelves and low prices. In each instance, the difference between expectation and reality has become the source of an intolerable political burden of expectations and an economic burden of subsidies.

Relinquishing price control, however, immediately establishes another political and economic burden, because consumer prices immediately rise, and painful labor market adjustments follow close behind. Yielding price control requires a focus on three policy areas to ameliorate undesirable effects. The first is to limit the effects of *monopoly*, which can raise prices well above reasonable costs. The second is to coordinate *relative price changes*. When the degree of decontrol varies from one sale to another, a price signal does not give accurate information. At the macroeconomic level, consumer goods price levels often are linked (indexed) to factor market prices so that they move relatively in tandem. Relative prices are equally important within these categories, i.e., where some "basic" prices are stable and subsidized but other "luxury" prices are free to rise. Finally, the burden is compounded by attempts to limit *inflation*, where price increases are uncontrollable.

The common thread in matters of price flexibility is a search for optimal security. While the security of citizens is an obligation of any state, economic security has been a particular province of socialism. Rigid prices have been a tool to guarantee employment and material security and to limit wealth accumulation, itself a kind of socialist public good. Public reassurance about the long-range gains of decontrol is a critical necessity. In the short run, the cost of price flexibility in insecurity is painfully evident, but the benefits to be gained, which may seem to be limited to a few vendors pejoratively named "speculators," are not obvious.

One decision facing the new market implementers is to decide which prices should be fixed, at what level, and with how much subsidy. Three issues seem to predominate. First, the creation of a safety net to give security to citizens who are dependent (children, the disabled, the unemployed, the elderly) has had a low priority in public actions, albeit not in discussions, but it eventually must occupy many minds, including those from the burgeoning religions.

Second, reformers must ask which monopoly controls are appropriate for the new market economy. Planning encouraged large enterprises over small. Thus, in a comparison of enterprise size in the Soviet Union, the Federal Republic of Germany, and the United States, the Soviet Union had more than twice as many enterprises with more than 1000 workers than its capitalistic counterparts.[7] The existing productive infrastructure predisposes post-Leninist societies to face many monopolies. The ordinary tools for controlling monopoly are price controls (already discussed), breakups into smaller units, and foreign competition. Breaking up the large monopolies by establishing domestic and foreign competition would seem to be the easiest policy, and it has the added advantage that a regional dispersion of firms would economize on transportation costs and offset losses from the economies of scale that were given up.

Banking and Currency Convertibility

In the Soviet socialist system, banking, foreign currency, and credit were centralized, and the allocations proceeded more on political than on economic principles. Bank credit was not easily distinguished from a subsidy, and currency transactions were heavily regulated. In a survey of Soviet farm managers, only 8 percent believed that credit should be repaid.[8] The consequence was that investment, which occurred through the state budget, was not directed to industries that could best use it, and some innovation was malnourished. Similarly, foreign currency flowed to planned uses and not necessarily to new opportunities. Entrepreneurship and private activity were poorly served, if at all.

In moving to the economic rules of a market and introducing flexibility into the economy, the monolithic socialist banking systems have been broken up into tiers -- a central bank with a number of commercial banks. The new banks' capital and portfolios, however, depend on the creation of private property in assets and financial instruments (stocks, bonds, and commercial paper) and on the institutions to make them transferable (bourses and markets). Although the instruments and institutions are now available by decree, the trust and faith have not yet emerged to implement them. A new social contract including such trust is pivotal for sustaining entrepreneurship and private property in the new market-oriented systems.

Creating and sustaining confidence in the new banking system requires several pre-requisites. First, the system must be managed by competent and honest staff who understand the goal of a market economy. The technical expertise probably can be obtained from professionalization relying on experience abroad and integration into world banking.

Honesty requires legal infrastructure and social acceptance of banking as a profession. Second, the banks need to work with enterprises who have a firm understanding of a bank's role. The development of commercial banking is held back when the legal status and authority of enterprises is in flux and when both institutions are learning to operate in a new system. The banks and enterprises can develop only hand in hand. Finally, banking regulation is a difficult agenda, as the United States' savings-and-loan crisis has shown. Too much regulation stifles growth through investment, but too little of it opens the system's integrity to attack. The choices are sensitive.

Currency convertibility is an indisputable requisite of entering into world markets for goods and financial instruments. All socialist economies have devalued their currencies, but open convertibility is restricted. Emerging economies face the decision of whether or not to establish their own untried currencies. The policy instruments require fine tuning. Gray[9] and Lavigne[10] found that in Poland a too-large devaluation left undesirable protection for inefficient domestic firms and slowed their reform, whereas East Germany found a too-small devaluation left the country with high unemployment. These circumstances are new and trying; some expertise can be gained only by experience.

Charges of "corruption" often accompany the introduction of macroeconomic reforms and financial markets. In some instances, the charge is truly one of fraud, which can be handled by a proficient legal system. In other instances, however, the charge simply reflects a changing social contract with high hopes and expectations accompanied by the search for a bargain. The case of "privatization from below" or "kleptocracy," where public property was appropriated by private persons, illustrates expectations gone awry in reality. Property rights were not specified and enforced by formal law, and informal law with questionable antecedents prevailed.

Temporarily, this confusion and even illegality is to be expected from a system in transition. Questionable incidents should be explored to highlight the basic issues to be resolved. For example, who should receive property or credit; what documentation should be required; what networks will dispense it: these questions need to be answered and understood at all levels of society and incorporated into the social contract. Such understandings diminish the cost of enforcement because the public accepts and supports the market principles that are involved.

Public Finance

Taxation and other fiscal policies such as monetary control and international trade regulations are also important features of evolving post-Leninist economies. The new market-oriented economies face particular problems and choices because of their recent past.

Taxes -- always a burden whether socialist or capitalist -- should ideally strive to discourage economic activity as little as possible. Socialist federal taxes have laid heaviest on enterprises (a profits tax) and consumer goods (a turnover tax). At the local level, the tax has fallen on agricultural goods and other small sources, such as the tax on unmarrieds -- the "bachelor" tax. A single tax on land, as espoused by Henry George, has attracted attention in Eastern Europe because it is simple to establish and administer. Tax reform, however, ultimately awaits political stability.

The primary problem, however, has been not the choice of fiscal instruments but their macroeconomic consequences, in that expenditures have exceeded income and fueled inflation. Instead of reducing expenditures, raising income, or restricting credit, federal expenditures were shifted to local governments without new revenue sources. In a local reaction, in the Soviet Union, the local governments have withheld from the center the revenues they collected at the periphery, resulting in macroeconomic destabilization.

Finally, establishing and sustaining the tools of macroeconomic stabilization -- fiscal policy, monetary practices, and international trade strategies -- engenders high hostility from the population. Fiscal stabilization is an elusive goal, monetary practices arouse an old hatred of bankers, and strategies for open international trade are untested. Regionalism and ethnicity complicate the matter, for they result in calls for autonomous and differentiated policies that compete for federal support and press for federal remuneration.

To relieve the hostile environment for change will be difficult. In a list of the main factors that generate a hostile environment for change, Brinkerhoff and Goldsmith, rank highly a distorted price system.[11] There is further difficulty inherent in valuing stabilization, and society finds it hard to rank conflicting policies because values are unclear. Conflicting elites, furthermore, value them differently and compete for control.

Despite pessimism, early reformers have indeed introduced the three major elements of macroeconomic stability and with some success. A sensitive point that remains for late reformers is the question of timing. Given the interdependency among elements, most economic advisors have suggested a "big bang" approach, where the elements are introduced simultaneously.[12] Others have espoused a more sedate course of continuous change and adaptation so that people's expectations and understanding may be engaged in the process.[13] The second path probably improves the stability and sustainability of change because it allows time to forge a new social contract; it has the drawback of diminishing momentum, incentive, and coordination. It is possible that the smaller and more homogeneous populations of some Eastern

European countries or of individual Soviet republics might, however, endure the faster and more turbulent process.

Democracy, Economic Reform, and the Social Contract

The foregoing discussion highlighted the challenges faced by post-Leninist societies as they shift to market-oriented economies. In particular, I have addressed not only technical economic concerns but also the need to transform the social contract of public expectations. Notions of justice, based on history, education, and culture, generate people's expectations concerning the social contract, especially concerning the state's and the economy's roles and functions. Yet, notions of justice are so idiosyncratic to a society that each social contract must also be different, i.e., it is not possible to import any one market system and impose it on another. For instance, even moving the West German market system to East Germany has proved difficult because the goals and attitudes that constitute the social contract differ so much. (A West German economist once confided to me that East Germans "didn't even seem German.")

Weintraub clearly identified the different theoretical underpinnings of democracy and the market, concluding that the marriage of the two may be necessary, yet inconvenient. My discussion of the social contract as it applies to economic matters illustrates a similar tension. The transition to a market-oriented economy promises to bring post-Leninist societies the benefit of impersonal self-regulation, whereby the "invisible hand" translates individual impulses into generally beneficial consequences for society as a whole. Yet, democratic processes (collective deliberations) may be the best means whereby the social contract can be reconstructed to conform to the requirements of a market-oriented economy.

For example, a pure market economy rewards people by the functions they perform and the market value of the functions. This means that functions whose money value is hazy, or whose costs are highly evident may not, in a pure market economy, generate much support. Poor citizens might not pay to educate their children, for instance, or defense of the environment might be abandoned. Ordinarily economists turn to arguments of public goods (producing for one person uses the same resources as producing for everyone; e.g., defense or technology) or "social" benefits (one person's expenditure benefits someone else; e.g., education or religion) to raise public awareness and generate support. Put differently, these are the areas where the collective decisions of the populace expressed through deliberative democratic processes must try to balance the market's logic.

The notions of justice surround public attitudes toward the distribution of wages, ownership and wealth, and other entitlements such as education, housing, and health. Socialists achieved much power and authority -- a strong social contract -- for wealth leveling and wage compression, and for the distribution of goods through the public sector. Leninism had the elements of a giant company town. A market-oriented economy must re-align or cancel these distribution policies if it is to incorporate individualistic decisions into the economy and introduce cost controls. The task of garnering acceptance for the ways of a market-oriented economy by altering the social contract falls to a large extent upon the political institutions of the emerging democracies, the persuasiveness of the reforming elites, and the support of other elements in civil society, such as voluntary organizations, the mass media, and churches. How well this social contract fits the requirements of a healthy market-oriented economy will vary from nation to nation, as is true among the existing democracies that might be considered to be consolidated. Just as there is no guarantee for the success of consolidating democracies, there is no easy recipe for institutionalizing a stable market-oriented economy.

Notes

1. The idea of social contract in formerly Leninist systems is explored in Jan Adam, *Economic Reforms and the Welfare System in the USSR, Poland and Hungary: Social Contract in Transformation* (London: Macmillan, 1991).

2. Amsden demonstrates the effectiveness of different state interventions in a cross-national comparison of economic growth and the diffusion of technology in East Asia. See Alice H. Amsden, "Diffusion of Development: The Late-Industrializing Model and Greater East Asia." *The American Economic Review* (1991) 81: 282-286.

3. Jim Butterfield. "Devolution in Decisionmaking and Organizational Change in Soviet Agriculture," in William Moskoff, ed., *Perestroika in the Countryside: Agricultural Reform in the Gorbachev Era* (New York: M.E. Sharpe, 1990), 19-46.

4. Don van Atta, "'Full-Scale, Like Collectivization, but without Collectivization's Excesses' - the Campaign to Introduce the Family and Lease Contract in Soviet Agriculture," in William Moscoff, ed., *Perestroika in the Countryside: Agricultural Reform in the Gorbachev Era.*

5. R. Schiller, M. Boycko, and V. Korobov, "Popular Attitudes toward Free Markets," *The American Economic Review* (1991) 81: 385-400.

6. J.H. Wigmore, "Property." *Evolution of Law*, Boston, 1923.

7. A. Iakovlev, "Monopolizm SSSR i faktory ego obslovluvaiushchie." *Voprosy Ekonomiki* (1991), 1: 4.

8. R.V. Ryvkina, "Management interactions and the Problem of Redistribution of Economic Power," translated in *Soviet Sociology* (1988), 42-56.

9. Cheryl Gray, "Economic Transformation: Issues, Progress, and Prospects," in *Transition* (1990), 5: 7-9.

10. M. Lavigne, *Financing the Transition in the USSR: The Shatalin Plan and the Soviet Economy* (New York: Institute for East-West Security Studies, 1990).

11. D.W. Brinkerhoff, and A.A. Goldsmith, *Institutional Sustainability in Agriculture and Rural Develoment: A Global Perspective* (New York: Praeger, 1990).

12. Cherl Gray, "Economic Transformation: Issues, Progress, and Prospects."

13. Karl Popper, "The Best World We Have Yet Had," interview by George Urban, *Report on USSR* (1991), 3(22): 20-22.

7

The Role of Law in Democratic and Economic Reform in Leninist States

Alice Erh-Soon Tay

The remarkable events that occurred in 1989-90 in what was then the Communist world threw into prominence an unprecedented widespread internal demand for breaking the Communist party's monopoly of power. Citizens now wanted guarantees that human rights would be observed and that the rule of law, independent of the party's will, would protect them and not exempt the state or its officials. They wanted and still want a pluralist society and economic system, an acknowledged multiplicity of parties, institutions and interests, freedom of association and expression, fragmented and varied forms of ownership and economic enterprise and a genuine internal and external market in labor and commodities.

For those who expressed these demands, the ideology represented by the American Declaration of Independence and the U.S. Constitution, with its separation of executive, legislative and judicial functions, continues to live as a vital goal and ideal not superseded or driven into obsolescence by what many now see as the unfortunate experiment with creating a new socialist stage of human historical development.[1]

This was, and still is, especially true of the elevation of free elections, the independence of the judiciary and its power to interpret law and review both government legislation and government action, and of the entrenchment of fundamental rights and liberties of the citizen as maintainable against the state, its officials and organs. Those goals and attitudes constituted the banner to which people rallied in Beijing and Shanghai, in the Baltic States, in Budapest, Prague, Berlin and Leipzig, Timisoara and Bucharest. These were the slogans that ensured or threatened electoral defeat for the Communist party from Poland to Albania.

Creating good laws to be fairly, justly and honestly applied has become a widespread demand in the former Communist states.[2] It is seen as a basic requirement for a good future; yet it is not predicted with confidence. To ask for the evidence for such generalizations is to show that one has little feel for the tragedy that populations under communism have passed through. It is to know nothing of their literature, little of their personal careers and to ignore the great popular demonstrations, the burgeoning newspaper literature, the rush to newly opened police files.

"What is 'law'?" I have been asked, and "What is 'the rule of law'?" Social thought and social criticism are not best furthered by the elevation of abstract social and political concepts, marked off and delineated to serve as pigeonholes into which whole societies, institutions, ideologies and events can be thrust. Law can mean many things. It can be contrasted with custom, with morality, with police regulations, with isolated decrees. It can be taken in other contexts, to embody all of these. It is not possible to understand the character of Western civilization, and not only Western civilization, without recognizing that it has contrasted specific laws, decrees and regulations, let alone arbitrary acts of power, with the actual reality and persistent ideal of an historical and concrete commitment to the elaboration of systematic legal principles, institutions and bodies of legislation or received authority that aim to judge fairly, but with reference to a host of competing interests and concerns. Law is thus a tradition, an historical institution, a system and a set of attitudes and beliefs that inform the work of judges, of advocates and, in many societies, the work of politicians and bureaucrats.[3] To understand law is to understand its history and its tradition; to do that is to pass beyond the need for and usefulness of an abstract definition. There are as many definitions of law as there are books written about it.

All this, let it be said, is partly consciously and partly implicitly understood by citizens in the former Communist world. When they now elevate the need for law, they are not elevating -- as Jeremy Bentham and some of the French revolutionaries of 1791 and 1792 did -- the desirability of a clear, rational and fundamental code that will lay down rules for society in the way that the Politburo, less honestly, used to do. They are yearning to acquire, to re-establish, or to regenerate, a tradition, a culture, a society in which law is not simply the will of the government and in which law counts even when the government finds it inconvenient. That is the starting point of our, and their, concept of the rule of law. The voluminous reports of the U.S. Supreme Court, of State Supreme Courts and of the courts of other common law and civil law jurisdictions show how complex and uncertain that concept of the rule of law is. It is not therefore an empty thing, a puff of wind. It constituted for many years the most important difference between the USSR on the one hand and the

United Kingdom or the United States on the other. One felt the difference on one's skin.

Democracy does not solve problems: it provides the necessary climate for discussing them seriously and tackling them with genuine involvement from below. On any scale larger than that of the village gathering and the town meeting, democracy requires law as a guarantee of rights, as a framework of stability, as a form of social pressure and control that is neither arbitrary nor irrelevantly selective. Such law incorporates and respects the concepts of reciprocity and justice on which relations between government and the governed should be based.

Given the widely acknowledged failure of the centralized command economy with its reliance on corruption to provide flexibilities and overcome shortages, the Communist world, too, now requires the rule of law and a legal culture to facilitate and control a freer, more competitive economic life. This is true not only of those states that have changed to democracies and market-oriented economies, but also of those, such as China, that are resisting change. But while these societies may need law, Communist traditions and, in the Soviet Union and China, earlier traditions of statecraft have done little to create and secure, among rulers and officials, respect for law, whether in theory or in practice.[4] To a surprising extent as recent revelations have fully confirmed, Communist officials operated as satraps or in satrapies, dependent above all on the goodwill and authority of the leader and their superiors and on mutual favors among equals.

The Centrality of Law and the Lack of Respect for It

The utopian Marxist vision of a society without government or law involved the equally utopian belief in a society without a conflict of interests or values. This would be a society in which politics had disappeared, replaced by mobilization at one stage and rational calculation at another. Hence, law, too, could disappear.[5] No one in the Communist world believes or wants to pretend to believe this theory any more -- unless their past privileges and promised security are directly threatened by change.

The difference between decree and law, between government proclamation and administrative power on the one hand and the genuine rule of law on the other, is perfectly well understood in all those countries where the rule of law is seriously threatened or has been abolished. It has been part of the legal education of humankind, keenly appreciated by people in those societies that have known despotism and trouble.

That Communist governments had no respect for law as an independent social institution, whether in theory or in practice, is not in serious dispute. Leaving aside the early utopianism of the period of War or Militant Communism from 1918 and 1921, and its belief in the speedy withering away of law and the elevation of revolutionary consciousness of justice exercised by "the masses" directly, Communists quickly came to use law as distinct from repression only where it suited them. For them, law was (1) a means of propaganda internally, i.e. a succinct and threatening formulation of party policy; (2) a means of propaganda externally, an assurance that Communist government had come to stay as part of the international order; and (3) a means of regularizing or appearing to regularize administration. All this was reflected in Communist practice, though very selectively, from the promulgation of the Codes of the Russian Soviet Federative Socialist Republic (RSFSR) from 1922 onward and in Communist theory from the 1936 Stalin Constitution onward. It came to less qualified theoretical expression with Khrushchev and his proclamation that the state was now no longer a Dictatorship of the Proletariat but an All-People's State representing the interest of everyone except a few criminals. More dramatically he revealed and continued to reveal publicly some of the most horrible crimes of Stalin and to proclaim that truth, kindness and sincerity were also moral virtues -- even under actual, real socialism. Such at least was the theoretical stance.

Law was given some, even if qualified, integrity and independence by the shift from seeing law as a weapon of class rule to seeing it, in the All-People's State, as a means of social control in the interests of the whole society. At various times, this elevation of law as proclaimed by the government has been reinforced, or even initiated, by various needs for law: 1) As a framework for economic activity both within the Plan (which used the contractual form) and outside it; 2) by attempts to strengthen legitimacy at home and respect abroad; 3) by the desire to consolidate trends alleged to amount to a new phase in socialist development.[6] 4) The search for foreign investment has at all times also demanded at least a semblance of legal protection for the investor and of legal regulation and determination of commercial activities and disputes.[7]

In virtually all Communist countries, the passage of time thus produced a shift from emphasis on the punitive and defensive functions of law to its organizational and administrative functions. Nevertheless, the proliferation of civil, criminal, administrative, labor, family, transport and other codes in every Communist country except (for a long time) China only served to hide the fundamental reality -- that all law was subordinate to political and administrative power and political and administrative policies and requirements. Laws, even constitutions, were promulgated and ignored. Exceptions were freely if secretly authorized by councils and ministers of state. Allegedly universal laws were applied in one part of the country and not in another. Law, in short, was a powerless handmaiden to administration, and both were totally subservient to politics, a point stressed and indeed demonstrated by the leading Soviet civil law expert -- now an emigré -- Professor O.S. Ioffe.[8]

The subservience of law to politics is crucial to understanding the nature and habits of administration, and even of police work and judicial determination, in Communist countries. When law was rigorously applied in Communist societies, it was applied at the behest and not against, the interests of those with power. With or without the use of legal form they could and did purge each other and each other's subordinates. They did not accept at any level but the verbal that power itself was subject to law. This applies even to the constitutions of the USSR and China. Long ignored in practice, they were ultimately but secretly proclaimed not to be citable or enforceable in court. Their provisions, the theory ran, were guidelines to legislation and did not have the force of law until such legislation had been adopted. It is on this basis that both China and the USSR have rejected the notion of a constitutional court, persisting in the view that a constitution is a statement of government policy, to be actualized by the government itself.[9] In the USSR, as it began to move to a more genuinely federal structure, the reliance was not so much on constitutions as on solemn contractual agreements among republics themselves and between republics and the center. By the end of 1991, the Union had been formally dissolved, the center abolished, and the Commonwealth of Independent States turned into a community resting on agreement alone.

Some changes in the earlier Communist situation, or at least in public response to it, began with Malenkov and Khrushchev. They were both responses to and promises of new internal threats to Communist party rule. Fitfully and only partially licensed from the top (most notably in the Soviet Union and more erratically in China), the new demands for "liberalization" received wider and more far-reaching internal support than the rulers expected. Such demands were still further strengthened by growing ease of communication and an international climate that increasingly emphasized human rights, self-determination and genuine redress against administrative arbitrariness. In the "good" periods, even Communist theoreticians began to emphasize and press for the importance of basic human values such as truth, sincerity and kindness, the importance of socialist legality as the proper observance of law by state and party organs and not only by citizens, and the inadmissibility of politically motivated repression and injustice.

The Demand for the Rule of Law

By 1990, the demand for honesty and decency had swept all Communist countries. The strength of that demand, its capacity for changing the situation, varied. So did the extent to which reformers and dissidents emphasized the concept of democracy as involving a legal order, a rule of law, or to which they first sought rather a religious, nationalist or ideological foundation for restoring human decency and concern for the people.

In the Communist world today there are those nations that were part of the (Continental) Western legal tradition, that valued and understood the rule of law until the Communists destroyed it. In the Republics of Latvia, Estonia and Lithuania, the Republic of Poland, the former German Democratic Republic, Hungary and even Romania, the overwhelming demand is quite simply for the restoration of the pre-Communist *Rechtsstaat*. There, when the relevant states were called People's Republics or Democratic Republics, the entire population ultimately came to know that the terms meant something non-popular and non-democratic. The Communist reinterpretation of democracy and of popular government, in short, is simply being pushed aside. Instead, appeals to the rule of law, the enforceability of constitutional guarantees, and international concern with preserving civil freedom and human rights are now openly made to reinforce internal demands for change.

Past legal tradition and culture do not lose their importance. In the territories of the former German Democratic Republic, in Hungary and Czechoslovakia, in the Baltic States, there is good understanding and strong appreciation of the role of the rule of law, of historic legal traditions, of honest legislation and of an independent legal profession. In Poland, the memory of those is less recent. In Romania and no doubt in Albania, this legal culture is confined to a small section of the population. In Yugoslavia the situation is as complex and varied in this respect as in other respects. Here, as in so many other questions about the future of countries that were dominated by communism for a period only, we must look to the historian and the student of the country's culture and literature, rather than to the sociologist and futurologist for guidance.

Legal sophistication, like other forms of sophistication, does not disappear overnight. For example, the Stalinist inspired Civil Codes of the Baltic Republics in the 1960s were more complex, even if marginally so, than those of the RSFSR and the Central Asian Republics. So were those of East Germany and Poland. In the USSR, the law against social parasitism, under which the poet Josif Brodski was sentenced after he had been dismissed from his job, required no proof that employment was available and had been wilfully refused. In the Polish People's Republic, the courts added that requirement.

The countries in which the Communist party's hegemony is less decisively threatened -- China, and perhaps Korea -- are those countries in which both the Western legal tradition and the associated historical reality of a pluralism of classes, institutions and courts not fully dependent on the state have been much more weakly established, if at all. Here, the Communist party could and did inherit both a tradition of state dominance internally and of imperial ambitions externally - an inheritance that has threatened to pass to sections of the military.

Strengthening the Role of Law

The Western legal tradition, with its intellectualization and its system-atization of the process of balancing and protecting interests as well as the claims of legal and individual persons, presupposes pluralism, pluralism of means and pluralism of ends. It aims at decisions that are reasonable, being fundamentally skeptical of the notion that a political or judicial judgment can claim to be ultimately, unconditionally, rational, or correct. It sees law as involving a complex set of dialogues: between counsel and counsel and the court, between all those and authorities to be cited, whether past or present, between the legal profession and the jury or the community,[10] between blackletter law and the system of law and legal interpretation through which it is to be understood.[11]

Fundamental to strengthening law and legal independence in the USSR and China where the task is even more difficult, is the need to foster the pluralist foundation and implications of law. This involves a sophisticated understanding of law as a system that balances internal competing requirements, principles and policies, not just external demands. Such an understanding of law necessitates the separation of sovereignty and ownership and the recognition of fragmentation in sovereignty itself. It requires the spread of social independence, of spheres of comparative self-determination and autonomy. It also requires the acceptance of open textured concepts, into which social expectations, notions of fairness and fair dealing, and rules of reasonable conduct can be built so as to tailor legal requirements to complex and shifting social and economic situations. This conception of the function of law requires laws and legal decisions sophisticated enough to make use of presumptions and shifts in onus of proof. Lawyers must recognize and yet limit the requirements of social policy, no longer subordinating individuals to the collective in theory and to the state in practice. The integrity of institutions must be recognized and respected. Voluntary associations and political parties must be allowed to flourish and to secure their existence. Republics must have democracy within and reciprocal rights vis-à-vis each other and in their relations to the Commonwealth center.

What is true of politics and social life, of parties, charities, parliaments and theaters, is also true of the economy. As Elizabeth Clayton noted in her excellent essay, the precise balance between market-driven economic activity and a state or public sector, between competition and external planning, can be a matter of dispute and of adjustment, in which profit need not be the only consideration. But the bankruptcy of the command economy does bring out that pluralism, security against administrative arbitrariness, and flexibility and responsiveness to consumer demands are as vital in economic life as they are in political life. Both areas depend in the end, on the existence of an honest and sophisticated legal system, an independent judiciary that commands social respect, and a legal profession capable of playing its part in the vindication of justice. They also require the total excision of the Communist habit of regarding any conflict of interests and of views as a contradiction to be sublated, that is, suppressed.

There are, in the Soviet Union, conspicuous areas where legal progress is possible. The contractual model for relationships between republics and the federal structure in which some of them choose to remain is an important and visible elevation of legal propriety and reciprocity. The development of standing orders for parliamentary assemblies and regional councils is another. The elaboration of a sophisticated system of commercial law, of contract and tort, is yet another. The international concern with human rights should lead to extensive criticism and revision of existing codes of criminal law and criminal procedure along lines that will make such law less state-centered and weighted against the accused. As sophistication grows in these matters, the sophistication, independence and integrity of a legal profession will also grow - especially if, in contrast to current Western democratic fashion, the control of its integrity is placed with the profession itself.[12]

Lawyers in both Russia and China have no great prestige or respect from the intelligentsia.[13] They come mostly from less educated families, seeking higher education through willingness to serve the government. Both their hands and their minds are seen as tainted by complicity in the ubiquitous work of repression. Their career choice, especially in Russia, was taken to imply acquiescence or even active participation. Yet, in the USSR and China, lawyers had been stressing both the need to meet international standards to facilitate commerce and the importance of making provisions against arbitrariness and injustice in wider areas of administration and social life. Some feel this more strongly than others and most feel it more strongly in relation to virtuous citizens than to criminals. China is perhaps the Communist or ex-Communist country in which the Western legal tradition is weakest. Yet, as I have reported elsewhere,[14] Chinese lawyers are beginning to see themselves as lawyers, to feel a certain kinship with other lawyers the world over and to rebel against what they see as an excessively circumscribed governmental conception of their role. They may not yet see themselves as predominantly protectors of the citizen but they are beginning to acquire a certain sense of professionalism in their functions. This means that they show some desire for independence from other organs and pressures and seek autonomy of organization and decision-making in their legal work.

There is also in China an increasing interest in comparative law, seen as opening new and relevant doors to China's perceptions of the demands that law makes on the operation of government. There is increasing recognition of and genuine concern about abuse of power by officials. This concern has led to the recent enactment of the Administrative Procedure Law, giving albeit limited opportunities to citizens to bring action against individual functionaries of the state for misuse or abuse of power. There is great interest, as there was earlier in the USSR, especially among legal practitioners, but also among judges and others, in the coming revision of the criminal law and criminal procedure law. Several lawyers have expressed to me the hope that new provisions would permit defense counsel to assist the client during investigation and not only after the investigation has been closed and the formal charge has been laid.

The negative aspects of both law and the legal profession in China are both weightier and of longer standing, although they are largely shared with the Soviet Union. The Chinese legal system, like the Soviet, has been bureaucratic in style and attitude in good times; it has been subject to brutal and unprincipled interventions including the purges of lawyers and judges on ideological grounds in bad times. Now, outside of political cases (and any case can be viewed as political) and so long as a law official is working within the written law and not deliberately seeking to uncover a can of worms that discredits the government or the powerful, all is well. But law is still seen as handed down from above, as a set of directives not subject to questioning or to uninvited interpretation, to debate or revision from below, to scrutiny from people not directly charged with the task of scrutinizing. The Chinese lawyer thus has little sense of being in constant debate with his colleagues, with the court, with the ministry, with the government. He sees himself and is seen by others as a state servant, though this is changing as commercial legal practices develop and as the profession seeks more independent status. But to a much greater extent than in the West, the lawyer still does most of his/her work, including his/her most important work, on the basis of *guanxi* relationships (i.e. of mutual exchanges of favors).

On the side of the government, whose attitude to law is at best totally pragmatic and often simply cynical, there is a strong tendency to substitute administrative regulation for laws which may tend to be inconvenient, especially since administrative regulations are not subject to procuratorial supervision in court. What is worse, powers that favor the government against the citizen are often ill-defined or open-ended. Thus, the Standing Committee of the National People's Congress has power to grant unlimited extensions to continue investigations in "complicated cases". It probably also has and exercises power to exempt whole areas of China, and whole complexes and institutions, from the operation of all sorts of laws that make no formal provisions for such exemptions. Further, every Chinese cadre receives and is bound by internal circulated instructions marked *neibu* (internal, i.e. not for publication or public circulation) which bind his conduct in the fullest legal sense and yet may not be mentioned to the non-official party in contractual negotiations, in public hearings or in academic writing.

Militating against these negative aspects is something I have written about elsewhere[15] -- the internationalization of law (in effect, of Western legal concepts, principles, and procedures) as part of the growing internationalization of economic endeavor, political arrangements, travel and the movement of labor, management of resources and protection of the environment etc. These social forces are both undermining the absoluteness of internal sovereignty and the isolation of past economic, political, cultural and legal arrangements and traditions. China's reluctant adoption or promulgation of significant and public codes of law came as part of her open-door policy in relation to foreign investment. Similarly, the (former) Soviet Union's democratization was, when viewed from the top, part of her attempt to end her isolation from Europe and from much of the rest of the world.

Law and Civil Society

There is much talk in Communist and former Communist countries today of civil society as the source and theater of political independence and economic development. Perhaps what was done badly, brutally and corruptly -- and in the end ineffectively -- from the top, will be done better from below.

The problem is both complex and simple. As Eugene Kamenka argues below, the totalitarian state in Russia and in China produced no real civil society -- no classes or institutions independent of the state, no judicial system that sought its strength not only from foreign models but from the *ius commune*, from the sentiments and habits of the people it set out to judge. Civil society in Russia and in China needs to be built just as all that part of law which is not purely administrative in spirit and aim needs to be built. What is more, the building cannot be done entirely from the top -- in the fashion in which Peter the Great strove to establish a *Landtag*. Nor can the building of civil society or of law take precedence: the two require each other and will grow together. It is for this reason that general principles cease to serve and political feel, historic sensibility and statesmanship have to take over. They will have to do so in many fields of endeavour simultaneously, concentrating on the specific while not losing sight of the whole. There is no panacea in words or formulas.

Political parties can help democracy and the growth of civil society or destroy it, its leadership, its members. Institutions may be less volatile, but they, too, can be taken over. Courts, for a long time, may be no better than the judges of which they are composed, and legislation will almost certainly seek too much of its inspiration and adopt too much of its style from the administrative manipulation and authority-mongering of the past.

While recognizing the weakness of civil society, of Western legal traditions and of what Russians call "civic courage" among large sections of the population of the USSR, we should not forget that the judicial reforms of the 1860s led surprisingly quickly to the emergence of a Russian Bar that fought tenaciously against the government and for political freedom and judicial and administrative integrity. That can happen again.

In China, the impediments are even greater and the isolation of westernizing intellectuals from the people is also even greater. Yet, economically, civil society is more active, though forced to rely on shameful accommodations with authority and its unending corruption.

Notes

1. Eugene Kamenka, "The French Revolution: A Universal Legacy?" 17 *Dialectics and Humanism*, No. 3, 71-82; "The Collapse of Communism", (1990) 34 *Quadrant*, No. 4, 20-24; *1990 Academy Annual Lecture: Revolution in the USSR and Eastern Europe*, Academy of the Social Sciences in Australia, *Annual Report 1991*, Canberra, 19-23.

2. Several leading legal journals have, in the past two to three years, devoted entire issues to considering concerns for law and the making of law in Communist countries, especially in the Soviet Union. Among these are: *Symposium: Perspectives in the Legal Perestroika: Soviet Constitutional and Legislative Changes*, (1990) 23 *Cornell International Law Journal*, No. 2; *Legal Reform in the Soviet Union*, (1990) 28 *Columbia Journal of Transnational Law*, No.1; *Symposium : "Perestroika" in Soviet Legal Institutions*, (1990) 15 *Law and Social Inquiry*, No. 3; *Law and the Gorbachev Era, Law in Eastern Europe*, No. 39, 1988. Individual articles run into the hundreds. A very detailed and useful one is Frances Foster-Simons, "Towards a More Perfect Union? The Restructuring of Soviet Legislation", (1989) 25 *Stanford Journal of International Law*, (Spring), 331.

3. See for a fuller discussion of this perception, A.E.S. Tay, "The Role of Law in the Twentieth Century: From Law to Laws to Social Science", the Lewin Chapel Lecture, Washington University in St. Louis, Missouri, 1990, 19 pp.

4. See, e.g., A.E.S. Tay, "Law in Communist China", Parts I-III, (1969) 6 *Sydney Law Review* 153-72 and 335-71 and (1976) 7 *Sydney Law Review* 400-23; *Law in China: Imperial, Republican, Communist: The Third Annual Lecture of the Centre for Asian Studies of the University of Sydney* (Sydney: University of Sydney Press, 1986) 45 pp.; "Law and the 'Legal Culture'", (1983) *Bulletin of the Australian*

Society of Legal Philosophy, No. 27, 15-26; "China and Legal Pluralism" in P. Sack and E. Minchin (eds), *Legal Pluralism*, Research School of Social Sciences, Australian National University, Canberra, 1985, 229-52.

5. Eugene Kamenka and A.E.S. Tay "Marxism, Socialism and the Theory of Law", (1985) 23 *Columbia Journal of Transnational Law: Special Issue on Marxism and Law in honor of Professor J.N. Hazard*, 217-249; "Socialist Legality or Administrative Justice in the U.S.S.R. and China?", George Ginsburgs et al. (eds), *Soviet Administrative Law: Theory and Practice* (Dordrecht/Boston/London: Martinus Nijhoff, 1989) 47-62; "Law, Legal Theory and Legal Education in the People's Republic of China", (1986) 7 *New York Law School Journal of International and Comparative Law*, 1-38.

6. Eugene Kamenka and A.E.S. Tay, "Beyond the French Revolution: Communist Socialism and the Concept of Law", in (1971) 21 *University of Toronto Law Journal*, 109-40.

7. In the PRC, see A.E.S. Tay "Introducing: China's Business Laws and Practice" in *China Laws for Foreign Businessmen and Investors*, CCH, (Australia), 1988, Vol. I, 1,011-2, 302 (being paras. 2-100 to 1-725); for the Soviet Union, see Christopher Osakwe, "The Death of Ideology in Soviet Foreign Investment Policy: A Clinical Examination of the Soviet Joint Venture Law of 1987", (1989) 22 *Vanderbilt Journal of Transnational Law*, No. 1, 111-125.

8. This theme appears repeatedly in all Ioffe's writings. See e.g. I.O. Ioffe and P.B. Maggs, *Soviet Law in Theory and Practice*, (London/New York: Oceana, 1983); Ioffe, *Soviet Law and Soviet Reality*, (Dordrecht/Boston: M. Nijhoff, 1985); Ioffe and Mark W. Janis, *Soviet Law and Economy* (Dordrecht/Boston: M. Nijhoff, 1986).

9. Eugene Kamenka and A.E.S. Tay, "Socialist Legality or Administrative Justice in the U.S.S.R. and China?", George Ginsburgs et al. (eds), *Soviet Administrative Law: Theory and Practice* (Dordrecht/Boston/London: M. Nijhoff, 1989) 47-62.

10. Bernard Rudden, "Courts & Codes in England, France and Soviet Russia", (1974) Tulane Law Review, 1010-28.

11. Benjamin N. Cardozo was the most distinguished exponent of this theme: *The Paradoxes of Legal Science* (New York: Columbia University Press, 1928); *The Nature of the Judicial Process* (New Haven: Yale University Press, 1924); *The Growth of the Law* (New Haven & London: Yale University Press, 1924).

12. See the discussion by Anatoly P. Fedoseyev, A.E.S. Tay, Georg Brunner and Olimpiad S. Ioffe, on the legal and constitutional prospects of a new Soviet Union, in Alexander Shtromas and Morton A. Kaplan (eds) *The Soviet Union and the Challenge of the Future*, Vol.1 *The Soviet System: Stasis and Change*, Part IV B (New York: Paragon House, 1987), 397-517.

13. A.E.S. Tay and Eugene Kamenka: "Law, Legal Theory and Legal Education in the People's Republic of China", (1986) 7 *New York Law School Journal of International and Comparative Law*, 1-38; and A.E.S. Tay, "The Struggle for Law in China", (1987) 21 *University of British Columbia Law Review*, No. 2, 561-80.

14. Report of the Australian Human Rights Delegation to China, 14-26 July 1991 (Canberra: Australian Government Publishing Service,1991), xiii + 83 pp.

15. A.E.S. Tay, "The Western Legal Tradition and the Internationalization of Law", (1991) 6 *Connecticut Journal of International Law*, No. 2, 529-43.

8

Civil Society and Freedom in the Post-Communist World

Eugene Kamenka

The remarkable upheavals that took place in the USSR, Eastern Europe and Central Europe in 1989 and 1990 have continued into the present. There is no doubt that they constitute what Marxists and Hegelians used to call a world-historical event. They also constitute a revolution, or a series of revolutions, as decisive as those of 1848. The 1848 revolutions achieved comparatively little in the short term. They have been seen by subsequent generations to stand as milestones on a Central, Southern and East European march to democracy and national self-determination. They were far from securing or even promoting immediate democracy; at best they constituted a "Springtime of the Nations" -- a reaffirmation of the rights of the citizens as against the passive loyalty imposed on subjects. They were a rejection of empires and a vindication of the bonds of language, culture and ordinary life at the level of the group, of civil society. Yet in France they produced the plebiscitory dictatorship of Louis Napoleon and his subsequent coronation.

The 1848-49 march to freedom at the popular level was sadly interrupted by the reviving power of reaction, at least in some countries, and by renewed Bonapartism in others. Now that is happening again. The years since 1989 have indeed achieved more spectacular successes than in 1848-49. The traditional power of an authoritarian and ubiquitous Communist party has been broken. The Soviet empire has collapsed, and so has its system of satellites. International military and political relations have undergone profound change. The future may be uncertain, but the past cannot be brought back to life. On that, it seems to me, contributors to this volume agree. It is in that sense and in that connection that the glorification of the state and the glorification of the party have given way to the exaltation of civil society -- the elevation not of the People, but of real actual people in their ordinary everyday lives.

Political revolutions have been defined (characterized would be a better word) as comparatively sharp, sudden transformations of social power, the basis of legitimacy and the structure of society, the economy or the state.[1] In Central and Eastern Europe, in Russia and Soviet Asia that has happened, though to varying degrees in different countries and regions and in different departments of political, social and economic life. A now largely consummated and unprecedented widespread, open, internal demand for breaking the Communist party's and the Communist state's monopolies of power -- political power, cultural power, economic power, power to decide without hindrance and to inform without fear of contradiction -- has triumphed. Multiple-party political systems and uncontrolled candidature for election, the dismantling of state ownership and control of the economy, the fragmentation of military structures and commands, the very break-up of the world's last major colonial empire, are completed or gathering pace. All that, too, is not in dispute.

As lovers of freedom, Sovietologists may find much comfort in this. As would-be social scientists, they should not. We have been urged to define, to measure and therefore quantify, to remember the techniques of micro-sociology and the insights of interest group and behaviorist social analysis. Yet those who predicted and understood the upheavals that have taken place in the Communist world were most significantly led by litterateurs, by novelists and artists, by historians and non-technical, independent philosophers. It is the latter, too, who have a livelier appreciation of the dangers of both opportunism and reaction.

Revolutions are times of extraordinary ferment, of rapid change, of the breakdown of traditional social groupings, of the rapid formation and transformation of styles of language, thought and action. (Consider only the central character in that splendid, bitter German film *Wir Wunderkinder* as he moves from the Kaiser, through Weimar, and the Nazis to the Allied Occupation. He becomes a different person at each stage.) Revolutions do not lend themselves well to social analyses that elevate one determining factor, that ignore culture, ideology and style but instead use theories of class and stratification which treat groupings and people as simply self-interested, static and given. It is the cultural tone of a society, its traditions and lifestyles, its languages as a repository of culture, morality and outlook, that provides the most important elements of continuity, re-emerging as terror retreats. Just as books of the "I was a Victim of Stalin's Terror" variety long gave us a much more accurate picture of the USSR than Sovietologists did, so internal dissidents and committed émigrés were better at predicting the imminent collapse of the Soviet Union than "fair" and "uncommitted" political scientists.

Factors Driving the Revolution

Four factors have driven the revolution in Communist countries insofar as it is a revolution from below.[2] One is the demand for democracy, freedom of speech and civil rights, strongest among the educated, and in those countries that have had a substantial past tradition of civil and political freedom, especially if that tradition was interrupted more recently, and if a unionized workforce has a past background of independent union discussion and activity. Second, and perhaps broader in its appeal but more decisive in its effects, is the demand for genuine national self-determination. Third, and in many countries again much broader in its appeal, is the demand for restoration of a personal or a national religion and its institutions and corporate life. Fourth, but by no means least important, is that great generator of revolutionary change, a sharp economic reversal against a background of rising economic expectations. Such expectations have risen even more sharply as Communist citizens became more aware of the standard of living of the Western, "capitalist" world. The economic reversals, and the growing lack of faith in the capacity of Communist governments to improve the situation, no doubt gave the democratic, national and religious protests their explosive power, but the three were also intertwined. What is more, the economic disasters of communism are widely perceived as having been exacerbated by economic and political isolation. Democratic reform and the building or rebuilding of a civil society outside the state, it is hoped by many, will make foreign aid and investment flow more freely, but also ultimately liberate and nurture enterprise within the society. There is fear, too, that without major political change, foreign aid and foreign investment will flow, as it does in China, into pockets already well-lined with the rewards of political power and corruption.

Explosive or not, revolutionary protest required something else for success -- weakness and lack of confidence among the rulers. It is possible to sit on bayonets; it is much more difficult to live with or stop a half-hearted process of reform or the growing realization from below that you have not the will or capacity to use force to its very limit. Many contingent factors, from the election of a Polish Pope to the increasing significance of international tourism, strengthened the protest movement in Communist countries. But the proximate cause of the revolution or revolutions was the withdrawal by Gorbachev of total (including military) support for past Soviet puppets.

The explosive factors that intertwine to produce revolution soon come apart, appearing to threaten each other. Democracy can threaten or appear to threaten national unity and economic development -- a tension Jeff Weintraub explored in his theoretical analysis. Economic decentralization and insistence on profits create social and class division, presenting challenges such as those Elizabeth Clayton discusses. And national and religious enthusiasm divide citizens and confront democratic freedoms. The break-up of the Soviet empire internally and externally has seen a remarkable revival of old-fashioned nationalism in every territory that had come under Soviet domination or continuing Soviet influence -- from Mongolia to Czechoslovakia, from Cuxhaven to Vladivostok. Much of the new nationalism is a liberating reaffirmation of national independence, both culturally and politically, of popular participation and home rule, of some earlier democratic institutions and traditions, which the Communists sought to destroy. It is in that sense an initial but far from lasting or secure affirmation of civil society. Much of it is less pretty than this -- insular, chauvinist, driven by hatred of near and often similar neighbors and ready to ape the pretensions and manners of the Soviet state to serve its own internal and external interests. Neither Catholicism in the East nor Russian Orthodoxy has succeeded, in this context, in becoming a force for universalism or reconciliation, or, at least, tolerance. Barbara Jelavich's contribution echoes these same themes for Yugoslavia in particular.

These threats are why revolutions so often prove unstable in their subsequent development and why contingency plays such a major role in determining the outcome. The future suddenly requires qualities quite different from those needed last year: moderation of national and religious bigotry, the blending of freedom with a willingness to help legitimate authority, accommodation and not only intransigence. Uncertainty about the future suddenly revitalizes romantic portrayals of a dreadful and recent past. The weakness of both civil society (that is independent social groupings and institutions) and democratic traditions in almost all the former USSR except perhaps the Baltic States makes the present and projected political and economic reforms far from totally secure.

The reasons for the collapse of will at the top fascinate. They do attract more general "social science" type explanations: the growing education and sophistication and foreign contact of a numerically increasing ruling elite; its realization that the post-industrial technology cannot be run on fear or by centralized, hierarchically transmitted command. The top levels of the KGB, from being the villain of the Soviet drama, were subsequently seen by some as a comparatively realistic, educated force, turning from thuggery to the promotion of Gorbachev. But the more closely we study this or any other revolution, the more suspicious we become of dominant factor explanations, of single process causalities, of the elevation of necessity and irresistible trends. Still, it is, I should think, too late for anyone in the USSR to reverse that policy and restore the previous political order or to save an internally centralized Moscow-controlled USSR. Regional dictatorship is possible; the restoration of

Marxism-Leninism, of a centralized Soviet empire and of monocratic socialism is not.

Revolutions may mark the end of an era: they do not inaugurate the millennium. They do not "supersede" conflicts; they substitute naked new conflicts for the suppressed or unacknowledged conflicts of the past. But the revolutions in Central and Eastern Europe and the territories of the USSR were fundamentally revolutions against the ideology and past reality of totalitarianism, of the ultimately all-powerful state, especially when that state was in various respects an external force and producer of horrors, from the Gulag to Chernobyl. That is why the word totalitarianism has become popular in the political thought and language of former Communist countries, just as its use declines in the West. This is why hope is invested in all that which is not the state -- in civil society. Civil society is a term, I shall argue, that has no great value as a tool of political analysis if divorced from history or from a theory and the reality of totalitarianism.

Civil Society Against Totalitarianism

The term *civil society*, now so popular in the former Communist world, emerged in the seventeenth and eighteenth centuries. It began as an affirmation or recognition of the human capacity to create political organization distinct from a state of nature. In the hands of Adam Ferguson, especially, it came to be used to emphasize the social or at least the economic rather than the political, the pursuit of economic goals or even of private interest as distinct from the elevation of public order or control. For Hegel, the less than truly universal interests of family and civil society had their own value, though they required ordering and completion by a state that represented the universal demands of reason or (in an allied version) of Rousseau's general will. For Marx, modern civil society was Hobbes's war of all against all, the unchecked pursuit of private interest in separation from any conception of the public good, of a universal human interest. It was the world of economic greed, of industry and trade. It was also the consummation of that historical process of alienation which drove universality and the pursuit of the common good out of the life of citizens and gave it a separate and illusory existence in religion, in the sovereign, in the state, in the bureaucracy. All of the latter could only be pretended carriers of the rational and the universal. All of them were unable to heal the split between public and private, universal and particular, created by private property in the means of production and the consequent differentiation of society into classes, without destroying the foundation of their own existence. In individualistic society, Marx thought, the human community had been banished into the blue mist of heaven. Civil society, the world of economic greed and competition, subjugated everything to its interest and way of working. Yet, it was unable to achieve coherence or stability; it carried within it the seeds of its own destruction.[3]

The philosophical underpinnings of these views and their theoretical and practical implications have been explored very thoroughly in the last 45 years. Even in quasi-Marxist circles, they are no longer accorded the respect they were once given. For the simple dichotomies of universal and particular, rational and self-contradictory, do not survive serious discussion or analysis. They are not a foundation for social theory. To speak of conflict and cooperation is to do serious social theory. But then we are no longer in the world of exclusively logical categories that know no problems of balance and no distinctions of degree.

The late twentieth century has come to view civil society in a more complex and also more favorable way. The free market is praised both economically and politically. Private vices, if not totally unchecked, are again held to produce public benefits. Even among socialists the difference between Marx's concept of civil society and Antonio Gramsci's has been influential.[4] For Gramsci, civil society was not atomistic or shaped only by greed. It was, as David Forgacs has put it, "an ensemble of organisms", of social activities and institutions.[5] It includes trade unions and other voluntary associations, church organizations and political parties not directly controlled by the state. Civil society, in short, is everything social that is not directly part of the government and its organs of repression, though the latter for Gramsci included the courts and not only the police.

Gramsci, of course, was Marxist enough to believe that civil society is shaped by a dominant social group, a ruling class, but he saw it as a sphere of both hegemony and consent, much of it unforced consent, and as a sphere in which opposition to a ruling class and a ruling system could similarly be organized. The strength of civil society in Western Europe, he thought, made the Leninist strategy of capturing power through conquest of the state machinery quite impossible -- one would have to capture a whole network of fortifications (schools, churches, newspapers, trade unions etc.) that lay around the bastion of the state and that were not simply dependent upon it for their existence and strength. Socialism, the Italian Communist Party later came to conclude, therefore required much more than the abolition of private ownership and a socialist state's control of the economy; it required a democratic culture built up in centuries of bourgeois development. It required a society not dominated by the state or shaped exclusively by its will. Can the same be said in reverse of the overthrow of "actual existing socialism"? Is civil society still too weak, in the former territories of the USSR at least, to make democracy safe?

Throughout the world, but especially in the formerly Communist world, there is today a collapse of confidence in the state as the organizer and controller of society, though there is in the West and in the East still no lack of demand for its help and protection, provided it is given without obligation. Those with a Marxist or quasi-Marxist education readily fall back on the term *civil society* as a way of indicating that there is worth and dignity, energy and political capacity, outside the state and its organs. The term *civil society*, popular in the USSR, Eastern Europe and among Chinese dissidents, is not there used as a term of art with specific reference to Hegel's or Marx's use of it. It is used to refer simply to all that in a society which is not created or controlled by the state as part of its operations. Political democracy, constitutionalism and the rule of law, it is now widely believed in the formerly Communist world, flow out of a vigorous and independent civil society; so do free trade unions, charitable and cultural institutions that are independent of the state, lawyers and colleges of lawyers, churches, autonomous universities, courts and parliaments, etc. All of these now have a romantic caché. They are the opposite of the totalitarian society and the totalitarian will.

The term *civil society*, like any other important social concept, needs not to be defined but to be understood in a multiplicity of often competing contexts. Both Marx and the neo-classical economists now known as free marketeers have tended to emphasize a concept of civil society that sees it as the sphere of private interest and pursuit of wealth. Others emphasize rather the concept of civil society as the field of operations for political and social pluralism that recognizes groups, traditions and organizations as much as it recognizes individuals. For the moment, the tensions between these two views are obscured in the West and in the East by ever-increasing suspicion of the state as controller and organizer, by a simple-minded faith in the virtues of privatization, especially if it postpones increases in taxation, and by a hope that the creative capacity of people will be liberated by matching effort and reward.

Less attention is paid to some frightening continuities in the former USSR: the elevation of "leaders", the organization of their staffs into personal retinues and of their spheres of influence into personal fiefdoms, the continued allocation of privileges and immunities.

Fundamental concepts in social thought, Max Weber reminded us,[6] are not well presented as classificatory concepts, as pigeonholes into which societies, social institutions and social ideologies are to be fitted on an all-or-nothing basis. They are rather "ideal types", logically interrelated complexes of attitudes, institutions and trends that are mutually supportive within each ideal type and strive to realize themselves in history. Further, many fundamental political concepts, like power, authority, control, are similarly porous, relative, incapable of clear-cut separation, distinction, absoluteness. They are points, often moving points, in a continuum that knows not truly absolute power and control, totally uncontested authority or the complete absence of those phenomena. No one sensitive or informed has any doubt about the difference between Stalin's Soviet Union and the situation that preceded and followed his period of power -- yet there are important continuities. It is plausible to say that Stalin's Russia and Stalin's practice and ideology were paradigmatically totalitarian, that Lenin was only an authoritarian with proto-totalitarian tendencies and that Khrushchev and his successors moved the Soviet Union back in fits and starts to an authoritarian society that nevertheless had continuing totalitarian structures and potentials. There is no great profit or interest in seeking to carve up the flux of history into formally separate segments; the important issue is the direction and strength of a development. Even the most fervent proponents of the concept of a totalitarian state do not believe that the dividing lines between the authoritarian and the totalitarian will not be blurred or problematic, a matter of degree, or that authoritarianism in fact knows no plurality of thinking or of action.

More recently, the discussion of totalitarianism has put more emphasis on the absence or presence of those factors in society which are, at least relatively, independent of the state and capable of confronting it on the basis of their own authority. Private enterprise and private property made secure by law are two such factors; a comparatively autonomous legal system, tradition and profession is another; democratic institutions, a multiplicity of parties, a church not created by or subservient to the state constitute others. The upshot of these wide-ranging discussions is not a listing of the essential factors of totalitarianism or the marking off of unambiguous borders between the totalitarian, the authoritarian and the pluralist-democratic. It does, however, suggest the rudiments of civil society and points to ways in which (contrary to the arguments of others in this volume) civil society as a sphere of action, of coordinated, principled and public action by citizens acting independently of the ruling party and the state, had to be created from the top, just as Peter the Great created the *Landraty*.

The Legacy of Russian and Chinese History

We are now more conscious of the political, legal, and social culture on which successful democracy rests and with which totalitarianism is incompatible. That is why democratically minded Russians and Chinese see their own history as a principal enemy. For various historical reasons, the state has been a pervasive force, a managerial state, taking responsibility for all social development, controlling or seeking to control everything that is politically relevant. In such states, classes were weakly developed

-- forms of stratification and not of independent power and organization. Property and, with it, law had no true independence or autonomy. Power, position and wealth were all fundamentally dependent on the state and its favor. As it was before communism, so it continued and, in conquered societies, came to be. To throw off communism in Russia and China, but not in Poland, Hungary or Czechoslovakia, therefore, was to throw off a thousand years of history, to join a new world community largely based on Western history, structures and development.

Analyzing the history of Russia and China is a complex and inexhaustible project, in which one has to steer between the Scylla of gross oversimplication and the Charybdis of missing the wood for the trees. There is no claim associated with the concept of an Asiatic mode of production or with that of a Russian or Chinese state always stronger than the rest of society that has not been challenged, in many cases seriously and responsibly. Yet the difference between the tsar as Autocrat of all the Russias and the emperor of China as Son of Heaven on the one hand and any European monarch on the other hand remains. Chinese Communists themselves, recognizing that the unification of China under the Qin and Han introduced a new and in many respects unique social form, have to call it bureaucratic feudalism as a way of accepting that direct social power lay primarily in the hands of a state-appointed and state-controlled bureaucracy. At least some of the continuing weakness of civil society in China, furthered by traditional and modern ideologies that have inculcated contempt for the merchant and made his position insecure, rests in the fact that almost all educated Chinese have seen their loyalty and their career opportunities as intimately bound up with state service, with the capital as the political and cultural center of China. For almost half of China's history, the capital's writ did not run throughout the provinces, or at least through all of them. There were times of trouble, of competing dynasties, of foreign invasion. But the ideal of a China unified under the emperor and a bureaucracy that served him remained stronger, far stronger than any competing ideal. In many ways, it still is.

In Europe, the emergence of Russia as a world power was as remarkable as that of Prussia. It, too, was based on the militarization of society and government -- on the building of a powerful state and army and the attempted pervasive regulation of social and political life for largely military purposes. That has a long history, a history that Russians themselves have seen as somber and tragic, as great and terrifying and as essentially different from that of Europe. The debate is not over that fact but over its causes and explanation.

Russia, some have argued[7], was for almost all of its history a great frontier -- a frontier whose armed struggle against invaders had a length, intensity, and ferocity unparalleled in the annals of any other nation. Secure existence on that frontier involved a continuous process of opening up and colonizing the vast spaces of Eastern Europe and northern Asia through unflagging migration and resettlement. (Between 1300 and 1600, the Muscovite state expanded from 20,000 square kilometers to 5,400,000 square kilometers and it continued to grow at the rate of 35,000 square kilometers a year.) Military service and migration, the colonization of the country, became the central features of Russian history. They called for effort on a scale undreamt of by Europe, but it had to be carried out under the most difficult circumstances -- meagerness of resources, shortage of manpower, lack of technological development and the harshest of climatic and physical conditions.

Others, more traditionally, have stressed the crucial role of the Mongol/Tatar yoke: first of the Mongol army, the terrible Golden Horde, and then of Mongol politics and statecraft, of the Mongol State Idea, according to which all men were equal in the totality of their duty to the state -- a state seen as exercising an irresistible, pervasive *Imperium mundi in statu nascendi*, an imperium before which all opposition or disobedience was an act of treason, to be punished as such.

More scholarly versions of Russian history -- see Professor Byrnes in this volume -- do not differ from this more popular and impressionistic version all that much. There is argument about the extent to which the Varangian Norse Kingdoms and princedoms in Russia were like or different from their northern and Western European counterparts. There is general agreement that these rulers had far less attachment, if any at all, to the territory or the people they literally acquired. Some ascribe the overwhelming powers and ambition of the Russian state as an instrument of autocracy to the Mongol-Tatar yoke and the influence of Mongol and Chinese statecraft. Others stress the Byzantine model of Caesaro-Papism in which church and state combine to rule, or in which the church is totally subordinated to the state. In Russia from early times, Richard Pipes has argued[8], the separation between sovereignty and authority exercised as ownership occurred very late and very imperfectly: the ruler was both the sovereign of the realm and its proprietor. No social class -- the peasantry, the *dvorianstvo* (the serving nobility that replaced the *boyars*) or the "missing bourgeoisie" -- was strong enough to challenge the state. True, in the nineteenth century, the tsarist government, in the central provinces at least, became captive to the landowning classes it had created, but those classes, threatened by the peasantry, were simply not strong enough to wrest formal power from the tsar. Deprived of a base in the power of property, Russian opposition to the autocracy became almost entirely intellectual, elevating ideas and, thus, encouraging the further extension of attempted ideological control by the state, but also the growth of an intelligentsia that defined itself by the belief that ideas could produce social change.

If the concept of communism as resting on an earlier Caesaro-Papism or Oriental Despotism in Russia and China is academically complex, it is -- in Russia and China, but not for Eastern Europeans -- also politically and psychologically difficult. Latvians and Lithuanians, Poles and Hungarians, let alone Czechs, have little difficulty, and indeed take much joy, in ascribing the unchecked excesses of communism to the servility and lack of freedom bred by Russian and Chinese political traditions. Some Russians and Chinese agree; many more would like to find and stress alternative traditions within their own society that do not doom them to servility and powerlessness vis-à-vis the state. But Russians have no political traditions from below that they can fall back on in any serious way. The revival of the old parliamentary assembly, the Duma, early in the twentieth century lasted less than ten years. The peasant commune, the Mir, was probably state-instituted for taxation purposes and was certainly not a vehicle of progress, whatever the Narodniks may have thought. Russians historically had been defined by three things, even in their own eyes: their capacity for suffering, their share in great power dominance that produced fantastic geographical expansion of their political rule, and their Russian orthodoxy. But only Protestants and Old Believers have any record of asserting religion against the state, of building independent religious communities and institutions.

Still, the Communist period, as we now see, after Stalin's death did witness important developments toward urbanization, westernization and even a "middle class"culture having more than only literary foundations. But all of these, in Russia, are still weak, and in the rest of the former Communist world materially poor. This is why an important element in the current amazing enthusiasm for building or restoring the institutions of civil society in the former Communist world is the more prosaic desire to attract foreign capital as charity, investment or loan. It is widely believed in Communist societies that foreign governments and foreign institutions will favor non-governmental organizations and institutions over governmental ones for these purposes; that civil society, in short, can be built with foreign help. A charitable trust has been established, officially under the control of citizens and not government officers, to collect funds at home and abroad to aid what is now admitted to be the enormous number of people living under the poverty line whom the state has not the money to help. A specifically Russian Cultural Foundation has been set up to receive donations and artifacts at home and abroad as part of a campaign to foster and invigorate the love and appreciation of the specifically Russian cultural heritage in art, architecture and religion. There will be, if there are not already, more such ventures. Dissidents and ex- or crypto-Communists vie with each other in arranging readings from Solovyev or Shestov, in making available Orthodox Easter food (*paskha* and *kulich*), in honoring non- and anti-Communists reviled until very recently.   Civil society, coupled with religion and nationalism (for Russians, the two are virtually one), now plays the role that *Volk* played in Germany: it separates culture and politics from the existing state authorities, but it still has little real content.

Democracy and Civil Society

Democracy is not the solution to problems.   It is a *sine qua non* for the sustained exposure of lies and illusions, of cynicism, dishonesty and incompetence in government.   For those who have just come out of the darkness, especially for the intellectuals among them, the first priority was to see the triumph of truth, the exposure of lies, and the end of the power to enforce compliance with evil.   For that, they needed what they called civil society (in the popular, non-theoretical sense) -- men and women, institutions and activities, not incorporated in the state apparatus, not subject to pervasive dictation from above.   In some countries such as Poland, the former East Germany and Hungary, there was more in the way of tradition and living actuality to draw on than in other countries, such as Russia, Bulgaria and Romania.   In some -- such as Serbia or Azerbaijan -- the non-state popular tradition was as suspect in its militant chauvinism as the state tradition.   In all countries, a total surrender of state power to civil society could easily lead to exacerbated conflict, tension and disunity, while facing the problem that the experienced were inevitably tainted by their participation in Communist administration and politics.   It is at this point that generalities cease to serve and national specificities and the presence or absence of stable institutions, stable mass parties and of statemanship come to the fore.

Here it becomes clear that civil society as a concept of practical and theoretical analysis has very limited value except as an initial slogan for rallying those not tainted by involvement with a discredited state.   At the political level, the countries formerly ruled by Communists need to create or recreate a *Rechtsstaat*, to impose the rule of law and respect for law on their citizens, their economic entrepreneurs and managers, their political parties and their political leaders and government officers.   They are aided in this, above all, by an international political and legal climate; they will be hindered, in some countries very seriously, by the lack of past traditions, by economic shortages and chaos, by chauvinism and national tensions, by the weak development of a legal profession, judicial independence and legal culture, as Alice Tay has argued.   They are even more hindered by a deeply ingrained political habit of meeting problems and opposition by giving orders, threatening or using force, and insisting that there is a "correct" solution rather than that there are two sides to any problem.   The battle for law and for the recognition of the legitimacy of social and political pluralism will be both necessary and difficult, for much of the population and the leadership still misunderstand law and politics by seeing them as consisting merely of a set of decrees.

Replacing the "Kingdom of Lies"

The "Kingdom of Lies" created by Communist rulers was successfully resisted only by three social phenomena the state did not succeed in controlling: the family, memory and cultural endeavour and tradition. These were the strongest elements of successful resistance on which much else, including the conquest of trade unions, depended. For citizens coming out of monocratic socialism, they represent the kernel of civil society. Both national consciousness and religious tradition can become and in many places have become intimately linked with them, expanding into the vacuum left by discredited state ideology -- though doing so in varying degrees in different sections of the population. Trade union consciousness is more limited in appeal and troublesome for governments bent on attracting investments and building up markets, but trade unions are and will be a significant element in the dispersion of power and the articulation of recognized interest groups that speak out freely. For even a people's revolution is always conducted and supported only by a section of the people, and conflicts of views and interests among the supporters themselves emerge as the excitement dies down. It is at that time that two perennial but ever-important questions acquire renewed urgency. One is the relationship between freedom and authority. Another is the possibility of creating structures that derive legitimacy from the character of civil society, of the community at large and not from the traditions of the command structure, the state and bureaucracy, against which people have rebelled. This is the central question in Eastern Europe today. Its solution requires a combination of principled understanding, tactical flexibility and responsiveness and a capacity to latch on to, reinterpret and create national and popular traditions. It requires statemanship, including a commitment to democracy and the willingness to defend it by exercising authority when necessary without making that into a way of life. Much of Eastern Europe is not doing badly in this respect; much of the former USSR is still not doing well.

The Future of China

In China -- politically, though not economically -- the situation at present is much less hopeful for democracy. The concept of monocratic socialism has not suffered the same death blow in the People's Republic of China as it has in the former Soviet empire and bloc. The intelligentsia, or significant portions of it, are perhaps as disaffected as they have ever been. Successfully crushed within the country, they are in danger of retreating to total cynicism. Those who still hope can only wait for a mistake, or a change of heart, at the top. When that happens, and it cannot be ruled out, symbolic revolution could break out again.

It is difficult, however, to see civil society doing more than protesting in order to cast down a bad emperor and promote the leadership ambitions of a good one, who will allow more discussion and adopt better policies, who will "bring the work of the government and the good of the people into greater harmony". China -- like the Soviet Union and the Soviet bloc -- needs the break-up of an empire that provided much of the foundation for monocratic rule. But China is an empire in a much more complex sense than the Soviet Union or the tsarist empire ever was. Its nationalities -- outside Tibet -- are predominantly minorities, surrounded by larger Chinese populations. Chinese or Han nationality is a matter of custom, lifestyle and political allegiance, not of spoken language. But the culture, including the political culture, has been so strong that rebel provinces and rebel warlords have not sought political independence, but simply backed their own candidates for emperor at the center. The division of China into independently governed South, East, West and North might well be the only way of erecting serious structural and ultimately cultural barriers against overwhelming central and centralizing power. Yet that course is not only fraught with practical difficulties, it would be quite unacceptable to the majority of Chinese and especially of Chinese intellectuals. China's status in the world as a great and unified civilization matters to them, at the ideological level, more than anything else. Otherwise one might as well emigrate. But Taiwan and Hong Kong do prove how great the potential of the Chinese people is, once they are liberated from the weight of that great tentacular Moloch of a state.

This is not to say that China has not been witnessing some of the tensions, expectations and hopes that have produced the momentous changes in Eastern Europe and the Soviet Union. It is to say that they have not gone as far politically (though they are more successful economically), that they have less conscious unideologized popular support and that the government has not given way, at home or abroad, to an extent that can undermine its capacity to control the situation. Communism still holds power in China. But as an ideology and a faith, it has lost the support of all sections of the community except the cynic and the opportunist. It is not now directly challenged by any major sections of the population that count in this connection except students and research workers because of fear, because they cannot see outside the party any force or group that can take over and hold China together, and because the party leadership is still willing to close ranks against any attempt to challenge its ultimate authority. For the moment, civil society in China remains as weak a force as it ever was.

Notes

1. See Eugene Kamenka, "The Concept of a Political Revolution", in Carl J. Friedrich, ed., *Nomos viii - Revolution* (New York: Atherton, 1966), 122-35, as well as the works there cited.

2. I draw here and in what follows on my "Revolution in the USSR and Eastern Europe" presented to the 1990 Annual Symposium of the Academy of the Social Sciences in Australia and printed in a shortened version in the Academy's *Annual Report 1991*. Canberra, Academy of the Social Sciences in Australia, 19-23.

3. Adam Ferguson's *History of Civil Society*, Hegel's further exploration of that theme and Marx's youthful and more philosophical writings, with their critique of alienation, have given rise to an enormous body of scholarship and criticism that commands respect and to an even larger body of useful exposition and scholarship. My own views were at first set out in the *Ethical Foundations of Marxism* (New York: Praeger, 1962) and have been restated in summary form in the E. Kamenka, ed., *The Portable Karl Marx* (New York: Viking Press, 1983). Readers of this volume will not need to be reminded of Z.A. Pelczynski's studies of Hegel and his comments on the Polish situation, "Solidarity and the Rebirth of Civil Society in Poland, 1976-81", in John Keane, ed. *Civil Society and the State: New European Perspectives* (London: Verso), 361-80; of Maximilien Rubel's life-long exploration of Marx's thought; of Leszek Kolakowski's massive 3-volume study, *Main Currents of Marxism: Its Rise, Growth, and Dissolution* or of the fact that the issue is explored by other contributors to this volume. Also see C. Kukathas and D.W. Lovell, "The Significance of Civil Society" in C. Kukathas, D.W. Lovell, and W. Maley, eds. *The Transition from Socialism: State and Civil Society in Gorbachev's USSR* (Melbourne: Longman Cheshire, 1991), 18-40 and Robert F. Miller, ed. *The Developments of Civil Society in Communist Systems* (Sydney: Allan & Unwin, 1992).

4. See the entry Gramsci, Antonio, in Tom Bottomore, *A Dictionary of Marxist Thought* (Oxford: Blackwell Reference, 1983), 193-6 and the literature there cited.

5. See D. Forgacs, ed. *A Gramsci Reader: Selected Writings 1916-1935* (London: Lawrence and Wishart, 1988), 420.

6. See E. Kamenka, *Bureaucracy* (Oxford: Blackwell, 1989), 2 and the literature there cited.

7. See E. Kamenka, *Bureaucracy*, 107-15 and the literature there cited.

8. R. Pipes. *Russia Under the Old Regime* (Cambridge, MA: Harvard University Press, 1972).

9

Civil Society in the Emerging Democracies: Poland and Hungary

Andrew Arato

This study discusses the concept of civil society in the transitions from Communist rule in two contexts, Poland and Hungary. The transition in Poland, representing the first of the series of struggles to dismantle a Soviet type regime, introduced a whole comprehensive strategy centering around the reconstruction of civil society. Through the successes and failures of this strategy we are now able to examine both the immense potential and the built-in problems of the whole political turn to civil society. Since models of the reconstruction of civil society were introduced (imported or reinvented) in several other countries of East and Central Europe, the important question arises whether the same approach could be applied elsewhere. The Hungarian case shows that the orientation of civil society could play a crucial role in a very different country and in a different period, that of the regime transitions or "revolutions" of 1989. This same case shows, however, that during and after the transitions, a previously organized civil society is demobilized and enters into a period of relative passivity, a point that has been made by Polish analysts as well. Hungarian developments after the change of government indicate both the causes of this decline, as well as the possible road of revival.

Defining Civil Society

Concepts have their careers. The category of civil society, central in the self-understanding of actors in the drama of the "end of communism", seems suddenly problematic after the events of 1989. Even if more widely disseminated than ever before and adopted by an increasing number of analysts, the centrality of the concept is now increasingly contested; according to some it has lost analytical relevance. It seems that a category developed from the point of view of critique and radical opposition, may be less well suited to understand and orient social construction and ordinary politics.

The concept of civil society is an undifferentiated one only in its polemical versions that juxtapose society against the state. A broader concept, however, not only allows us to differentiate between its own use in the milieu of oppositional movements where the polemical dualism has important mobilizing functions *and* theoretical utilization that makes civil society a part of a far more complex topography of society, but provides for the possibility of an internal differentiation of the category. Let me refer to my own *theoretical* understanding of the concept of civil society:

> I understand civil society as a sphere of social interaction between economy and state, composed above all of associations and publics. Modern civil society is created through forms of self-constitution and self-mobilization and is institutionalized through laws, especially subjective rights that stabilize social differentiation. It would be misleading to identify however civil society with all of social life outside the administrative state and economic processes in the narrow sense. Firstly, it is necessary and meaningful to distinguish civil society from a political society of parties, political organizations, and political publics in particular parliaments. The latter to be sure generally arise from civil society and share with it both forms of organization and communication. But directly involved with state power, which they seek to control and in part obtain, the structures of political society cannot afford to subordinate strategic criteria to the patterns of normative integration and open-ended communication characteristic of civil society. Even the public sphere of political society, rooted in parliaments, involves important formal and temporal constraints in processes of communication. The political role of civil society in turn is not directly related to the control or conquest of power but to the generation of influence, through the life of democratic associations and unconstrained discussion in the cultural public sphere. Such a political role is inevitably diffuse and inefficient. Thus the mediating role of political society between civil society and state is indispensable, but so is the rootedness of political society in civil society.
>
> Secondly, the differentiation of civil society from the economy on the one hand and political society/state on the other seems to suggest that the category somehow should include and refer to all phenomena of society, outside of the state, the economy and political society in the narrow sense. But this is the case only to the extent that we focus on relations of association, of self-organization and organized communication. Civil society in fact represents only a dimension of the sociological world of norms, roles, practices,

competences and forms of dependence, or a very particular angle of looking at this world from the point of view of conscious association building and associational life.[1]

This definition is derived from the modern history of the concept, from both East European and Western contemporary usage, as well as from systematic considerations. Its main components involve a temporal differentiation between civil society as movement and civil society as institution, a distinction not generally made by the actors who use the category. Along with many East Europeans today I consider the movement form to be fundamental for the institutionalization of civil societies, with the type of movement influencing the character of the civil society in formation. At the same time, along with West European students of the new social movements, I consider movements, less global, potential as well as actual, to be crucial for maintaining the spirit of democratic and liberal institutions, indeed for their further development.[2] Furthermore, I distinguish not only as did Gramsci between civil society, economy and state, but, in line with some contemporary analysts, between political and civil society as well.[3] Finally within an institutionalized civil society especially, I consider, in a neo but not orthodox Hegelian manner, laws and rights, associations and cultural publics to be the central institutions. Against orthodox Hegelians, but in line with the modern development of the framework of rights, I would place the institution of property in an economic society, protected by primarily pragmatic considerations of policy, and only in a more limited and partial manner by a cluster of fundamental rights. The differentiation of civil society today is less protected by absolute property rights than by the rights of personality (private sphere) and communication (public sphere). In my conception the institutions of property and contract, protected by a secondary framework of rights, represent core components of an *economic society* that mediates between civil society and market economy in a manner analogous to political society, between civil society and the state.

This definition, while not developed merely by the interpretation of East European politics, is largely compatible with the trajectory of the project of the reconstruction of civil society as it emerged in this region. In effect it combines an interpretive perspective that relies on what the concept of civil society is to the actors (including intellectuals) who use it, and an analytical, objectifying perspective that focuses on institutions and practices from the point of view of an external observer. More than a mere reproduction of the views of the actors, such perspective allows us to focus on the internal contradictions and external constraints of their relevant projects.

Civil Society and Radical Reform

Though not without earlier anticipations[4], the East European project for the reconstruction of civil society was born in Poland in the mid and late 1970s. In the writings of Adam Michnik[5] this strategy was based on negative and positive learning experiences. According to Michnik, in the given geo-political constellation dominated by an intact imperial system under Soviet hegemony, complete social transformation on the patterns of the Hungarian revolution from below (1956) and the Czechoslovak reform from above (1968) were still impossible. This was the case not only because of almost absolutely certain Soviet military response often stylized as "the Brezhnev doctrine", but also because the ruling elites in each country have learned that all serious reformism from above leads to internal splits in the ruling parties, social mobilization and loss of control by the reformers. Nevertheless, Polish experience, in particular the workers' protests in 1956, 1970, 1976 has shown that, within limits significant change can be achieved in at least some of the societies of the Soviet type.

For Michnik, an opposition interested in such a change must formulate a program of *radical reform from below*, addressed to independent "society" or "public opinion" which through its pressure should be able to achieve some significant concessions as long as these stay well within the limits of the geo-political interests of the Soviet Union, and the control by the existing ruling party of the central positions within the sphere of the state. In such a struggle, Michnik argued, party moderates or pragmatists might become reluctant reformers, ad hoc partners though never genuine allies. The actual force for reform must come from below. But where exactly?

Interestingly Michnik's argument, in an apparently contradictory manner, both appealed to an independent society, and postulated the formation of such a society as the goal of a dualistic program that would radically transform the social sphere and leave that of the party-state intact. The last phrase reveals a second potential contradiction, the obverse of the first. In the totalitarianism theory assumed by Michnik, the party-state penetrates and controls *all* of society, and thus any carving out of an independent social sphere could not leave the rule of the party in the state intact.

Michnik's own answer to these contradictions, and that of the new organization KOR (Committee in Defense of Workers) he helped to found, was first of all political-existential. We should act as if we already had the freedoms of association, assembly, and communication (the central rights of civil society), and thereby contribute to the institutionalization of just these rights. Under such an assumption KOR not only organized itself, but proceeded to facilitate the self-organization of select constituencies of workers to whom they provided legal, journalistic, economic and organizational support. This program amounted to the self-organization and defense of civil society in the form of a movement or proto-movement of which KOR was only one important organ. KOR played an important role in the strike movement of the summer of 1980 that led on August 31 and in the subsequent days to the apparent legal institutionalization of some of the key rights of civil society, first and foremost the right to form free unions.

In Poland a self-organizing society could rely on micro-structures, learning experiences as well as institutional models. It was the unique combination of these givens that distinguished Poland from all other contexts in the Soviet imperium. Even if civil society in the sense of stabilized institutions existed at best in the case of the Catholic church, various levels of independent or rather partially independent social life existed throughout the whole society, some of which (in particular workers and intellectuals) were already tested in political and social conflicts. The project of organizing civil society in the form of a movement aiming at its institutionalization presupposed these levels and appealed to individuals who were already associating and communicating, and were quite different than the atomized, entirely state dependent individuals stylized by the totalitarian theory. The Communist regimes indeed tried to create such individuals, but in the long run unsuccessfully.

Thus, KOR's strategy initially sought "only" the transformation of de facto existing forms of social independence, that could be organized in the form of a movement for reform,[6] into legally institutionalized structures. Purely theoretically at least, it was possible to postulate without self-contradiction that such a transformation would not reduce the actual framework of authority of the party state but only transform the status of the societal sphere which this ruling structure already did not control. What was not yet clearly realized however, or was "tactfully" suppressed, was that this could not happen unless the status of the party-state sphere itself was transformed.[7] Even the formal granting of some of the rights constitutive of civil society was legally (though not politically, as long as the movement was very strong) meaningless as long as the structure of the state was based on the prerogative power of the ruling party rather than constitutionalism, at the very least in the form of an authoritarian *Rechtsstaat*.[8]

Thus, in my view the term "self-limiting revolution", invented by Kuron and popularized by Jadwiga Staniszkis[9] best characterized the kind of change required by the new strategy. As Michnik and Kuron often repeated, the "revolution" they aimed at ought to be self-limiting not only because of the obvious geo-political constraints for the countries of the imperial periphery, but also because of the very negative experiences of all unlimited social revolutions of the Jacobin-Bolshevik type. In order to avoid the unintended emergence of a new, authoritarian state, once again incompatible with the building of a democratic civil society, the classical instruments of social revolutions, their elitism, their violence, their semantics, all linked to the desire of an impossible total rupture with the past, should be consistently avoided. Such learning from the history of revolutions was an essential dimension of the new orientation to civil society.

Solidarity and the Self-Limiting Revolution

To be sure the term "new evolutionism" reflected a period (1976-1979) in which the small democratic opposition in Poland was on the defensive. The idea of "the self-limiting revolution" presupposed an offensive strategy based on the existence of a rapidly growing, remarkably united social movement, Solidarity. Evidently this movement was not simply the product of the new strategy, or of the organizing activities of intellectuals. It took the dramatic decline of Poland's economic situation in the late 1970s, and the opportunity presented by the government's administratively ordained price rises in 1980, to produce a vast, initially spontaneous industrial strike movement most of whose participants were entirely new in politics. Nevertheless, groups of intellectuals and workers actively involved in the development of political networks and forms of communication on the pattern of the new strategy played a decisive role in the organization of the movement, in the formulation of the central demands, in the negotiations with the authorities, and in leadership and expert-advisory roles. It was due to their influence that Solidarity, the first independent and self-managing union in the whole Soviet imperium, came to be the first legally secured institution of an independent civil society. Never a revolutionary movement, nor merely a social movement on behalf of its own worker constituency, Solidarity was above all a "movement for the liberation of society".[10]

And yet Solidarity could not simply stay within the original program for the reconstitution of civil society. To begin with, the vast strata mobilized had in large part no experience in earlier protests and dissident activity. While in the beginning it was easy enough to accept the strategy of self-limitation, this did not in all likelihood apply to its principled, normative post-revolutionary dimension. Very soon, the simultaneous growth of the organization and the deepening of the economic crisis was to produce a fundamentalist movement within the movement, and to some extent a split between a pragmatic leadership and many rank and file groups. As a result the Solidarity leadership was alternatively (and I believe inconsistently) criticized as insufficiently democratic or radical. Equally important, the growth and the central role of the organization for all social conflict brought the adherence of new groups of intellectuals with different programs than the civil society orientation of the most important early experts and advisors.

The program of the reconstruction of civil society through the vehicle of the one great movement within a framework of dualistic self-limitation had serious internal weaknesses. First, there was an obvious conflict between the goal to establish a pluralistic civil society and the formula of the one unified movement. Not a political party, Solidarity was on the same plane of interest articulation and identity formation as all the other proto movements, associations and initiatives, but on this plane there could be no competition between the giant movement and its tiny offsprings and allies. Any social proposal, any economic initiative could become serious in this context only if it was first adopted by Solidarity. I believe it was this structural situation and not the supposed authoritarianism of the Solidarity leadership that led many intellectuals, especially after the defeat of December 13, 1981, to remember the movement as monolithic, authoritarian or even neo-Bolshevik and "totalitarian".

Second, the project of a dualistic reconstruction of society reluctantly leaving the sphere of the state intact and in the hands of the ruling party, perhaps impossible in itself, was all the more untenable in the context of a vast, largely unified, increasingly politicized movement of society. Vast democratic mobilization from below but within definite limits led to a situation where one side continued to possess administrative power but without legitimacy; the other side came to have significant democratic legitimacy but without administrative power. As a result neither could generate policy. There was, as a result, no social actor capable of undertaking a radical reform of the economy, a project that would inevitably involve new austerity. Without legitimacy the regime could no more institute economic changes involving sacrifices in 1981 than in 1980 when the strike movement first challenged the price rises. But without power in the state, Solidarity could not initiate economic reforms, or even accept the responsibility for programs arrived at without its participation.

This situation led not only to impasse, but in my view to some significant if tacit support for the only one violent solution geo-politically possible. On the one side, organized society remained potentially powerful, but increasingly also fearful of its own power and its consequences: political stalemate and unresolved economic crisis.[11] This power could only block solutions without being able to generate alternative ones. Solidarity remained popular, yet its negative power left society in the midst of economic collapse without any perspectives. Anyone with a plausible scenario of extrication had to have some support, and no one outside of Jaruzelski had such a scenario, however unattractive it was and however implausible it now appears in retrospect. Moreover, in spite of the claims of the fundamentalists, a revolutionary option was feared all the more when the logic of the situation began to point to it. There was still widespread agreement among groups as diverse as the moderate leadership of Solidarity, the episcopate of the Catholic Church, and the military leadership that revolution was equal to the worst evil, namely Soviet intervention that was in any case continually threatened. Finally, the regime, given the growth of Solidarity, increasingly had no other resource than military violence, and even this resource, exposed to the potential discontent of enlisted men and junior officers, could be lost if not used quickly.

The defeat of Solidarity in the martial law regime of December 13 demonstrated that the sustenance of civil society in the form of a highly mobilized movement and in the absence of adequate institutionalization was highly unstable. It became clear moreover that institutionalization relying on a single isolated legal act, the legalization of the union, was entirely insufficient in context of an intact prerogative party-state capable of reversing without due process any and all legal guarantees. A constitution in a society without constitutionalism offered no protection for the central rights of civil society: association and assembly. And a social movement, even the strongest, could be a functional equivalent for constitutionalism at best only through the upward phase of its life cycle.

In spite of the defeat of the movement, the organization of Polish society in the first Solidarity epoch was not in vain. The martial law regime and even its Soviet backers never could feel themselves powerful enough to terrorize society into submission. Moreover, the unprecedented involvement in the movement of large parts of society, as well as its decentralization, made the job of normalization all the more difficult. Throughout the 1980s, the earlier program of organizing an alternative sphere of public communication was not only resumed, but was vastly expanded.[12] Gradually, new groups, organizations, forums appeared, concerned with ecology, peace, draft resistance, defense of consumer interests, economic, educational projects and above all free and independent publishing efforts.[13] Solidarity as an organization also survived, first as a largely decentralized underground led by a few important national leaders. Later, after the 1986 amnesty of its imprisoned leaders, it was to move from a double existence, both underground and semi-open, to a largely open though not yet legal operation. Attempts on the part of the government to work out a bargain with the episcopate alone never really succeeded, despite some initial willingness on the part of some bishops, and the Church soon resumed a role of collaborating with independent social and cultural activities on the local level, and a potentially mediating posture on the national one.

The civil society in formation in the 1980s was both more extensive than that of the 1970s, and far less oriented to an organizational center than in 1980-1981. Not only the organizations but even more the ideologies of this period became much more pluralistic; there were attempts to formulate different versions of liberal, nationalist, social democratic ideologies many of which were explicitly critical of the earlier Solidarity.[14] In this context the remnants of Solidarity, its underground activists, intellectuals as well as its undisputed leader Walesa had a privileged position only in that the regime attempted to exclude (through 1987) this group more emphatically than all others from any possible political negotiations.[15] This negative privilege, the memory of the earlier Solidarity, as well as the unrivalled political experience of the still cohesive group made it into a kind of democratic counter-elite that alone had the aspiration for comprehensive political action in independent society. Thus the self-organizing society of the second half of 1980s was not only more pluralized in the horizontal sense than its predecessor in 1980-1981, but now began to exhibit vertical differentiation between the civil and the political. When in 1988 regime reformers led by Kiszczak and Jaruzelski, facing a continued economic and legitimacy crisis, the revival of working class discontent, and the probable loss of their ultimate Soviet guarantee, sought partners for undertaking radical economic reform, it was to this political counter-elite, born of civil society, that they were to turn.[16]

In its new political reincarnation Solidarity was socially much weaker, yet more capable of unified action than its great predecessor in 1980-1981. It was both less threatening to the authorities, and more capable of bargaining and negotiation. But, most importantly, after almost a decade of struggling for an independent civil society, it was the only political organization in Poland with the important resource of legitimacy. Significantly, Solidarity was mistaken about its identity and the limits of its possibilities. The political organization continued to see itself as intimately connected to a program oriented to civil society. Thus the relegalization of the union was its primary demand, and participation in the political system was at first only a reluctant concession. It was only unexpected strength in both negotiations and subsequent elections that confirmed the shift of Solidarity to the level of political society, eventually under the new name of Citizen Committee. The subsequent difficulties of generating a plurality of political parties from this body, and even the eventual fragmentation of the parliamentary party political landscape, both indicate the difficulties inherent in the glorious heritage of the one great movement for the reconstruction of civil society.

Pluralistic Civil Society in Hungary

In the 1980s, the strategy of the reconstruction of civil society was imported or reinvented in other East European countries. In Hungary, the pride of place belongs to the "post-Marxist" democratic opposition, organized around the early samizdat projects of the late 1970s and 1980s. The dualistic Polish project was in particular first adopted by János Kis and György Bence, who were, however, clear that the model had both internal problems and special difficulties when applied to Hungary. They saw in particular that the combination of a fully self-organized society and an intact party-state was logically and politically self-contradictory. More immediately relevant was the fact that Hungary had no ongoing history of a working class or any other social movement to which a democratic opposition could refer and respond.

Significantly, Hungary had neither a model for independent civil society like the Polish church, nor series of learning experiences like 1956, 1970, and 1976 in Poland for a movement to learn that radical action within limits could make significant gains. Indeed the key learning experiences of Hungarians were 1956, which seemed to teach that radical, collective action leads to disaster, and the Kadarist reform of 1968, implying that only individual and private pursuit of self-interest can lead to relative success. It was this whole unpolitical trend in Hungarian learning, ingrained in the population, that the small opposition sought to counteract by example, by exhortation and by the proposal of programs.

Fortunately, due to the partial modernization of Hungarian society by the economic reform of 1968 and the related relaxation of the private sphere, in Hungary, perhaps even more than in Poland, independent groupings, networks, practices, and forms of communication existed around which an alternative or second public sphere could be organized. Increasingly dependent on Western good will, and wishing to avoid a climate that would endanger independent economic activities, the regime found it difficult to use sufficient force to entirely suppress this support system. As a result "the second public sphere" was not only not suppressed despite some administrative sanctions against its organizers, but its interaction with parts of the official framework of communication, especially in the social sciences and the humanities could not be prevented.[17]

The plans and proposals of the early samizdat, in particular the editorials of Kis in *Beszélö* in the early 1980s, consciously operated with a dualistic Polish model, in spite of the defeat of Solidarity. Kis in particular insisted already in 1982 that the defeat of the Polish democratic opposition was not like the defeats of 1956 and 1968, that in particular the Soviet Union did not have the economic strength to normalize Poland.[18] This analysis was connected to the contemporary one of Tamás Bauer, an economist close to Kis and *Beszélö*, who was the first to systematically outline the reasons for the beginning of the general economic crisis of the whole Soviet-centered CMEA bloc.[19]

In the absence of a social movement, Kis was forced to decisively modify the Polish model. In Hungary, the much smaller democratic opposition could not hope to directly support the self-organization of an already active society against the party-state; and aside from creating a few islands of independent activity (the *samizdat*, the "independent university", and a group dedicated to helping the poor, SZETA) it was forced to address semi-independent, groups and networks *between* itself and the regime.[20] Kis had in mind primarily social scientific intellectuals, tolerated and even used by the regime as independent experts, as well as "populist" writers and their followings at uneasy peace with the regime whose ideology and insufficient "national" character they rejected. These groups were, each in its own way, critical of the regime, but on the whole they still accepted the Kadarist assumption that any overt political action or pressure is impossible and counter-productive. To counter their fears, Kis insisted in a debate that the mere existence of the *samizdat*, establishing an alternative public sphere was not enough, and that in the new situation political programs for change, radical yet plausible, were needed.

Accordingly, *Beszélő*'s first formulations of a new program were certainly minimalist. Let us merely fight, Kis argued, for the conversion of our existing spaces of autonomy, and our privileges into rights. Of course, this formula already contained the assumption that the regime can hope to legitimate itself under conditions of economic difficulty only by taking some steps toward the rule of law. Subsequently this notion was generalized in a new version of dualism: Hungarians should aim at the establishment of rights in the sphere of private law, a sphere understood somewhat more narrowly than the Poles understood civil society, and the rule of law in the state sphere.[21] Addressed to a 1985 meeting of the democratic opposition with the social scientists and the populist writers, this model clearly sought to overcome the rigid dualism of the older Polish formula. It counted among other things on the revival of reformism within the ruling party. Finally in 1987, in the pamphlet *Social Contract*[22], Kis and the editors of *Beszélő* made a wide ranging proposal whose main features involved a comprehensive constitutional regulation of a society increasingly autonomous and self-organized, a state divided into a genuine parliamentary sphere and a sector (itself bound by rules) reserved for the ruling party, and an economy whose main pillars were private property and industrial democracy. This proposal, the most radical version of the Polish model, came at a time when the decline of the Hungarian economic model was clearly visible, when social initiatives had begun to mushroom, when, in response to the requests of a part of the ruling party, radical economists had already (1986) produced their own comprehensive proposal for economic reform.[23] The extended discussion in 1987-1988 of *Social Contract*, *Fordulat és reform* and several other proposals presupposed and expressed the existence of a dynamic new public sphere as the central organ of a self-emancipating civil society.

The new civil society, whose highest point of development was reached in 1988, while open to the discussions and proposals of the democratic opposition and of critical social scientists, was the result of largely spontaneous forms of self-organization. In Hungary, no single organization like KOR, Charta 77, or Solidarity ever played the pre-eminent role in the organization of other groups. Those however who claim that there is no civil society in Hungary today should take another look at the year 1988.[24] The colorful picture of associational life and civic initiatives from that year require several different headings[25]:

Clubs, Circles, "Colleges"

In the first half of the 1980s ("the era of circles") there was a mushrooming of intellectual, primarily university-based circles and clubs dedicated to the study, discussion and debate of a variety of issues, including the economic, social and political problems of the day. By 1985, the need for coordination was felt, and the first council of clubs included representatives of almost 20 clubs.[26] Professional "colleges", anticipated by a forerunner in the 1970s, were organizations combining university training with the life of small academic communities of intellectuals dedicated to both intellectual pursuits and ideals of public service.[27] Initially eschewing direct political participation, the clubs, circles and colleges came to see themselves by the second half of the 1980s in terms of the program of reconstructing civil society from below.[28]

New Social Movements

The relative modernity and openness of Kadarist Hungary to the West made it a likely place for the emergence and proliferation of the most modern social movements, especially ecological and youth movements, but to a lesser extent pacifism as well. Significantly, all three tended to emerge from the organizational matrix of circles and colleges; thus the self-organizing forums of youth had a catalyzing role for social movements.[29] Both peace and ecology movements initially eschewed, however unconvincingly, any general political intentions.[30] The youth movement, with the creation of FIDESZ in 1988 by members of the college movement, followed by a new national umbrella organization of youth (MISZOT), was the first to deliberately pass through the political threshold.[31]

Given the politicization of the youth movement at the same time it became comprehensive, and the general weakness of pacifism, the ecology or environmental movement was the Hungarian new social movement par excellence, not a remarkable fact given the ecological disaster in the wake of state socialism. Politically, this movement was a great success story, absorbing for a time the energy and some of the best people of other movements, including not only those of youth but also the democratic and populist oppositions. Organized by members of the club "movement" from 1984 around one national movement battling against a potentially disastrous dam project on the Danube (Gabcikovo-Nagymaros Dam)[32] and a variety of locally-based single issue movements, ecology and environmentalism generated a variety of organizations (clubs, foundations, action committees) and activities (forums of discussion, demonstrations, petition campaigns, campaign for a referendum, campaigns for the recall of deputies). Even before the government and parliament were forced to finally suspend the Danube dam project in 1989, the battle for and in an independent public sphere was won by the ecologists and their support-ers.

Interest Representations and Professional Associations

Unlike Poland, in Hungary, very likely because of the individualistic consequences of the second economy, independent interest representations came into being relatively late.[33] Nevertheless, in 1988, an independent organization of entrepreneurs (VOSZ) and several small, eventually affiliated unions of "intellectual workers" did emerge, playing an important role not only in exploring the legal and constitutional possibili-ties of association and coalition building, but also in social movements like ecology. Of the latter TDDSZ (Union of Scientific Workers) was the first and most important, playing a role in organizing new, independent unions of film makers and teachers, and a new umbrella organization, the Liga (or FSZDL: League of Independent Trade Unions). This organization was followed by two others, Workers' Solidarity and the Alliance of Workers Councils (MOSZ). All these organizations of the defense of worker interests, influenced by different aspects of the model of Polish Solidarity, understood themselves as promoting a fabric of "thick" social self-organization from below, as building and fighting for a civil society with important elements of participation in economic and political life.[34]

Two professional associations, founded in 1988, were especially important not only because by their existence they expanded the space of civil society, but because they were dedicated to the institutional protection of dimensions of civil society presupposed by all other movements. The Publicity Club was organized by journalists, lawyers and scholars (who included a member of the democratic opposition, an ecologist and two reform social scientists) to promote the full freedom of speech, information, communication, and press, in order to provide all the requisite forums for independent opinion and criticism, a life necessity for the new movements and initiatives to which the founders of the club explicitly referred.[35] The Independent Forum of Jurists was founded by

135 lawyers in order to help inform society about the legislative projects of the authorities, and to propose legal and constitutional alternatives capable of securing rights, expanding democratic participation, and promoting the establishment of a sturdy civil society along with the controlling function of the public sphere.[36] Both of these organizations played a crucial role in the legal and political changes of the next year, with the Publicity Club continuing its activism in 1990-1991 as well.[37]

Political Umbrella Movements for Reform

While it is true that in Hungary no comprehensive movement for reform ever emerged, many of the hopes of those who formulated reform proposals were tied to such a possibility. To be sure, the various social movements were interlocked through common memberships, networks, and events like the important meetings, debates and discussions at the Jurta theater.[38] Yet this fact indicated also that the over-all membership was rather small both in context of the whole society, and compared with Solidarity in its ascending phase. Not only was there a need for the coordination of many diverse activities, but also for their politicization, if the population at large, not able to identify with the existing movements, were to be given any realistic alternative outside of the illusory one of a reform carried out entirely from above. Politicization was also necessary to avoid a polarization of society in the style of Poland in 1980-1981.

The one and only major attempt to create an overarching political movement to include the democratic opposition, the social scientific intellectuals, and the populist writers and their following at Monor in 1985 did not succeed in bridging historically inherited differences, as well as differences in the degree of radicalism. After the populist intellectuals formed their own movement (Hungarian Democratic Forum or MDF) in 1987 at the conference of Lakitelek, to which representatives of the democratic opposition (with three cosmetic exceptions) were not invited, political umbrella organizations became inevitably more partial. Such was the caucus of the primarily democratic-liberal, social democratic and alternative organization, the Network of Free Initiatives, in which the intellectuals of the democratic opposition played a leading role, and from which the social liberal Alliance of Free Democrats (SzDSZ) was to emerge within less than a year. Of lesser importance was the reform-Communist New March Front that was unable to make the full step to politics, but which was to help nevertheless to activate the reformers within the ruling party. Evidently MDF and SzDSz were proto-political organizations able to become political parties, even if this was not the inclination of some members (especially of the Network, but the same was true of many of the populist literati). The same was true of FIDESZ (Alliance of Young Democrats) emerging from the youth college movement, eventually unwilling to integrate itself into a non-political umbrella organization of youth. Nevertheless, all of these three organizations were originally part of the ferment of movements in and for civil society, and never completely lost their movement character. For the early FIDESZ for example the Polish model of Solidarity was decisive.[39] Indeed, FIDESZ was to play a central role in promoting the freedom of self- organization in the context of existing constitutional and legal loopholes. The eventual outcome after a long struggle for public opinion, the entirely modern liberal and democratic laws of association and assembly of January 1989 represented a victory for civil society analogous to (though far more comprehensive than) the legalization of Solidarity in 1980.[40]

The public discussion of the draft of the law of association, perhaps intended as sham or controlled democracy, turned out to be the first democratic political discussion of legislation in Hungary in over forty years.[41] Yet, in spite its successes, the method oriented to public discussion alone could not be relied on in an ongoing fashion, even from the point of view of the organizations of civil society. First, it was too time consuming: a whole constitution (which was increasingly recognized as necessary) could not be created by a method that took six or more months with respect to merely two fundamental rights (association and assembly). Second, the ruling party could and did try, after its defeat, to manipulate the time and procedure of "societal debate," depriving the process of all participatory character. Third, Hungarian society and its organizations were already too plural to speak with one voice on issues other than the few fundamental rights all parts of civil society required. Fourth, even after a few signal victories for the groups of civil society, it was very risky for the old parliament, under Communist control, to remain in the position to legislatively establish the parameters of a new political system. As it became clear in the draft of a new electoral law proposed in 1988, but received with total antipathy by society[42], it was possible to come up with a formally democratic procedure and timetable that would allow the ruling party to convert its monopolistic power in one system into a hegemony in the next. Here the civil society-based strategy was ultimately defenseless. Yet the regime was also in a poor position to merely impose new rules, since its own formal instance of legislation and constitution making, the undemocratically elected Parliament, was now highly unpopular because of its well publicized and criticized role in the conflict over the Danube dam, and certainly did not have the legitimacy to act on its own. As in Poland somewhat earlier in 1989, in Hungary too, a new forum of negotiation and compromise became indispensable not only for a quasi-legitimate road to democratic system, but for a way out of potential stalemate.

The Erosion of Civil Society

Paradoxically, the legal and constitutional victory of civil society in Hungary concerning the law of association actually closed its most dramatic period of self-organization. Of course the road to the institution-alized development of civil society was now more open than ever before, as the continued mushrooming of small clubs, associations, and organizations was to show. Yet, among the major beneficiaries of the conflict over the law of association were the so-called historical parties, first the Independent Smallholder Party (FKgP) followed by the Hungarian Social Democratic Party (MSZDP) which announced their re-constitution in 1988 and 1989, groups that neither had roots in the civil society of the 1980s nor had any of the technical means at the time (people, resources, ideas) to be even proto-parties. Nevertheless, their famous names to which those questioned in public opinion surveys seemed to respond and the possibility of their manipulation in a new pseudo-multi party system produced by the current parliament presented the political movements arising from civil society with a new challenge. This challenge, made possible by the loophole in Hungarian law concerning political associa-tions, now reinforced the earlier rigidification of the separation of the democratic opposition and the populist intellectuals by the formation of the MDF at Lakitelek, preparing an important shift in the politics of 1989, which became the year of political rather than civil society.[43]

The year of revolution in East and Central Europe, 1989, saw negotiated transitions in Poland and Hungary. For such processes actors of political society were indispensable. Indeed, the very legal and constitutional framework needed to institutionalize civil society now required the strategic, bargaining and legal skills of political actors, a political counter elite in Poland, and a plurality of parties in Hungary. Significantly, rival political actors, capable of strategic considerations, were necessary to provide enough security and guarantees for the ruling parties to be able to disengage and surrender most of their power. A mass movement, always having a fundamentalist wing, could not provide such guarantees. Such a mass movement was increasingly the much feared *idée fixe* of leading Hungarian reform Communists, and the events in Czechoslovakia eventually seemed to prove how right they could have been. Moreover, political parties could be possible partners in future governments, able to share in the burdensome responsibility of difficult economic decisions. Having relatively low legitimacy, they could not turn the struggle into the older Solidarity formula of legitimate society vs. immoral power, "us" against "them".

While inevitably weakening civil society at least transitionally, the turn to political society did not in itself have to lead to the disorganization of civil society and its elimination from the processes of change. The shift was compatible with forms of institutionalization involving demobilization but expansion as well. Such is the evidence of rural Hungary, where even in the epoch dominated by party formation the creation of local organizations, and especially local initiatives (primarily in the area of ecology) continued to expand.[44] Equally important, 1989 saw a further development of independent unions, whose pressure in context of the now more tightly controlled "social discussion" of the strike law draft managed once again to produce a modern piece of legislation, comparable to West European precedents.[45] Indeed when it came to the formation of the Round Table of the Opposition (EKA) and its negotiation with the ruling party and its allies at the National Roundtable (NKA), the importance of free unionism was recognized by the participatory status of the Liga (as a member of the EKA, and an observer at the NKA). We should also note that it was in this period that the ecological campaign for the discontinuation of the Danube dam was successfully ended, to be sure with the support of all parties of the opposition. Finally the links of at least some of the new parties to civil society remained very much in evidence during the September-November 1989 petition and referendum campaign against the direct election of the president *before* parliamentary elections, organized primarily by FIDESZ and SZDSZ, and using specifically the networks, methods and the style of the ecological movement against the Danube dam.[46] By bringing civil society back in, FIDESZ and SZDSZ not only re-energized their own organizations, but helped to legitimate the whole constitutional package arrived at by elite agreement at the NKA, and voted in (with a few remarkable modifications!) by an illegitimate parliament.[47]

Nevertheless, the petition and referendum campaign also showed that now the leading activists were in political parties. In the case of ecology, for example the best known moderate leaders and activists tended to join one of the three major parties arising from civil society, FIDESZ, SZDSZ or MDF, which established environmental or green sections, committees or caucuses. Such a development had to initially impoverish the ecological organizations proper.

There were also processes where the exclusion of civil society was more intentional. At the NKA, at the insistence of the representatives of the ruling party, it was agreed to exclude the press and the public from all the sessions of the committees, followed by their exclusion, without prior agreement, from middle-level bargaining as well. Public participation in the negotiation was more or less non-existent, and even press coverage, was, as it turned out, remarkably poor, in contradistinction to the Round Table in Poland, as well as the Hungarian standards of the preceding year.[48] While the ruling party's motivation seems clear in this matter, it is hard to avoid the feeling that at least some of the parties of the opposition did not fight hard enough for publicity.

The negative trend toward the marginalization of civil society, and the reinforcement of a new étatism was very much reinforced after the emergence of the post-Communist governments. Several different motivations seemed to be at play. Some political actors were and are frankly étatistic and believe that all power must be in the hands of those who legitimately control the state. This view has been openly advocated by many members of the Hungarian Democratic Forum, some of whom are, moreover, attracted to a new-old, hierarchical authoritarian view of society on principled old conservative lines.[49] More pragmatic (if more confused) are those who believe that the transition from a state socialist economy requires a strong state and a strong government (the two are wrongly identified) capable of maintaining a course harmful to the short run economic interests of large sectors of the population.[50] Finally, some politicians, mistakenly identifying the 1989 retreat of civil society in the context of party formation with its absence, seem to believe that the highly desirable, but inevitably long term institutionalization of civil society must be primarily the function of constitutional and legislative provisions for which parliament alone can take the responsibility.[51] Even this last position is caught in a quandary, overlooking potential allies in civil society, wherever the parliamentary structure is in control of forces that do not share the normative view concerning the desirability of the institutionalization and expansion of a thick, autonomous fabric of independent social life. This seems to be increasingly the case in Hungary.[52]

Let me consider several Hungarian contexts of the attack on civil society, and, if relevant, indicate counter-trends and the present state of the battle:

1. Formalized societal discussion of pending legislation has been abolished. This late Kadarist device, by intention providing only pseudo-democratic participation, had, as we have seen, important democratizing potential during the transition, especially before being restricted. Following an agreement by the leading governmental party (MDF) and the major party of the opposition (SZDSZ), the provision was eliminated as entirely pseudo-democratic and unnecessary, given a democratically elected parliament.[53] Since then, even vast movements of public opinion have not been able to influence legislation. What is interesting is how little the opposition parties, deprived of the institutionalized support of public opinion, have been able to block legislation which surveys have shown to be quite unpopular.

2. Ever since the election, the government and the main governing party have tirelessly attacked the press and sought to governmentalize the electronic media. The counterattacks of some privately owned newspapers, chambers of journalists, and most spectacularly the Publicity Club have managed to produce a stalemate in this area.[54] The situation is

much worse in the case of television, where the president Elemér Hankiss has not been able to establish a second news program to this day to balance the existing one that is aggressively pro-government and pro-MDF. Where the situation is somewhat better, in the case of radio, the attacks on its president Csaba Gombár have been correspondingly uglier, though Hankiss gets his share of hate as well from leading MDF figures. Two factors may counteract the statist trend in the electronic media: eventual private stations (at present there is a "frequency moratorium"), though the government might be able to fully control the choice of buyers, and the learned response of the Hungarian citizenry to disbelieve what is said on television.

3. Local government. The central government has attempted to install a centralized, authoritarian structure of local government, reviving some institutions and symbolism from pre-war hierarchical Hungary. Being a matter of legislation constitutionally requiring a 2/3 majority, the opposition was able to greatly moderate, though not entirely eliminate the centralist elements of the program. In the fall of 1990, the government was rewarded by local level Hungary with a resounding defeat in city, town and village elections, to the benefit of SZDSZ, FIDESZ in larger communities, and to the benefit of independents (often old Communist officials) in smaller ones. The new self-governments were in turn rewarded by the government with harsh budgetary restrictions.

4. The government pays little attention to unions, including the National Alliance of Workers Councils (MOSZ), earlier friendly to the MDF. In spite of the complaints of all independent unions, and the protest of the new Round Table of Unions (SZKA), the ministry of labor held elections for enterprise councils, hoping to facilitate the entry of its own people into key managerial positions.[55] The Council for Interest Aggregation (ÉT), where employee, employer and government representatives are to consider social and economic legislation and policy, has been allowed to languish, with the exception of the crisis caused by the taxi and truckers' strike of October, 1990, that was solved in effect by ÉT negotiations covered by television! The question of dealing with the property of the old official union, now called National Alliance of Hungarian Unions [MSZOSZ] has been so long delayed that the old union, more interested in social demagogy than democratic, horizontal organization building, has been decisively strengthened. The new unions have actually grown through the whole period, but without much interest on the part of the government to offer them organizational trade-offs there will not be much they will be able to counterpose to the wage demagogy of MSZOSZ. A creative line of thought[56], corresponding to positions of the Liga and the workers' council movement, according to which unions could participate in controlling the privatization process and receive some employee shares for their members, has fallen on deaf ears.

5. In spite of the importance of ecological concerns for the MDF as a movement party, the government and the Christian Democratic minister for the environment have done very little to reverse earlier patterns of growth and industry. Indeed it took a struggle to save the ministry in defense of the environment and to establish a relevant parliamentary committee. Little attention has been paid to the fact that some of the foreign investments for Hungary project the use of substandard technologies excluded from Western Europe for ecological reasons (for example an Austrian manufacturer of asbestos, or a Dutch manufacturer of lead-based paints, banned from the Netherlands). The government is at least as closed to consultation with ecological groups as its predecessor was, if not more so. There is a very slow revival of the older and newer ecological groups, and given the situation of the environment, new battles are foreseeable in this area.[57]

Old Friends and New Antagonists

It would be misleading to put the blame for the difficult situation of civil society in the post-Communist societies on their enemies alone. In my view the problem is as much with earlier friends. In the dualistic formula for the reconstruction of civil society, a unified society was arrayed against an unchanged party-state as its enemy; "us" against "them". In such a context, it has been not only easy but even necessary for very different ideological orientations to join the side of a unified, self-limiting societal movement if they wanted to participate in politics at all. Yet there were always reservations, which came out in the open in the free public sphere in Poland after the weakening of Solidarity: the civil society-oriented program was too collectivistic for the liberal economists, too cosmopolitan and not communitarian enough for the nationalists, too defensive for the revolutionaries, too liberal for the neo-Marxist advocates of class interests, too populistic for the *Realpolitiker*. With the enemy gone, all these trends turned against one another, and against the advocates and the very program of a democratic civil society that could have been a minimum basis of a consensus among many of them.

In Hungary of course the civil society-oriented program never corresponded to a single, unified movement. Nevertheless, in 1988 a remarkable number of independent groups emerged and formed a variety of complex, interwoven coalitions, all under the new East Central European banner of a democratic civil society driving for political democratization and the establishment of a genuinely modern, market economy. Even in the elections of March 1990, 55% of the population voted for parties that came out of this tradition. Had they united for a first government of transition, as János Kis and FIDESZ among many others hoped, Hungary would be a better place today, certainly with a stronger government, with a less divided culture, further down on the road to a market economy, and probably with a less threatened civil society.

It did not happen, and in part did not because there was a failure of political theory. Instead of focusing on their own project and achievement, the participants came to focus on either Europe's present or Hungary's past as alone worthy of imitation. But in Hungary too, some of the friends of civil society in 1988, turned out to have, by 1990, other apparently incompatible agendas. I believe that many of the intellectual objections to the use of the category of civil society reflect one or more of these agendas. For the revolutionaries, who want to purge and punish, the idea of a self-limiting revolution is too limiting, the orientation to civil society was too legalistic and gradualist. For the new professional politicians, keeping channels of communication open to groups outside of parties and parliaments violates their narrow conception of democracy derived not so much from Western ideals as from Western elite democratic practice. Cynically put, it also threatens their imagined new monopoly of power. For the liberal economists, who imagine themselves as bourgeois, after having called for civil society in their pamphlets as the only possible environment for a market economy, a society of unions, ecologists, consumer associations etc. came to appear to be a luxury only for developed market economies. For now a minimal civil society organized around the protection of property will do. Thus they are allied with the elite democrats wishing to keep politics isolated from societal inputs. Neither is apparently conscious of the fact that the paper thin legitimacy acquired through a democratic election alone is not going to be sufficient for a population undergoing deep economic hardships. On the other side, the nationalists are interested in the imagined community of the whole, living off issues of the past, and not in the real communities that are confronting the challenges of the next century. They fear the modern post-material values around the new social movements most of all. Along with the advocates of class, they tend to channel social protest inadvertently or deliberately in populist directions, as we have found out in the case of the one class-based party of Hungarian society, the small holders (FKGP) and may yet find out in the case of the reviving ex-official labor union.

Can the program of a democratic civil society revive in the face of so many old friends who have become antagonists? First of all, it is not yet dead, and is already gathering some energy in response to the artless statism of the new regime. There is not a day when someone in the Hungarian press does not defend not only the threatened forms of self-organization and communication I have listed, but defend them from the point of view of civil society, implicitly assuming the internal connection of these forms. What is missing for the moment is a new ideology capable of rearticulating the politics of civil society, demonstrating that only an institutionalized civil society can serve as the secure foundation for a genuinely modern social liberalism, and bringing together in an original fashion the values of freedom, solidarity and participation.

Notes

1. A. Arato, "Social Movements and Civil Society in the Soviet Union" in J. Butterfield and J. Sedaitis, *Perestroika from Below* (Boulder, CO: Westview Press, 1991). See A. Arato and J. Cohen, *Civil Society and Political Theory* (Cambridge, MA: MIT Press, 1992) for a full development of this conception of civil society. I am inclined to think that one needs a notion of economic society as well, as a form of mediation parallel to political society.

2. See especially A. Touraine, *The Voice and the Eye* (Cambridge: Cambridge University Press, 1982).

3. See e.g. A. Stepan, *Rethinking Military Politics* (Princeton: Princeton University Press, 1988) and J. Weintraub, "Democracy and the Market: a Marriage of Inconvenience" in this volume. I hesitate however to identify as does Weintraub civil society with the institutional framework of the market economy (for this latter sphere I now prefer the separate category of "economic society"), and political society with the republican dimension of public communication and deliberation. This second identification leaves out of consideration the party political sphere of strategic actors stressed by Stepan, which in my view also is best placed in the sphere of political society. Moreover instead of putting the public sphere in the manner of Hannah Arendt in the political realm exclusively, we would do better if we followed Habermas's early work in locating publics, and consequential communication and deliberation in all institutional realms. Unlike Habermas however I would insist on the different structure of the public in the political and the civil-cultural spheres.

4. L. Kolakowski, "Thèses sur l'espoir et le désespoir" [1971] in Z. Erard and G.M. Zygier, *La pologne: une société en dissidence* (Paris: Maspero, 1978).

5. See "The New Evolutionism" [1976] in *Letters from Prison* (Berkeley: Univ. of Cal. Press, 1988); as well as *L'Église et la gauche: le dialogue polonais* (Paris: Seuil, 1979).

6. Jacek Kuron, "Pour une platforme unique de l'opposition" in Z. Erard and G.M. Zygier, *La Pologne: une société en dissidence.*

7. The editors of *Beszélö*, "Társadalmi Szerzödés" [Social Contract] (Budapest, 1987). The same point has been made in many of the earlier editorials of Kis in this underground journal.

8. A. Arato, "Critical Sociology and Authoritarian State Socialism" in J. Thompson, D. Held, *Habermas: Critical Debates* (Cambridge: MIT Press, 1982).

9. J. Staniszkis, *Poland's Self-limiting Revolution* (Princeton: Princeton University Press, 1982).

10. Alain Touraine, François Dubet, et.al., *Solidarity. Poland 1980-1981* (Cambridge: Cambridge University Press, 1983).

11. This crucial idea of "society's fear of itself" was developed by J. Corradi and his collaborators.

12. D. Ost, *Solidarity and the Politics of Anti-politics* (Philadelphia: Temple University Press, 1990).

13. For a useful summary of these activities see *Reinventing Civil Society: Poland's Quiet Revolution 1981-1986* (New York: The U.S. Helsinki Watch Committee, 1986).

14. For excellent presentations of these criticisms, from two different sides, see the articles by Aleksandr Smolar and Adam Walicki in F. Fehér and A. Arato eds., *Crisis and Reform in Eastern Europe* (New Brunswick: Transaction Press, 1991).

15. Conversation with J. Kuron, Warsaw, February of 1987.

16. See Ost's excellent *Solidarity* chapters seven and eight.

17. Elemér Hankiss has given us a pioneering analysis of the "second society" in Hungary under late Kadarism in *Diagnózisok* 2. (Budapest: Magvetö, 1986).

18. "Gondolatok a közeljövöröl" in *Beszélö* (Budapest, 1982), No. 3.

19. T. Bauer, "A második gazdasági reform és a tulajdonviszonyok" in *Mozgó Világ* (Budapest, 1982), Vol. 8, No. 11. The editorial board of the journal was purged after this issue.

20. "Magyorország 1983 tavaszán" *Beszélö*, (April 1983), No. 7.

21. "Korlátainkról és lehetöségeinkröl" speech at Monor meeting, June 14-16, 1985 (mimeographed samizdat publication).

22. "Korlátainkról és lehetöségeinkröl" speech at Monor meeting.

23. *Fordulat és reform* (1987 final text) in *Medvetánc* (Budapest, 1987) # 2.

24. Well represented in the first volume of S. Kurtán, P. Sándor, L. Vass,eds.,*Magyarország politikai évkönyve 1988* (Budapest: R-Forma kiadó, 1989).

25. I am combining, reducing and slightly altering the typologies presented in two excellent articles by I. Stumpf: "Rendszerkritika, alternativitás generációs köntösben" in *Magyarország politikai évkönyve 1988*; and "Pártosodás 89" in S. Kurtán, P. Sándor, L. Vass, eds., *Magyarország politikai évkönyve* (Budapest: Aula-Omikk, 1990).

26. I. Stumpf, "Rendszerkritika, alternativitás generációs köntösben".

27. I. Stumpf, "Political Socialization of New Generation -- Alliance of Young Democrats" in *How to be a Democrat in a Post-Communist Society* (Budapest: Institute for Political Science, Hungarian Academy of Science, 1991).

28. E. Bilecz, "Szárszó '88" in *Magyarország politikai évkönyve 1988*.

29. E. Bilecz, "Szárszó '88" in *Magyarország politikai évkönyve 1988*, 334.

30. For the latter, see László Sólyom, "A társadalom részvétele a környezet-védelemben" in *Medvetánc* (Budapest, 1988); interview with János Vargha in K. Bossányi, *Szólampróba: Beszélgetések az alternativ mozgalmakról* (Budapest: Láng kiadó, 1989); and G. Lányi, "A kuvik éve - környezetvédelmi jelzések" in *Magyarország politikai évkönyve 1988*.

31. See two previous articles by I. Stumpf as well as interviews with L. Kövér in *Szólampróba* and in A. Richter, ed., *Ellenzéki kerekasztal* (Budapest: Ötlet kft., 1990).

32. For some of its documents: see "Duna Kör" in *Magyarország politikai évkönyve 1988*, 704-712.

33. L. Bruszt, "Az érdekképviseleti monopóliumok alkonya" in *Magyarország politikai évkönyve 1988*.

34. For the founding documents: TDDSZ in *Magyarország politikai évkönyve 1988*, 770-779; FSZDL and MOSZ in *Magyarország politikai évkönyve [1990]* (Budapest: Ökonomia Alapitvány, 1991) 712ff; 727ff. See also the interviews with P. Forgács in *Szólampróba*; and with L. Bruszt in *Ellenzéki kerekasztal*.

35. For documents see "Nyilvánosság Club" in *Magyarország politikai évkönyve 1988*, 752-755; as well as G. Bányai, J. Bercsi, eds., *Lel-Tàr* (Budapest: Tudósitások kiadó, 1989), 133-141.

36. "Független Jogász Fórum" in *Lel-Tár*, 49-53.

37. The founding document foresaw its self-dissolution on the day when press and communication were perfectly free and guaranteed in a new constitutional state, and when the pluralism of opinions was fully established: *Magyarország politikai évkönyve 1988*, 753. That time has not yet apparently come, in the view of the Club!

38. See the vivid description in the interview with M. Haraszti in *Uncaptive Minds* (January-February 1989), Vol. 2, No. 1.

39. See the interviews with Kövér and especially Viktor Orbán in *Ellenzéki Kerekasztal*; as well as I. Stumpf's recollections in "Political Socialization".

40. L. Bruszt, "1989: The Negotiated Revolution in Hungary" in *Social Research* (Summer 1990) Vol. 7, No. 2, 372-374; G. Halmai, *Az egyesülés szabadsága* (Budapest: Atlantisz, 1990), 97-107.

41. On this problem of "societal debate" see L. Bruszt, "1989: The Negotiated Revolution in Hungary", 373-374.

42. I. Kukorelli, "The Birth, Testing and Results of the 1989 Hungarian Election Law" in *Soviet Studies* (1991), Vol, 43, No. 1, 138.

43. The second 1989 volume of S. Kurtán, P. Sándor, L. Vass, eds., *Magyarország politikai évkönyve* (Budapest: Aula-Omikk, 1990) shows this distinction very well indeed, with articles about parties almost completely displacing those dealing with civil society in the preceding volume.

44. See in particular E. Bilecz "Helybenjáró helyi társadalmak-1989" and A. Telekes, J. Rechnitzer, "Megmozdult a vidék!" both in *Magyarország politikai évkönyve [1989]*.

45. G. Halmai, *Az egyesülés szabadsága*, 192-194; L. Bruszt, "1989:The Negotiated Revolution in Hungary," 373-374; as well as the interview with Csaba Öry in *Ellenzéki kerekasztal*, 109-110.

46. E. Babus, "Népszavazás-1989" in *Magyarország politikai évkönyve 1989*.

47. See A. Arato, "Revolution, Civil Society and Democracy" in *Praxis International* (April & July 1990), Vol. 10, No. 1-2. For the modifications in the agreement imposed by the last Kádárist parliament, see the interview with P. Tölgyessy in *Ellenzéki kerekasztal*, 152.

48. A. Bozóki, "Ut a rendszerváltáshoz: az Ellenzéki Kerekasztal" in *Mozgó világ* (1990), No. 8, 35; for a contrary position see the interview with Sólyom in *Ellenzéki kerekasztal*, 140, whose recollections however tend to support the view expressed by Bozóki and most of the FIDESZ and SZDSZ delegates, as well as by I. Kónya, one of the key organizers on behalf of the Independent Forum of Jurists, later parliamentary fraction leader of MDF. For the latter, see the interview in *Ellenzéki kerekasztal*, 21. Evidently, the MDF at the time was not unhappy with the

exclusion of the public, as the remarks of Sólyom, then a key MDF negotiator, indicate.

49. The étatist turn in the politics of the Hungarian government has been documented by many texts, first and foremost and repeatedly in the journal, now of course legal, *Beszélö*. For a useful English analysis of the first phase see: M. Bihari, "Change of Regime and Power in Hungary (1989-1990)" in *Magyarország politikai évkönyve [1990]*, 33ff. See also the somewhat different diagnosis of A. Agh in "The Year of Incomplete Changes" in the same volume.

50. Jadwiga Staniszkis seems to hold such a view in her essays on political capitalism in Eastern Europe, in "Dilemma der Demokratie in Osteuropa" in F. Deppe, H. Dubiel, et.al., eds. *Demokratischer Umbruch in Osteuropa* (Frankfurt: Suhrkamp, 1990) and most recently in a somewhat chastened form in: *The Dynamics of Breakthrough in Eastern Europe. The Polish Experience* (Berkeley: Univ. of Cal. Press, 1991).

51. See the interesting debate in SZDSZ between Kis and G. Tellér, reproduced in *Beszélö*, February 2, 1991 and February 9, 1991.

52. In Poland, similar trends have been documented. See Lena Kolarska-Bobinska, "The Changing Face of Civil Society in Eastern Europe" in *Praxis International* (October 1990-January 1991), Vol. 10, No. 3-4.

53. See the text of the MDF-SZDSZ agreement in *Magyarország politikai évkönyve [1991]*.

54. Z. Farkas, "Allóháború" in *Magyarország politikai évkönyve [1990]*.

55. For the documents: *Magyarország politikai évkönyve 1991*, 712-730.

56. See especially the genuinely pluralistic conception of privatization in E. Szalai's work, *Gazdaság és hatalom* (Budapest: Aula kiadó, 1990).

57. Z. Illés, "Piros jelzés a zöldeknek" in *Magyarország politikai évkönyve [1990]*.

10

Transforming East Germany: A New German Question

Stephen F. Szabo

Rather than closing the German question, the unification of Germany has reopened it once again. In particular, that part of the German question posed over thirty years ago by Ralf Dahrendorf in his classic study of democracy in West Germany, *Society and Democracy in Germany*[1], of why Germany has had such difficulty establishing liberal democracy, has to be reexamined for guidance on the prospects for the democratization of Eastern Germany.

Unlike the western two-thirds of Germany, the eastern third has never sustained a successful democracy. Its only experience with democracy ended with the Weimar Republic in 1933. With its incorporation under Article 23 of the Basic Law into the Federal Republic, it is now again a democracy. Yet Eastern Germany, like the other new democracies of Central and Southern Europe, faces serious challenges and questions, not only about its own viability, but about its impact on German democracy.

The incorporation into the larger and successful democracy of West Germany gives it an advantage not shared by the other new European democracies and few doubt that this will insure the viability of democracy in the East. But in some important ways democracy in Eastern Germany could have a decisive impact on the overall balance of German politics. The recent decision to move the German capital from Bonn to Berlin is an example of how the presence of the new legislators from the East decided an emotional and hard fought national political issue.

In order to assess the prospects for democracy in the former German Democratic Republic (GDR), a look back to the reasons both for the failure and the later success of democracy in Germany should prove instructive. The key factors both in explaining the demise of Weimar and the democratization of the Federal Republic can be found in the following broad factors: the political culture, the party system, the constitutional and electoral arrangements, and the broader international constellation.

Political Culture

Explanations for political behavior which rely upon political culture too often run the risk of using culture as a last resort to account for outcomes which cannot be explained by other factors. If we don't know why Weimar failed we can blame it on "culture." Keeping this in mind, most examinations of the fall and rise of democracy in Germany turn to political culture. Weimar was a republic without republicans.[2] It is plausible to argue that Weimar was bound to fail because of the combination of economic depression and nationalist resentment against the Versailles system, but Britain, the United States and France all went through the social and economic crises of the 1930s without sacrificing democracy. Once the Weimar system encountered rough waters, it had no cultural reservoir of constitutionalism in either the general public, or more crucially, among the intelligentsia. The turn toward authoritarian alternatives was not seen as unnatural or un-German.

Conversely, studies of the political culture of the early years of the Federal Republic, such as those of Almond and Verba and of the Allensbach Institute, found thin support for such key institutions and practices of democracy as a multiparty system and free speech.[3] On the contrary, support for a single party state remained high in the early 1950s, as were positive evaluations of aspects of National Socialism. Most studies of the political attitudes and values of the citizens of West Germany would conclude that, prior to the 1970s the legitimacy of democracy was "performance-based", i.e. resting on support for the strong performance of the West German economy, and that the Federal Republic was, therefore, a "fair weather" democracy. It was only during the decade of the 1970s that evidence of a deeper-based democratic political culture began to emerge.

Students of democracy in the Federal Republic pointed to a number of reasons for this transformation. First was the long period of economic growth and a stable society which reinforced performance-based legitimacy. Germans came to realize that the trains can run on time in democracies.

Second was the turnover of power from the Christian Democrats (CDU) to the Social Democrats (SPD) in 1969 (and then the second turnover of power back to the CDU in 1982). The openness of the system to the opposition converted the supporters of the SPD to a system they had feared was only a *CDU Staat* (a CDU state).

Third was generational change. The socialization of two generations in a democracy created a basis of legitimacy beyond performance and extended the participatory elements of what had been an elitist style of democracy.

Turning to the state of Eastern German political culture today, although it seems reasonable to expect that it will take at least a generation to develop a mature democratic political culture, the East Germans have several advantages over their West German compatriots. While the West Germans had the assistance of the West, especially of the United States, the Eastern Germans have in place a functioning German democracy with proven institutions and patterns of political behavior, most critically a functioning party system. They will benefit from forty years of democracy and will not have to reinvent the wheel.

A recent survey of public opinion commissioned by the Times-Mirror Foundation throughout Europe and the Soviet Union provides some interesting insights into the emerging East German political culture. First, the survey found the East Germans to be the most optimistic about the future of all the East Europeans polled. Forty-eight percent believed that they were better off as a result of unification, while only 23 percent felt they were worse off. More importantly, 79 percent believed that they would have a better life in five years as a result of unification, while only 5 percent expected things to be worse because of unification.[4]

Second, there is little evidence in the survey to support fears of a Weimar syndrome. Ninety-one percent of Eastern Germans approved of the change to a multiparty system, while only 4 percent disapproved. This figure of approval is the highest among the other former "People's Democracies," which tend to have approval ratings in the 70 percent range. It is also higher than figures from similar questions posed to West Germans in the early 1950s. In April 1991, for example, 70 percent of Eastern Germans believed that democracy was the best form of government, while only between 66 and 74 percent believed this to be the case in West Germany in the 1970s.[5] This broad support for political pluralism is mirrored by strong approval of efforts to establish a free market. Despite massive unemployment in the former GDR, 86 percent of Eastern Germans in the survey supported efforts to establish a free market.

To be sure, resentment exists against the *wessies* and their domination of the unification process. The Times-Mirror survey found that about three-fourths of Eastern Germans feel that East Germany was "overwhelmed and taken over" by West Germany and about half felt a great deal of resentment over this. Only a third believed that West German leaders care about East Germany and 58 percent thought of themselves as East Germans as compared to only 38 percent who viewed themselves as Germans. Yet this does not change the overall support for unification.

Questions about whether unification was worth the cost are raised much more often in Western Germany than in the eastern states (*Laender*).[6]

Overall, the first indications about the state of political culture in the former GDR are surprisingly good, far better than we would have expected based on the West German experience. The reasons for this state of affairs probably have to do with the accumulated experience of over twenty years of watching West German television. Close to 90 percent of East Germans followed West German and Western politics from their living rooms every evening and had compensated at least to some extent for the lack of a democratic political culture at home.

Beyond this foundation for democratic culture is the exhaustion of authoritarian alternatives to democracy. For almost all East Germans, authoritarian and totalitarian models of social and political organization are completely discredited. The East German Revolution was not simply about the D Mark and the achievement of the benefits of Western consumer society, it was also about ridding East Germans of the leaden hand of the paternalistic state. Protests were directed at a failed and corrupt leadership and, beyond that, at a state which watched over every aspect of private life. Few Germans over the age of fifteen who lived through this are likely to forget it or to have any nostalgia for an escape from freedom. This experience stands in marked contrast to that of the Weimar era during which left and right extremists could offer totalitarian types of alternative societies with credibility to large segments of the public.

Democracy will not be without its tests in the new political culture. Resentment toward foreign minority groups has emerged as a serious problem. Once again, turning to the Times-Mirror survey, anti-foreign attitudes are striking. Anywhere from 50 to 60 percent of Germans have unfavorable views of gypsies, Poles and Romanians and 30 to 40 percent have negative images of Soviet émigrés and Turks. Jews are less disliked (with 52 percent having favorable attitudes as compared to 24 percent with unfavorable ones). These are disturbingly high levels of what the Germans refer to as *Auslaenderfeindlichkeit* (animosity toward foreigners), although lower than those found in the Times-Mirror surveys in the newly liberated countries of Central Europe. The influx of 2.5 million immigrants into Germany between 1989 and the end of 1991 has increased feelings that the boat is full. The increase of people seeking entry on grounds of political asylum (estimated at 250,000 for 1991) largely from Third World countries has also awakened a new brand of racism.

This xenophobia is not a larger problem in Eastern Germany than in Western Germany in terms of public opinion, nor for that matter is it more or less a source of concern in Germany than in other parts of Europe. Despite the palpably higher level of anti-Polish feelings in the former GDR and the more visible presence of skinheads and neo-Nazi groups in the former GDR, there is no evidence in surveys that the *ossies* are any worse than the *wessies* when it comes to anti-foreign feelings.

Yet the Fascist temptation will surely be stronger in the East than in the West, both in Europe and in Germany. Ralf Dahrendorf in his thoughtful essay, *Reflections on the Revolution in Europe*, warns that the greatest risk to democracies in post-Communist Europe is fascism. In his words, "By that I mean the combination of a nostalgic ideology of community which draws harsh boundaries between those who belong and those who do not, with a new monopoly of a man or a "movement" and a strong emphasis on organization and mobilization rather than freedom of choice."[7]

The disturbing rise of skin head and neo-Nazi groups in Eastern Germany, while not surprising, is troubling nonetheless and an example of what concerns Dahrendorf. There was a dramatic increase in reported incidents of violence against foreigners in the fall of 1991. Federal authorities, who reported 26 incidents of such attacks during the first quarter of the year, listed the number at 220 by mid-September. The attacks in the fall tended to be concentrated in the new eastern states.[8] German authorities estimate a hard core of about 2,000 neo-Nazis in the former GDR and a broader group of sympathizers to number about 15,000. Social scientists estimate that about 50,000 young Eastern Germans are open to the appeals of this deviant behavior.[9] The population in the eastern *Laender* are more vulnerable to these types of appeals than those in the West for a number of reasons. Unemployment is much higher, creating a larger clientele for radicalization. The collapse of a society, even one as corrupt and debilitating as was that of the GDR, creates feelings of dislocation and anomie. The decollectivization of the "niche society" of the GDR and what the political scientist, Christoph Butterwegge calls "the reprivatization of social risk" is especially disorienting to many.[10] Finally, police forces in the East have not been rebuilt and law enforcement is consequently much weaker than in the western states.

In addition, the different approach taken to German responsibility for Hitler and the Holocaust in East Germany as compared to West Germany has had consequences for the potential of extreme right groups. While the Federal Republic accepted responsibility for the crimes of the Nazi regime and made restitution payments to Jews and serious efforts to educate their public about what really happened in the Third Reich, the Communist regime in the GDR did not. They took the position that fascism was a legacy of capitalism and not of communism. East Germans were liberated by the Soviets, and the Nazi period was, therefore, not treated as a historical predecessor to the East German regime. This has left a vacuum on the right which is larger than in the West. Four decades of suppression of nationalism and patriotism in the name of proletarian internationalism only increases the potential for right wing extremism.

Although there has been a serious rise in violence against foreigners beginning in the fall of 1991 and, given all these warning signals, it is still true that Eastern Germans have shown no greater proclivity to vote for right wing extremist parties than Western Germans. *Die Republikaner* (the Republicans) and other new right groups have had even less electoral impact in the East than they had in the West. Voter turnout in state and national elections remains high. All in all, given their starting point, the political culture of Eastern Germans seems quite promising for the consolidation of democracy.

Political Institutions

The democratization of the political culture is likely to be further supported by the stability of the political institutions transplanted from the West. Here again the Eastern Germans have a great advantage over the new democracies of Eastern and Central Europe which are struggling to create functioning democratic institutions in short order during a period of system overload because of the economic and social policy demands facing these new polities. In contrast, the East Germans have the advantage of adopting a system which has proven itself to be among the most stable and democratic in Europe.

The new constitution (the Basic Law of West Germany) should fit the requirements of integration comfortably. The decentralized federal system in which states play an important autonomous role in administration, cultural policies and law enforcement should allow the "new states" to have adequate flexibility to adjust in their own way to the varying demands they will all face. Certainly a system which has accommodated the varying interests and cultural traditions of Hamburg and of Bavaria can deal with those of Brandenburg and Saxony. Not that such searing national issues as abortion will not try the system, but some sort of state-level solution could help to defuse even these divisions.

Similarly, the adoption of the West German party and electoral systems will also ease the transition to democracy. Besides a fragile political culture, the Weimar Republic failed because of its fragmented and ideologically polarized party system and the consequent weakness of the executive facing an uncontrollable legislature. The Weimar party system was one characterized by a multiplicity of parties, each with narrow constituencies, which became dominated by extreme anti-democratic parties.

The party system of the Federal Republic, in contrast, has been one in which centrist, democratic parties have dominated. There has been a long term trend toward a consolidation of a three party system in which the centrist Free Democrats have held the balance of power. The addition of the Greens as a fourth party has not altered a party system which continues to produce stable, centrist coalition governments.

In contrast to the party constellations of Weimar and the early Federal Republic, Eastern Germany begins its democratic experience with democracy with a stable centrist party landscape, reinforced not only by the domination of the Western German parties and politicians, but also by the electoral system of the West German republic with its five percent clause. This clause, which requires a party to gain at least five percent of the national vote to enter the Bundestag, has proved to be as effective a hurdle against splinter parties in the East as it has in the West.

A more serious problem for the new democracies of the East, including the former GDR, is the lack of professional and experienced political leaders untainted by collaboration with the old regimes. The leadership vacuum is especially acute in the GDR due to a number of factors. Unlike Poland, which developed an experienced leadership within Solidarity, any dissident in the GDR was quickly jailed and then exported to the West for D Marks. Second, the police state was quite effective in controlling dissent and identifying and isolating potential opposition leaders. When the revolution came, it did not produce a Walesa or a Havel, let alone a Solidarity. Third, the police and party state was much more extensive than in Hungary, Poland or Czechoslovakia. Over 500,000 people are estimated to have been employed by the secret police (*Stasi*). It is estimated that about two million East Germans collaborated with *Stasi*, and the East German Communist party (the Socialist Unity Party or SED) had a large membership.

This is not to say that there was no civil society separate from or in contradiction to the official society of the SED. The "niche society" was based upon a wide variety of small private networks of people who cooperated with each other to better cope with the privations and demands of the state.[11] The Lutheran Church, in particular, provided a haven from the official GDR for people to discuss environmental and peace issues as well as other topics which were tabu in open discussion. It was the network of church related groups which provided the infrastructure for the organized opposition to the SED which erupted in the fall of 1989.

Yet, the weakness of East German civil society as compared to that of Poland and Hungary and the lack of effective leaders became quickly apparent in the inability of East Germans to fill the vacuum which was created by the fall of the Communist party. Not only were Erich Honecker and his successors swept away, but so also was the group which was most prominent in the German Revolution of 1989, New Forum. The incompetence of the only democratic government in the history of the GDR led by the Christian Democrat, Lothar de Maziere, further underlined this problem and opened up East Germany to a "friendly take-over." Many of the current leaders in the eastern *Laender* are West Germans who have either been appointed or elected by Easterners and who direct many of the policies of the East. This should also prove to be a short term problem which will be resolved by an education in democratic politics through democratic practice.

As for the problem of collaborators, the Germans will have to follow the example of West Germany at the end of World War II which attempted to identify and punish the worst offenders of the Nazi regime while keeping on many former members and collaborators in the transition to democracy. Too many are guilty to sweep with too broad a broom. The trial of East German border guards for the murder of people attempting to flee the GDR is likely to be a painful remainder that it is difficult to punish subordinates for carrying out the policies of the state. A series of trials of prominent East German leaders including the former head of counter-intelligence, Markus Wolf, and possibly of Honecker himself if he is returned to Germany, can also be expected. Unlike after the Nazi period, however, the collaborators of the GDR have few usable skills which can be put to use either in administration or the economy.

Furthermore the parliament has given the victims of the *Stasi* the right to access to the files which were kept on them and to information about who reported them to the police, although it has limited media access to these records. The German government will also establish a special office to administer the six million files which the secret police compiled on East and West Germans as well as some foreigners. The office will be administered largely by Eastern Germans and will have a staff of 2,500 and an annual budget of 98 million D Marks ($60 million).[12]

In short the institutional framework for democratization in Eastern Germany is much more stable and tested than that with which the West Germans or the other new democracies of Central and Eastern Europe began.

Economic Transformation and Democratization

Economic prospects and performance will play an important role in the stabilization of democracy in the eastern states. Recent surveys of public opinion in Eastern Germany have found that two-thirds of those asked believed that democracy can only function in a growing economy, while only 17 percent believed that democracy could work in a poor economy.[13] This association of support of a political system with economic performance is a traditional German characteristic, and thus the state of the economy in the East will be crucial in the early stages of the development of democracy in the East.

While the prospects for economic reconstruction seem good, they are not immediate. The October, 1991 report of the five leading German economic institutes concluded that, while the bottom had been reached in the drop of production in the East and that substantial growth is to be expected in 1992, inflation will rise in the East to an annual rate of 12 percent and, most importantly, unemployment is likely to continue to increase from 950,000 to over 1.4 million in 1992, while those on shortened hours will decline from 1.6 million in 1991 to 750,000 in 1992. This means that about 30 percent of the Eastern German workforce is predicted to be either unemployed or underemployed by the end of 1991. Furthermore the institutes warned that the increase in growth in the East is due to the assistance from the West and not from increased private investment or eastern competitiveness. Privatization has been substantial in the small business sector but slow in both the industrial and agricultural sectors.[14]

The longer term (five years) prospects are much better. As in politics, the Eastern Germans have a great advantage over their eastern neighbors in the economic realm as well. The West Germans have begun a massive transfer to Eastern Germany of investment and economic assistance greater than the Marshall Plan aid received by the West Germans. Estimates of the extent of this aid range from 100 billion D Marks (about $60 billion) annually for the next ten years on up. In 1992, public transfers from West to East will reach 10,800 D Mark (about $6,000) per person living in the East.[15] While this assistance will strain the German economy and push up public sector deficits and possibly taxes, it will help to transform the former East Germany within five years. By then infrastructure will be modernized, the old state structure privatized and new plants and equipment will be in operation. This modernization should significantly raise labor productivity and ease unemployment. Already by the end of 1991 signs of construction and renewal were visible through the new states.

What is important is how Eastern Germans view the situation and their own prospects. It still seems safe to conclude that by the time of the next federal elections in December 1994 the economy in the East will be on the clear upswing and most people will believe that they are better off than they were four years earlier.

The International Environment

Finally a comparison of the international, and specifically European, milieu in which the new democracies of the East are taking root is much more favorable than that of the inter-war period. The Weimar Republic failed in part because it was associated with what was seen by many Germans as a vindictive peace imposed by outsiders and was tested during a period of general crisis in Europe where fascism, communism and other forms of totalitarian and authoritarian ideologies were on the rise. Today, while Europe may not have reached the End of History, the clear trend is toward democracy. Attempts to restore non-democratic forms of government would go against the current of trends in Europe and lead to isolation and exclusion from the promise of the European Community. Similarly, the openness of societies to others through the media and the limits such exposure places on political regression, most recently apparent during the Soviet coup, add yet another check on authoritarian tendencies.

Eastern German Impact on German Democracy

The clear conclusion from the recent experience of unification is that, while its impetus came from the East Germans, its management and the reconstruction of Eastern Germany was and is "Made in West Germany." The flow has been largely in one direction. Yet the Eastern Germans will have an impact on German politics and democracy and will not only be an object but will also become participants in the new German democracy. The addition of about 12 million new voters into the German electorate and of 140 Bundestag representatives from the East as well as of five state elections will have important consequences for the national political balance. East Germans now comprise about 20% of the German electorate, and the political leadership in Berlin cannot afford to ignore these voters who may hold the balance in future elections. The majority of members of the Liberal party (FDP) which holds the balance of power in the current government in Bonn, for example, now are from the East. What impact are they likely to have?

First, the citizens of the five new *Laender* are likely to strengthen the social side of the Social Market economy, expecting and demanding greater state intervention in the economy and defense of the broad net of social services. This means that both the SPD and the left of the CDU will have at least the prospect of more influence than they did in the old Federal Republic.

Second, the anti-foreign sentiments in the East will probably strengthen those tendencies in the West and push Germany toward a more restrictive immigration policy in the future. The strong pacifist feelings in the East will probably also have a broader impact in the West.

Third, the distinctiveness of the East will probably strengthen the already strong federalist and decentralist tendencies of the Federal Republic, at least in education and cultural policies. There is some conflict between the social agenda of the eastern *Laender* and this desire to have flexibility to deal with regionally specific problems and traditions, but federalist politics are likely to be more prominent in the future.

Finally, the inclusion of the East has, as the debate over Bonn versus Berlin showed, reopened yet another discussion of the German identity. In this sense, the changes in Europe as well as those in Germany will force a major reexamination of fundamental assumptions about security policy, foreign policy and Germany's role in the new Europe. Here too, the Eastern Germans will have a voice.

As the new Federal Republic defines itself once again, the question about the degree of continuity and change remains open. Will the Federal Republic be simply a continuation of the old Federal Republic with five new states? To a large extent the answer will be yes, especially in terms of its institutional structures and political practices. However, the changing European milieu in which Germany is centered will not allow it to maintain continuity in its foreign and defense policies. With the implosion of the former Soviet Union, the instability in Eastern and Central Europe, the movement toward integration in the European Community and the prospect of a marginalization of the American role in Europe (at least in the crucial area of European security), many of the fundamental assumptions of postwar German foreign and defense policies are being challenged.

German Atlanticism is likely to be tested and reshaped if it survives these transformations, and a more European Germany will emerge. Germany is once again the Land of the Middle, facing East and West and probably South as well. It is fully sovereign and will eventually be unified in fact as well as in law. Thus change will come, and this will once again reshape what has always been a malleable German identity. Whatever the contours of the new Germany in the new Europe may be, it seems sure that it will shape its new role and identity on the basis of a stable democratic foundation.

Notes

1. Ralf Dahrendorf, *Society and Democracy in Germany* (New York: Doubleday, 1967).

2. For an exposition of this theme see Peter Gay, *Weimar Culture: The Outsider as Insider* (New York: Harper Torchbooks, 1968).

3. Gabriel Almond and Sidney Verba, *The Civic Culture* (Princeton: Princeton University Press, 1963); see also David Conradt, "Changing German Political Culture," in *The Civic Culture Revisited*, edited by Gabriel Almond and Sidney Verba (Boston: Little Brown, 1980); The Allensbach surveys can be found in a series edited by Elisbeth Noelle-Neumann, *The Germans* (Allensbach: Institut fuer Demoskopie).

4. Times Mirror Center for The People and The Press, *The Pulse of Europe: A Survey of Political and Social Values and Attitudes* (Washington: Times Mirror Center for The People and The Press, 1991).

5. Elisabeth Noelle-Neumann, "Die Vorzuege der Freiheit stehen noch nicht im Mittelpunkt, *"Frankfurter Allgemeine Zeitung*, September 30, 1991, 13.

6. In a survey conducted by the Allensbach Institute in April 1991, 59% of Eastern Germans believed that German unification was a reason for joy while only 26% believed it to be a reason for concern as compared to 44% Western Germans finding it an occasion for joy and 39% one for concern. See Renate Koecher, "Im Neuen Staat Nicht Zu Hause," *Rheinischer Merkur*, November 15, 1991, 10.

7. Ralf Dahrendorf, *Reflection on the Revolution in Europe: In a Letter Intended to have been Sent to a Gentleman in Warsaw* (New York: Random House, 1990), 111.

8. "Lieber sterben als nach Sachsen," *Der Spiegel*, September 30, 1991, 36; and "Dann macht er dich kalt," *Der Spiegel*, October 14, 1991, 37; Stephen Kinzer, "Klan Seizes On Germany's Wave of Racist Violence," *The New York Times*, November 3, 1991, 16.

9. Bartholomaeus Grill, "Auferstanden aus Ruinen," *Die Zeit* (North American edition), June 21, 1991, 3.

10. Quoted in B. Grill, "Auferstanden aus Ruinen," 3.

11. For a discussion of the conflict between the "official" political culture and the "dominant" political culture of the GDR see Christiane Lemke, *Die Ursachen des Umbruchs 1989: Politische Sozialisation in der ehemalige DDR* (Opladen: Westdeutscher Verlag, 1991).

12. "Der Bundestag billigt das Stasi-Unterlagengesetz," *Frankfurter Allgemeine Zeitung*, November 15, 1991, 1.

13. Noelle Neumann, "Die Vorzug der Freiheit," *Frankfurter Allgemeine Zeitung*, September 30, 1991, 13.

14. See "Im kommenden Jahr in den neuen Laendern Wirtschaftswachstum von zwoelf Prozent," *Frankfurter Allgemeine Zeitung*, October 27, 1991, 1; Stephen Kinzer, "Facing Down Protest, Eastern Germany Goes Private," *The New York Times*, November 3, 1991, A16; Quentin Peel, "Germany is given grim warning on economy," *Financial Times*, October 22, 1991, 1.

15. Quentin Peel, "Autumn of Discontent," *The Financial Times*, October 24, 1991.

11

Transition to Democracy in Czechoslovakia, Hungary, and Poland: A Preliminary Analysis

Andrzej Korbonski *

The opening of the Berlin Wall on November 9, 1989 ultimately paved the way for the end of Communist rule in the German Democratic Republic and the unification of both German states roughly a year later. Although the downfall of Nicolae Ceausescu in Romania was still two months off and there were still Communist regimes in Albania, Bulgaria, and some Yugoslav republics, in November, 1989 it was clear that the days of Communist rule in East Central Europe were numbered.

Although, according to some scholars, the events in Eastern Europe "have resulted in Himalayas of print,"[1] two years are certainly not enough time to produce a systematic analysis of the reasons behind the process of revolutionary change in the region which brought about the end of the 40-year long Communist political and economic systems.[2] Although the basic facts and key watershed events in the process are reasonably well known, the last few months have witnessed the appearance of hitherto unpublished secret documents which throw additional light on the critical decisions taken in the different East Central European countries in the course of 1989.[3] Because of that, the limited purpose of this chapter is to present only some preliminary ideas on the process of systemic transformation in three key East Central European countries -- Czechoslovakia, Hungary, and Poland -- in the hope of

*   *Research for this paper was aided by a grant from the UCLA Academic Senate Committee on Research, whose support is hereby gratefully acknowledged.*

expanding somewhat our knowledge of the dramatic transition in the region.

The choice of the three countries was not accidental: The three states not only are located in a well-defined geographical area of East Central Europe, but in the past four decades they have shared several essential features, including political and economic structures and institutions; patterns of socioeconomic changes; and membership in two important regional organizations, the Warsaw Pact (WTO) and the Council for Mutual Economic Assistance (CMEA). Moreover, they have also enjoyed a lengthy common historical heritage, antedating for centuries the Communist takeover in the wake of World War II.

Also, the three countries have shared a substantial economic dependence on the Soviet Union, a deep political dependence characterized by a need to coordinate their foreign and domestic policies with the Kremlin, and a direct military vulnerability based on geography, recent history, and Soviet military power.

The differences among the three are less easily observable. On the one hand, they derived from many deeply rooted cultural and socioeconomic phenomena that have created national political cultures which continue to influence the respective countries' external and internal policies, even after more than forty years of Communist efforts to eradicate them. On the other hand, as will be shown below, other differences relate to the way the individual states have faced various developmental and systemic crises.

I am prepared to argue that, on balance, systemic similarities seem to outweigh the differences. At the same time, the presence of persisting and even growing differences among them continues, making Czechoslovakia, Hungary, and Poland a fascinating focus of research.

The approach used in this paper is based on my work on the process of change in East Central Europe, which I began about twenty years ago.[4] It reflected my growing unhappiness with the attitude of many Western social scientists who for years have studiously ignored changes in Communist Europe, claiming that the traditional totalitarian model, which they assumed was still applicable to East Central Europe, long after its demise, by definition precluded change.

It was only after the explosions in Hungary and Poland in October-November, 1956 that scholars in the West began to pay some attention to the region, but even here I can only think of a single authority in the field who first began to notice the effects of de-Stalinization and its impact on the process of political and then economic differentiation in what used to be viewed at that time as a monolithic bloc. It was Zbigniew Brzezinski who emphasized such key factors in the process of change as the depth of internal socioeconomic crisis, the degree of alienation of the working class and the intelligentsia from the Stalinist regime, and the availability of alternative leadership.[5] After a hiatus of several years, there was a new outburst of interest in the process of change in Communist societies associated, on the one hand, with the growing belief that the traditional totalitarian model was no longer applicable for the study of Communist systems, and on the other with the developments in East Central Europe in the 1960s, culminating in the Prague Spring of 1968. As a result, there was an effort to replace the totalitarian syndrome with a syndrome of another hue, with many scholars embarking on a two-pronged study of "Comparative Communism" and change in Communist systems.[6] The various efforts assumed, either explicitly or implicitly, a unidirectional aspect of change, the objective of which was liberalization and/or democratization of Communist systems. While the definition of the concept of change appeared unambiguous and non-controversial, the same could not be said of the concepts of "liberalization" versus "democratization." One possible way of avoiding some of the conceptual pitfalls would be to disaggregate the major synthetic variables used by Brzezinski and others, and to take a look at the component parts. The final conclusion may very well be identical to that reached by using aggregate variables, but in addition to offering a more detailed insight into the workings of the Communist systems, the disaggregated model is likely to lend itself better to research.

The suggested approach is not without pitfalls of its own. The application of a dozen or so variables instead of three or four may indeed give a more detailed picture of the situation on the eve of the major systemic change, but the final judgment is still not devoid of a certain degree of arbitrariness. The same applies to the selection of the "strategic" variables, some of which can hardly be considered independent. Finally, disaggregation alone -- without assigning relative weights to particular variables -- is not very helpful since the various conditions that obtained in individual countries had an unequal impact on the process of democratization. To sum up, the "model" presented below should be considered, above all, as a rather simplistic effort at model building and at postulating some hypotheses regarding the democratic transformation in selected East Central European countries.

The Dynamics of Transition to Democracy

Before suggesting an approach that would more systematically explain the process of transition to democracy, some observations must be made about the controversy regarding the character of that change, as between "liberalization" and "democratization."[7] The former may be viewed as being simply synonymous with de-Stalinization: the essentials of the system remain unchanged, the impulse for the reforms comes usually from above, the stimulus for change often comes from the outside, and the whole process meets with relatively little resistance from the rulers. In contrast, at least until most recently, "democratization" has been a much less frequent phenomenon, characterized by far more drastic political and institutional changes, by strong grass roots pressures and by often fierce resistance from within the system. Rather than deal with the controversy, I shall define a "democratized" system, seen as a culmination of the process of democratic transition, as a system providing for free and regular elections; containing a significant measure of pluralism, including the presence of independent parties; a high degree of political and economic decentralization, and freedom of expression by the system's participants.[8]

In order to trace the path taken by the three polities to reach their goal of a democratized system, some time ago I postulated a "paradigm of democratic transition" or a check list of twelve variables divided into two broad groups and three major categories.[9] Table 11.1 presents the variables involved in this paradigm of democratic transition:

Table 11.1 Paradigm of Democratic Transitions

Exogenous Conditions
1. Changing Attitude of the Soviet Union

Endogenous Conditions

Background Conditions
2. Economic Difficulties
3. Divisions within the Party
4. Re-emergence of Civil Society
5. Political Reforms

Changeover Conditions
6. Changes in the Party
7. Changes in the Government
8. Changes in the Economy

Democratization Conditions
9. Emergence of Pluralism
10. Free Elections
11. Freedom of Expression
12. Economic Decentralization

The two broad groups refer to exogenous and endogenous conditions, embracing two sets of external and internal variables. The first narrower category, "background conditions," lists the conditions and processes existing or taking place on the eve of a major change in the system. It is implicitly assumed that, taken together, these conditions and processes trigger a transition to the second stage in the democratic transformation, which I call "changeover conditions." This category includes various steps which occur throughout the system and which ultimately cause the appearance of the final stage in the process, that of democratization itself. The subset of "democratization conditions" lists the key changes in the system which in the final analysis determine whether democratization has a chance of becoming consolidated.[10] In other words, democratization in this context may be seen as a dependent variable with the other twelve variables assumed to be independent of each other.

In Table 11.2, which follows, each variable of the paradigm is assigned a rank of "high," "moderate," and "low," and similar rankings are given to each of the three major categories of conditions. Finally, an overall judgment is made with regard to the main question -- the chances of a lasting and successful democratization in each of the three states.

One of the major problems connected with the use of the paradigm is the time dimension. For example, in discussing the background conditions, should one consider one, two or three years? Clearly, the larger the time span, the longer the number of conditions one is bound to consider and the greater the divergence or similarity between the developments in each country. It is also obvious that the rate of change in different countries, however measured, was different. Whatever the ultimate choice, it was likely to involve considerable arbitrariness.

Rather than having to choose among different degrees of arbitrariness, I decided to cut the Gordian knot and limit the "background conditions" to the period 1981-1985, the "changeover conditions" to the three-year period from 1985 to 1988, and the "democratization conditions" to the critical two year period, 1988-1990. The imposition of martial law in Poland in 1981 may be seen as a reaffirmation of Moscow's hard line vis-a-vis its junior allies in an attempt to maintain the cohesion of the bloc. Gorbachev's ascent to power in the Kremlin in March 1985 was obviously an important watershed event with critical implications for the region as a whole. Finally, 1988 witnessed the beginning of the process of democratization, as shown by the ouster of Janos Kadar in Hungary, coming on the heels of a similar ouster of Gustav Husak in Czechoslovakia, and the announcement of Round Table negotiations between the government and Solidarity in Poland in September of that year. Finally, the process of dismantling the Communist system hit its stride in 1990 in every single East Central European country except Albania and, to some extent, Yugoslavia.

Table 11.2 Democratization in Czechoslovakia, Hungary, and Poland
1981-1990

	Czechoslovakia	Hungary	Poland
Exogenous Conditions: 1981-1990			
1. Changing Attitude of the Soviet Union	low	moderate	moderate
Endogenous Conditions: 1981-1990			
Background Conditions: 1981-1985			
2. Economic Difficulties	moderate-low	moderate	high
3. Divisions within the Party	moderate	moderate	moderate
4. Re-emergence of Civil Society	moderate	high	high
5. Political Reforms	low	moderate	moderate-high
Total judgment	moderate-low	moderate	moderate-high
Changeover Conditions: 1985-1988			
6. Changes in the Communist Party	moderate-high	high	moderate-low
7. Changes in the Government	moderate	moderate	moderate
8. Changes in the Economy	moderate	high	high
Total judgment	moderate	high	moderate
Democratization Conditions: 1988-1990			
9. Emergence of Pluralism	high	high	high-moderate
10. Free Elections	moderate	high	high
11. Freedom of Expression	moderate	high	high
12. Economic Decentralization	moderate	moderate	high
Total judgment	moderate	high	high
Probability of Achieving a Democracy	moderate	high	high

The Process of Democratization: Exogenous Conditions

Changing Attitude of the Soviet Union

Much has been written about Soviet attitudes and objectives vis-a-vis East Central Europe prior to the 1980s.[11] It is generally agreed, however, that at the beginning of the eighties, East Central Europe was no longer the primary target of Soviet interests and that its centrality to the Kremlin gradually declined. This is not to say that the region was no longer important for the USSR; it only meant that, as Soviet interests and capabilities expanded, East Central Europe diminished in relative importance. The strategic weapons buildup, the development of a blue water navy, and the creation of long-range airlift capacity had transformed the Soviet Union into a global power whose interests ranged far beyond its immediate periphery.

With this in mind, the four year period 1981-1985, which saw four successive leaders in the Kremlin, is even today hard to categorize. Andropov was viewed, at least by the Hungarians, as essentially sympathetic to East Central Europe, and the opposite appeared true for Chernenko, who was generally seen as Brezhnev's *alter ego*.

It was assumed that Gorbachev would pay more attention to the region than his predecessors. The early signals out of Moscow suggested that the new Soviet leader might assume a tough stand vis-a-vis East Central Europe. It was thought, for example, that Gorbachev would give top priority to the replacement of most local leaders, who could be easily blamed for the difficulties faced by the respective states. Surprisingly, even though several East Central European Communist parties held their congresses in 1985 and 1986 -- which would have provided an opportunity for a wholesale ouster of the aging leaders -- no one was actually forced to retire. The common explanation was that Gorbachev had his mind set on other things -- rapprochement with the United States, Western Europe and China and *perestroika* at home -- and that East Central Europe was again relegated to the back burner, at least for the time being. The Kremlin's seeming indifference toward the region was also interpreted by some of the local leaders as giving them a free hand to pursue their policies at will, without Moscow's interference. For Hungary and Poland this meant continuing their policies of liberalization. While in Czechoslovakia things appeared frozen, it was obvious that even there the seeds of discontent were being planted with increasing frequency.

The remainder of the eighties has shown rather conclusively that there has been a veritable sea change in the Kremlin's *modus operandi* vis-a-vis East Central Europe, in the style and manner of making policy by the Soviet leadership, especially on the bilateral level, and in the general atmosphere of conducting business in the Warsaw Pact and CMEA. Gone was the arrogance of Brezhnev allowing his military overlord, Marshal Kulikov to treat Poland as Moscow's fiefdom, in a manner reminiscent of Stalin's days. Chernenko's disapproval of East Central European bridge-building to West Germany was replaced by a much more permissive Soviet attitude. Moreover, serious questions have been raised in both East and West challenging the continuing validity of the "Brezhnev Doctrine" which was perceived as governing Soviet-East Central European relations ever since 1968. Although Gorbachev for a rather long time rather carefully avoided making unequivocal statements about the "Doctrine," his advisers and spokesmen went to great pains to create the impression that the "Brezhnev Doctrine" was essentially dead. Gorbachev himself, by formally denying Soviet primacy in the Warsaw Pact, at least implicitly confirmed that view.

The "new thinking" in the general area of Soviet-East Central European relations affected also the relationship between the USSR and the individual countries. A truly striking change, for example, could be observed in the relationship between Moscow and Warsaw. General Jaruzelski, who only a few years earlier was viewed by the Kremlin as a black sheep in the East Central European flock, became Gorbachev's strongest and closest friend. Kadar also continued as Gorbachev's close ally, at least until his replacement by Karoly Grosz. In contrast, there was no change in Gorbachev's attitude toward Husak, which continued cool on both sides. It may be assumed that it was that coolness that contributed to Husak's ouster from Czechoslovak party leadership and his replacement by Milos Jakes in December, 1987.

By mid-1988 the official Soviet attitude toward the region could be summarized as follows:[12]

-- economically, East Central Europe was rapidly approaching a critical stage, and only massive foreign economic aid (a new "Marshall Plan") could avert total disaster;

-- the USSR, itself faced with growing economic difficulties, was not in the position to provide such aid, which had to come from the West;

-- despite its economic problems, East Central Europe continued to be a key factor in the matrix of US-Soviet relations and an economic collapse in the region could seriously affect the future of East-West detente. If Washington were interested in maintaining and enhancing that detente, the United States and Western Europe had to bail out East Central Europe in order to prevent a catastrophe;

-- if economic reforms necessitated political reforms in the region, the Kremlin implicitly promised not to interfere with the process of liberalization in the name of maintaining political stability in the bloc.

The tenor of the message, especially of its last part, was unmistakable and obviously not lost on the inhabitants of the region. Starting with Poland, the strikes led by Solidarity in the spring and early fall of 1988 resulted in the initiation of a dialogue between the government and the opposition, which received the tacit blessing of the Kremlin, clearly concerned with the threat of the growing political and economic unrest in the country. The dialogue, which ultimately ended in the so-called Round Table negotiations, led to the striking Solidarity victory in the June, 1989 elections and the establishment of the first non-Communist government in East Central Europe in more than forty years. Soon thereafter the world was treated to the rather extraordinary spectacle of Vladimir Kryuchkov, the head of the KGB, bestowing official Soviet blessing on Prime Minister Tadeusz Mazowiecki.

The crucial decision by the Hungarian government in May, 1989, to open the country's border with Austria, which resulted in a mass exodus of East Germans to West Germany and which ultimately contributed in a major way to the downfall of the Honecker regime, must have been made with Moscow's tacit approval. Also, the parallel disintegration of the

Hungarian party, followed by the elections of March-April, 1990, was met with seeming indifference on the part of the Kremlin.

It was then Czechoslovakia's turn. Initially, it was assumed throughout the region that, despite the obvious coolness between Gorbachev and Jakes and despite the impact of the East German exodus, some of which was channeled through Prague, the conservative Czechoslovak government, which until then paid only reluctant lip service to *perestroika*, would manage to survive at the expense of some minor concessions. This was not to be. When the end of the Communist regime came in November, 1989, it came swiftly. So swiftly, in fact, that for some time after that there were rumors that the ouster of Jakes was somehow either engineered by, or orchestrated with, the Soviets.[13]

To conclude, this short summary strongly suggests that early in the second half of the 1980s, the new Soviet leadership under Gorbachev decided to unburden itself of East Central Europe, for reasons spelled out above. It may also be postulated that, while giving green light to the reformers in the individual countries, Gorbachev never expected that this decision would amount to issuing a death warrant to the ruling Communist parties. Most likely, he assumed that having embraced *perestroika* the parties would retain their leading role. This proved to be a fatal mistake from Moscow's point of view. It simply opened the door to democratic transformation of the East Central European political and economic systems.

The Process of Democratization: Endogenous Conditions

Background Conditions

Economic Difficulties Although all three countries in question suffered from a deteriorating economic situation, there were some interesting contrasts among them.

Despite the fact that in the early eighties Czechoslovakia lost its lead to East Germany as the most efficient economy in CMEA, it succeeded rather well in maintaining a reasonable living standard for its population, thus avoiding mass discontent so characteristic of Poland and, to a much lesser degree, of Hungary. Unlike its neighbors, Czechoslovakia borrowed relatively little from the West during the 1970s and, as a result, unlike Hungary and Poland was not saddled with a huge burden of hard currency debt. On the other hand, the Czechoslovak industry, deprived of Western know-how and technology, was becoming rapidly obsolete, with the resulting loss of efficiency and competitiveness in foreign markets. Being also more dependent than Hungary and Poland on the USSR as a source of raw materials and purchaser of its industrial products, Czechoslovakia suffered more from the vagaries of Soviet economic policy.

Once a pioneer in economic reforms, Czechoslovakia in the early 1980s fell behind the other two countries in trying to modernize its industry and to enhance the organization and management of its economy. Despite occasional calls for reforms, reminiscent of the period 1963-1966, the government, still largely run by the enemies of the "Prague Spring," refused to budge, afraid of a potential spillover from the economic to the political arena.

To sum up, although hardly an economic basket case such as Poland, Czechoslovakia in the first half of the decade entered a period of stagnation, with few prospects for improvement. That the living standard did not decline sharply was largely due to the fact that the country's population remained practically stationary. Still, the future looked bleak and Czechoslovakia's economic deterioration was not lost on its intellectuals and its youth, the two groups that spearheaded the democratization drive of 1968.[14]

It was Hungary that replaced Czechoslovakia in 1968 as the leader in the economic reforms. The country also borrowed heavily from the West in the course of the 1970s, so much so that a decade later it ended up with the highest per capita hard currency debt in East Central Europe. Nonetheless, the economic reforms have continued, although the ultimate result proved to be disappointing.

The failure of reforms to achieve greater progress was due to both internal and external causes. At home, after more than fifteen years, the reformers still refused to face such fundamental issues as privatization, establishment of a competitive free market system, or full convertibility of Hungarian currency. Apart from standard bureaucratic resistance, there was a deeply rooted fear of unemployment accompanied by inflation which, in the final analysis prevented the implementation of the reforms.

Of all the CMEA members, Hungary was the country most dependent on foreign trade and credits and, therefore, it was particularly badly hit by the Western credit squeeze in the wake of Polish martial law of 1981, by trade restrictions gradually being imposed by the European Economic Community, and by the failure of CMEA to expand trade among its members.

The ultimate result was a steady decline in Hungary's economic performance in the first half of the 1980s, reflected in a decline of its GNP, a reduction in the volume of foreign trade, and growing difficulties in obtaining key imports of energy and raw materials from the USSR. At the same time, there was a visible increase in the rate of inflation. Hungarian consumers, who until then enjoyed a living standard second only to East Germany, greeted the decline with considerable dismay. There is little doubt that they blamed the Kadar government for their plight.

The striking deterioration in Poland's economic situation in the aftermath of martial law has been well documented in the literature.[15] Probably the most shocking was the staggering decline in the country's GNP, caused mainly by a sharp fall in industrial production. Despite the rather impressive performance of the farm sector, which showed a steady growth throughout the period, there was a significant reduction in the living standard and household consumption, pushing them back to the levels of the 1970s. To add insult to injury, food rationing was introduced by the Jaruzelski regime amid growing fears that it may not be possible to maintain the meager rations in the long run.

On top of that, Poland's huge hard currency debt kept growing, mostly because of the country's inability to keep up with interest payments. The US-sponsored embargo on credits and various punitive trade sanctions made the situation worse. The government tried to deal with it partly through drastic price reforms intended to reduce inflationary pressure, and partly through the announcement of an economic reform modeled after that of Hungary. During martial law, in contrast to its strong opposition to prior reforms in the past, the Polish population sullenly accepted the steep rise in consumer good prices without offering any resistance. It was soon apparent that both measures proved ineffective. By the middle of the 1980s the overall economic situation was worse than ever.

Thus, there was little doubt that the economic deterioration in all three countries was beginning to have a serious impact on the mood of the respective populations. Whereas Czechoslovakia and Hungary were faced with the problem of relative deprivation, Poland had to deal with the challenge of absolute deprivation. There was little or no hope of an early improvement. To no one's surprise, there was growing tension throughout the region.

Divisions within the Party Following the purge of the party in the aftermath of the Soviet invasion in August, 1968, which resulted in a sharp reduction in its numerical strength, it appeared that the cleansed Czechoslovak party succeeded in re-establishing unity. This was not the case, however, and under the surface the old antagonisms and resentments, which antedated the "Prague Spring," survived, albeit at a lower level of intensity. The post-1968 purge got rid of the liberal faction identified with Alexander Dubcek; it did not really affect the centrist and conservative factions, which for the next decade or so managed to maintain an uneasy coexistence, carefully avoiding a direct confrontation.

The centrist group, led by Gustav Husak, enjoyed the support of Moscow, and as long as Brezhnev remained in power, it felt reasonably secure. The hardliners, headed by Vasil Bilak, were waiting in the wings, hoping that an imminent changeover in the Kremlin would propel them to power in Prague. In time, a third faction made its appearance on the political scene. Led by Prime minister Lubomir Strougal, it consisted primarily of technocrats who from the outset presented themselves as pragmatists, while maintaining a low political profile. Thus, although superficially the Czechoslovak party managed to display a high degree of unity, it soon turned out that the tension within the oligarchy was rising steadily.

The situation within the Hungarian party was less dramatic, but in the early 1980s it became clear that the unity so carefully engineered by Janos Kadar as part of his post-1956 reconciliation campaign was falling apart. The source of the growing discontent was Kadar himself, who was approaching the 30th anniversary of his rule in 1986. While his success in largely healing the wounds caused by the 1956 revolt could not be denied, it was becoming obvious that Kadar was losing his touch. He was no longer capable of pursuing a policy of innovation and reforms, so characteristic of his earlier days. Yet, in a fashion reminiscent of other Communist leaders, he refused to quit, thus blocking access to power of younger, more pragmatic, yet no less ambitious members of the new Communist elite.

Not surprisingly, his stubborn clinging to power caused considerable resentment within the oligarchy. Although during the first half of the 1980s none of the potential aspirants felt confident enough to challenge Kadar, his days were clearly numbered. It was only a matter of time before a new leadership was to assume power in Budapest.

The imposition of military rule succeeded in defusing much of the intra-party conflict, so visible in Poland in 1980-1981. Despite some resentment of the military rulers, both the party's *apparat* and its rank and file realized only too well that, but for martial law, their situation in the post-1981 period would have been much more difficult.

The seeming party unity did not last long, and soon the old differences between the hard- and softliners appeared as wide as ever. The former group was closely identified with Moscow, and as long as Brezhnev was alive, it could not be touched. With the changeover in the Kremlin, the traditional links began to weaken. Neither Andropov nor Chernenko raised serious objections to Jaruzelski's purge of the hardliners in the wake of the highly publicized assassination of Reverend Jerzy Popieluszko. The Tenth Party Congress in June, 1986, attended by Gorbachev, which witnessed a major reshuffling in both the Politburo and the Central Committee, seemed to provide a good testimony to Jaruzelski's ability to control the party. This proved to be a false impression when less than two years later, several members of the ruling oligarchy, viewed as loyal and reliable, strongly resisted the opening of a dialogue between the party and the opposition. Hence, many appearances to the contrary, the Polish party was as deeply divided as ever.

To sum up, while the intra-party squabble in Czechoslovakia was kept under wraps by the leadership, the rising divisions within the Hungarian and Polish parties could not be contained and came to the surface in the mid-1980s. Even at that time, however, no one could predict that the intra-party conflict would ultimately lead to a demise of communism in the region.

Re-emergence of Civil Society   Although the notion of civil society has been correctly characterized as "highly unclear and contested,"[16] the gradual re-emergence of civil society, defined as a "web of autonomous associations, independent of the state, which bound citizens together in matters of common concern, and by their existence or action could have an effect on public policy,"[17] strongly reflected in a progressing alienation of intellectuals and youth, has been a constant feature of the political and cultural scene in all three countries since the mid-1950s.[18] After all, it was the intellectuals and the youth who contributed signally to the events of "Polish October" and the outbreak of the revolt in Hungary in 1956. In the same vein, the origins of the "Prague Spring" of 1968 were rooted in the growing dissatisfaction of Czechoslovak intellectuals and students. Although in time the leadership of the anti-Communist opposition, at least in Poland, was handed over to the workers, the largely passive resistance on the part of the intellectual elite, often supported by the increasingly frustrated and disillusioned youth, continued to play an important political role in all three countries.

Although several best-known Czechoslovak writers and film makers decided to emigrate to the West after the defeat of the "Prague Spring," many equally known individuals remained. Soon they became the focus of anti-Communist resistance, as manifested by their founding of "Charta 77." In time, their undisputed leader became Vaclav Havel, the future president of the country, who despite several prison terms succeeded in defying the authorities until the end of the Communist rule. The intellectual opposition continued to be supported by the youth, which soon brought on itself the wrath of the regime, as illustrated by the fierce attack against the youthful Czechoslovak jazz players, which ultimately proved to be a major embarrassment to the regime.

The intellectual ferment among Hungarian intellectuals was just as strong.[19] Kadar's policy of benign neglect, including relaxation of censorship, allowed the writers, journalists and other intellectuals to voice their discontent without much fear of retribution. As a result, for the first time in three decades, such previously banned topics as the origin of the Hungarian revolt of 1956 and the role of Imre Nagy, began to be freely discussed, initially among the narrow circles of intellectuals, but in time in mass media, resulting in the symbolic reburial of Nagy and a fundamental reappraisal of the revolt. The government's belated efforts to limit the discourse only added fuel to the escalating discontent. Although there is not much evidence of the Hungarian youth being actively engaged in opposition activities, there were increasing signs that it also was rapidly politicized on the side of the opponents of the system.

Polish intellectuals, who seemingly lost the leadership of the opposition to the industrial workers at the time of the Baltic Coast riots of December, 1970, returned to the forefront of anti-regime activities as the moving spirits behind the Worker's Defense Committee (KOR), formed in 1976. Not surprisingly, many of the leading intellectuals acted as advisers, editors or spokesmen of Solidarity. Again, not surprisingly, most of them were arrested by the *junta* in December, 1981, and kept interned for some time.[20]

As part of a comprehensive house cleaning, the martial law authorities ordered the dissolution of various associations representing intellectuals and students and replaced them with the discredited "transmission belts," a throwback to the Stalinist days. Following their release from imprisonment, most of the intellectuals continued their resistance underground, and several of them were ultimately rearrested. As a result, the alienation of both these key groups in the mid-1980s was higher than ever.

The escalating discontent among the intellectuals and youth groups in all three countries represented a major threat to the established regimes. The Communist rulers understood only too well the special position of the intellectuals in their respective societies, and the rulers also remembered the crucial role played by intellectuals and the youth in the previous crises. All attempts to modify or bribe them failed. A head-on collision appeared inevitable.

Political Reforms It may be assumed that at least some members of the East European ruling oligarchies were aware of de Tocqueville's prophetic statement that no authoritarian government is more vulnerable than that which begins to offer concessions to the disgruntled population.[21] Possibly because of that, with the exception of Poland, and, to some extent, Hungary, none of the countries attempted to introduce political reforms despite mounting pressure from the re-emerging civil society.

The best example of a seemingly well-entrenched regime which hoped to be able to ride out the storm was provided by the Husak government, which steadfastly refused to offer any political concessions, not even cosmetic ones.[22] However, even there some cracks began to appear on the seemingly monolithic surface, as illustrated by the openly voiced dissatisfaction with the stationing of new Soviet missiles being deployed on Czechoslovak territory in 1983. This surprising reaction strongly implied that Prague was no longer willing to maintain the traditional submissive stance vis-a-vis the Kremlin. Although the objection to missiles was not followed by any political reforms, it created a climate favorable to future changes.

Hungary continued its step-by-step, cautious approach to political and economic reforms. July, 1983, witnessed the approval of an amendment to electoral law making multiple candidacies obligatory in national and local elections. In March, 1985, the Thirteenth Congress of the Hungarian Communist Party went on record confirming the importance of the reform course. Altogether, there were strong indications that, in the foreseeable future, the country would pursue its incremental pragmatic policy of reforms.

The Polish situation was strikingly different. Within a year of the imposition of martial law, it became clear that the Jaruzelski regime, right from the start, was trying to restore some degree of political normalcy. Among the most important steps in that endeavor were the suspension and then the abolition of martial law; a continuing flirtation with the Church; the drastic purge of the security apparatus in 1984; and plans for a reform of the electoral laws, including the possibility of a popular referendum, the first one since 1946. Finally, the far-reaching amnesty resulted in freeing some of the best-known opposition leaders. It was a most surprising event and a good testimony to the *junta* leaders' eagerness to resume some kind of a dialogue with the opponents of the regime.

Looking back at the first half of the eighties, one got the strong impression that whereas Poland was clearly experiencing a snowballing crisis on all counts, the situation in Czechoslovakia and Hungary resembled a deceptive calm before the storm. The economy in all three countries was ailing. The party seemed hopelessly divided and the two key groups -- the intellectuals and youth -- were as alienated as ever, if not more so. The attempted political concessions led nowhere and it was becoming increasingly clear that a second stage in the democratization process was about to begin.

Changeover Conditions

Changes in the Party While the three-year period, 1985-1988, produced relatively few changes at the top of the Polish party hierarchy, it witnessed momentous reshuffling in the leadership of the Czechoslovak and Hungarian parties.

In Czechoslovakia, Husak's relinquishing of the party leadership in December, 1987 preceded Kadar's departure in Hungary by six months. However, his replacement by Jakes, one of the most conservative survivors of the "Prague Spring," did not augur well for the chances of liberalization -- far from it. On the other hand, Husak's willingness to step down after 18 years in power was bound to have serious repercussions on the ruling party as much, if not more so, than Kadar's resignation after almost 32 years as Hungarian leader. By hindsight, during his tenure in office Husak has managed rather skillfully to play both sides -- the conservatives and the moderates -- against the middle. His successor would not likely prove equally adept at the balancing act. Still, Jakes' open refusal to accept *perestroika* strongly suggested that the hardliners would not give in.

In Hungary, the process of the party's disintegration began in 1986 when the disgruntled intellectuals staged a frontal attack on Kadar on the occasion of the 30th anniversary of the revolution of 1956. Growing dissatisfaction with Kadar's stubborn resistance to quit his post ultimately resulted in his being forced out in May, 1988. The new party leader, Karoly Grosz and his largely new Politburo were described as being "hesitant and low in authority,"[23] with the result that, toward the end of the year, new actors such as Imre Pozsgay and others began to attract public attention.

In Poland, most of the members of the party hierarchy, elected with Gorbachev's blessing at the Tenth Party Congress in June, 1986, were strongly conservative and opposed to an opening of the Round Table discussions which were to begin in early 1989. Jaruzelski, who continued as party leader, and who, in sharp contrast to the past, was able to develop cordial relations with the new occupant of the Kremlin, was ready for a showdown. In January, 1989 he succeeded in packing both the Politburo and the Central Committee with several of his liberal allies who favored a dialogue with Solidarity.

To sum up, between 1985 and 1988, the intra-party conflict which continued escalating in the early part of the decade finally surfaced, especially in Czechoslovakia and Hungary, with incalculable consequences for the democratic transition.

Changes in the Government   In Czechoslovakia, Prime Minister Strougal, who held his job for 18 years and who was generally viewed as the leader of a pragmatist faction favoring reforms, was ousted in October, 1988. In contrast to the changes in the Hungarian and Polish governments, which also took place in 1988, both of which were interpreted as victories for the reformers, Strougal's departure and his replacement by Ladislav Adamec, identified as a technocrat and a member of the post-1968 *nomenklatura*, could hardly be seen as an important step in the direction of democratization.

Hungary also experienced changes in its government. In June, 1987, Grosz, the future party leader, became Prime Minister. After his elevation to the party leadership, his place at the head of the government was taken by the relatively unknown Miklos Nemeth. The presence in the government of such well known reformers as Pozsgay and Rezso Nyers provided a guarantee that the new regime would maintain if not strengthen its commitment to liberal political and economic reforms.

The period 1985-1988 also witnessed two major changes in the Polish government. In 1985 General Jaruzelski, while retaining his party leadership, was replaced as Prime Minister by Zdzislaw Messner, who three years later was forced to resign in favor of Mieczyslaw Rakowski. He, in turn, finally agreed to open a dialogue with the opposition headed by Solidarity leader, Lech Walesa. The new Premier made no changes in the key ministries of defense and interior, which strongly suggested that the two generals in charge -- Czeslaw Kiszczak (Interior) and Florian Siwicki (Defense) supported the bridge-building policy favored by Jaruzelski. In fact, it was Kiszczak who not only endorsed the Round Table negotiations but also made sure that they were brought to a successful conclusion in April, 1989.

In light of the above, it may be concluded that the significant changes in the government, as much as the changes at the top of the party hierarchy, provided a powerful stimulus to the process of democratization, especially in Hungary and Poland, much less so in Czechoslovakia. By the end of 1988, it was becoming increasingly clear that, at least in the former two countries, the end of communism was in sight, save for a last minute intervention by the Kremlin which, alas, was not coming. While the process of systemic disintegration in Czechoslovakia was less visible, the events of November, 1989 pointed to the fact that also in that country the 40-year long Communist rule was on the verge of collapse.

Changes in the Economy   The only thing that could be said about the economic situation in all three countries was that it showed little or no improvement between 1985 and 1988 and that the malaise continued unabated.[24] Neither the economic reforms supposedly being implemented or promised, nor various ad hoc income and price policies managed to stop the rot. The government in Prague, Budapest, and Warsaw, sharply divided and lacking in confidence, appeared simply too weak to implement tough measures needed to produce an economic turnaround. Still, at least in both Czechoslovakia and Hungary, the economic deterioration did not reach the crisis level experienced by Poland.

In that country, toward the end of 1988 it was clear to all, including the authorities, that unless some drastic measures were taken soon, Poland might well face another round of angry explosions and confrontations in the coming winter, comparable to the strikes in the spring and early fall of 1988, which were settled with considerable difficulty with the help of Solidarity. The government's proposal to start Round Table negotiations in early 1989 must be seen in that light. As has been the case in the past, in this particular respect Poland was once again ahead of its neighbors, but as time went on, the gap between it and the other two countries was narrowing rapidly.

Democratization Conditions

Emergence of Pluralism The dialogue between the Communist regime and the opposition in Poland in the form of the Round Table negotiations, resulted in April, 1989, in an agreement to hold parliamentary elections in June of that year. The announcement of a new electoral law provided a powerful stimulus to the formation of new political parties and organizations. Although the law still largely favored the Communist party and the two "satellite" parties, nonetheless it provided an opportunity, in the spring and summer of 1989, for a veritable explosion in the number of political parties, clubs, associations and interest groups of all hues, which mushroomed following the passage of a new law on associations. As a result, in the second half of 1989, Poland appeared for all practical purposes to be a free, pluralistic polity, with political parties and clubs, labor unions, and youth associations competing with each other for support and membership. The process of recreating civil society was essentially completed.

The same was largely true for both Hungary and Czechoslovakia. In Hungary, the Round Table conference which met in June, 1989, reflected the presence of powerful pluralistic tendencies, representing a wide spectrum of opinions. No less than nine opposition groupings sat across from the Communist party, not to mention various other groups which also demanded to be heard.[25]

In Czechoslovakia, the pluralistic explosion followed rather than preceded the collapse of the Communist rule in November, 1989, but once it got under way it soon caught up with the situation in Hungary and Poland. The presence of an increasing vocal Slovak minority further strengthened the growth of political pluralism.

Free Elections The most important result of Round Table discussions in Hungary and Poland and intra-party negotiations in Czechoslovakia was the agreement to hold parliamentary and presidential elections in 1989-1990. The first country to hold parliamentary elections was Poland. However, in contrast to the other two countries, the elections which took place in June, 1989 were technically not entirely free. The anti-Communist opposition, Solidarity, was allocated only 35% of the seats in the lower house (*Sejm*), the rest going to the Communists and their allies. Only the election to the upper chamber, the Senate, was left unrestricted. The results of the elections surprised everyone. Solidarity swept the senatorial races and also achieved striking success in the *Sejm* elections. The Communist party performed poorly and, as a result, its heretofore loyal puppet allies switched sides and allowed Solidarity to form the first non-Communist government in Eastern Europe in more than 40 years.

Parliamentary elections held in Hungary in March and April, 1990 were contested by 28 parties, among which only six received a significant share of popular vote.[26] The center-right party, the Hungarian Democratic Forum, which gained the plurality of the vote, managed to form a government in alliance with two smaller parties.

Finally, 22 parties competed in the Czechoslovak parliamentary elections in June, 1990.[27] Predictably, the big winner was the Civic Forum and its Slovak equivalent, Public Against Violence, which between them gained absolute majority in the Federal Assembly.

The other step in the electoral process in all three countries was the presidential election. In Czechoslovakia it actually preceded the parliamentary elections and to no one's surprise, at the end of December, 1989 the well-known leader of the anti-Communist opposition, Vaclav Havel, was elected president by the Federal Assembly, in which the Communists still retained majority. In Hungary, the newly elected National Assembly chose Arpad Goncz, a well-known dissident leader, to be president in August, 1990.

The most exciting election took place in Poland in November-December, 1990. Lech Walesa, the leader of Solidarity, running in the field of six candidates, including Prime Minister Mazowiecki, astonishingly enough was forced into a run-off by a dark horse candidate, who succeeded in attracting enough votes to defeat the Premier. In the second round, Walesa easily defeated his opponent, thus becoming the first popularly elected president in the region.

Thus, it can be seen that holding free elections, seen as one of the necessary conditions for consolidation of democracy, was amply fulfilled in all three countries. The only disquieting aspect of it was the rather low voters turnout, especially in Hungary and Poland, which did not augur too well for the future of the parliamentary system.

Freedom of Expression It has long been accepted that strict governmental control over mass media and all other artistic and cultural activities was one of the fundamental principles of Communist rule. It is also equally well known that it was the relaxation of those controls that largely precipitated the 1956 upheavals in Hungary and Poland and that the "Prague Spring" of 1968 was often referred to as a "revolution by mass media."

The record shows that, at least in Hungary and Poland during the 1980s, the censors behaved selectively, allowing different degrees of freedom to different mass media. Moreover, in Poland, the first half of the decade witnessed an explosion in the number of clandestinely published books and periodicals, known collectively as the "second circulation." As a result, on the eve of the momentous changes in 1988-1989, censorship in Hungary and Poland *de facto* disappeared in the case of books and periodicals, and its use with respect to daily newspapers and some weeklies became even more selective and less oppressive than in the past. In Czechoslovakia, the process of jettisoning government media controls got under way in 1989, but it was not really until after the overthrow of the Communist regime in November of that year that the censorship disappeared for good.

Thus, the overthrow of communism and the beginning of the new democratic rule did not really bring about radical changes in this respect. The few remaining government controls over the media were lifted and in Poland the distinction between the legal and semi- or illegal publications ceased overnight.

The process of democratization, accompanied by a rapid proliferation of political parties and interest groups, was paralleled by an equally fast growth in the number of newspapers and periodicals representing all points of view, from left to right. The administration of state television and radio networks was purged and replaced by new personnel, committed to the upholding of democratic values and to the freedom of the press and the airwaves, which in itself represented a significant political reform.

Economic Decentralization As pointed out earlier, during the changeover period of 1988-1989, it appeared that the various governments were so preoccupied with their own survival that they had little or no time to do something about the deteriorating economic situation. This was particularly true in the case of Czechoslovakia and Hungary which, as suggested earlier, were not in such dire economic straits as Poland. Nonetheless, both countries, and especially Hungary, were aware of the need to get rid of the Soviet-type economic system. The question of radical economic reforms, which were to emphasize decentralization and marketization, was high on the agenda in both states.

As economic conditions in Poland continued deteriorating from 1988 to 1989, ways of improving the economy formed one of the most important topics of the Round Table negotiations. After the Communist defeat in the June, 1989, elections and the creation of the first non-Communist government in the region in more than forty years, perhaps the most important single decision taken by the newly elected parliament concerned the introduction, on January 1, 1990, of a competitive free market system, the freeing of prices and wages, abolition of most of the governmental subsidies, and introduction of internal convertibility of Polish currency. This was strong and unprecedented medicine, but after years if not decades of indecision, the leaders of all political parties and labor unions agreed that extraordinary measures were needed to restore some semblance of normalcy to the economy. The impact of that decision on the future of democracy in Poland could not be underestimated.

Conclusion

The question raised at the outset and discussed throughout this paper concerned the probability of the various changes, processes and reforms taking place in Czechoslovakia, Hungary, and Poland since 1985 resulting in the emergence of a democratic system in all three countries. As was discussed above, the period 1985-1990 was not the only period in the post-World II history of these three nations in which an attempt was made to introduce liberal or democratic reforms. Similar efforts were undertaken in Czechoslovakia in 1968, in Hungary in 1956, and in Poland in 1956, and 1980-1981. As is well known, they all met with failure rather than success. The question is why?

In trying to answer this question as well as the question regarding the chances of success in the post-1990 period, one must focus on the similarities and differences between now and then, between the conditions in 1956, 1968, and 1980, and those existing at the end of the 1980s.

I am prepared to argue that the strategic variable present in all four cases that ultimately seemed to guarantee the success of the most recent democratic endeavor was the attitude of the Soviet Union. Neither Khrushchev nor Brezhnev were obviously ready and willing to allow the democratization of East Central Europe, for reasons that are well known and need not to be repeated here . The guardians of the orthodoxy in Moscow, as a rule, exercised tight control over the party leaders in the respective countries and seldom, if ever, allowed divisions within the oligarchies to go too far. Also, as a rule, the successive occupants of the Kremlin tended to maintain a rather conservative stance and, hence, they opposed radical economic and political changes, while providing a safety valve for the growing popular discontent in the form of largely cosmetic and superficial reforms.

One frequently neglected aspect of the rigid Soviet policy toward the three countries concerned Moscow's ability at any given time to manipulate and mobilize its junior allies against a reformist country. The Soviet-led invasion of Czechoslovakia, which included military contingents from several WTO members, provided a good illustration of the Kremlin's policy, as did the fierce opposition by several East Central European states to the 1980-1981 democratic experiment in Poland, spearheaded by Solidarity.

All this changed with the arrival of Gorbachev on the Soviet scene. The hardliners within the various ruling oligarchies could no longer count on being bailed out by their counterparts in the Kremlin and ultimately had to succumb to the pressure of the opposition. Moscow no longer raised objections to economic and political reforms and, in fact, often encouraged their implementation. Finally, whereas in the past nearly all WTO members marched in unison to the Soviet drummer, after 1985, the Warsaw alliance began falling apart and many of its members started going their own way. This, among other things, meant that the spillover effect which in the past tended to hamper democratic reforms, in 1989 actually stimulated them, as illustrated by the example of the Polish Round Table or that of the East German refugees in Prague being allowed to leave freely for West Germany. Thus, there is little doubt that the strategic variable that had a major impact on the process of democratization in the region was the dramatic change in the attitude of the Soviet Union.

Despite its crucial importance, the attitude of benign neglect on the part of the USSR toward the dramatic changes in Eastern Europe was a necessary albeit not a sufficient condition of successful democratization. Had this been the case, the preceding discussion would have been essentially meaningless.

The basic premise of the whole analysis was that although Soviet indifference, reflected in the Kremlin's unwillingness to intervene in the region throughout 1989 ultimately played a crucial role in allowing democratization to succeed, it was clearly not a sufficient condition of success.

To start with, until almost the very end of the Communist downfall in late fall 1989, culminating in the collapse of the German Democratic Republic, the democratic reformers could never be entirely certain about Moscow's intentions. Thus, while *ex post facto* the Soviet inactivity proved critical, it could never be taken entirely for granted.

With this in mind, the presence or absence of endogenous conditions, favoring or deterring democratic transition, appeared equally crucial. It also helped to explain the differences in the rate and character of democratization among the three countries under discussion. Had our analysis embraced also the remaining states in Eastern Europe, the existence of various endogenous conditions would go a long way in clarifying the reasons for democratization in Albania or Romania proceeding at a much slower pace than in Hungary or Poland.

A couple of other questions deserve some attention. One of them is the question of the impact of the West on the democratic transformation of East Central Europe. While this issue deserves a separate treatment, which cannot be accomplished here, it is my view that the direct influence of the West on the process of democratization was relatively insignificant and that its main significance lay in the ability of the West to "mellow" the USSR by making it less paranoid and insecure and more willing to let go of the East Central European buffer zone.

The other question concerns the lasting character of the democratic rule in the three countries. As stated at the very beginning, the purpose of the suggested paradigm was to trace the process of democratic transition with the help of a number of selected variables. The overall conclusion that emerged from the exercise was that, by 1989, that process was essentially accomplished in Czechoslovakia, Hungary, and Poland, where democratic governments were established after more than forty years of Communist rule. However, it would be foolhardy and irresponsible on my part to predict the future of democracy there only two years after its birth. I leave it to others to address this issue and to answer the question whether democracy in East Central Europe is likely to succeed in the foreseeable future.

Notes

1. Leszek Kolakowski, "The Postrevolutionary Hangover," *Journal of Democracy*, Vol. 2, No. 3, Summer 1991, 70.

2. The adjective "revolutionary" has now become the standard Soviet description of changes in East Central Europe. See, Vladmir K. Vokov, "Revolutsionnye Preobrazovaniia w Stranakh Tsentralnoi i Yugo-Vostochnoi Evropy," *Voprosy Istorii*, No. 6, June, 1990, 21-35, and Yuri S. Novopashin, "K Voprosu o Prichinakh Revolutsionnykh Sobitii 1989 g.v. Stranakh Tsentralnoi i Vostoichoi Evropy," (Paper Presented at a Conference on "East Europe and the USSR at a Historical Turning Point," Institute of Slavonic and Balkan Research and the All-Union Znanie Society, Moscow, June 2-9, 1991).

3. See, for example, Hans Modrow, *Aufbruch und Ende* (Berlin: Konkret Literatur Verlag, 1991); Günther Mittag, *Um jeden Preis* (Berlin: Aufbau Verlag, 1991); Gyula Horn, *Freiheit die ich meine* (Hamburg: Hoffmann & Campe, 1991); Krzysztof Dubinski, Magdalenka: Transakcja Epoki (Warsaw: Sylwa, 1990); Mieczyslaw F. Rakowski, *Jak to sie stalo* (Warsaw: BGW, 1991).

4. See, Andrzej Korbonski, "Comparing Liberalization Processes in Eastern Europe," *Comparative Politics*, Vol. 4, No. 2, January, 1972, 231-249; "Liberalization Processes," in Carmelo Mesa-Lago and Carl Beck, eds., *Comparative Socialist Systems: Essays on Politics and Economics* (Pittsburgh: University of Pittsburgh Center for International Studies, 1975), 192-214; and "Reform in Poland," in Ilpyong J. Kim and Jane S. Zacek, eds., *Reform and Transformation in Communist Systems: Comparative Perspectives* (New York: Paragon House, 1991), 241-259.

5. Zbigniew Brzezinski, *The Soviet Bloc*, rev. ed., (Cambridge, MA: Harvard University Press, 1967), 205-206.

6. See, for example, Chalmers Johnson, "Comparing Communist Nations," in Chalmers Johnson, ed., *Change in Communist Systems* (Stanford, CA: Stanford University Press, 1970), 1-32.

7. For an interesting discussion, see Adam Przeworski, *Democracy and the Market* (Cambridge and New York: Cambridge University Press, 1991), 51-88.

8. Philippe C. Schmitter and Terry Lynn Karl, "What Democracy Is. . . and Is Not," *Journal of Democracy*, Vol. 2, No. 3, Summer 1991, 75-87. See also, Valerie Bunce, "The Struggle for Liberal Democracy in Eastern Europe," *World Policy Journal*, Vol. 7, No. 3, Summer 1990, 398-401.

9. For the original paradigm, see Korbonski, "Comparing Liberalization Processes in Eastern Europe," 236.

10. Przeworski, *Democracy and the Market*, 51.

11. The most comprehensive analysis can be found in Sarah Meiklejohn Terry, ed., *Soviet Policy in Eastern Europe* (New Haven and London: Yale University Press, 1984). For a recent Soviet view, see "Sovetskii Soiuz i Strany

Vostochnoi Evropy: Evolutsia i Krusheniie Politicheskikh Rezhimov," (Kruglyi Stol), Istoriia SSSR, No. 1, 1991, 3-68.

12. In early July, 1988, a group of U.S. and Soviet specialists met in Washington, D.C. to discuss the topic of "The Place of Eastern Europe in the Relaxation of Tensions between the USA and the USSR." A partial summary of the Soviet position can be found in "The Soviet Perspective," *Problems of Communism*, Vol. 37, No. 3-4, May-August, 1988, 60-67.

13. R.W. Apple, Jr., "A Soviet Warning on Foot-Dragging is Given to Prague," New York Times, November 16, 1989, and Jim Mann, "Moscow's Push Seen in Prague," Los Angeles Times, November 25, 1989.

14. Vladimir V. Kusin, "Husak's Czechoslovakia and Economic Stagnation," *Problems of Communism*, Vol. 21, No. 3, May-June 1982, 24-37.

15. A latest example can be found in Bartlomiej Kaminski, *The Collapse of State Socialism: The Case of Poland* (Princeton, N.J.: Princeton University Press, 1991).

16. Grzegorz Ekiert, "Democratization Processes in East Central Europe: A Theoretical Reconsideration," *British Journal of Political Science*, Vol. 21, part 3, July 1991, 300.

17. Charles Taylor, "Invoking Civil Society," in Greg Urban and Benjamin Lee, eds., *Working Papers and Proceedings of the Center for Psychosocial Studies* (Chicago, 1990), 1, as cited in Gail Kligman, "Reclaiming the Public: A Reflexion on Recreating Civil Society in Romania," *East European Politics and Society*, Vol. 4, No. 3, Fall 1990, 420.

18. For an interesting discussion of civil society under communism, see Giuseppe de Palma, "Legitimation from the Top to Civil Society:Politico-Cultural Change in Eastern Europe," *World Politics*, Vol. 44, No. 11, October, 1991, 63ff.

19. For a study comparing Hungarian and Polish intellectuals, see Michael D. Kennedy, "The Intelligentsia in the Constitution of Civil Societies and Post-Communist Regimes in Hungary and Poland," The University of Michigan, CSST Working Papers, No. 45, July, 1990.

20. For a comprehensive discussion, see Z.A. Pelczynski, "Solidarity and the 'Rebirth of Civil Society' in Poland," in John Keane, ed., *Civil Society and the State* (London and New York: Verso, 1988), 361-380.

21. ". . . generally speaking, the most perilous moment for a bad government is one when it seeks to mends its ways." Alexis de Tocqueville, *The Old Regime and the French Revolution* (Garden City, N.Y.:Doubleday & Company, 1955), 177.

22. For a discussion of the situation in Czechoslovakia prior to 1988, see Vlad Sobell, "Czechoslovakia: The Legacy of Normalization," *East European Politics and Society*, Vol. 2, No. 1, Winter 1988, 36-68.

23. George Schopflin, "The End of Communism in Eastern Europe," *International Affairs* (London), Vol. 66, No. 1, 1990, 7.

24. For a superior analysis of the economic situation in the three countries, see Pressures for Reform in the East European Economies; Study Papers submitted to the Joint Economic Committee 101st Congress, 1st Session, Vol. II (Washington, D.C.: U.S. Government Printing Office, 1989), 1-51; 84-151; and 186-241.

25. Barnabas Racz, "Political Pluralism in Hungary: the 1990 Parliamentary Elections," *Soviet Studies*, Vol. 43, No. 1, 1991, 112.

26. Janos Kis, "Postcommunist Politics in Hungary," *Journal of Democracy*, Vol. 2, No. 3, Summer 1991, 3-15.

27. Karel Vodicka, "Die neue Parteilandschaft in der Tschechoslovakei," *Osteuropa*, Vol. 41, No. 2, February, 1991, 150.

12

Democratization in the Multinational State of Yugoslavia

Barbara Jelavich

Although the end of Communist rule throughout Eastern Europe has inevitably been accompanied by internal stresses and strains, in Yugoslavia political change has resulted in civil war and a breakup of the state. This discussion will center on the steps which led to this condition with particular emphasis on the elections which brought to power republican governments whose chief aim was the accomplishment of long-term national goals, all involving the destruction of the Yugoslav state as it existed after 1945. With the removal of the Soviet restraining hand and with the end of any hope that socialist economic systems would indeed bring the glorious future previously promised, the public throughout Yugoslavia returned to the one concept that had remained untarnished -- nationalism in the traditional nineteenth century sense -- an attitude shared by the revived religious institutions.

The convictions of the voters in each of the six Yugoslav republics were reflected in two sets of elections: the first, on the establishment of new governments, were held in Slovenia, Croatia, Macedonia, Bosnia-Hercegovina, Serbia, and Montenegro; the second, on independence, in Slovenia, Croatia, Macedonia, and Bosnia-Hercegovina. The voting commenced in Slovenia in April, 1990 and was concluded by the actions of the Bosnian and Macedonian legislatures in October and November, 1991. Although the emphasis in the next pages will be on these elections and their consequences, some comment will be made on other issues, such as the economic crisis, the civil war, and the European intervention. There will be, however, no attempt to describe these in detail, nor will events after Christmas, 1991 be included.

Historical Background

Yugoslavia has perhaps been the least successful of the political creations of the Versailles settlement. Although designated as the national home of the South Slav Serbs, Croats, and Slovenes, the state was never able to win the primary allegiance of its citizens, who uniformly remained attached to their historical roots. In addition, few serious attempts were made to bring into the political life of the state the other component nationalities who today play such a prominent role, for instance, the Albanians, Bosnian Muslims, Hungarians, and Macedonians, among others. A major cause of this condition lay in the fact that, unlike neighboring Albania, Bulgaria, Greece, Romania, and even Turkey, the Yugoslav state did not come into existence as the result of a national movement with a long tradition and a unifying concept that could command the loyalty and allegiance of its people. Instead it was based on a union of three nations -- the Serbs, Croats, and Slovenes -- each with a distinct national character and historical experience.

Of these, the Serbian national movement most closely approximated that of the other Balkan people. With a long historical heritage, reaching back to the Middle Ages, the Serbian people had participated in a revolution, lasting from 1804 to 1815, and then by stages had won a position of autonomy within the Ottoman Empire, followed by independence in 1878. United by their Orthodox faith, the Serbs were further joined together by a common view of their past history and their goals for the future. The aim of "uniting all Serbs," a slogan which is so prominent in the present crisis, was similarly the major goal of the pre-1914 Serbian government.

The Croats, too, had a long and unique heritage. An independent kingdom in the tenth and eleventh centuries, their fate was thereafter closely associated with that of the Hungarian crown and the Habsburg Monarchy. Catholic in religion, they were thus closer to events in Central and Western Europe and, therefore did not experience the long period of Ottoman domination undergone by the other Balkan Slavs. Although they shared a common literary language with the Serbs over the last century, they had few other historical experiences in common. In 1918, Croats lived primarily in Dalmatia, which was joined to Austria in the Dual Monarchy, and in the Kingdom of Croatia-Slavonia, which had an autonomous status as part of the Hungarian lands. The Slovenes inhabited areas under Austrian administration. Although Catholic, they did not share a common language with the Croats.

Before 1914, all South Slavs had some experience with constitutional governments, although the degree to which elections were in fact free and representative differed considerably. After 1830, Serbia adopted a number of constitutions and had a multiparty system. However, political life was closely controlled by a centralized bureaucracy which assured that the real political power remained in the hands of the court, the army, the politicians, and the police. In Croatia-Slavonia, there was similarly a multiparty system, but the franchise allowed only about 8 percent (after 1910) of the population to vote. By 1914, the Croats in Dalmatia and the Slovenes all enjoyed the benefits of the universal manhood suffrage in effect in Austria.

Although political life centered around parties with a national base, some leaders, particularly students and intellectuals in the Habsburg Empire, called for the creation of a state which would unite the South Slavs. Unlike Serbia, which was primarily Serbian in population, at least until the conclusion of the Second Balkan War in 1913, the Croatian areas of the monarchy had a large proportion of Serbs. By 1914 many Serbian and Croatian parties within the empire had learned the advantages of cooperation, but there was certainly no major organized Yugoslav movement with a program aiming at the destruction of Austria-Hungary and union with Serbia. As far as Serbia was concerned, certainly many Serbs, particularly among the educated, saw the advantages of union. However, the primary enthusiasm was for the creation of a Greater Serbia, whose lands would embrace large Habsburg areas in which the Croats were, in fact, in the majority. The Serbian national claims today are a direct reflection of the convictions held before World War I.

The Kingdom of Serbs, Croats, and Slovenes created on December 1, 1918 was the result of negotiations carried on by émigré South Slav politicians from the Habsburg Empire with representatives of the Serbian government-in-exile during the war. In the declaration of Corfu of 1917 it was agreed that a South Slav state would be created and that it would be a constitutional monarchy under the Serbian Karadjordjević dynasty. This understanding, which was unofficial and not binding on the participants, dealt only with the cooperation of the Serbs, Croats, and Slovenes, with no mention of the status of the other nationalities. It also did not deal with the vital question of whether the future state should have a federal or centralized administration.

The immediate impulse for unification came at the end of the war when the Habsburg Empire dissolved into its national constituencies and when the South Slav leaders came to feel increasingly threatened by Italian claims to their territories. At that time, the National Council, representing the South Slavs of the monarchy, decided on an immediate union with Serbia, an action which was accepted on December 1, 1918 on behalf of Serbia by Prince Regent Alexander, who became king in 1921. Difficulties, however, arose almost immediately. A constituent assembly was indeed elected, but the divisions within the new state were clearly apparent. The Croatian Peasant Party, with 50 representatives, and the Communist Party, with 58 (which was subsequently outlawed), did not participate. In the final vote on the constitution, only 258 representatives attended; of the 419 delegates originally elected, 223, or 53 percent, approved the document. This Serbian victory meant that the state would be organized on the basis of the centralized system favored by this nationality rather than on a federal organization preferred by the other nationalities.

This unfortunate beginning makes clear why the history of the interwar state, which was called Yugoslavia only after 1929, was characterized by recurrent crises. In January, 1929, King Alexander abolished the constitutional government, disbanded the political parties, and instituted a personal dictatorship which lasted until his assassination in 1934. In these years he introduced a new constitution and political organization, but it was little more than a cover for his authoritarian rule, which favored Serbian interests. After his death, a regency was established under Prince Paul until Peter II became of age. The constitution was kept and, as before, carefully managed elections were held. In June, 1935, Milan Stojadinović formed a government which maintained relative political calm over the next years. It was also recognized that an understanding would have to be reached with the Croats. In August, 1939, after complicated negotiations, an agreement was concluded which established an autonomous Croatia with considerable political rights. Its territory included Dalmatia, Croatia, Slavonia, and some territory at present a part of Bosnia-Hercegovina. The outbreak of World War II, of course, prevented a test of the viability of the new arrangement.

The Communist Regime

The depth and bitterness of the national animosities were clearly evident during the war. After the defeat by Germany and Italy in 1941, a government-in-exile, representing the prewar regime and King Peter II was established in London. Its home army, the Chetniks under Draža Mihailović, represented the Serbian national camp. In Croatia, the Ustaša regime of Ante Pavelić worked with the German and Italian occupying forces and carried on measures of extreme violence against Serbs and Jews under its control. Under the conditions of civil war which existed at the time, the only effective organization with an all-Yugoslav program was the Communist party, under the leadership of Josip Broz Tito. His Partisan Army received direct Western aid and the support of the Soviet Union. When the war drew to a close, this force had complete military control of the country.

Although the Communist victory in Yugoslavia was not obtained by peaceful or democratic methods, the party did have a program which met some of the urgent needs of this divided and impoverished land. The Communist economic program did not stand the test of time, but at first at least the new regime could offer the promise of modernization and an improvement in general conditions of life. The party introduced a basic social welfare network, including improved health care, basic education, and, initially, a promise of full employment. The Communist leadership also attempted to meet the national question by the reorganization of the country into a federation of six republics -- Serbia, Croatia, Slovenia, Bosnia-Hercegovina, Macedonia, and Montenegro. Within Serbia, two autonomous districts, Kosovo and Vojvodina, were established.

Despite the fact that the Croats, Macedonians, Montenegrins, Serbs, and Slovenes had their own republics, and the interests of the Albanians and the nationally diverse population in Bosnia-Hercegovina and Vojvodina had been taken into account, this division did not solve the major problem. Unfortunately, the Yugoslav nationalities did not live in neat territorial compartments. Thus, 24 percent of the Serbs and 22 percent of the Croats lived outside of their republics. Only the Slovenes to the north had relatively stable ethnic frontiers.

Having achieved this settlement, the Tito regime subsequently firmly squelched any expressions of nationalist sentiment deemed dangerous for the union. Thus, in 1966, in Serbia and, in 1971, in Croatia, Tito moved to stifle expressions of national passion. At the same time, more power was given to the republics. Although the Yugoslav Communist Party was at first a centralist organization, changes were made in 1952 which shifted more authority to the parties of the republics. The party was now called the League of Communists of Yugoslavia (LCY). In 1974, a new constitution also reflected this move to decentralization.

As long as Tito was alive, the Communist regime, although facing many difficulties, did not have to resort to the measures of extreme repression common to other socialist bloc countries. Tito's refusal to bend to Soviet demands was popular. Moreover, as time went on, fewer attempts were made to control the population. Yugoslav citizens could travel freely; over a million went as laborers to Western Europe, particularly to Germany. In general, books and periodicals circulated with relative freedom, at least in contrast to other bloc states. In addition, although his control of the situation declined with time, Tito, the president for life, did remain as a figure of authority and of final appeal.

After Tito's death in 1980, the political and economic difficulties became more severe. With the intent of preserving the balance among the republics, the state was governed by a very complicated system. The executive branch consisted of a collective presidency of eight, representing the six republics and the two autonomous provinces. The leadership of this body rotated each year among the representatives of the republics. At the same time, the links among the Communist parties weakened, with more control devolving to the republics. Added to this situation, the economic conditions, which will be discussed later, became catastrophic.

In 1989 the rate of inflation rose to 2,700 percent. The weak central leadership and the declining economy, together with the collapse of Communist control in 1989 throughout Eastern Europe, were important elements in the dramatic events of the next years. However, national antagonisms were on the rise well before this time.

National Tensions

The responsibility for the first steps towards the unraveling of the national situation in Yugoslavia is generally attributed to Serbia, in particular, to the new leadership which emerged at this time. Serbian nationalists had always held strong feelings of grievance over what they felt was a sharp decline in their position after 1945. Strongly disliking the autonomous status assigned to Vojvodina and Kosovo within Serbian territory, they felt that their interests were also not served by the creation of the Macedonian, Montenegrin and Bosnian republics. This bitterness was ably exploited by a skillful politician, Slobodan Milošević, who took over the leadership of the Serbian League of Communists in 1987. In the subsequent months, he and his followers were able to subvert the leadership of the party in Vojvodina, where the Serbs had a majority of 55 percent, and replace it with his partisans. In his speeches, he made promises of reform, but he instituted strict control over the media. The major Serbian newspaper, *Politika*, degenerated from being a respected source of news on Yugoslavia to a propaganda tool for his supporters. Serbia thus received a rejuvenated Communist leadership, but one whose program was to split the federation.

Since little could be done to salvage the faltering economy, Milošević used the Serbian national question to rally support and justify the suppression of opposition opinion. The first focus of attention was the province of Kosovo, where the population had become about 90 percent Albanian. The Serbian government had already used measures of repression in the area, which was overwhelmingly Albanian but where the Serbian nationalists had claims based on past history and national mythology. In 1981, troops had been sent to repress Albanian demands for increased autonomy, including perhaps a separate republic. Claims were made that the Albanians sought union with Albania and that they had used terror to force the migration of the Slavic population, which had indeed declined. Thereafter, the Serbian authorities turned to weakening the legal position of the province. Amendments introduced into the Serbian constitution in March, 1989 limited the autonomous rights of the province. This action was met by demonstrations, which were suppressed by the Yugoslav army and resulted in 29 deaths, all Albanian. Further amendments in the constitution ended the autonomy of both Vojvodina and Kosovo in September. Thus, at the time that the other East European socialist states were adopting democratic reforms, the Serbian LCY went in the opposite direction. The introduction of a military regime in Kosovo had a strong effect on the other republics. The old fears of Serbian hegemony left from the interwar years were easily reawakened. These suspicions contributed to the collapse of the central organization of the LCY, an event that opened a period of intense political activity.

In January, 1990 the Extraordinary 14th Congress of the LCY was opened.[1] The intention was to formulate a reform program leading to the introduction of a multiparty system and a market economy, but the sessions broke up almost immediately on the national issue. The Slovenian representatives, supported by those from Croatia, Bosnia-Hercegovina, and Macedonia, demanded that the LCY become a union of independent parties. Unable to secure their desires, the Slovenian delegates left. Although Milošević wanted the sessions to continue, the other representatives also returned home and the congress was declared "suspended." This action, however, did not affect the state administration. Both the prime minister, Ante Marković, a Croat, and his deputy prime minister, Živko Pregl, a Slovene, declared that the federal government could function without the LCY.

The congress was scheduled to reopen on May 26. However, with the absence of delegates from Slovenia, Croatia, and Macedonia, only a three hour session was held. On November 19, the LCY was reorganized as the LCY-Movement for Yugoslavia (LCY-MY), with a program calling for the defense of socialism and the preservation of Yugoslav unity. Its membership was drawn from the ranks of the army officers and others who had benefitted from the previous system.

Electoral Challenges to Unity

The major events of 1990, however, were the elections held in all of the republics, with the first in Slovenia and Croatia, all on a multiparty basis.[2] In Slovenia, in elections in April and May, the opposition coalition Demos received 55 percent of the votes as against 17 percent for the reformed Slovenian Communist Party; it thus held 126 of the 240 seats in the legislature. However, in a runoff election, a Communist, Milan Kučan, a popular figure who had led in the changes in the Slovenian party, was elected as president with 58.5 percent of the vote. A similar result was obtained in Croatia, where the Croatian Democratic Union won 58 percent of the vote and thus controlled 205 of the 365 seats in the three-chamber assembly. It defeated the Croatian Communist Party, now renamed the Party for Democratic Change (PDC).

Whereas Slovenia acquired a reformed Communist leader as its president, Croatia elected Franjo Tudjman, formerly a Communist but now a strong nationalist, who was 68 years old at the time. During the war he had joined Tito and fought with the Partisans. Rising to the rank of general, he served in Belgrade. In 1961, with a change in the direction of his career, he returned to Zagreb, where he received a doctorate in history and subsequently published four books. Joining the Croatian nationalist movement, he was sent to jail for a year in 1971 and again ten years later. During the campaign, he proved to be a good political organizer and his message was simple. As the *Economist* wrote, "He beat the nationalist drum louder than anyone else."[3] His party called for Croatia to become either a sovereign state or a member of a weak confederation. In the campaign, the party used past historical associations, including the display of the Croatian flag, coat-of-arms, and similar symbols and slogans. Similarly, there was an emphasis on the Catholic Church. In fact, after the first session of the new assembly, the 28 member government attended a mass.

With non-Communist governments in place, both Croatia and Slovenia joined to call for a reorganization of Yugoslavia into a confederation of sovereign states, in which each would conduct its own foreign relations and control its own armed forces. There would, however, be a central parliament, a monetary union, and a common market. These proposals brought the northern republics into direct opposition to Serbia, which stood behind the authority of the central government. The first open confrontation involved Slovenia. In October, the Slovenian assembly passed constitutional amendments giving Slovene laws precedence over federal regulations and transferring the control of the republic's defenses from the Yugoslav state presidency to the Slovenian presidency. In reply, the central executive ordered the federal forces to act. On October 5, a sixteen man unit of the Yugoslav military police seized the administrative building of the Slovenian militia. Although this incident did not provoke a major crisis, it resulted in a sharpening of the Slovenian stand. In December, the assembly announced that a plebiscite would be held on the question of independence. At the same time, the antagonists took economic measures. In October, Serbia placed duties on Croatian and Slovenian goods; these republics in turn responded with similar actions.

In November, elections were held in Macedonia and Bosnia-Hercegovina. Here, too, the local Communist parties lost to those representing a distinct national identity. In Macedonia, with 120 seats in contest, the victors were the Internal Macedonian Revolutionary Organization (IMRO) with 37, the reformed Communists with 31, and the Albanian Party of Democratic Prosperity with 25, and the Alliance of Reform Forces (a party with a Yugoslav program led by Ante Marković) with 19.

In Bosnia-Hercegovina, where the electoral divisions also reflected the national composition of the population, the major parties appeared at least temporarily to have worked out a satisfactory accommodation. With a population consisting of 43 percent Muslims, 38 percent Serbs, and 18 percent Croats, the parties representing these nationalities -- the Muslim Party for Democratic Action, the Serbian Democratic Party, and the Croatian Democratic Community -- won 80 percent of the seats in the assembly, with the percentages roughly approximating the divisions. Following this pattern, a Serb was chosen president of the assembly and a Croat became prime minister. The collective presidency was composed of two Muslims, two Croats, and two Serbs, with one additional member. Alija Izetbegović, a Muslim, became state president.

The last elections were held in Serbia and Montenegro in December. In Serbia, the presidency and the 250 member legislature were in contest. In the two rounds of voting, Milošević obviously held the most advantageous position. Leading a reformed Communist party, whose name was changed to Socialist, he had an organized constituency and he controlled the media. Nevertheless, he did face an opponent in Vuk Drašković who threatened to beat him at his own nationalist game. Drašković was already well known as the author of five books concentrating on the "genocide" of the Serbs during World War II. His party, the Serbian Movement for Renewal, placed a strong emphasis on Serbian historical and Orthodox themes. On the platform he surrounded himself with paintings of Serbian kings, and he portrayed the choice at issue as that between "the cross and the red star."[4] Reflecting the extreme nationalist position, he wished to redraw the Serbian frontiers to include large sections of Croatia and Bosnia-Hercegovina as well as all of Montenegro and Kosovo. As far as the non-Serbian population of these areas were concerned, he believed that these people should either accept Serbian control or leave.

Although there were recognized irregularities, most of the observers of the elections in Serbia and Montenegro considered them fair and free. In Serbia, Milošević received 65 percent of the vote for the presidency as against 16 percent for Drašković. In two rounds of voting, the Socialists won control of the Serbian assembly of 250. In Montenegro, similar results were obtained. In the next months, the two Serbian states, with their Communist governments, were to stand together.

The elections thus served to weaken further the relations among the republics. In the coming period of crisis, the Serbian position became the strong defense of the federal relationship of the republics as it existed at the time. In control of the votes of Montenegro and of Vojvodina and Kosovo, whose autonomous rights had been suppressed, the Serbian authorities could expect to have the predominant position in the state. Should the federation dissolve, they demanded that the Serbian frontiers be changed to enclose areas designated as Serbian. At the same time, relations were strengthened with the Serbs living outside of the republic, particularly those in Croatia and in Bosnia-Hercegovina, and their national sentiments were strongly encouraged.

Increasing Antagonisms

In contrast to the Serbian support of the centralist position, both Slovenia and Croatia moved further along the road to loosening their ties with the rest of country. In December, 1990, a plebiscite was held in Slovenia on the issue of the establishment of a sovereign and independent state within a Yugoslav confederation, or, if that could not be achieved within six months, a declaration of complete independence. With 93 percent of the electorate voting, 88 percent supported the proposition.

Although the federal presidency declared the Slovenian action unconstitutional, the republic continued along its independent path. Its government began to take over offices and functions previously filled by the federal authorities. In February, 1991, the assembly passed a constitutional amendment suppressing federal laws that applied to the republic and a resolution which "disassociated" Slovenia from Yugoslavia. At the same time, the leadership called for a general discussion among the republics about how the separation could best be accomplished. It was willing to assume a share in the repayment of the national debt.

Similar actions were undertaken in Croatia: The federal laws were declared invalid. A referendum on a reorganization of Yugoslavia or a declaration of independence was, however, not held until May, 1991. Both Croatia and Slovenia agreed that Macedonia and Bosnia-Hercegovina should make their own decisions about the future. For their part in these months of crisis, the leaders of these two republics made strong efforts to mediate between Serbia and the northern republics.

Meanwhile, Milošević faced increasing difficulties. In January, a financial scandal made relations with the other republics even worse. At the time, federal officials made public the fact that on December 28, 1990 the Serbian assembly had illegally and secretly adopted a measure which forced the Serbian-controlled state bank to issue 1.8 billion dollars of unbacked new money without the federal approval which was required. The money was used to ease the desperate financial position of the republic and to provide funds for pensions, subsidies, loans to enterprises, etc. It was generally believed that Milošević had used the money to buy support in the elections. This action, which severely undercut the effort at general economic reform, was denounced in particular in Slovenia and Croatia as theft.

Although he had won the election by a convincing majority, Milošević still had to deal with continued challenges from Drašković. The economic situation in the republic remained desperate; unemployment had risen to above 16 percent, and many enterprises could not pay their workers. In addition, there was much discontent over the continued control of the media. On March 9, a mass demonstration, with Drašković's followers as the chief organizers, was held. With a strong representation of students and intellectuals, the participants demanded a change in the directorship of Belgrade television. The Serbian police employed violent methods, including the use of tear gas, live ammunition, and water cannons, to break up the crowd. At the same time, the federal presidency, without the approval of the Croatian and Slovenian representatives, agreed to the use of Yugoslav army tanks and soldiers, which were, however, withdrawn after 24 hours.

This use of military force, accompanied by the arrest of the leaders of the demonstration, solved nothing. Milošević's supporters organized a counter-demonstration in New Belgrade, across the Sava River, which was attended mainly by workers from the state factories. Milošević, however, could not afford a further confrontation. On March 12, he agreed to the demands for a change in the editorial direction of *Politika* and Belgrade television. Drašković, who had been imprisoned, was now released and was greeted by a crowd of supporters estimated at around 100,000.

Throughout this period of tension, a major question was what role the Yugoslav army, which received 30 percent of the federal budget, would play. As we have seen, federal troops had already acted in Slovenia and Serbia, and, as will be explained later, in the conflict between the Serbs and Croats in Croatia. The national and political divisions within the army, however, raised questions about its effectiveness in a domestic crisis. The approximately 200,000 man army had at its head an officer corps which was 70 to 75 percent Serbian or Montenegrin. Moreover, the officers, of whom 95 percent had been of the LCY and who formed a major part of the leadership of LCY-MY, had a personal stake in both the survival of the old political system and the unity of Yugoslavia. Enjoying a privileged position, including relatively high salaries, subsidized housing, vacation homes and access to other advantages, they had no interest in change. The soldiers, however, were in the majority one-year draftees from all the republics, with their members reflecting the general composition of the population.

The use of the Yugoslav army to preserve the political status quo became a major issue shortly after the March crisis in Serbia. On March 12, Borislav Jović, the Serbian head of the collective presidency, at the request of the defense minister, General Veljko Kadijević, called a special session of the body to discuss the use of the military and whether a state of emergency should be declared. When the proposal on intervention was defeated five to three (Slovenia, Croatia, Kosovo, Bosnia-Hercegovina and Macedonia against Serbia, Montenegro, and Vojvodina), the army command declared that it would follow the constitution and not act without the approval of the majority in the collective presidency. Although he supported this decision, General Kadijević, on March 19, issued what was in fact an ambivalent statement: "The Yugoslav People's Army, as in the past, will not interfere in political talks on the country's future," but that it would "under no circumstances allow armed inter-ethnic conflicts and civil war in Yugoslavia."[5]

Units of the Yugoslav army were, however, used to suppress the bloody confrontations which took place between the Serbs of Croatia and the republic's authorities.   With the increase of strong nationalist sentiment and the victory of parties with nationalist programs, it could be expected that the Serbian population of Croatia, numbering 600,000 of a total of 4.5 million, or 12 percent, would be affected by conflicting sentiments.   Milošević, with his pan-Serb program and the local Serbian remembrances of the massacres of World War II, stirred up strong reactions.   In August, 1990, the Serbian population created what it declared to be an autonomous region called Krajina, a section of southern Croatia where 90 percent were Serbs.   In March, 1991, Krajina announced its independence from Croatia, and on April 1 it declared itself a part of Serbia.   This action was paralleled by a series of clashes between armed Serbian groups and the Croatian police, which, in turn, brought in the Yugoslav army.

Incidents occurred in March, April, and May.   In March, local Serbs took control of a police station in Pakrac.   Federal troops entered the area, where they worked with the Croatian police.   A more serious action occurred on March 31, when armed Serbs blockaded a Croatian police convoy in Plitvica national park and opened fire.   After several hours of fighting, the Croatian police were able to take control of the park, but again the Yugoslav army intervened.   A third incident occurred at the beginning of May at Borovo Selo, when Croatian police were ambushed in a predominantly Serbian area, resulting in the deaths of 12 police and three civilians.   Once again, federal troops and tanks were brought to the scene.   These events emphasized the difficulties of controlling a situation where the local population on both sides was heavily armed, and where each national group was determined to defend its own enclave.

By May, the position of the two major contenders in the political struggle -- Croatia and Slovenia against Serbia and its client regimes in Montenegro, Vojvodina and Kosovo -- had become firm.   On May 19, a vote was held in Croatia on the question of independence and member-ship in a loose Yugoslav confederation; as previously in Slovenia, over 90 percent approved this proposal.   Meanwhile, in Slovenia preparations were made for eventual independence.   The authorities introduced their own system of compulsory military service, and they continued in their efforts to take over federal services. Both of the northern republics, it will be remembered, had non-Communist governments, and they supported the transformation of Yugoslavia into a loose association of sovereign states.

In contrast, Milošević's Serbia retained its Communist leadership, and it continued to support a tight federal system which it hoped to dominate. In the voting in the presidency, as we have seen, it could count on the support of Montenegro, also with a Communist administration, and Vojvodina and Kosovo, whose autonomy had been suppressed. If Yugoslavia did indeed break apart, Milošević and his nationalist supporters demanded the redrawing of the borders of the republic in order to "protect all Serbs." This very dangerous claim could also be made by other nationalities and could only lead to civil war. The Croats could also demand similar rights for their people in Bosnia-Hercegovina and Vojvodina. Even more serious was the possibility of outside intervention, with Hungary concerned about its nationals in Vojvodina, Albania about the Kosovars, and Bulgaria about its historical interests in Macedonia. In this conflict, it should be noted that Bosnia-Hercegovina and Macedonia, well aware of the implications of the quarrel, made great but unsuccessful efforts to mediate the dispute.

Economic Difficulties and Civil War

In this period of crisis, it is remarkable how little attention the contending parties paid to the economic disaster which these events directly affected. Yet, after 1980, the Yugoslav economy entered a period of sharp decline, reaching a critical level by 1988. In March, 1989, Ante Marković became prime minister at a time when inflation had reached a record high. In December, he introduced a series of reform measures; in six months he was able to bring the inflation rate down to almost zero by the introduction of a new currency and by freezing prices, wages, and salaries. For the future, his reforms depended on the preservation of a unified economy and a degree of centralization. He also formed the only truly "Yugoslav" party, the Alliance of Reform Forces, which was not successful in the elections. Throughout this period he continued to argue for the maintenance of a unified Yugoslavia. His efforts were widely appreciated abroad, where both the European Economic Community and the United States realized the importance of the continuation of his program. His efforts, while acknowledged elsewhere, received support neither in Serbia nor in the other republics.

The division between the republics that elected democratic regimes and those that remained Communist, of course, affected the attitude of their governments toward the introduction of a market economy. In fact, the condition of crisis meant that reforms of any kind could not be introduced and that all of the republics faced economic disaster. For example, state enterprises in Serbia, suffering their worse recession in four decades, could not pay salaries or buy raw materials for future production. At the end of January, 1991, a fourth of the firms were judged insolvent. Milošević and his supporters attempted to solve the immediate problems by using the profits of successful enterprises to pay for those which were failing and to cover the costs of state services. As the situation worsened, he took the easy road of blaming the Croats, the Slovenes, and the Catholic Church.

The northern republics, despite their better economic position, suffered similarly. Most important was the collapse of the tourist industry, which in 1990 had brought in $2.7 billion and which was of vital importance for the balance of payments of the country. With all of the nationalities suffering, the conflicts, as the *Wall Street Journal* concluded, did indeed make:

> ". . .a farce of efforts to transform the economy from socialism to the free market. What once was one of the most promising reform programs in Eastern Europe is now one of the most hopeless."[6]

The disregard of the economic implications of internal political turmoil by the leaders of the contesting factions was to continue throughout the crisis.

As has been seen, until May there had been repeated crises, but all of the parties had hesitated about going too far. This situation was now to change. On May 15, Jović should have surrendered his position as federal president to Stipe Mesić, a non-Communist Croat, according to what had been the regular procedure since the death of Tito. Serbia, however, was able to block this succession by controlling the votes of Montenegro, Vojvodina and Kosovo and thus preventing Mesić from receiving the majority which he needed. Yugoslavia was now without a chief executive, important because the president was both head of state and commander of the army. In the next weeks continual efforts were made to break the deadlock. The representatives of Bosnia-Hercegovina and Macedonia, as well as Prime Minister Ante Marković, all attempted to mediate a solution.

After long, futile discussions it became apparent that a solution by negotiation was not in sight. At this time, Marković continued to warn of the consequences of secession, including civil war and economic ruin. He, however, declared that legal means and not force should be used to keep the country together. Meanwhile, the date set by both the Croatian and Slovenian governments for independence approached. On June 22, Kučan and Tudjman met to coordinate their actions. They both made it clear that they were willing to continue to negotiate and that their goal remained the transformation of Yugoslavia into a loose federation of sovereign states. Finally, on June 25, both Slovenia and Croatia declared their independence. The Slovenian statement was the more decisive. This government had already approved measures leading to independence, including the taking control of border posts, the issuance of a national currency, and the suppression of federal laws. The action of both republics was taken against the advice of the European Community and the United States, which announced that the declarations would not be recognized nor would economic assistance be given. Although both states considered themselves independent, it was obvious that many problems remained to be settled.

The immediate problem which arose concerned the possibility that the Yugoslav army might intervene, with the major questions those of the control of the international border checkpoints in Slovenia and the tense relations between Serbs and Croats in Croatia. Fears were also expressed that the army would act on its own, under the influence of the Serbian-dominated officers corps, and that the civilian authorities would not be able to control its actions. The situation was made more dangerous by the fact that, although the army was under the authority of the collective presidency, particularly under its president, the failure of that body to accept Stipe Mesić had paralyzed its actions.

Despite this lack of clarity concerning the situation, the Yugoslav army on June 27, in an action that far exceeded previous interventions, entered Slovenia in force, employing tanks, helicopters, air force planes, and heavy weapons. It is not clear exactly on whose authority the action was initiated or if, as later charged, the army exceeded its instructions. Marković, despite his previous declarations on the use of force, did, however, sanction the action. The main attack was on the border checkpoints, but also on the Ljubljana and Maribor airports. The Slovenian forces were well prepared to resist the attack. They blocked the roads with trucks, buses, and cars, and they also had effective means of defense, including anti-tank weapons, machine guns, rifles, and surface-to-air missiles. The Yugoslav army, unable to achieve its military objectives and with the capture by the Slovenes of thousands of prisoners, suffered a humiliating defeat.

The fighting finally was ended by a European intervention and an agreement covering both Slovenia and Croatia, which dealt with the immediate situation, but not with the larger issues. The two republics were to suspend further moves towards independence for a short period; Yugoslav army units were to return to their barracks; the militias were to disband; and Mesić was to be accepted as the head of the collective presidency. International observers were to oversee the implementation of the conditions.

Through its successful resistance, it was generally recognized that Slovenia would eventually achieve independence. Certainly, the Serbian government had no reason to oppose the secession of a republic without a Serbian minority of significance and whose independence would actually strengthen Serbian preponderance in Yugoslavia. On July 18, the federal presidency agreed to the withdrawal of all troops from Slovenia. It was later announced that recruits for the army would no longer be taken from Slovenia.

The Slovenian episode marked the first of what were to be numerous active European interventions in the Yugoslav crisis. The agreement was the result of negotiations led by a mission from the European Community composed of the foreign ministers of Luxembourg, Italy, and the Netherlands. For the European governments and the United States, the Yugoslav dispute had implications for other sensitive areas. The principle of self-determination was also at issue, for instance, in Spain with its Basque and Catalan problem, in France with the Corsican question, and in the rapidly disintegrating Soviet Union with its major national and religious divisions. With their primary concern for stability, the E.C. and the United States at first expressed opposition to the breakup of Yugoslavia, although they would agree to changes in the political structure in the unlikely case that these could be achieved by peaceful means. A division of opinion, however, soon occurred.

Although at first France, Britain, Italy, and Spain were clear supporters of Yugoslav territorial integrity, Germany and Austria showed more sympathy toward the Croatian and Slovenian positions. Pressed by opinion within his own Christian Democratic Party, the Catholic Church, and the general German reaction, Chancellor Helmut Kohl came out clearly in favor of the two republics. In fact, there was little that the E.C. could do since armed intervention was not an option. The only available weapons were those of economic sanctions and the withdrawal of aid money. In this connection the German government did have some advantages; 20 percent of Yugoslav foreign trade was involved and the remittances of the 600,000 Yugoslav workers in Germany were essential to the Yugoslav economy. How little economic considerations affected all of the parties in the Yugoslav disputes, however, has already been noted.

As the Croatian government had feared, the ending of the Slovenian crisis marked the almost immediate beginning of a major offensive by Serbian paramilitary groups, encouraged by the Serbian government and backed by units of the Yugoslav army to control territories which Serbian nationalists claimed. These forces advanced in Kajina and in Eastern Slavonia until they occupied about a third of Croatia. Despite constant negotiations and the conclusion of numerous cease-fires which were subsequently broken, E.C. mediators, later joined by those from the United Nations, were unable to stop the fighting. The conflict increased in intensity at the end of September and in October. The Croatian forces laid siege to the army garrisons in their territory; the Serbian and Yugoslav military attacked Croatian and Dalmatian cities, including Dubrovnik and Zadar. On October 5, air force jets bombed the presidential residence in Zagreb at a time when not only Tudjman but also Mesić and Marković were there. It was obvious by this time that the central Yugoslav government had lost its authority, although Mesić did not resign as president until December 5 and Marković as prime minister until December 21. Under the circumstances, the E.C. members uniformly blamed the Serbian leaders for the political and military breakdown and were more willing to consider a recognition of the republics who wished to become independent.[7]

The Slovenian resistance and the fighting in Croatia naturally affected the attitudes of the two other republics, Macedonia and Bosnia-Hercegovina, which had repudiated their former Communist regimes. Of these, Macedonia, unwilling to remain part of a Serbian-dominated state, held a plebiscite on September 8 on the question: "Are you in favor of a sovereign and independent state of Macedonia having a right to enter into a future alliance of sovereign states of Yugoslavia?" It has been estimated that of those who voted, 72 percent of the electorate, 95 percent accepted the proposition. The Albanians, 20 percent of the population and the Serbs with 2.3 percent, boycotted the elections. On November 20, a new constitution was proclaimed which declared Macedonia an independent state. This action had implications not only for Yugoslav domestic politics, but also for inter-Balkan relations and the interests of Bulgaria, Greece, and Albania in Macedonian territory.

Of the Yugoslav republics, the situation was most difficult in Bosnia-Hercegovina, with its delicate national and religious divisions. Although a referendum was not held, the events in the neighboring republics ended the compromise between the nationalities worked out previously. It was natural that Bosnian Muslims and Croats would be joined by a common interest in opposing Serbian domination. On September 12, in a step similar to that taken by the Serbs of Croatia, local Serbs established an "autonomous region of Hercegovina," an area of 3,000 square miles bordering on Hercegovina. In October, in a counter-measure, the Croatian and Muslim parliamentary deputies voted for independence. After 73 Serbian representatives left, the final vote was 133 in favor with 15 abstentions.

One other election should be mentioned, although it did not have the international significance of those previously discussed. Despite the suppression of Kosovo's autonomy, local leaders from the province, joined by those in exile, scheduled an election, beginning on September 26, on the organization of a separate and independent republic within Yugoslavia. Once again the Serbian authorities reacted with violence, declaring the referendum illegal and harassing and arresting the participants. It has been estimated that, nevertheless, an overwhelmingly favorable vote was obtained.

Democracy and Disunity

As can be seen, democratization in the multinational state of Yugoslavia by December, 1991 had brought that country to the edge of complete dissolution. As an official commented: "Democracy in this part of the world is a Pandora's box. Although with the good things, you get the side effects, including nationalism."[8] Free elections did indeed allow the electorate to express its prime concerns, largely suppressed under the Tito regime. The Serbs and Montenegrins elected strongly nationalistic but Communist governments. The Slovenes and Croats voted for non-Communist parties which sought a reorganized Yugoslavia. In Macedonia and Bosnia-Hercegovina national but democratic parties were victorious. Subsequently, Slovenia, Croatia, and Macedonia held further elections and chose independence, although their leaders appeared willing to join in a loose confederation of sovereign units. Bosnian independence was affirmed by parliamentary action. With the breakdown of the central administration, the Yugoslav state was thus split apart. On the one side, Serbia, controlling the decisions of Montenegro, Kosovo, and Vojvodina, and also with paramount influence in the army, supported the maintenance of a centralized, Serbian-dominated state, or, should that not be possible, a redrawing of republic frontiers to create a greater Serbia. In opposition, Croatia, Slovenia, Macedonia, and Bosnia-Hercegovina stood for either a federal reorganization or independence for the republics with their borders unchanged. Although the elections did reflect the predominant sentiments of the voters and did bring out the fundamental structural weaknesses of the previous Yugoslav union, their results by Christmas of 1991 faced the republics with the disasters of civil war, economic breakdown, and an uncertain future.

Notes

1. The discussion of events from 1989 on is based primarily on the accounts in the newspapers *Chicago Tribune, Financial Times, Indianapolis Star, New York Times, Wall Street Journal* and on material in the *Economist* and the publications of Radio Free Europe. Among the many accounts of the events of 1989-1991, see in particular, Milan Andrejevich, "The End of an Era, New Beginnings?" RFE/RL *Report on Eastern Europe,* II: 1 (January 4, 1991), 38-44; Ivo Banac, "Political Change and National Diversity," *Daedalus,* Winter 1990, 141-159; Robin Allison Remington, "The Federal Dilemma in Yugoslavia," *Current History,* December, 1990, 405-408,

429-431; Dennison Rusinow, "Yugoslavia: Balkan Breakup?", *Foreign Policy*, No. 93, Summer 1991, 143-159, and the chapter on Yugoslavia in J. F. Brown, *Surge to Freedom* (Durham: Duke University Press, 1991), pp. 199-220.

2. The figures on election results usually are taken from newspaper accounts. They should not be regarded as final or official.

3. *Economist*, April 28, 1990.

4. *Washington Post*, December 9, 1990, A29, A34.

5. *New York Times*, March 20, 1991, A3.

6. *Wall Street Journal*, May 22, 1991.

7. This shift can also be seen in the policy of the United States which had previously preferred to see the Yugoslav crisis mediated by the E.C., but which also at first favored maintenance of a Yugoslav state. However, on September 26, Secretary of State James A. Baker delivered a strong denunciation of the Serbian position before the U. N. Security Council: "The government of Serbia and the Yugoslav federal military bear a special and indeed growing responsibility for the grim future which awaits the peoples of Yugoslavia if they do not stop the bloodshed." *New York Times*, September, 27, 1991, A4. At the same time, the Yugoslav military added the United States to its list of enemies, accusing it of seeking Albanian bases.

8. *Chicago Tribune*, June 27, 1991, 8.

13

Economic Decentralization and Democratization in the USSR

Peter Toumanoff

This chapter focuses on efforts to carry out decentralizing economic reforms in the USSR. Unlike the situation in China, Hungary, and Poland, no significant political reforms aimed at democratization were even attempted before *perestroika*. Many attempts to decentralize economic decision-making have been made, however, and all have failed. Their history suggests that the Soviet government was either unable or unwilling to decentralize the economy. In another chapter of this book, Robert Byrnes suggests that the USSR was unable to decentralize because the population is culturally and traditionally unsuited to non-authoritarian decision-making. I am more convinced that the centralized and bureaucratic political leadership was unable to conceive of appropriate decentralizing economic reforms. Besides being unable to decentralize, these same officials were unwilling to change because decentralizing the economy would take power from the politico-economic apparatus and ultimately threaten the position of the Communist party, as proved the case once Gorbachev's political reforms took root.

This history of failure suggests that economic reform could not succeed without related democratizing political reform. Although the dissolution of the USSR and the creation of the Commonwealth of Independent States already supports this claim of the importance of democratic political reform, the future survival of the individual republics as well as the Commonwealth itself will provide a better test for the relationship between political and economic reform. This chapter suggests that a powerful and simultaneous relationship between economic and political decentralization exists. Therefore, we expect that successful decentralization of the economy will not take place unless it is accompanied by democratization of the republics (and vice-versa).

As events in the early 1990s demonstrated, political democratization in the Soviet Union proved difficult as long as it was opposed by the party along with the KGB and the Red Army. For the successful transition from Leninism to democracy and a market-oriented economy to occur in the Commonwealth of Independent States and its constituent republics, either these institutions must themselves democratize or they must somehow be overcome by democratic forces within the union or the individual republics. The ill-fated putsch of August 19, 1991 appears to have removed the party and the KGB as obstacles to reform in the USSR, contributing to the end of that empire in December, 1991. Whether remnants of the military and party apparatus in individual republics can oppose the forces of democracy remains to be seen.

Economic Decentralization and Political Democratization

In an earlier chapter, Jeff Weintraub suggests that capitalism can exist without democracy. While this is undoubtedly true, as many historical examples attest, it is an observation that does not illuminate the problem of how to decentralize a Soviet-type administered economy. There are at least two reasons for this. First, capitalism can exist without being particularly decentralized. In fact, the same historical examples which confirm the coexistence of capitalism with dictatorship tend also to be examples of extremely concentrated and centralized capitalist economies. State capitalism in Germany and Japan in the end of the 19th and the beginning of the 20th centuries fostered highly concentrated industry. Capitalism in third world dictatorships is typically characterized by an extreme degree of monopoly and concentration of wealth. One could easily imagine a monopolistic capitalist economic structure inheriting the existing administrative apparatus of a formerly Communist state and changing it very little.

Second, the problem faced by reforming Communist states is not the identity of the ultimate political and economic systems that may evolve, but rather the process by which change in those systems will occur. The appropriate question to address is not "Can an authoritarian polity coexist with a market economy?," but rather "How do political factors influence the process of economic decentralization?" The process of economic decentralization abets the process of political democratization, and *vice versa*, because of the simultaneous relationship between them.

Several factors which link the processes of democratization and economic decentralization are described in Figure 13.1. Five factors are pictured, two of which influence democratization and economic decentralization simultaneously, two of which imply an influence of economic decentralization on democratization, and one of which implies an influence of democratization on economic decentralization. The simultaneous influences are the reliance by both processes on the rule of law and pluralist decision-making, and the need for a relatively self-reliant citizenry. The factors through which economic decentralization influences democratization are the lack of economic levers available to an authoritarian government from a decentralized economy, and the increased demand for democracy that may be fostered by accelerated economic growth. The factor through which democratization influences economic decentralization recognizes that the political system is the mechanism by which economic institutions are chosen. A democratic political system is more likely than a Leninist system to be able to identify an appropriate pace and composition of economic reform. Each of these factors is described in more detail below.

Rule of Law and Pluralism

Democracy is frequently described as including 1) on-going participation of all members of a society in political decisions; and 2) the primacy of the rule of law over administrative authority in the decision-making process. Economic decentralization can be described as the devolution of economic decision-making power from the center to those agents in the economic system responsible for carrying out the decisions. Sometimes this implies replacing centralized administrative authority with the rule of law. For example, the *khozrashchet* system of economic accountability replaces ministerial oversight of enterprises with the rule that, whatever their decisions, enterprises must be financially self-sufficient. Similarly, the contract responsibility systems in the People's Republic of China replace ministerial decision-making authority with the rule that contracts negotiated by intermediate production units must be fulfilled.

This connection between the economic system and the political system recognizes that the boundary between these two categories of social organization is not well-defined. Societies make decisions in a wide range of overlapping spheres, including economic and political. To the extent that some economic decisions have a political component to them, increased rule of law and/or pluralism in the economic system increases the level of political democracy. For example, laws providing for freedom of choice in labor markets permit the population to exercise political

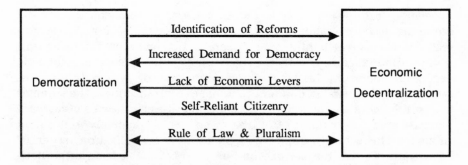

FIGURE 13.1 The Relationship Between Economic Decentralization and Political Democratization

influence through their choices. Individuals could choose, for example, not to work in military plants, or not to work in jobs which they consider environmentally damaging.

Likewise, to the extent that some political decisions have an economic component to them, increased political democracy can increase the degree of economic decentralization. Delegating the political authority over items of collective consumption to local government bodies simultaneously decentralizes the economic provision of those items. For example, local control over education decentralizes the supply of education, and increases the variety and choice of educational opportunities available to consumers. Because political and economic decisions cannot be entirely separated, decentralization in one sphere necessarily and simultaneously decentralizes the other.

Self-Reliant Citizenry

Just as economic decisions and political decisions often have common elements, they also share the same agents. That is to say, the same people make them. Decentralization, both political and economic, requires vastly increased participation in decision-making by individual members of society. The processes of democratization and economic decentralization are hindered by a citizenry which is unaccustomed and unable to take responsibility for economic and political activity. Decentralizing the economy requires economic agents who are willing and able to make their own production and consumption choices which, in the past, have been largely made for them by the state. Democratizing the polity will require citizens with the energy and will to engage in and accept collective, pluralistic, political decision-making. In the short-hand of Figure 13.1, I call these traits of character "self-reliance".

Another part of what makes a citizenry capable of independent political and economic decision-making is the support system of social institutions frequently referred to in other chapters as "civil society." The market economy needs the institutions of the civil society, such as church, organizations of culture, recreation, neighborhoods, etc. not only for the communication and networking which they encourage, but also for the checks they impose on the destructive potential of atomistic self-interested behavior.[1] Civil society provides a mechanism for recognizing and influencing the effects of individual behavior on society at large. Similarly, when economic interests gain a foothold in political society, elements of civil society may mitigate the destructive aspects of democratic political action. For example, Mancur Olson, among others, argues persuasively that small special interest groups can pass legislation in a democratic polity which generates large social losses but large personal gains for the members of the special interest group.[2] Public interest groups and other organizations in civil society may organize to counteract such biases. To the extent that the processes of democratization and economic decentralization nurture the institutions of civil society, both processes are encouraged.

These first two links between democratization and economic decentralization work in both directions. Democratization facilitates decentralization and vice versa. This suggests that a synergy exists between the two processes which means that we can expect to see one accompany the other. It should be more difficult for an undemocratic and authoritarian government to decentralize the economic system than for a government which is either already democratic or in the process of democratizing. Conversely, a centrally administered economy should find it more difficult to democratize than one which is already decentralized or in the process of decentralizing. Claims that it is too much to ask of a Communist society to transform both the political system and the economic system simultaneously are contradicted by this argument. China's current strategy of economic decentralization unaccompanied by political democratization is also not supported. On the other hand, this theory fits the experiences of many of the transitioning countries of Eastern Europe as well as that of the USSR under Gorbachev. Once genuine political reforms such as ending the leading role of the party occurred, the momentum for both democracy and economic reforms increased.

Lack of Economic Levers

In an authoritarian state such as the Soviet Union under Communist rule, means must exist for the elite group in power to impose its political will over the general population. Military force, charisma, fear of external threats, and economic control are among the means that have been employed in the USSR. Centralized economic power is a particularly effective tool of political repression. Control over income, production, communication, transportation, and trade are means by which political will can be imposed over a society. Decentralization of the economy removes economic levers from the set of controls the Communist party leadership has over society.

When economic decision-making power is decentralized, something must take the place of the economic tools which so effectively repress political opposition. In some cases, a charismatic personality commands the loyalty of the populace. In other cases, a more overt and active secret police replaces economic power as an instrument of political control. Without something to replace economic levers, the authority of the elite is weakened, and democratization may result. The point is that centralized economic power is an efficient means of maintaining authoritarian political power. Without it, authoritarian power is less easily maintained, and democratic forces have more chance to survive and grow. Therefore, this is a link by which economic decentralization encourages political democratization.

Economic Growth Increases the Demand for Democracy

It has long been an article of faith within the comparative economic systems' literature that, while centralized command economies may have advantages in promoting economic growth in less developed economies, decentralization is necessary for continued growth as economies become mature and more sophisticated. In addition, command systems are demonstrably ineffective at responding to the increasingly sophisticated demands of the consumer sector as the economy develops.

In fact, as the economic systems of communism have modernized, once spectacular economic growth rates have declined and stagnated. The rapid early growth in centralized Soviet-type economies is generated by mobilizing the labor force and by extraordinary investment in heavy industrial capital. As the labor force participation becomes nearly universal, and capital requirements become more sophisticated and less obvious, growth rates decline. Continued growth must come from productivity increases and from growth in the consumer sector. Centralized methods of allocating resources have not proven effective at increasing productivity or producing for the consumer. The USSR could only increase the pace of technological change and innovation, as well as improve consumer welfare, by decentralizing its economy.

If economic decentralization does result in perceptible gains in consumer well-being, one consequence is likely to be an increase in demand for political democracy. Political democracy is a normal good; i.e. demand for democracy increases as real income rises. A population that is preoccupied with meeting very fundamental requirements for survival is not likely to spend resources seeking a democratic government. As consumer welfare improves, demand for normal goods, including political democracy, increases. In this way, effective decentralization of the economic system may increase the demand of the population for a democratic government.

A Democratic Polity Identifies Decentralizing Reforms

Decentralizing the planned Communist economy requires de-bureaucratizing it. As Alice Tay noted, administrative rule must be replaced by the rule of law. Rights determined by position within a hierarchy must be replaced by private property rights. The sheer complexity of laws necessary to cope with the nuances of private property rights in different contexts suggests that some horizontal, participatory legislative process is appropriate. An authoritarian government is unlikely to possess sufficient information to enact appropriate legislation even if it were motivated to do so.

What private property is, and what rights are associated with it depend not only on the type of property, but also on the custom, culture, and history of the locality, as Elizabeth Clayton also mentioned in this volume. For example, the particular rights associated with land will depend on whether its uses are primarily residential, agricultural, mining, tourist, manufacturing, etc. Even land used for the same purposes will have different rights associated with it in different places depending on the history and tradition of the locality in which it is situated. Other forms of property, including intellectual, financial, productive, corporate, personal, etc., can provide similar legislative problems. Identification of the appropriate rights for various types of property is a task for which democratic institutions at a local level are better suited than authoritarian institutions.[3]

Another argument for a democratic government's ability to implement decentralizing economic reform is especially relevant in the Soviet context. The Communist party and its Leninist form of government commands very little respect or loyalty within the population. Even if it were able to identify the appropriate set of decentralizing reforms for each particular locality in the USSR, those reforms would not be likely to be well received by the populations they affect simply because they emanated from Moscow. The oppressiveness and ineffectiveness of communism has left a legacy of deep and understandable distrust that even appropriate and well-intentioned reforms could not overcome. Therefore, I argue that this particular link suggests that political democratization can positively influence economic decentralization.

Past Attempts at Economic Decentralization

In this section I trace the history of decentralizing reforms in the USSR. This history tends to support the description of the relationship between democratization and decentralization. We see that in each case, decentralization without democratization was not successful, because reforms were ill-chosen, the population was ill-suited, or because the power and prestige of the Communist party was ultimately threatened. I also show that the final collapse of the USSR fits the model of the synergistic relationship between democratic reform and economic decentralization, with both of these undermining the power of the military and the party and resulting in the end of Leninism.

New Economic Policy: 1921-1928

Lenin's New Economic Policy (NEP) describes the period of experimentation with a part privatized, part socialized economy following Russia's civil war and the confiscatory policies of War Communism. While NEP can be considered a short term success, its several unique features caution against inferring too much from its history. These unique features are a) the relatively primitive and war-ravaged state of the Soviet economy; b) the newness of the Communist regime; and c) the succession crisis which began with Lenin's illness in 1922 and was not ultimately resolved until Stalin terminated NEP.

Under NEP, agriculture, light industry and consumer services were left to private trade, while the "commanding heights" of the economy, banking, trade, and heavy industry, were nationalized.[4]   Growth of national income per capita averaged an impressive nine percent per year from 1921 to 1928, but this growth was characterized by extreme volatility of prices and output.   Unemployment also fluctuated considerably, becoming a serious problem by the end of the NEP period.[5] NEP ended with Stalin's first five year plan in 1928.

What conclusions may be drawn from the NEP experiment? On the positive side, a hybrid economy, with one sector decentralized in markets and the other under centralized administrative direction can experience rapid short run growth. Because NEP was instituted early in Soviet history, before the centralized, command style system, there was no resistance from a powerful, entrenched bureaucracy to sabotage it. The people responsible for carrying out economic activity had experience with change and risks in a decentralized economic environment. Elements of an emerging civil society carried over from pre-revolutionary Russia to support the decentralized sector.

On the negative side, the economic growth tended to be unbalanced and unstable between the private and socialized sectors with respect to prices and employment. The instability and unemployment may have been a reflection of the inability or unwillingness of the authoritarian elite to identify and implement more comprehensive economic reform. The economic instability, along with the perceived threat of the NEPmen, or growing bourgeoisie, to Communist power contributed to the abandonment of the NEP and the complete socialization and collectivization of the economy.

These conclusions must be tempered by the realization that the initial ravaged state of the USSR's economy made early rapid growth relatively easy. The growth up to the beginning of 1927 had the effect of restoring the nation's economy to 1913 levels. The volatility of the economy was certainly affected by the political struggles taking place at the time, both the struggle to consolidate power by the Communists and the struggle for succession within the Communist party.

Some may cite the recent experiences of the People's Republic of China to refute my hypothesis of the interrelationships between economic decentralization and democratization. For this reason, it is instructive to draw some parallels between the experience of the USSR during the NEP and China since 1978. China's reforms have created a dual sector economy similar to the USSR under the NEP, with a decentralized agricultural and consumer sector, but a planned, administrative heavy industrial sector. In the following chapter, Kjeld Erik Brødsgaard makes these observations regarding China's reforms. (1) Economic decentralization in the country-side and the consumer sector developed China's civil society and had the effect of democratizing the polity. (2) The form that economic reform took in China resulted in significant volatility of macroeconomic indicators, with high inflation rates from 1986 to 1988. (3) China's Communist leadership recognized the threat posed by a significant private sector and retrenched in the economic reform process and cracked down politically. These experiences mirror the experience of the USSR and are consistent with the relationships I posit. I agree with Brødsgaard that it is not yet possible to predict the ultimate outcome of the conflict between authoritarian polity and decentralized economy in China.

Khrushchev's Sovnarkhoz Experiment

A *sovnarkhoz* is a regional economic ministry, responsible for formulating and implementing economic plans for a region. Prior to 1957, when the regional ministries were instituted, the ministries were organized on a functional basis and were criticized for failing to coordinate economic activity across industries within a geographic region. The *sovnarkhozy* relocated economic decision-making out of Moscow to the provinces. This move decentralized economic power at the ministerial but not at the enterprise level. The change in location strengthened Khrushchev's political power but was not judged to be an economic success, possibly because the political subdivisions to which the *sovnarkhozy* were attached were too small for rational economic allocation of resources.[6] Econometric measures of the effect of regional ministries on industrial productivity show it to be negligible.[7] Even the political advantage was short-lived. Resentment by bureaucrats sent out of Moscow contributed to the forces which ousted Khrushchev in October 1964.[8] Consequently, the *sovnarkhoz* experiment was abandoned when Brezhnev and Kosygin came to power.

The *sovnarkhoz* experiment illustrates the importance of administrative power in the USSR, emphasizing the need for simultaneously decentralizing politically and economically. Although Khrushchev's economic reforms were accompanied by a thaw in the political climate (for example, increased freedom of speech), this represented a change in policy, not a democratizing political reform. This organizational experiment also provides an example of the inability of the center to choose appropriate economic reform. The *sovnarkhozy* traded lack of coordination at the regional level for lack of coordination at the functional level. Besides, the size of the regional ministries was such that even the regional problems were not solved.

Kosygin Reforms

In the fall of 1965, a year after Brezhnev and Kosygin succeeded Khrushchev, a comprehensive set of changes known as the "Kosygin" reforms was announced. The reforms were a frequently contradictory mixture of centralizing and decentralizing features. Industrial managers were subject to closer scrutiny on more plan targets, but at the same time were expected to demonstrate more initiative on investment decisions, innovations, supply links, and cost-cutting measures. As the reform was carried out, the decentralizing features were sacrificed for the centralizing. Direct links with intermediate suppliers have never taken root in Soviet industry. An enterprise's use of retained earnings was strictly controlled. The freedom to engage in decentralized investment had to be limited because of its tendency to promote autarkic vertical organization in firms seeking to insulate themselves from the uncertainty of centrally directed supply.

What remained of the original reforms were new targets in the annual plan, a strictly controlled fund from retained earnings, and the price revision which included a charge for the use of capital. The result was that by the early 1970s the organization of Soviet industry resembled fairly closely its pre-*sovnarkhoz* predecessor. Econometric estimates of the effects of the Kosygin reforms on industrial productivity are again statistically insignificant.[9] Like Khrushchev's *sovnarkhozy*, the Kosygin reforms illustrate the difficulties an authoritarian government has attempting to decentralize economically due both to its incompetence in choosing appropriate reforms and its unwillingness to sacrifice administrative power.

Brezhnev's Organizational Reforms

From 1970 until his death in 1983, Brezhnev's regime attempted to perfect Soviet socialism by tinkering with organizational details. Two of the more significant decentralizing reforms were the **production associations** and the **labor brigades.**

The production association, or *proizvodstvennoe obedinenie* began to emerge as a new organizational form in 1970. The associations are a varied group of horizontally and vertically integrated conglomerates of enterprises. A special sub-category is the scientific-technical production association (*nauchnoe-tekhnicheskoe proizvodstvennoe obedinenie*) which integrates research institutes with enterprises in an effort to speed the pace and assimilation of invention and innovation in industry.[10] While the integration of enterprises represents increased centralization of economic power, at the same time the production associations are on *khozrashchet* (that is, they are self-financing) and represent a devolution of power from the ministries.

Joseph Berliner, citing Professor A. M. Birman, suggests that the decentralization of power from ministry to association has been effectively resisted by ministry bureaucrats, and that few actual changes have occurred at the enterprise level.[11] The data show that the adoption of the association by Soviet industry increased rapidly at first but has leveled off to the point where 58% of all industrial production was by production associations in 1989.[12] Again, econometric analysis fails to discern any significant effect of the production association on industrial productivity.[13]

In 1979 the labor brigade (*brigada*) began to be officially encouraged as a unit of production in Soviet industry. The labor brigade is a relatively small group of workers who work as a somewhat independent subcontracting production unit. In 1989, for example, each brigade averaged 13.6 workers. By 1989, almost three-quarters of all industrial workers were members of a brigade.[14]

The degree of independence varies among the type of brigade. The most independent form of brigade is self-financing; that is, it works under conditions of *khozrashchet*. This form is the most effectively decentralized. Other forms of the labor brigade are not self-financing and are more dependent on the enterprise both for management and inputs. They are, therefore, less decentralized production forms than the *khozrashchetnaya brigada*. Darrell Slider notes that implementing the brigade system in industry has been strongly urged by Communist party leaders, and that many reported brigades are purely cosmetic in nature. Where introduction of the brigade system has been forced, they have not been effective.[15] While it is still too soon to judge the effectiveness of the brigade, econometric results indicate that the self-financing brigade form may have a positive effect on industrial productivity, while the less decentralized form appears to affect performance negatively.[16] On balance, the brigade has not had a positive impact on Soviet industrial performance. Brezhnev's organizational experimentation once again demonstrates that centralized Leninist form of government has great difficulty decentralizing its economic system due to ill-chosen reforms, lack of implementation by unsympathetic and incapable bureaucrats, and little support from society at large.

Perestroika

With the exception of the thaw during the Khrushchev period, none of the decentralizing economic reforms attempted in the Soviet Union were accompanied by political reforms until Gorbachev, and these occurred only when he realized that decentralization would be impossible without political changes. Gorbachev's program of economic reform, *perestroika*, has undergone three phases since his succession of Chernenko in 1985. The first phase closely resembled reforms of the past, with similar ineffectual results. The second phase coupled more radically decentralizing economic reform with democratizing political reform. The third phase saw economic change thoroughly subordinated to the political struggle between democratizers and the existing governmental and economic apparatus. This third phase climaxed in the failed putsch on August 19, 1991 and eventually culminated in the disbanding of the USSR in late December.

The initial phase of *perestroika* included an anti-alcohol and worker discipline campaign, an investment drive to modernize industrial technology, and continued reliance on production associations and labor brigades as organizational innovations. A "super-ministry" was formed (*Gosagroprom*) to oversee agriculture and agricultural industry. A quality control agency was formed (*Gospriyemka*) with the power to reject as output substandard products. These measures did not represent new solutions, nor were they particularly decentralizing. Not surprisingly, they had no long-term positive results.

The next phase saw many announcements of radical and decentralizing economic reforms, with apparently little effect. For example, in 1987 we saw announcements of bankruptcy laws and one actual bankruptcy, as well as radical decrees issued at the party congress in June giving enterprise managers authority to set their own production plans and choose their own suppliers as well as determine prices.[17] We saw aggressive attempts to attract foreign partners in joint ventures and more autonomy given to enterprises to engage in foreign trade. We saw a plan to make all Soviet enterprises self-financing by the end of 1989. We saw liberalization of the laws on cooperative enterprises and growth of this organizational form in the consumer services sector. We saw at the same time resistance to all of these measures and little change in plan formation, pricing policies, and the frustrations faced by Western partners in joint ventures. The economic reforms were accompanied by streamlining of the ministries,*"glasnost"*, and some steps toward democratization which included contested party and government elections. The economic results showed continued decline and stagnation of economic growth, while the political reforms sowed the seeds for the demise of the Communist rule that was to follow.

The final phase of *perestroika* reflected all of the contradictions, frustrations, and polarities inherent in the six-year attempt to decentralize the economy via an authoritarian polity. It began in early 1990 when Gorbachev assumed extraordinary centralized presidential power for the expressed purpose of implementing decentralizing economic reform. This step may have been taken in order to circumvent obstructionists in the party apparatus, because party influence in the new governmental structure was reduced. The constitutional guarantee of the Communist Party's "leading role" was removed. Despite these measures, it transpired that extraordinary presidential power was no more effective than the party apparatus at decentralizing the economy. By the summer of 1990 it was evident that the government's inability to formulate an economic mechanism to replace the failing administrative system would result in economic crisis.

The crisis atmosphere gave birth to two competing economic plans. The "500-day" program, initially embraced but ultimately rejected in October, 1990 by Gorbachev, represents one polar extreme, while Pavlov's "anti-crisis" program, implemented in the winter and spring of 1991, represents the other. The former was a radical plunge into privatization and marketization; the latter provided for administrative confiscation of large ruble notes and an arbitrary tripling of many consumer good prices. "500-days" was truly decentralizing; the anticrisis plan was a centralizing, administrative response. As the history of reform in the USSR indicates, decentralizing reforms have always been scrapped in favor of centralizing, and this is what happened in the fall of 1990. The result of the polarized political debate was an economic debacle: a precipitous decline in GNP over the first six months of 1991 and widespread shortages in such basic goods as foodstuffs, medical supplies, and heating fuel.

The contradictions and polarities that were so evident in the last phase of *perestroika* were perhaps inevitable. Because of the inability of the authoritarian polity to implement an appropriate set of decentralizing economic reforms, Gorbachev responded by centralizing political power to a greater degree. While his formal powers had never been greater, his ability to implement *perestroika* continued to decline. Recognizing that "500-days" would result in the loss of economic levers and ultimately the demise of Communist power, the party forced Gorbachev to reject the decentralizing reform in favor of Pavlov's ill-conceived anti-crisis measures. Ironically, the August putsch, engineered by the very conservatives whom Gorbachev had spent a year appeasing, finally closed the curtain on *perestroika*, clearing the path for the twin processes of economic decentralization and democratization, and the demise of the USSR.

Perestroika teaches us that even Mikhail Gorbachev, a relatively youthful, energetic, and very capable Communist reformer was unable to decentralize the economic system within the context of a centralized, authoritarian state apparatus. He proved unable to conceive a coordinated and rational plan for reform, and the Soviet state proved unwilling to decentralize in any but cosmetic ways.

The Commonwealth of Independent States

If the failures of Gorbachev's *perestroika* support the hypothesis that the Leninist system was unable to decentralize its economy in the absence of political reform, the events from August through December, 1991 support my arguments for the synergistic relationship between economic and political reform. The failed putsch catalyzed support for democratic reform and catapulted Yeltsin ahead of Gorbachev in political influence. It also eliminated the major impediments to economic decentralization and democratization. Those impediments were, of course, those groups in the USSR which were especially favored by the Leninist form of government; i.e. the Communist party, the Red Army, the KGB, and the *nomenklatura*. At the same time, the attempted putsch finally destroyed the central political authority of the USSR, which had been waning in the months prior to August, 1991. Despite these dramatic changes, Gorbachev remained unwilling to abandon the Soviet political and economic structure completely in his attempt to retain his power as well as the Union. Thus, the formation of the Commonwealth was an "end run" around the remaining vestiges of Communist power that stood in the way of the ever growing momentum of the forces for democracy.

The Lessons of the History of Economic Reform in the USSR

The fact that no decentralizing economic reform had unambiguous success in the Soviet era is an indication that the Soviet polity was unable and/or unwilling to choose effective economic institutions. The fact that decentralizing aspects of the reforms tended to be abandoned or diluted in their implementation is an indication of the long-run incompatibility of decentralizing economic reform with an authoritarian government. While the history of Russia and the USSR cannot disprove the contention of Robert Byrnes and others that the Russians are better suited for centralized government than for democracy and decentralization, the history of *perestroika* and the collapse of the center in August 1991 lend support to the notions that economic decentralization and political democratization are best carried out simultaneously, and give some reason to hope that the major political impediments to democratization have disappeared.

At the time of this writing, the uncertain status of the Commonwealth of Independent States makes it apparent that the political future of the former USSR depends largely on the republics, not the Union. Both my theoretical and historical analyses suggest that we look for objective conditions which favor the simultaneous evolution of democracy and economic decentralization in order to assess that future. Such an examination of the republics may provide insight into the prospects for the success of the different independent states and the Commonwealth as a whole to develop and maintain stable democracies and market-oriented economies.

I have argued that the motivation for economic decentralization comes from the level of economic development and the desire to increase the well-being of the consumer in a country. This suggests that the higher the level of economic development, the greater the likelihood of economic decentralization.

I have also suggested that democratic political institutions are better suited to identifying appropriate collective choices than authoritarian institutions. On the other hand, authoritarian polities are better suited to implementing collective decisions than democratic ones, because less negotiating by autonomous and equal parties is necessary when authoritarian decisions are imposed.[18] As the population of a state rises, the problems of implementation rise more than proportionally if the political environment is democratic because of the number of multilateral contacts that must be made in order to negotiate a majority vote. In an authoritarian environment implementation costs rise proportionally with the number of participants, as the authority need only communicate and enforce its collective choice to each member of the group. Therefore, population is an objective condition influencing the likelihood of successful democratization. The lower the population, the more democratization is favored.

Finally, one may also argue that homogeneity of the population will also influence collective decision-making. A society composed of a relatively homogeneous citizenry tends to face fewer problems in both identifying and implementing collective choices. The population is more homogeneous when it shares a common culture and ethnic background. This condition makes collective decision-making less costly in any political environment. The autonomous and equal citizens in a democratic environment are likely to find negotiating and enforcing political transactions easier the more homogeneous they are as a group. A republic seeking to remake its fundamental institutions will find it easier the more homogeneous its population. Therefore, the greater the ethnic homogeneity within a republic, the greater the likelihood of economic decentralization and democratization.

Table 13.1 ranks the 15 republics of the former USSR by level of economic development (capital assets per person, ranked from highest to lowest), population (thousands, ranked from fewest to most), and ethnic homogeneity (percentage of population in largest ethnic group, ranked from highest to lowest). For each category the top third of the republics are considered to have a relatively "high" likelihood of reforming. The middle third are considered "moderate." The bottom third are considered to have a relatively "low" likelihood of reform. The raw data are given in parentheses in each category for each republic. We can expect that the republics with the highest level of economic development have the greatest motivation to decentralize and democratize, while the republics with the lowest population and the highest ethnic homogeneity have the greatest capability of democratizing.

The order of the Republics in Table 13.1 is somewhat arbitrary. There is no sound theoretical basis for weighting the relative importance of the economic and demographic indicators in assessing the likelihood of reform. I have chosen a roughly lexicographic ordering, in which the level of economic development is primary. The reasoning for this is that this variable is intended to measure the motivation to decentralize. Without the motivation to reform, the capability of reforming is not as important.

Examining the data leads one to anticipate that the republics of European Russia, including Russia, the Baltic states, Byelorussia, and the Ukraine, along with Kazakhstan have the greatest economic incentive to decentralize and democratize. Of these, Lithuania features the best combination of size and homogeneity to be able to transform itself into a democracy, while Byelorussia lags in both categories. The other Baltic states are disadvantaged relative to Lithuania due to their ethnic heterogeneity (Estonia and Latvia both have large Russian populations). Russia and the Ukraine are disadvantaged due to their size. Kazakhstan

Table 13.1 Likelihood of Decentralizing and Democratizing Reform,
According to Selected Economic and Demographic Data
Republics of the Former USSR
(Raw data appear in parentheses)

Republic	Wealth per capita (thous. 1989 rubles)	Population (thous. persons)*	% Dominant Group
Lithuania	High (7.25)	High (3723)	High (80)
Estonia	High (8.21)	High (1583)	Low (62)
Latvia	High (7.44)	High (2687)	Low (52)
Russia	High (7.86)	Low (148041)	High (82)
Byelorussia	Moderate (6.24)	Low (10259)	High (78)
Kazakhstan	High (6.65)	Low (16691)	Low (40)
Ukraine	Moderate (5.54)	Low (51839)	Moderate (73)
Turkmenistan	Moderate (4.97)	High (3622)	Moderate (72)
Georgia	Moderate (4.77)	Moderate (5456)	Moderate (70)
Moldavia	Moderate (4.59)	Moderate (4362)	Moderate (64)
Armenia	Low (4.56)	High (3293)	High (93)
Azerbaijan	Low (4.07)	Moderate (7131)	High (83)
Kirghizia	Low (3.21)	Moderate (4367)	Low (52)
Uzbekistan	Low (3.10)	Low (20322)	Moderate (71)
Tadzhikistan	Low (2.48)	Moderate (5248)	Low (62)

*Remember that the inverse relationship between the size of the population and the ease of democratization means that republics are ranked higher when their population is lower.

Data on population and wealth are from Tsen'tralnoe Statisticheskoe Upravlenie, *Narodnoe Khozyaistvo SSSR*, 1989, pages 17 and 278.
Data on ethnic homogeneity are from CIA, *USSR: Demographic Trends and Ethnic Balance in the Non-Russian Republics*, GI 90-10013U, April 1990, page 8.

is the most ethnically diverse republic in the Union, and the third largest in population. While other republics, notably Armenia, have demographic characteristics which give them favorable conditions for democratizing, their level of development gives them less economic incentive to do so.[19] Armenia and Azerbaijan are presently engaged in a bloody ethnic and border conflict, a crisis situation which tends not to favor the development of democratic institutions.

The principles developed in this chapter suggest that democratization and economic decentralization best go hand in hand. Since all the republics appear to desire economic decentralization to some degree, we can expect some long-term movement towards democratization, although Table 13.1 suggests that the consolidation of democracy will be easier for some than for others. Of course, as has been pointed out throughout this volume, many other factors influence the success of transitions from Leninist states to market-oriented democracies, including historical foundations, the status of civil society and the rule of law, and certainly political leadership. My predictions are based on only a narrow set of three factors.   Yet, even these predictions must be tempered by the extreme economic crisis in which all the former republics of the USSR find themselves in the immediate future.   Crisis conditions usually favor authoritarian government.

What might be said of the prospects for the Commonwealth of Independent States? At the time of this writing, even the nature of the Commonwealth is too uncertain to allow for any meaningful predictions. Yet, perhaps one observation can be made in response to the rather pessimistic characterization of the Russian people offered by Robert Byrnes and others in this volume. How dare a people so historically ill-suited for decentralized rule attempt to break the USSR into independent nations bound together into a loose Commonwealth? Given the failures of centralized government in the region, such a confederation may not only be possible, but necessary, in order that appropriate and feasible economic restructuring take place. As long as there is an economic infrastructure including a common currency to facilitate exchange, less central control should favor greater economic growth. And, as I have argued throughout this chapter, although economic decentralization and its accompanying growth are not sufficient conditions for democratization, they certainly reinforce its progress.

Notes

1.   Of course, actors in a market-oriented economy may themselves be considered as elements of civil society.

2. See Olson, Mancur, *The Logic of Collective Action*, Cambridge: Harvard University Press, 1971; and *The Rise and Decline of Nations*, New Haven: Yale University Press, 1982.

3. See Toumanoff, "Institutional Change in Communist Countries," Bradley Institute for Democracy and Public Values Working Paper, July 1991, for further development of this argument.

4. See Alec Nove, *An Economic History of the USSR* (Baltimore: Penguin Books Inc., 1969), 85.

5. Alec Nove, *An Economic History of the USSR*83-118.

6.   See David Dyker, *The Future of the Soviet Economic Planning System* (Armonk, New York: M.E. Sharpe Inc., 1985), 43.

7. See Peter Toumanoff, "The Use of Production Functions to Investigate Soviet Industrial Reform," *Comparative Economic Studies*, Fall 1987, 94-111; and "Economic Reform and Industrial Performance in the Soviet Union: 1950-1984," in Susan Linz and William Moskoff, eds., *Reorganization and Reform in the Soviet Economy* (Armonk, NY: M.E. Sharpe Inc., 1988).

8. See Philippe J. Bernard (I. Nove, trans.), *Planning in the Soviet Union* (Oxford: Pergamon Press, 1966), 108-136; and Mikhail Heller and Aleksandr Nekrich, *Utopia in Power: The History of the Soviet Union from 1917 to the Present* (New York: Summit Books, 1986), 553-554.

9. See Toumanoff, "The Use of Production Functions to Investigate Soviet Industrial Reform," and "Economic Reform and Industrial Performance in the Soviet Union: 1950-1984."

10. See Joseph Berliner, *The Innovation Decision in Soviet Industry* (Cambridge: The MIT Press, 1976), 129-147; Paul Cocks, "Organizing for Technological Innovation in the 1980s," in Gregory Guroff and Fred V. Carstensen (eds.), *Entrepreneurship in Imperial Russia and the Soviet Union*, (Princeton: Princeton University Press, 1983), 306-46; and John H. Moore, "Agency Costs, Technological Change, and Soviet Central Planning," *Journal of Law and Economics* 24, 2:189-214, October, 1981 for informative discussions of production associations.

11. Joseph Berliner, *The Innovation Decision in Soviet Industry*, 144.

12. See Goskomstat, *Narodnoe Khozyaistvo SSSR 1989* [*NARKHOZ*], (Moscow, 1989), 331.

13. See Toumanoff, "Economic Reform and Industrial Performance in the Soviet Union: 1950-1984."

14. See *NARKHOZ 1989*, 369.

15. Darrell Slider, "The Brigade System in Soviet Industry: An Effort to Restructure the Labor Force," *Soviet Studies* 39, No. 3, 388-405, July 1987, 394-403.

16. See Toumanoff, "Economic Reform and Industrial Performance in the Soviet Union: 1950-1984."

17. See "Gorbachev Economic Plan Called Radical," *Wall Street Journal*, Monday, June 29, 1987, 2.

18. See Toumanoff, "Institutional Change in Communist Countries," Bradley Institute for Democracy and Public Values Working Paper, July, 1991, 13. In this paper I suggest that the horizontal relationships in market and democratic institutions have a comparative advantage in identifying appropriate economic and political transactions, and that the vertical relationships in hierarchic and authoritarian institutions have a comparative advantage in implementing economic and political transactions. The economic and demographic conditions I suggest favor democratization are those which minimize implementation problems but emphasize identification problems.

19. I do not intend to suggest that only economic incentives motivate a desire for democracy. It is beyond the scope of this paper to examine other possible motives, including cultural, philosophical, and psychological.

14

Civil Society and Democratization
in China

Kjeld Erik Brødsgaard

In the 1980s, China experienced what appeared to be a substantial reform of the existing economic and political system.[1] Economic reforms resulted in significant departures from central planning and the emergence of various forms of market regulation of the economy. New economic forms, such as individual and private economy emerged and new social groups arose such as private entrepreneurs and businessmen. Political reforms, although less radical, signified an initial retreat of the party from its traditional all-dominating role. Similarly, the state allowed more space for debate on the future direction of Chinese society. On several occasions, there were demonstrations and mass critiques of the regime. Although the party often reacted with repressive measures, in general these new autonomous forces grew stronger and stronger.

The present paper will analyze the process of reform in Post-Mao China. Some of the major events and documents will be discussed, but the main concern is to view the Chinese reform process from the perspective of the emergence of civil society and from the perspective of the possible democratization of Chinese society. It will be argued that the emergence of civil society and initial steps to democratize the polity signified a transition from authoritarianism. The "thaw" of authoritarian rule brought about by the "soft-liners" in the party created a sharp increase in general politicization and popular activities, which formed the background of the people's movement in Beijing and other cities in China in the spring of 1989.

The June 1989 military crackdown abruptly halted the transition away from authoritarianism in China. However, it appears that the new order post-Tiananmen Square cannot be characterized as a reversal to pre-1976 totalitarian rule. Rather, what has gradually evolved over the last two years is a system which combines political repression and economic liberalism. Is this a viable combination in the long run or has the reform process already created a civil society sufficiently strong to eventually force the transition from "authoritarian rule" to a more democratic society? This aspect will be discussed towards the end of the paper. But first it is necessary to put the discussion of civil society in China in a theoretical perspective.

Civil Society

The term *civil society* has been used in several senses throughout this volume and elsewhere in the scholarly literature.[2] When the discourse of civil society was reinvented in Poland in the 1970s, it was based on Antonio Gramsci's conception which stressed the state as a massive structure in contrast to autonomous spheres of activities that were emerging.[3] The most notable of these activities was, of course, the independent trade union Solidarity, but this was, in fact, only one example of a number of networks that emerged, creating a new public discourse beyond the control and limits of the party-state.

Recently Moshe Lewin has pointed out that civil society can penetrate the state, thereby in a sense abolishing or raising to a new level (in German: *aufheben*) the sharp confrontation between state and civil society. Lewin defines civil society in the following way:

> By "civil society" we refer to the aggregate of networks and institutions that either exist and act independently of the state or are official organizations capable of developing their own, spontaneous views on national or local issues and then impressing these views on their members, on small groups and, finally, on the authorities. These social complexes do not necessarily oppose the state, but exist in contrast to outright state organisms and enjoy a certain degree of autonomy.[4]

Lewin argues that independent or informal trends and groups also may appear in the Soviet state bureaucracy. Similarly public opinion and sentiments penetrate the state and may solicit sympathy from state officials. This concept of a civil society operating within the state apparatus is different from the Polish type of civil society and would more correspond to an alternative of Gramsci's where the state encompasses civil society.

The following use of civil society will take its inspiration in the Polish type, i.e. our use of the concept refers to the organization of a plurality of interests outside the state and party in an increasingly independent or autonomous social sphere. However it is also informed by Lewin's interpretation of the Soviet example, where civil society penetrates the state or emerges from within the state.

Democratization

The term democratization appears to be linked to civil society. Thus, David Held has coined the concept "double democratization".[5] This concept signifies an attempt to reform the state and civil society through both a restructuring of state institutions and the expansion of autonomy in civil society. These processes must be interdependent; the state and civil society must become the condition for each other's democratization:

> Without a secure and independent civil society, goals such as freedom and equality cannot be realized. But without the protective, redistributive and conflict-mediating functions of the state, struggles to transform civil society are likely to become fragmented, or the bearers of new forms of inequality of power, wealth or status. The central issue today is not the old alternative between liberalism or Marxism, reformism or revolution to abolish the state. Rather, it is the question of how to enact the "double-sided" process of creative reform protected by state action and innovation from below through radical social initiatives.[6]

John Keane also maintains that civil society and the state must become the conditions of each other's democratization. He understands democratization as "the pluralization of power within a civil society protected and encouraged by an accountable framework of state institutions" and rejects the assumption that the state could ever replace civil society in any legitimate sense.[7]

In the following we will analyze the Chinese reform process post-Mao. The primary objective will be to evaluate whether this process in any meaningful way has initiated democratization and pluralization in an economic and political sense and whether there are corresponding signs of the emergence of a civil society.

The Democracy Movement, 1978-1979

Following the death of Mao Zedong, China was in a deep crisis. Although the economy was picking up again after having recorded negative growth in 1976, it was clear that sustained growth was threatened by a lopsided development process placing too much emphasis on heavy-industrial growth and high accumulation rates. The strong emphasis on accumulation had adverse effects on social conditions. Thus, the real income of the peasants had not registered any improvement from the mid-1950s to Mao's death, the city populations were living in housing conditions which were significantly worse than in the 1950s, most consumer goods were still rationed and often of poor quality, etc. Politically, the country was in the midst of a succession crisis which had split the leadership into antagonistic factions. The factional fight did not end with the arrest of the Gang of Four in October 1976. It only intensified the struggle which eventually would end in the demise of Mao's designated successor, Hua Guofeng. Since the political system was held responsible for allowing the Cultural Revolution to happen and for generating political phenomena like the Gang of Four, it had lost most of its legitimacy. In short, the old system and the old development strategy seemed to have lost out, and reforms were urgently needed.

As the debates among the leadership on the future direction for China intensified, a democracy movement began to emerge outside the immediate reach of state and party. The movement started as a wall poster campaign in November 1978, with individual protesters putting up their complaints and demands on the democracy wall in Beijing.[8] But already in December, the protesters began to organize and form groups which published their own journals. Their rallying point was the modernization and improvement of democratic conditions and, in particular they demanded civil liberties, basic economic rights and a higher degree of freedom vis-à-vis state and party. Based on these demands and the fact that the various democratic groups were formed spontaneously and independently of the state, it can be argued that one sees here the first signs of the emergence of a civil society in China.[9]

It appears useful to distinguish between two major groups in the democracy movement. One group, "the socialist democrats", argued for reform within the existing political and economic structure of China. Thus, they hesitated to question the authority and legitimacy of the state and party. In fact, a number of "socialist democrats" were party members or members of the Communist Youth League.[10] In contrast, the other main group, the "abolitionists", sought a complete transformation of the existing order in China. In their opinion, China was a class society ruled by a new class which had emerged, rooted in the special privileges of the bureaucratic and technocratic strata. Thus, this group had a clear anti-state orientation. They wanted to abolish the dictatorship of the proletariat and called for a multiparty system. Wei Jingsheng's group, which published the underground journal *Tansuo* (Exploration) is the most well-known in this category.[11]

Wei Jingheng's three-part article on "The Fifth Modernization" in *Tansuo* can be regarded as one of the main "abolitionist" documents. The article contains strong arguments for democracy and human rights, and points to the need to prevent the state from encroaching on civil society. On democracy and democratization Wei says:

> What is true democracy? It means the right of the people to choose their own representatives to work according to their will and their interests. Only this can be called democracy. Furthermore, the people must also have the power to replace their representatives anytime so that these representatives cannot go on deceiving others in the name of the people.[12]

Wei maintains that democratization by no means is the result of social and economic progress and development. On the contrary, democracy is the precondition for the realization of the Four Modernizations. In order to underline the importance of democracy in the modernization process, Wei dubs it the "Fifth Modernization." Wei further argues that true socialism should secure "equal rights for individuals in their livelihood" and "these rights can be realized only through free organizations and coordination with democratic politics."[13]

Another important document that seems to indicate the emergence of a civil society in China is the nineteen points Human Rights Declaration of the Chinese Human Rights League (*Zhongguo Renquan Tongmeng*) published on January 17, 1979, in Beijing.[14] The declaration demands freedom of thought, freedom of speech and the release of everyone convicted for offenses connected with these two freedoms (point 1). Moreover, according to the declaration, the citizens must have freedom to subscribe to foreign newspapers and magazines and to listen to foreign television and radio stations (10). Citizens must also have the right to choose their own vocations and freedom of movement (11). There are also demands for a pluralization of the political system. Various parties and groups should be allowed and have right of access to the National People's Congress (3). Finally, the Human Rights League calls for a national referendum to be held to elect state leaders and leaders at all levels in various areas (4).

In the beginning of 1979, the democracy movement had developed autonomous as well as autocephalous traits. So what the party could envisage was the development of a civil society composed of groups and associations which not only defined their own order, but also elected their own leaders independently of the formal leadership of state and party. This was unacceptable to the leadership, and even Deng Xiaoping, who had originally appeared to appreciate the participatory political disposition of the movement, could no longer support it.[15] Deng and his reform coalition presumably also made the calculation that they had already succeeded in their efforts to out-maneuver Hua Guofeng and the "whateverist" faction and no longer benefitted from the "extra-parliamentary" activities in the streets. In fact, they feared that they themselves might become targets of criticism.

The first sign of a split came when Deng, at a meeting of a group of high-ranking cadres on March 16, 1979, warned that the democracy movement had "gone too far" and that, in the future, all discussions were to uphold the socialist road, the dictatorship of the proletariat, the leadership of the Communist Party, and Marxism-Leninism-Mao Zedong Thought (the so-called "Four Fundamental Principles"). An official notice was later posted in Beijing banning all *dazibao*, books, and publications opposed to the "Four Principles."[16]

When Wei Jingsheng responded to this development by publishing a special issue of *Tansuo* entitled "Democracy or New Dictatorship", which stated that Deng had turned into a dictator no longer "worthy of the people's trust and support," he was promptly arrested. During the following days, other leaders of the democracy movement were arrested, among them Ren Wanding from the Human Right's League. Over the next year, further repressive steps were taken, and in April, 1980, the Standing Committee of the National People's Congress crowned the final crackdown by passing a decision to delete the right to "speak out freely, air views fully, hold great debates, and write *dazibao*" ("Four Greats") from the Constitution.[17]

To Deng, the Democracy Movement represented "factors of instability" that could not fit into his vision of a new political order. It is noteworthy that Deng took great pains to reassure the intellectuals while clamping down on the Democracy Movement. In fact, although Deng had broken with the young activists, he had not abandoned the notion of political reform. But to him it had to come from above -- it had to be led by the party.

The reform discussion was brought into the party fold. But within these parameters the debate was quite open and nuanced in terms of different policy positions on the major issues. Since our definition of democratization ("the double democratization") involves both a restructuring of state institutions as well as an expansion of autonomy in civil society, this is of course of major importance.

Gengshen Reforms

In August, 1980, at an enlarged meeting of the Politburo, Deng delivered an important speech on reform of the leadership systems of the party and the state.[18] The speech was not published at the time, but the Chinese press was full of allusions to it. The debate which followed and the policy proposals which were formulated came to be known as the *Gengshen* reforms.[19]

In his August, 1980 speech, Deng identified five major obstacles to political reform: bureaucracy, over-concentration of power, patriarchal methods, lifelong tenure of leading posts, and various kinds of privileges. The major problem, according to Deng, was the over-concentration of power which primarily manifested itself in the form of the concentration of all power in party committees. This was a major problem, because the power of the party committee usually was in the hands of party first secretaries, thereby, in fact turning leadership by the party into leadership by individuals.

Deng admitted that historically there had been too much emphasis on ensuring centralism and unification by the party, and on combatting decentralism and any assertion of independence. In this way there had been too little emphasis on ensuring the "necessary degree of decentralization, delegating necessary decision-making power to the lower organizations and opposing the over-concentration of power in the hands of individuals."[20]

At about the same time, Deng delivered an even more "internal" speech where he clarified his views on the role of the party in Chinese society:

The Party organization neither equals the government nor the organ of state power. The method of the Party ruling over the country cannot be practiced any more.[21]

This is a very categorical statement, and what is meant by it is probably not that Deng envisions doing away with the leading role of the party; rather he wants to pull the party and its cadres out of daily administration in order to "strengthen the party's leadership over the ideological and political fields." Deng warned that if the party neglected to introduce reforms to solve these problems, it would be placed in a position "antagonistic to the masses". He pointed out that when the Polish Communist Party had failed to redefine its position in society, the Polish workers had reacted by establishing their own independent trade unions.

At a seminar on party history held by the national party school system in October of 1980, Liao Gailong, a member of the Policy Research Office of the Central Committee, further elaborated on these reform proposals.[22] Liao Gailong's *Gengshen*[23] reforms entail a loosening of party control over Chinese society and an increase of the autonomy of other organizations. Concerning the leadership system of the party, he proposed two specific reforms. The first was that the Central Committee no longer should enjoy absolute power. Instead the next party congress should elect three parallel central committees which would "mutually supervise and impose constraints on one another." These three bodies could be called Central Executive Committee (the former Central Committee), the Central Discipline Inspection Committee and the Central Supervisory Committee. The members of the last committee would be "the revolutionaries of the older generation, who have rich experience, will still be able to work, but are rather weak physically". Along the same line Liao Gailong proposed to divide the NPC into two houses; one house should be based on territorial representation and the other should represent social and functional interests. These two houses would jointly execute legislative power, jointly supervise the work of the government, and jointly exercise state power. They would impose a constraint on each other so that neither house would have the final say. Meetings would also have to be convened more frequently, so that people no longer could call the NPC a "rubber stamp". There should also be an independent judiciary which would mean that when a court passed a verdict, it would not have to send it to any party committee for examination and approval. The workers should be permitted to elect the officials of the trade unions, otherwise the working class might rise in rebellion as had happened in Poland.[24]

In sum, Liao Gailong proposed the introduction of pluralistic elements into the Chinese political system. He envisaged a system characterized by "checks and balances" between various political institutions and organs rather than by the exclusive dominance of a strong and centralized party.

In the course of discussion and ratification, Liao Gailong's reform proposals seem to have encountered strong resistance. This, in combination with a general moratorium in the reform process from December, 1980, caused by economic retrenchment and consolidation, made Deng reluctant to pursue the *Gengshen* reforms. From the beginning of 1980, Deng's faction also seemed to focus more on organizational development rather than political rethinking.[25] Finally, Jaruzelski's coup in 1981 in Poland appeared to have capped the Polish dissident movement which caused the Chinese leaders to be less concerned with the Polish situation.

Renewed Reform Efforts

In the summer of 1986, after 5 years' concentration on economic issues, political reform again was placed at the top of the political agenda in China. Again the issue was opened by Deng Xiaoping, and in August, 1986, excerpts of his August, 1980, reform speech appeared in the Chinese media.[26]

The 1986 debate explicitly connected political reform to economic reform. In particular, two reform proposals had a direct bearing on the economy as well as on the political arena. One concerned the reduction of the power of local governments and local party committees. The other concerned reducing the power of the enterprise party committee in order to strengthen the management role of enterprise directors and managers.

It was expected that the reform process would be further accelerated at the 6th Plenum in September, 1986. However, the plenum adopted a resolution that stressed that reform of the political system represented "a very complicated task" that only could proceed step by step and with "proper guidance".[27] The term "proper guidance" clearly denotes that the leading role of the party would not be abandoned.

But the renewed reform process was not easily capped. The debate in the party and among prominent party and state leaders relaxed central control and created space for a reemergence of civil society. Thus, following the 6th Plenum, a new series of demonstrations erupted. They started in Hefei and had by December reached Shanghai and Beijing. Whereas the 1978-79 democracy movement was led by workers (many of whom were Red Guards), this time the students took the initiative. Many students were primarily motivated by frustrations with their living conditions on campus, but there were also widespread demands for democratic reforms, and the movement in fact started with the issue of selecting candidates for the local people's congress at Hefei University.[28] In Wuhan students demanded the right to establish independent student associations and to choose their own cadres.[29] There were posters to the same effect in both Beijing and Shanghai.

To be sure, no clear political program emerged from the demonstrations, nevertheless, the events proved that social forces still could organize and act independently of the state.

The demonstrations caused Deng to once again reflect on developments in Poland. At a meeting with a number of party and state leaders on December, 1986, he underlined the importance of being clearheaded and resolute when faced with unrest and demonstrations, just as the Polish leaders had been in 1981. The Polish leaders were faced with a united opposition from the trade unions and the church, and they resorted to military measures to bring the situation under control. In Deng's view "this proves that it won't do without the methods of dictatorship," only one should use these measures carefully and arrest as few people as possible and in as bloodless a manner as possible.[30]

General Secretary Hu Yaobang was blamed for not taking such a clear stand against the student demonstrations and for having allowed things to take their own course. He was consequently dismissed at an enlarged meeting of the Politburo on January 16, 1987.

Hu Yaobang's dismissal meant a temporary setback to the reform process. The conservative wing of the party orchestrated a campaign against bourgeois liberalization which in fact was an anti-reform campaign. However, from the early summer of 1987, Deng Xiaoping and the new party leader Zhao Ziyang reversed the process by warning against the danger of leftism rather than rightism. This indicated that, although Deng had agreed to oust Hu Yaobang, he still believed in reform. But once again he had been confirmed in his conviction that the reform process had to be led by a strong and unified party and could not rely on forces associated with an emerging civil society.

Party Reform

In 1980, in his speech to the Politburo on the reform of leadership systems, Deng had stated that party and state were too interconnected and some kind of reform in this area was needed so that the party would no longer "take on and intervene in everything."[31] The same position was taken by Liao Gailong who said that the old system had caused a system of individual dictatorial and arbitrary rule by the party committee secretaries.[32]

However, the proposals on the separation of party from government remained on paper for quite some time. This was not only because the reform encountered major systemic opposition among party bureaucrats and cadres, especially at the local level, who rightly feared they might lose power if the reform was implemented. Another important factor was that major changes had to await the completion of the party rectification campaign.

Party rectification had started in the winter of 1983-84 and it was projected that the campaign would proceed by stages over a period of three years.[33] It would start with the leading organs and cadres and then proceed down to lower levels. At the end there would be a re-registration of party members, and those who failed to meet the requirements after having gone through education would be expelled from the party.[34]

The about 2.5 million party organizations' 40 million members, including more than 9 million cadres, would be affected in two stages. During the first stage work would focus on the party organizations of the leading bodies at the central, provincial, and autonomous regional level, including the party organs of the various ministries, commissions and departments of these two levels and the PLA headquarters and regional commands. During the second stage, beginning in the winter of 1984-85, the campaign would be extended to the remaining party organizations.[35]

In May, 1987, after three and one-half years of party rectification, Bo Yibo summed up the results of the campaign.[36] He revealed that in addition to the 400,000 people that had been "ferreted out" in the pre-rectification period, more than 200,000 were expelled from the party or were not allowed to renew their membership and about 325,000 others had their registration postponed or received various disciplinary actions. This means that about 600,000 had been expelled from the party in the post-Mao period. Given the fact that about 18 million were recruited into the party during the Cultural Revolution decade, this is perhaps an indication that the effect of elite conflict on the party rank-and-file membership was less serious than could have been anticipated.

With Bo Yibo's report, the rectification campaign was completed. The focus of party work was now to be directed towards the issue of separating party from government, which was regarded as the key to political reform. Consequently, separating party from government came to occupy an important position in Zhao Ziyang's important reform-oriented report to the 13th Party Congress in October 1987.[37]

First, Zhao Ziyang proposed that the party should no longer duplicate and overlap existing government organizations and that the system of party groups (*dangzu*) within government units should be abolished. Secondly, the General Secretary proposed to reform the personnel system relating to cadres by instituting different management systems for different categories of cadres. The crux in his proposal was to make the party relinquish its control over the nomenklatura, according to which all cadre appointments are subject to the approval of the party, and to establish a system of public service.[38] In the future, cadres should be classified in two categories, a political-administrative category and a professional work category, and only the former category should be managed by the party.

Small Government Big Society

Following Zhao's report, several concrete proposals on how to separate party and government and to limit central control in order to stimulate local initiative were formulated. One of the more interesting was put forward in 1988 when Hainan Island was appointed a special economic zone and given provincial status. The proposal was advanced under the name "small government big society," and its implementation was supposed to be monitored by the central government in order to obtain experiences which could be used in the rest of the country.[39]

The "small government big society" plan envisaged the establishment of a new government structure consisting of only four systems. The first system would be a political guarantee system, which should include courts of law, police, matters concerning staff and personnel, etc. The second system, the social service system, was to consist of civil administration, labor relations, health, education, etc. The third system, called the economic development and organization system, was supposed to deal with matters in agriculture, industry, commerce, energy, communication and science and technology. Finally, the plans operated with an economic coordination and control system, which would manage economic planning and control, taxes and environment issues.[40]

In addition to a reform of state and government functions, "small government big society" entailed the recognition of the enterprises' right to run their own affairs. But the most important and inventive part of the program was the proposal to set up various trade unions, business associations and consumer organizations. They were supposed to represent the interests of their members and to function as a bridge between the state organs and the citizens. Self-governing associations in the villages, townships and at the local level in major cities were also to form. Moreover, "little government big society" involved the establishment of various institutions and organizations which should assist individual persons, such as law and accounting offices and labor employment bureaus.[41]

Finally, leading proponents of "little government big society" projected that the implementation of the new plans would require the establishment of some form of market economy to substitute for the planned economy, which would disappear as a result of the abolishment of most of the provincial government apparatus.

In short "little government big society" involved a substantial cutback of government functions and, instead, an autonomous sphere consisting of the independent activities of the citizens and their own associations and organizations would be established. A full implementation of these plans would lay the foundation of civil society introduced from above.

Economic Reform

The concept of civil society is often said to have two dimensions. One refers to non-state private economic activities. New forms of market activity and the emergence of social groups of capitalist entrepreneurs is the first step in the direction of such a civil society. The other dimension, which we have documented above, designates public and voluntary associations, independent journals and newspapers, autonomous social movements, occupational and professional societies, and local self-government. This dimension could also be called "political society."[42] Although repressed in 1979-1980, "political society" benefitted from the loosening of the party's and the state's control over society which gradually took place during the 1980s as a result of the political reform process.

The economic reforms of the 1980s also strengthened the process towards the emergence of a civil society in China. The Chinese economic reforms involve adopting measures to (1) decentralize decision-making power to the production units, whether enterprises in the urban state sector or households in the rural sector, (2) enhance material incentives to stimulate economic efficiency and productivity, (3) substitute administrative planning methods with economic levers (jingji ganggan), e.g. credit control, interest rates, taxes, and prices, (4) allow the market mechanism to play a role in resource mobilization and allocation, and (5) change the ownership system.

It is beyond the scope of the present article to address all of these issues. Therefore, the discussion will be limited to questions relating directly to the retrenchment of the state's and of the party's direct control over the economy.

Chinese economic reforms were only slowly unfolding in the beginning of the 1980s (with the exception of agriculture). To be sure, there were experiments with granting expanded decision-making power to enterprises, coupled with profit-retention schemes for selected enterprises and initial reforms of financial institutions and the wage and labor systems in the urban sector. Also in mid-1983, a major tax reform was introduced according to which the profit-retention scheme would be replaced with a new enterprise taxation system.[43] Nevertheless, in 1984, Xue Muqiao rightly complained that reforms had only resulted in partial and minor alterations of the economic system.[44]

At the Third Plenary Session of the 12th Party Congress in October, 1984, a major reform program was adopted.[45] This program, "The Decision on Reform of the Economic Structure", called for reform of every aspect of the entire economic structure. It involved the introduction of a whole range of reforms, including planning, pricing, economic management, and the labor and wage system, which should be accomplished within five years.

The Decision recommended a three-tiered pricing system which would reflect and also support the tripartite planning system: planned prices for essential products covered by the state plan (mandatory planning), floating or negotiated prices for products under guidance planning, and free prices for products circulated in the free market.

Suggestions to pay more attention to what the Chinese call economic levers (pricing, taxation, credit, etc.) were combined with suggestions to implement wage and labor reform. Along these lines there was also a call for an enterprise management system where the director or manager assumes full responsibility.

The Decision pointed out that a thorough reform of the economic structure badly needed a contingent of managerial and administrative personnel, and especially managers who were knowledgeable in modern economics and technology. It was therefore necessary to promote a new generation of managerial personnel. This was called "reshuffling of leadership in enterprises", and was to be completed before the end of 1985.

The 1984 reform document was given wide coverage in the media in China as well as abroad. The Chinese used phrases like "great practical importance" and "far-reaching historical significance" in order to emphasize that this time the reform process did not aim at partial and minor alterations of the system, but rather had entered a stage of comprehensive reform.

Following the adoption of the reform program, important changes took place in the realm of planning. In industrial production, the number of products controlled by the mandatory planning of the State Planning Commission were reduced from 123 to 60, and the number of materials allocated through unified state distribution by the State Planning Commission and the State Bureau of Material Supply went down from 256 to 65. The types of agricultural and sideline products covered by mandatory plans declined from 29 to 10, and, in late March, the Central Committee issued a *zhongfa* that consolidated the shift from state planning to market regulation in farm production. State purchasing quotas were to be abolished, and instead the state would buy grain and cotton according to contracts and allow farmers to sell their surplus production on the open market. Other agricultural goods would be allowed to float at free market prices.[46]

The following year there was further experimentation with wage and labor reform, and industrial enterprises were given permission to keep their depreciation funds. Finally, an important reform of the Science and Technology management system was announced in March, 1985, when the Central Committee issued its "Decision on Reform of the Science and Technology Management System."[47]

All these reform measures contributed to the creation of an economic environment favorable to the expansion of the market and the emergence of new forms of economic activity independent of the state.

Private Sector

Of primary importance in this context is that the economic reforms created the conditions for the emergence of a private sector in the Chinese economy. The private sector which was legitimized by article 11 in the 1982 constitution is mostly found in service and repair trades, cottage handicrafts, commercialized farming, transportation and animal husbandry. It can be divided into the urban private sector and the rural private sector. The urban private sector started from a minuscule base of 0.15 percent of the urban labor force in 1978, but has grown so rapidly through the 1980s that in 1987 it exceeded 4 percent of the urban labor force.[48] There is a great regional variation in the relative size of the individual and private sector.[49] In 1989 the individual sector made up 1.3 percent of Beijing's urban work force and 1.9 percent of Tianjin's, but constituted 7.5 percent of Anhui's, 7.6 percent of Guangdong's and 9.7 percent of Guizhou's.[50]

The rapid development of individual/private enterprises is a major factor in the rural industrialization process.[51] In 1988, private enterprises comprised 33 percent of total output value of rural industry.[52] They numbered 17,291,651 (92% of all rural enterprises) and had a workforce of 46,515,317 (48.7 percent of total labor force in rural industry).[53]

It appears that these statistics underestimate the actual size and weight of the private sector. There are several reasons for this. Many big private enterprises often register as collective enterprises because of fear that policies may change. Smaller enterprises often try to pass for specialized households, thereby trying to avoid paying sales tax. Enterprises in operation for less than three months annually are not required to register and pay taxes and, therefore, many entrepreneurs claim that they operate for less than three months. Some reports suggest that about 50 percent of all private enterprises are not included in the statistics.[54]

In short, the post-Mao period has seen a rapid expansion of the private economy, causing the center to lose considerably in its control over the economy. As a consequence of this development, a new social group of capitalist entrepreneurs has emerged in China, especially along the coast in Fujian and Guangdong provinces. They establish wholesale trading companies, hire up to hundreds of employees, and operate in both commerce, services and manufacture.[55] The private economy is supplemented by various new forms of property rights such as leasing, contracting and partnership arrangements with state units. It is mostly private entrepreneurs who enter into these arrangements with the state, but often they cooperate with local cadres who in a discretionary fashion possess the infrastructural power in their area. In this fashion the entrepreneurs make further inroads into the state structure.

Based on fieldwork among urban entrepreneurs in Xiamen, David Wank maintains that capitalist entrepreneurship in China is embedded in *guanxi* with local cadres and that capitalist growth has been stimulated because of, not in spite of this embeddedness. As a consequence entrepreneurs are more interested in developing alliances with cadres than in autonomy seeking. Furthermore, according to Wank, in contradistinction to the situation in Eastern Europe where social groups in civil society form horizontal alliances with other social groups to push back the state the entrepreneurs in China seek to establish vertical alliances with the local level of state and party. In this way the private economy does not challenge the authority of the state. The line between market and plan, state and the private sector is anything but clear in David Wank's view. In fact it is rather "blurred" and the "binary logic" involved in the state/society dichotomy does not appear to apply to China.[56]

Walder is also of the opinion that there is close cooperation between local cadres and private business. Local political rule in China is still a clientelist system and cadres and entrepreneurs are tied together in mutual dependency. Therefore the notion of civil society in China "is fraught with difficulties and ambiguities".[57] Lucian Pye, who also stresses the importance of particularistic relationships and *guanxi* in China, takes the argument even further and claims that "it makes little sense to speak of state-society relations because the Chinese never had a national civil society."[58]

However, David Strand has shown that in urban China in the pre-1949 period, there existed a civil society and a public sphere which made possible a pluralistic politics which periodically subjected the rulers to popular pressures. It is precisely such a configuration of pressures which was revived in China in 1989.[59] Moreover, that there is mutual dependency between cadres and entrepreneurs appears to correspond to the definition of civil society advanced by Moshe Lewin, namely that civil society does not have to be in direct opposition to the state (as in the 1970's Polish case), but can emerge from within the state. In the Chinese case, the increasing profit and commodity orientation of cadres running state offices and enterprises is an example. That *guanxi* networks operate within the state structure is another example of this transformation from within.

Although Walder and others do not meet with universal approval for their skepticism concerning the usefulness of the concept of civil society, they emphasize an important point, namely that in China the line between state and society is often "blurred." It is difficult to find associations and organizations which are not to some extent penetrated by or part of the state structure.

The 1989 Student Demonstrations and Civil Society

Ten years after the decision to introduce basic reforms in China was taken at the important Third Plenary Session in December, 1978, China had changed considerably. Political relaxation had weakened the institutions of control and numerous new associations and publications had sprung up -- some of them quite independently of the state. Economic reforms had weakened central planning, and, instead, market elements were being introduced into the economy, creating space for private and individual activities. New social groups arose based on the new economic opportunities, and they articulated interests often opposed to the state and party. Clearly, the economic and political conditions for the further strengthening of civil society were present.

As a result of the retrenchment of state and party from society, at the end of the 1980s, many intellectuals were able to organize their own discussion clubs (salons) and meetings and new independent publications appeared. For example, in 1986 the American business man George Soros, with Zhao Ziyang's support, set up the Fund for the Reform and Opening of China, which officially was supposed to operate independently of the Chinese government.[60] The Shanghai *World Economic Herald*, although nominally under the jurisdiction of the Shanghai Party Committee, developed into a critical voice calling for more radical reform. Another sign of a nascent civil society was the establishment of a number of independent research organizations, such as Stone Company's Institute for Social Development. Also, some of the institutes which had been formed as a part of the official system, such as the Economic System Reform Institute under Chen Yizi and the Rural Development Research Institute under Du Runsheng, began to operate relatively independently and at the same time served as vehicles for bringing the new thinking into the heart of the state and party structure.

The many discussion clubs or salons which appeared were important for the emergence of an independent public sphere. In January, 1989, Su Shaozhi and Fang Lizhi organized a so-called "neo-enlightenment salon" at the Happiness Bookstore in Peking. In February Fang and Chen Jun arranged a "winter jasmine get-together" at the Friendship Hotel where democracy and human rights were discussed. Among the students, discussion clubs also proliferated. Wang Dan, for example, organized a "democratic salon" which sponsored talks and lectures. One of the guest speakers was Ren Wanding, head of the Human Rights League which had been active in 1978-79.

Intellectuals also began to write open letters to the leadership with their grievances. Thus, on January 6, 1989, Fang Lizhi called for the release of political prisoners including Wei Jingsheng, thereby linking the new movement with the democracy movement of 1978-79. On February 16, 33 intellectuals supported Fang's open letter, and later in the same month, 42 scholars and scientists followed suit and demanded the release of political prisoners.[61]

The student movement of Spring 1989 emerged against this background. Following the death of Hu Yaobang, the student protest developed like an explosion, and on April 18 the first autonomous student organization was set up, followed by the formation of the Capital Federation of Autonomous College Students' Organizations (*Gaozilian*) on April 26. In May, several other independently formed organizations such as the Beijing Intellectuals' Association (*Beizhilian*) and the Capital Workers' Autonomous Federation (*Gongzilian*) joined the movement.[62]

These organizations achieved much prominence in Beijing and abroad in the spring of 1989. However, perhaps just as important for the mobilization of hundreds of thousands of demonstrators all through May were the formation of many hundreds and perhaps well over a thousand associations by ordinary citizens. They ranged from self-defense groups to political associations and embryonic labor unions. These groups of organized citizens did not merely reiterate or support student demands, but formed their own distinct demands.[63]

Of particular interest is the role of the private sector in the people's movement of 1989. In the massive street demonstrations of May 17 and May 18 more than 700 work units sent organized delegations. The private sector was less conspicuous since it did not participate in an organized form with banners and slogans. Nevertheless, the *getihus* may have constituted up to a third of the participants. Two of the students' most important support groups came from the private sector. First, there was the so-called Flying Tiger Motor Brigade, which functioned as the students' liaison and information group. Second, there was the Stone Computer Company, which provided the students with financial funds and advanced communication systems.[64] Thus, the state and party was confronted with a plethora of independent organizations and activities, which signified the emergence of a civil society of the Polish type.

Compared to 1979, the movement had grown considerably. In 1979, only a few thousand workers and city people, among whom were many former red guards, were involved. In 1989, the movement was much broader and involved more social sectors of society. In the big demonstrations in May not only students participated, but also workers, shop assistants, *getihu*, journalists and other media people, etc. Even police officers could be seen protesting in the streets. In the Tiananmen Square several thousand students were tightly organized in different groups and in another corner of the square the *gongzilian* was organizing the workers into departments for logistics, liaison, organization and propaganda. They also established a "workers' picket corps" and "dare to die" brigades. In addition to these sectors of the population, thousands of state and party officials were involved as sympathetic middle men between the students and the leadership at different levels, and even those who were not directly involved often went to the square to watch and perhaps take part in discussions with other onlookers. That sections of the state and party apparatus were sympathetic to the movement indicates that civil society was making inroads into the very fortress of statism in the way it had done in the Soviet Union.

However, compared to the kind of civil society in Hungary which Andrew Arato describes elsewhere in this volume, the Chinese version is still rather weak. The differentiation into different groups and associations is not as sophisticated as in Hungary and the movement is certainly not as strong as to constitute an alternative to the party-state as was the case in Poland.

Moreover, although hundreds of thousands were involved, it is important to note that the movement was dominated by *shimin* (city people) and hardly affected the huge Chinese countryside.[65] Thus Mark Selden observes that the inability to build significant bridges outward from the cities to the rural areas was one of the most critical weaknesses of the democracy movement throughout the 1980s.[66] In fact, unless

China's democrats will be able to establish these bridges, they will not be able to effectively claim to represent the Chinese people and will continue to be vulnerable to state repression.

China After Tiananmen Square

After the crackdown, the new leadership coalition of veteran party and state leaders adopted a number of important measures to stamp out autonomous political activity and organized opposition. They ousted a number of important party leaders, notably General Secretary Zhao Ziyang, and promoted new leaders who would restore the old order. They increased political indoctrination and conducted a new campaign against harmful Western influence. They reduced the student intake at major universities and introduced a 9 month military training for first year students at Beijing University. They introduced new economic austerity policies in an attempt to bring down inflation. Most important, they tried to abolish the social and political basis for civil society in a number of ways. First, they came down heavily on the different autonomous organizations that had sprung up and arrested their leaders. Second, they reversed the policies announced by Zhao Ziyang in October, 1987, on the role of the party and its relationship to the government apparatus. Thus, they reinstituted the dominating role of the party group in the different organs of the state. Third, they reversed the process towards a substantial change of the economic planning system and restressed the dominating role of the state sector in the economy.[67] This meant that private enterprises would be squeezed for funding, raw materials and energy supplies, and that the possibilities to operate on the free market would be reduced. As a result the private sector and private entrepreneurs would find it difficult to operate, and the economic foundation of civil society would be severely restricted.

Authoritarianism Versus Democratization

In characterizing Post-Mao China's political system many different labels have been used.[68] Perhaps the concept of "authoritarian rule" is the most fitting.[69] In authoritarian regimes there is often a conflict between "hard-liners" and "soft-liners".[70] The "hard-liners" believe that the "perpetuation of authoritarian rule is possible *and* desirable."[71] They usually reject democracy outright or they try to erect some facade behind which they maintain the hierarchial and authoritarian nature of their power. The "soft-liners", on the other hand, are aware that the regime, in which they usually occupy high positions, will have to change or liberalize. This realization may be due to the existence of political opposition, an economic crisis, international pressure, etc.

The "opening" or "thaw" of authoritarian rule brought about by the "soft-liners" usually creates a sharp increase in general politicization and popular activities (the resurrection of civil society).[72] This wave may crest or it may grow, and eventually it may even threaten to overwhelm the "soft-liners" so that the agenda they established is superseded by a new agenda and they in fact become dispensable. It is also possible that the "hard-liners" are prepared to force a return to the "old order", in which case the result may be the restoration of a new, and possibly even more severe, form of authoritarian rule.

To complicate matters, hard-liners and soft-liners may split into subgroups. That is, some soft-liners may be soft-liners on issues relating to economic reform while being hard-liners on political issues and vice versa. If this is the case, which aspect is dominant depends on the concrete situation.

In China in 1988-1989, Zhao Ziyang and his reform group were the soft-liners, and they argued for both economic and political reform. Deng Xiaoping, who most Western analysts all the way through the 1980s had characterized as a soft-liner, was a hard-liner on political issues and would not give up on the leading role of the party, the socialist road, the dictatorship of the proletariat and Marxism-Leninism-Mao Zedong Thought (the so-called Four Fundamental Principles), whereas he was a soft-liner on economic issues. Chen Yun, Peng Zhen, Bo Yibo and most of the other octogenarians lived up to their reputation and were hardliners both on economic and political issues.

The military crackdown in June, 1989 appears to show the failure of the transition from authoritarian rule to democracy and freedom in China. Although the result has been the restoration of a more severe form of authoritarian rule compared to the 1980s, it has not meant a restoration of the totalitarian rule of the past.[73] In fact, the present rule in China appears to combine political authoritarianism with economic liberalism.[74] In China it is called "socialism with Chinese characteristics," and today it constitutes the political platform of the Deng Xiaoping faction.

In line with its belief in political authoritarianism, the regime will continue to reject Western-style democratic institutions with a multi-party system, electoral competition, etc. The struggle for political democratization is, therefore, likely to continue.

Over the years the democracy movement, which first appeared in 1978-79, has grown stronger and stronger. First, it was former red guards (many of whom were workers), then the students took to the streets in 1985, 1986 and in 1989, and finally the intelligentsia (authors, professors, researchers, etc), after 30 years of almost complete public silence, articulated a critique of the leadership and the system. In short, the democracy movement has solidified its roots in important sectors of the urban population. Thus there exists a foundation for the re-emergence of civil society, although this may not happen as easily and successfully as it did in Poland.

Of late the Chinese economic reform process has resumed momentum. Price reform and reforms of the planning and ownership systems are again being comtemplated.[75] The *getihu* and the private sector, which was restricted in 1989-1990, is experiencing a relaxation of central control. The new climate is bound to benefit private entrepreneurs and other social groups operating outside the realm of central planning. A continuation of the economic reform process will reproduce the economic and social base for the re-emergence of civil society. The *getihu* and the private sector, the floating population, the aspirations of the coastal provinces will all combine to constitute an alternative to the old system. The urge for political liberalization to secure the rights and freedom of these new forces and groups will grow.

Thus, the conflict between the forces of authoritarianism and the forces of reform and democratization is still present and is likely to intensify even though the ultimate trial of strength may have to await the passing away of Deng and the old guard.

Notes

1. I wish to thank the following people for their helpful comments on an earlier draft: Margaret L. Nugent, Mark Selden, Andrew Walder, and Mairfair Mei-hui Yang. I am also grateful to the Carlsberg Foundation for financially supporting the collection of materials for the project.

2. Conceptually, civil society can be positioned in at least six different discourses: (1) the traditional; (2) the classical-liberal; (3) the Hegelian; (4) the Marxian; (5) the Gramscian; and a (6) newer one which transcends Marx and Gramsci and takes its inspiration in the East European and Soviet transition to post-communism. Since this paper is not primarily concerned with an investigation and discussion of the concept of civil society, we will not attempt to take all these discourses into consideration. Important works on civil society include Andrew Arato and Jean Cohen, "Social Movements, Civil Society, and the Problem of Sovereignty," *Praxis International*, Vol. 4. No. 3 (October 1984), 266-283; Perry Anderson, "The Antinomies of Antonio Gramsci," *New Left Review*, No. 100 (1976-77), 5-78; Jean L. Cohen, *Class and Civil Society* (Oxford: Martin Robertson & Company, 1983); Alex Demirovic, "Zivilgesellschaft, Öffentlichkeit, Demokratie," *Das Argument*, No. 185 (1991), 41-55; John Keane, ed., *Civil Society and the State* (London: Verso, 1988); Salvador Giner, "The Withering Away of Civil Society?" *Praxis International*, Vol. 5, No. 3 (1985), 247-267. For a short but good discussion of some of the literature on the subject see Volker Gransow, "Zivilgesellschaft und demokratische Frage: Ein Literaturbericht," *Das Argument*, Vol. 32, No. 2 (1990), 249-254.

3. See Andrew Arato, "Civil Society against the State: Poland 1980-81," *Telos*, Vol. 47, 1981, 23-47.

4. Moshe Lewin, *The Gorbachev Phenomenon* (Berkeley: University of California Press, 1988), 80.

5. David Held, "Liberalism, Marxism and the Future Direction of Public Policy," in Peter Nolan and Suzanne Paine, *Rethinking Socialist Economics* (Oxford Polity Press, 1986), 13-34.

6. David Held, "Liberalism, Marxism and the Future Direction of Public Policy," 27.

7. See John Keane, *Democracy and Civil Society*, 15 and 61.

8. See Kjeld Erik Brødsgaard, "The Democracy Movement in China, 1978-79: Opposition Movements, Wall Poster Campaigns, and Underground Journals," *Asian Survey*, Vol. XXI, No. 7 (July 1981), 747-774.

9. Other examples of literature pertaining to the issue of civil society in China include Tom Gold, "Party-State versus Society in China," in Joyce K. Kallgren, ed., *Building a Nation-State: China after Forty Years* (Berkeley: Institute of East Asian Studies, 1990), 128; David Strand, "Protest in Beijing: Civil Society and Public Sphere in Beijing," *Problems of Communism*, Vol. 39, No. 3 (May-June, 1990), 1-19; Laurence Sullivan, "The Emergence of Civil Society in China," in Tony Saich, ed., *The Chinese People's Movement* (New York: M.E: Sharpe, 1990), 126-144; Mayfair Mei-hui Yang, "Between State and Society: The Construction of Corporateness in a Chinese Socialist Factory," *The Australian Journal of Chinese Affairs*, No. 22 (July, 1989), 31-60; William T. Rowe, "The Public Sphere in Modern China," *Modern China* (July, 1990), 309-329. A number of papers from the recent conference "American-European Symposium on State versus Society in East Asian Traditions" held in Paris, May 29-31, 1991, discuss the concept of civil society in relation to China. However, most of them neglect to put the discussion into a comparative perspective. Another weakness from our point of view is that the focus is on pre-1949 Chinese history with hardly any references to contemporary China.

10. Yan Jiaqi, for example, wrote two articles under pseudonym in *Beijing zhi chun*. See Andrew Nathan, "Chinese Democracy in 1989: Continuity and Change," *Problems of Communism* (September-October), 16-29.

11. Kjeld Erik Brødsgaard, "The Democracy Movement in China, 1978-1979," 768.

12. James D. Seymour, *The Fifth Modernization: China's Human Rights Movement, 1978-1979* (New York: Earl M. Coleman Enterprises, 1980), 52.

13. James D. Seymour, *The Fifth Modernization: China's Human Rights Movement, 1978-1979*, 62.

14. James D. Seymour, *The Fifth Modernization: China's Human Rights Movement, 1978-1979*, 83-86.

15. On this aspect see also Nina P. Halpern, "Economic Reform and Democratization," in Richard Baum, ed., *Reform and Reaction in Post-Mao China* (London: Routledge, 1991), 38-59.

16. Kjeld Erik Brødsgaard, "The Democracy Movement in China, 1978-1979," 770.

17. Kjeld Erik Brødsgaard, "The Democracy Movement in China, 1978-1979," 772.

18. Deng Xiaoping, "Dang he guojia lingdao zhidu de gaige" (Reform of the leadership systems of the party and state). The text appears in *Sanzhong quanhui yilai zhongyao wengao xuanbian* (Beijing Renmin Chubanshe, 1982), 510-535. This is a two-volume *neibu*-collection of speeches published in September, 1982 for use in the party rectification campaign. An excerpt appears in another *neibu*-collection *Shiyi jie sanzhong quanhui yilai jingji zhengce wenxian xuanbian* (Beijing: Renmin Chubanshe, 1986), 64-75. A public version appeared in the summer of 1983 in *Deng Xiaoping wenxuan, 1975-1982* (Shanghai: Renmin Chubanshe, 1983), 280-302. The last version will be used in this paper.

19. For a discussion of the *Gengshen* reforms, see also Kjeld Erik Brødsgaard, "Economic and Political Reform in Post-Mao China," *Copenhagen Papers in East and Southeast Asian Studies*, No. 1 (1987), 31-56.

20. Kjeld Erik Brødsgaard, "Economic and Political Reform," 289.

21. "A Speech of Deng Xiaoping for Restricted Use Only", *FBIS-CHI-86-117* (June 18, 1986), W1-2.

22. Liao Gailong's speech "Lishi de jingyan he women de fazhan daolu" (Historical experience and our development path) has not been openly published in China. However, a photolithographic version of the Chinese text appears in *Zhonggong Yanjiu*, Vol. 15, No. 9 (September 15, 1981), 108-177. Part 4 of the speech has been translated into English and published in FBIS, *Daily Report: China* (hereafter FBIS-CHI), March 16, 1981, U 1 -19. Here the Chinese version will be used.

23. Most of the year 1980 was called *Gengshen* according to the traditional Chinese 60-year calendar cycle.

24. Liao Gailong, "Lishi de jingyan he women de fazhan daolu," 164-171.

25. Liao Gailong was transferred from the Policy Research Office of the Central Committee to the Party History Research Center.

26. For example in *Beijing Review*, 1986, No. 32 (August 11, 1986), 15-19.

27. "Resolution of the Central Committee of the Communist Party of China on the Guiding Principles for Building a Socialist Society With an Advanced Culture and Ideology" (Adopted at the 6th Plenary Session of the 12th Central Committee of the Communist Party of China on September 28, 1986), *Beijing Review*, 1986, No. 40 (October 6, 1986), I-VIII.

28. The students were partly acting under the inspiration of astrophysicist Fang Lizhi, who at that time was vice-president of the university in Hefei.

29. See Göran Leijonhufvud, *Going Against the Tide: On Dissent and Big Character Posters in China* (London: Curzon Press, 1990), 92-97.

30. The speech appears in "Feidang zhongyang you guan "fan ziyouhua" douzheng zhongfa wenjian huibian" (Collection of Central Documents on the struggle against liberalism issued by the CCP Central Committee) (Taibei: n.d.). This is a collection of six *neibu* documents pertaining to the fall of Hu Yaobang in January, 1986. For a more detailed analysis of the documents, see Kjeld Erik Brødsgaard, "Economic and Political Reform in Post-Mao China," 46-51.

31. Deng Xiaoping, "Dang he guojia lingdao zhidu de gaige", 289. See also "A Speech of Deng Xiaoping for Restricted Use Only", W 1-2.

32. Liao Gailong, "Lishi de jingyan he women de fazhan daolu," 169.

33. See Kjeld Erik Brødsgaard, "Party Reform in Post-Mao China," *East Asian Institute Occasional Papers*, No. 6 (University of Copenhagen: East Asian Institute, 1990), 67-76.

34. See Hu Yaobang, "Quanmian kaichuang shehuizhuyi xiandaihua jianshe de xin jumian" (Create a New Situation in All Fields of Socialist Modernization) (Report to the 12th National Congress of the Communist Party of China, September 1, 1982), *Renmin Ribao*, September 8, 1982.

35. See "Zhonggong zhongyang guanyu zheng dang de jueding" (The Decision of the Central Committee of the Communist Party of China on Party Consolidation), *Renmin Ribao*, October 10, 1983.

36. The report, entitled "A Basic Summary of Party Rectification and the Further Strengthening of Party Building", appears in *FBIS-CHI-87-105* (June 2, 1987), K3-18.

37. See Zhao Ziyang, "Yanzhe you Zhongguo tese de shehuizhuyi daolu qianjin" (Advance along the road of socialism with Chinese characteristics), *Renmin Ribao*, November 4, 1987. See also Zhao Ziyang, "On Separating Party from Government", *Beijing Review*, No. 50 (December 14-20, 1987), 14-16. For a detailed analysis of Zhao's speech to the Party Congress, see T. Manoharan, "Current Rural Organizational Structure in the PRC: An Overview", *Copenhagen Discussion Papers*, No. 2 (December 1988).

38. For a discussion of the *nomenklatura* system and translations of some of the relevant documents, see Melanie Manion, ed., "Cadre Recruitment and Management in the People's Republic of China", *Chinese Law and Government*, Vol. 17, No. 3 (Fall 1984); and John P. Burns, ed., "Contemporary China's Nomenklatura System", *Chinese Law and Government*, Vol. 20, No. 4 (Winter 1987-88). Detailed information on the *nomenklatura* system after 1984 is not publicly available.

39. Not much research has been done on this reform proposal which cast important light on the Chinese reform process and the possible emergence of civil society. A notable exception is a Danish M.A. thesis written by Susan Aagaard Petersen and Mads Kirkebæk entitled "Hainan som provins og særlig økonomisk zone" (East Asian Institute, University of Copenhagen, October, 1990).

40. Susan Aagaard Petersen and MadsKirkebæk, "Hainan som provins og særlig økonomisk zone", 209.

41. Susan Aagaard Petersen and Mads Kirkebæk, "Hainan som provins og særlig økonomisk zone", 210-211.

42. See John Keane, *Civil Society and the State*, 19-20 and 368. See also Yang, "Between State and Society: The Construction of Corporateness in a Chinese Socialist Factory," 31-60.

43. See Kjeld Erik Brødsgaard, "Political and Economic Reform," 32-40.

44. Xue Muqiao, "Keep Abreast of the New Situation, Improve the Planned System," *FBIS, JPRS-CEA-84-085*, 2-6.

45. See "Decision of the Central Committee of the Communist Party of China on Reform of the Economic Structure," *Beijing Review*, No. 44 (1984), I-XVI.

46. See Kjeld Erik Brødsgaard, "Economic and Political Reform in Post-Mao China," 39-40.

47. Kjeld Erik Brødsgaard, "Economic and Political Reform in Post-Mao China," 39-40.

48. See *Zhongguo Tongji Nianjian 1988.*

49. Often there is a distinction in Chinese sources between individual enterprise (*geti hu*) and private enterprise (*siying hu*). Enterprises owned by individual households and employing more than seven workers are referred to as private enterprises while enterprises with less than seven workers are classified as individual. But since *geti hu* and *siying hu* both belong to the private sector, this distinction will not be made in this article.

50. See *Zhongguo Tongji Nianjian 1990*, 121 and 127.

51. The term rural private economy actually comprises three types of enterprises. "Joint" (*lianhu qiye* or *lianying qiye*), "individual" (*getihu* or *geti qiye*) and "private" (*siying qiye*). One might add a fourth type, the "specialized households" (*zhuanye hu*), which often are engaged in enterprise acitivities. See Kjeld Erik Brødsgaard, "Planning, Administration, and Management in Chinese Agriculture with Particular Reference to the Post-Mao Period," in Magnus Mörner and Thommy Svensson, eds., *The Transformation of Rural Society in the Third World* (London and New York: Routledge, 1991), 295-313.

52. *Zhongguo Nongye Nianjian 1989*, 346.

53. See *Zhongguo Tongji Nianjian 1989*, 339 and 340.

54. See Susan Young, "Policy, Practice and the Private Sector in China," *The Australian Journal of Chinese Affairs*, No. 21 (January 1989), 57-80. See also Ole Odgaard, "Inadequate and Inaccurate Chinese Statistics: The Case of Private Rural Enterprises," *China Information*, Vol. 5, No. 3 (Winter 1990-1991), 29-38.

55. See, for example, David L. Wank, "Merchant Entrepreneurs and the Development of Civil Society: Some Social and Political Consequences of Private Sector Expansion in a Southeast Coastal City," (Paper prepared for the Annual Meeting of the Association for Asian Studies, April 1991).

56. David L. Wank, "Merchant Entrepreneurs and the Development of Civil Society.

57. See Andrew Walder, "Social Structure and Political Authority: China's Evolving Polity," in Ramon, H. Myers, ed., *Two Societies in Opposition: The Republic of China and the People's Republic of China after Forty Years* (Stanford, California: Hoover Institution Press, 1991), 341-361.

58. See Lucian W. Pye, "The State and the Individual: An Overview Interpretation," *The China Quarterly*, No. 127 (September, 1991), 443-466.

59. Strand, "Protest in Beijing," 2. See also David Strand, *Rickshaw Beijing: City People and Politics in the 1920s* (Berkeley: University of California Press, 1989).

60. See Andrew Nathan, "Chinese Democracy in 1989: Continuity and Change."

61. For a good account of the background and development of the student demonstrations in Beijing in the spring of 1989, see Tony Saich, "The Rise and Fall of the Beijing People's Movement," *The Australian Journal of Chinese Affairs*, No. 24 (July 1990).

62. The most detailed chronology of the demonstrations in Beijing appears in Guojia jiaowei sixiang zhengzhi gongzuosi, ed., *Jingxin dongpo de 56 tian* (56 soul-stirring days) (Beijing: Dadi chubanshe, 1989).

63. See Andrew G. Walder, "City People in the 1989 Democracy Movement: Popular Mobilization and Political Mentalities" (Paper presented to the Regional

Seminar, Center for Chinese Studies, University of California, Berkeley, April 27, 1991).

64. See Saich, "The Rise and Fall of the Beijing People's Movement," 204-205.

65. It is interesting to note that the concept most often used by Chinese social theorists in translating the concept civil society is *shimin shehui* (the society of city people). The two other translations which are used are *gongmin shehui* and *minjian shehui*.

66. See Mark Selden, "The Social Consequences of Chinese Reform: The Road to Tiananmen," Ravi Palat, ed., *Pacific-Asia and the Future of the World System* (Westport Ct.: Greenwood Press, 1992) (forthcoming).

67. The economic policy guidelines for Post-Tiananmen China were formulated in the important 39-points document adopted at the Fifth Plenum in November, 1989, but not made public until January, 1990. See *Renmin Ribao*, January 17, 1990.

68. See Kjeld Erik Brødsgaard, *Studies of Chinese Politics* (University of Copenhagen: Copenhagen Discussion Papers, No. 8, 1989).

69. See Edward Friedman, "Theorizing the Democratization of China's Leninist State," in Arif Dirlik and Maurice Meisner, eds., *Marxism and the Chinese Experience* (Armonk, New York: M.E. Sharpe, 1989), 171-189. Harding argues that China with the beginning of the reform process in the early post-Mao period passed from totalitarianism to a form of "consultive authoritarianism". See Harry Harding, "Political Development in Post-Mao China," in Doak Barnett and Ralph N. Clough, eds., *Modernizing China: Post Mao Reform and Development* (Boulder and London: Westview Press, 1986), 13-37. Paraphrasing Edwin Winkler one could perhaps advance the proposition that China in the Post-Mao period is best understood as a "gerontocratic-authoritarian" regime in the midst of a generational change and beginning a systemic transition from "hard" to "soft" authoritarianism. See Edwin A. Winckler, "Institutionalization and Participation in Taiwan," *China Quarterly*, No. 99 (September, 1984), 481-499.

70. For the following observations on "authoritarian rule" I draw strongly on O'Donnell and Schmitter's work on transitions form authoritarian rule. See especially Guillermo O'Donnell and Philippe C. Schmitter, *Transitions from Authoritarian Rule: Tentative Conclusions* (Baltimore and London: The Johns Hopkins Press, 1989).

71. Guillermo O'Donnell and Phillippe C. Schmitter, *Transitions from Authoritarian Rule: Tentative Conclusions*, 16.

72. Guillermo O'Donnell and Phillippe C. Schmitter, *Transitions from Authoritarian Rule: Tentative Conclusions*, 26.

73. On this point Professor Su Shaozhi would probably disagree with me. He has recently argued that a combination of "feudal-despotism" with Stalinism turned China into a system of "all embracing totalitarianism". According to Su, the reform efforts of the 1980s were not able to secure the transition to a qualitatively new system. See Su Shaozhi, *Understanding Democratic Reform in China* (Bradley Institute for Democracy and Public Values, Marquette University: Papers on Democracy, March 20, 27 and April 3, 1990). See also Professor Su's contribution to this volume.

74. See also Manoranjan Mohanty, "State and Socialist Freedom in China" (Paper presented at the Seminar "China in the 1990s," Center for the Study of Developing Societies, Delhi, February 15-17, 1991).

75. Kjeld Erik Brødsgaard, "China's Political Economy in the Nineties," *China Report*, Vol. 27, No. 3 (1991), 177-196.

15

The Prospects for Transitions from Leninism to Democracy

Su Shaozhi and Margaret Latus Nugent

As we have seen, the transition from Leninism to freedom is complicated and perilous. It is influenced in so many ways by the particular historical, economic, political, and cultural circumstances in each country. As Edward Friedman warned, there is no guarantee of success -- especially in the short run. According to Stanislaw Gomulka's metaphor, "the reform process looks like a long swim from one island to another in a water visited by crocodiles."[1] Among the largest crocodiles are extreme nationalism, economic hardships, and political instability. This concluding chapter assesses the prospects for transitions (eventually) in Eastern Europe, the Commonwealth of Independent States, and China, and it explores the possible alternatives if the transitions falter or fail.

A New Kind of Democratization

The transitions from Leninism to democracy and market-oriented economies present challenges to social scientists as well as to the world because such dramatic changes are new phenomena and because the nature of Leninism has been poorly understood. The world has experienced democratization of totalitarian and authoritarian regimes, but the transformation of Communist regimes has heretofore been deemed unlikely, if not impossible.

After World War II, the three defeated totalitarian states of Nazi Germany, Fascist Italy, and militarist Japan were guided along the process of democratization by the Allies. Fascist parties were banned and multi-party systems established. Monopolistic military bodies were replaced with free elections, congressional systems, and democratic constitutions, allowing these three countries to effect the transition to democracy in a relatively short period of time.[2]

Nazi Germany, Fascist Italy, and militarist Japan all exhibited characteristics which were fairly consistent with Carl Friedrich's classic definition of totalitarianism: a totalist ideology, a single party committed to this ideology, a fully developed secret police, and three kinds of monopolistic control -- of mass communications, of operational weapons, and of all organizations, including economic ones.[3]   Although the economies of these regimes were controlled, however, they were based upon a system of private ownership. This fact, together with the influence of external forces plus the resumption and development of their internal democratic forces, enabled them to achieve the difficult transition from totalitarianism to democracy.[4] Thus, it appeared that the transformation of a totalitarian regime to democracy could only be achieved with the help of external forces, never as the result of a peaceful evolution based upon internal factors alone.

The 1970s saw the authoritarian regimes of Greece, Portugal, and Spain replaced by democratic systems. Meanwhile, the bureaucratic authoritarian rule of some Latin American countries began to be democratized. In the 1980s, some Asian countries also embarked on the transition from authoritarianism to democracy. The transition from authoritarian rule to democracy is easier than that from totalitarian rule to democracy, because authoritarian control of power does not penetrate everywhere, as totalitarian control does. Its control is limited to some specific areas, especially to the political realm.[5] Therefore, despite the political and often tyrannical dictatorship in some of these regimes, the existence of economies that were largely market-oriented enabled these countries to finish their transitions to democracies relatively peacefully (although the threat that non-democratic regimes may return in some of these countries remains).

By the end of the 1980s, therefore, the force of an apparent democratic trend had influenced non-Leninist totalitarian regimes as well as countries under various authoritarian rules. While scholarship on such transitions multiplied, the study of the possibility of the democratization of Leninist[6] states was neglected. Beyond the points already made by Edward Friedman, the reason for such neglect was the lack of adequate study and awareness about the true nature of the Leninist state. Study of Leninist states is often inadequate because scholars within such states are constrained by ideology, and because Western academics are blinded by their biases, misperceptions, or lack of access to information.

Within such states, the ideological control of the Communist party allows scholars to say only what officials allow them to say. The democratization of their regimes need not be explored because socialism is presumed automatically to create a higher form of democracy than that in capitalist countries. Even in cases of crisis, the Communist party chooses to ascribe the blame to alleged imperialist conspiracies rather than to limitations inherent in the Leninist system. For example, former member of the Soviet Politburo Alexander Yakovlev told the February 6, 1990 plenum of the Communist party of the Soviet Union that "alarm signals" had already surfaced in 1953, 1956, 1968, and 1980, but were ignored.[7] In the People's Republic of China, only after the political disaster of the Cultural Revolution did the Chinese Communist party admit that there had been no real establishment of democratic politics since 1949.

In some cases, Western academics have ignored the possibility of democratizing Leninist states because they are leftists who share the ideological view of the Leninists. In other cases, such scholars have overestimated the legitimacy, material achievements, stability, and control of Leninist systems or underestimated the discontent of the people governed by them.[8] The Communist revolution's pretense of universal ideology and myth of irreversibility so influenced our century that change in Communist countries appeared impossible.[9] In 1984, Samuel Huntington claimed, "The likelihood of democratic development in Eastern Europe is virtually nil.[10]

In 1989, a book on the progress of worldwide democratization did not include any Communist countries because "there is little prospect among them of a transition to democracy."[11] Paul Hollander has since explained, "The study of these systems convinced most of us that their radical transformation, let alone collapse, was not a realistic possibility in the foreseeable future.[12] Because no one expected Communist systems, considered to be totalitarian precisely because of their immutability, to collapse suddenly and peacefully, Adam Przeworski asserts that "the "Autumn of the people" was a dismal failure of political science."[13] Only Hannah Arendt raised the issue of the pattern for democratizing the Leninist state after the Hungarian democratic revolution in 1956. She found that a succession crisis (a structural inevitability in Leninist tyrannies) could unleash factional struggles for power that could readily lead to "competition for mass popularity. This competition was likely to take a democratic turn."[14]

The Nature of the Leninist State

The nature of a Leninist state is determined by the nature and history of the Communist party in power. The Communist party led by Lenin originated in the tsar-ruled tyrannical Russia, which Robert Byrnes and Eugene Kamenka have already argued predisposed the Russian people to authoritarian rule. To preserve its existence, the party needed to operate in secrecy, and its secret activities required a centrally organized system for making decisions and appointments. After the Communists came into power, they faced a serious combination of civil war and class struggle. In response, the Leninist state was born, featuring a highly centralized one-party dictatorship, the merging of the party with the government, and the unified tyrannical control of the party and the country. In such a system, democracy within the party and the country was banned. Instead, personality cultism was encouraged, and governmental power was seized by the party at the same time that the power of the party was put into the hands of a few people. Even Lenin admitted, "We say 'Yes, it is a dictatorship of one party. That is what we stand for and we shall not shift from that position'."[15] He also stated, "That in the history of revolutionary movements, the dictatorship of individuals was very often the expression, the vehicle, the channel of dictatorship of the revolutionary classes has been shown by the irrefutable experience of history. . . Hence, there is absolutely no contradiction in principle between Soviet (*that is* socialist) democracy and the exercise of dictatorial powers by individuals."[16]

The emergence of the Leninist state in the Soviet Union resulted in two triads, according to Moshe Lewin: party-state-economy and power-ideology-culture.[17] We prefer to consider it an all-inclusive, unified entity of party-state-economy-military-law-ideology-culture. This monopolistic union of the party and state results in command politics, a command economy, and a command society. The party/state interferes with and controls virtually every aspect of society, even individual thoughts and behavior. Thus, the Leninist state is a version of totalitarianism where the control of the state is even more comprehensive, because it abolishes private ownership and adopts state ownership as its economic foundation. That is why Michel Reiman calls it "all-embracing totalitarianism."[18] That is also why some proponents of a civil society-based movement for democracy in these countries have understood civil society simply as any social structure that is independent of the state.

Perhaps Leninism has persisted into the 1990s in part because this kind of all-embracing totalitarian state has the advantage of gathering major resources in a relatively short time to achieve a specific objective. For example, after 1922, great improvement occurred in the economy of the Soviet Union. Productivity increased rapidly. In 1954, Isaac Deutscher said, "No major Western country could achieve the industrial revolution in such a short period of time and under the condition of so many difficulties."[19] Barrington Moore, Jr. even thought that dictatorial communism had become the late 20th century's route to modernization.[20] Other contributors to this volume have mentioned similar apparent successes.

But as the Goldmans noted in their introductory chapter, such economic and social progress was accompanied by factors that have since contributed to the demise of Leninism in recent years. The imposition of Leninist regimes sows the seeds of their very destruction. For example, the Soviet people paid the price of Stalin's dictatorship and terror, whereas the Chinese people suffered the tyranny of Mao-Zedong's Cultural Revolution. Political means of achieving industrialization excluded the role of the market, replacing economic rules with administrative orders. Personal arbitrary decisions often caused serious mistakes that limited the increase of productivity. State-controlled industrialization was imbalanced, preferring heavy industry, especially military industry, to agriculture and light industry. And serious shortages of resources resulted from the command economy. Centrally controlled industrialization also tended to expand production by increasing investment and labor power rather than by adapting to today's scientific and technological revolution. As Peter Toumanoff argues, today's sophisticated and internationally interdependent economies are too complex to be managed centrally. Finally, the poor standard of living of the working people, in contrast with the corruption of those in absolute power, seriously hurt their creativity and initiative.

In addition to those mentioned above, the economic disadvantages of the Leninist system are many: The policies of individual officials often lack rational calculation of the effectiveness of capital investment, resulting in waste in investments, resources, and management. Because a state ownership system is "ownership by the people" in name only, no one can be held responsible for it. This lack of accountability results in "organized poor management" and extremely ineffective productivity.

The political disadvantages of Leninism are also obvious: The power of the party/state is over-centralized, producing bureaucratism and a privileged class. The democratic and other civil rights of the people are abused or denied, and even slight dissents are seriously suppressed. The people become divided into rulers and the ruled in what is supposed to be a classless society. Such conflicts are increasingly intensified. Despite the existence of elections and so-called people's congresses, there is no real democracy in Leninist states.

Transitioning from Leninism to Freedom

Others in this volume have already explored the many theoretical and actual considerations for the transition from a Leninist state to a market-oriented and democratic one. These include not only economic reform and the creation of democratic institutions, but also the strengthening of civil society and the establishment of the genuine rule of law. How these factors are defined and interrelated is a matter of dispute, as can be seen even by comparing the views of Jeff Weintraub, Andrew Arato, Edward Friedman, and Peter Toumanoff in this volume. What follows, therefore, represents our synthesis of the ideas presented and not the consensus of the contributors.

We are inclined to favor Weintraub's distinction among the state, political society, and civil society. In a democratic country, the state is that greater entity which exercises power to preserve order and the common welfare and generally reflects the shared aspirations of its people. Civil society is that realm which is reserved to individuals and organizations for their own endeavors: the enjoyment of family life, the exercise of civil liberties, economic activities, artistic and spiritual pursuits, and such. Mediating between these two realms is political society and law. In a democratic society, the law is used by the state to establish the procedures for the functioning of political society and to regulate the activities of political society and civil society for the sake of the common good. Because this common good includes a healthy economy, the state must use law to provide the infrastructure needed to sustain the economy (such as contracts and property rights) and the limits on economic activities (such as monopolies or environmental abuses) needed to preserve the public welfare. But the role of law in a democratic society also includes the rule of law -- the understanding that law also binds the state and its officials and preserves fundamental rights to individuals and organizations in civil society. Respect for the rule of law means that actors in civil society have access to law as a means to limit state intervention as well as to regulate the actions of other individuals and organizations. Finally, political society is composed of the organizations and processes concerned with making democratic decisions about the common good and giving direction to the state and its laws. It is our contention that transitions from the all-embracing Leninist states require the emergence and strengthening of civil society, political society, and the rule of law to accompany the decentralizing and privatizing of the economy and other reforms.

There is no recipe for how each Leninist state has or can accomplish the tasks required for the transition to and consolidation of a market-oriented economy and democratic government. In many cases, the process is likely to occur in a long evolutionary period, with intermediate stages that blend socialism with economic decentralization and perhaps even authoritarianism with democratization. The move to a market-oriented economy also requires several conditions, such as those discussed by Elizabeth Clayton in this volume and by Jan S. Prybyla:

> To get to the market system, a legal infrastructure has to be put in place, property has to be privatized, a free market has to be established. The

economy has to be demonopolized, monetary and fiscal levels of government intervention in the market process have to be introduced, and the
system has to be decommunized in the structure and personnel.[21]

Many political and social changes must also take place not only to
facilitate the transition to democratic rule but to adapt to the transformation of a socialist economy. Just as there may be intermediate economic
systems between total centralization and total capitalism, the path from
totalitarianism to democracy may include a period of authoritarianism.
In authoritarian regimes, the control of the party/state over other mass
organizations and the economy is limited. Hence, even the transformation
of the Leninist state into an authoritarian one may be progress, as it may
allow for the strengthening of civil society and the emergence of the rule
of law. The erosion of the Leninist state must also involve the breakdown
of the hold of Communist ideology on the people. Ultimately, however,
the political transformation must progress beyond authoritarianism, or the
consequences will be disastrous.[22] Political decentralization must
accompany economic decentralization. Just as the Communist party must
surrender its monopoly control of property, it must also allow for the
emergence of pluralism and the creation of a multi-party system with free
elections. And it must provide the foundation for the preservation of civil
liberties, transforming from "the rule of men" to "the rule of law."

Obstacles to Reform

Evolutions from Leninism to market-oriented economies and democracies face challenges, as most of the authors in this book have noted.
According to Gomulka, the stages along the process of transformation:

> ". . .are found to involve efficiency losses due to the presence of elements
> of different, mutually incompatible systems. In such mixed systems the
> allocative and disciplinary roles of central authorities are already substan-
> tially relaxed, but competitive market pressures are not yet developed.
> During such a transition high inflation may appear in addition to low
> efficiency and slow innovation."[23]

There are also political, ideological, intellectual, and societal obstacles
to the successful transition, as both Edward Friedman and Elizabeth
Clayton noted. Politically, party/state leaders will resist transferring the
power to make decisions about production and resource distribution from
the party leaders of various levels to the managers of enterprises
(including workers' committees). Ideologically, orthodox Marxist-Leninists
always see any form of a market economy as capitalism, and see
marketization as revisionist reform. Intellectually, after decades of

socialism in the USSR, China, and Eastern Europe, people have very little knowledge of the functioning of the market or trust for its economic levers. Finally, as a society, people in Leninist states have been insulated from enterprise risks. They may resist a market economy out of fear of bankruptcy, unemployment, inflation, and other economic risks.

Many of these obstacles to economic reform have their counterpart obstacles to political reform. The vested interests and ideological convictions of the rulers cause them to be resistant to any manifestations of civil society and pluralism, including trade unions such as Solidarity, religious institutions, or any fragmentation of the unified party-state-economy-military-law-ideology-culture. If reforms are attempted, they may fall prey to a repeated cycle of reform-rectification as hard-liners reassert their power, such as happened in the PRC. Furthermore, as Robert Byrnes noted, the absence of historical experience with democratic rule or the lack of knowledge among the people about the functioning of democracy can also weaken the prospects for successful reform. Finally, the economic complacency of the people may cause them to forego political change in exchange for bread and butter. This was apparently behind the Soviet coup leaders' appeals for support when they claimed that they alone could restore the economy, and it partially explains the quiescence of the Chinese people after the Democracy Movement of 1989.

Assessing Transformations from Leninism to Democracy

Despite the seeming pessimism of many of the contributions in this volume, the events of the 1980s and early 1990s in Eastern Europe and the former Soviet Union demonstrate that the people of Leninist states are not dissuaded from seeking economic and democratic reform despite the many obstacles in their way. Why? Because as a social, political, and economic system, the Leninist state has failed. The traditional socialist pattern has exhausted its potentialities. There seems to be no alternative but to abandon the Leninist state in favor of a democratic political system and a market-oriented economy. But just as the nature of Leninism in each country was affected by its unique historical, political, and cultural circumstances, so shall it be for the path to democracy.[24]

A major distinction must be made between internally-directed and externally-guided Leninist states.[25] The former, mainly the USSR and China, had systems formed via internal revolutions. The Communist party and its leaders had rather high legitimacy. The development of these states relied primarily on their own political and economic resources, evolving over a series of ideological twists and turns. Both countries do not belong to the West, and both are influenced deeply by a history of feudal despotism.[26] As a consequence, they resisted Western democracy and a market-oriented system for a long time -- especially in China, where mass ideology intentionally equates the West with imperialism in order to provoke resistance to reforms. Although the collapse and disintegration of the USSR and CPSU happened suddenly, the Commonwealth of Independent States still faces a long and difficult transition to democracy.

Externally-guided Leninist states include those in Eastern Europe. Their existence was established and supported by external forces. Except in Yugoslavia, the Communist parties in power in these countries have never had legitimacy; therefore, they collapsed easily once the support of external forces (e.g. Moscow) was withdrawn. Most of these countries originally shared in European culture, including a legal tradition with respect for the rule of law. Thus, abandoning Leninism and turning to democracy and freedom constitute a "return to Europe" for them.[27] The ideological obstacles are few. These countries may be able to develop rapidly and to be integrated into regional capitalist economic systems such as the European Community.

The transitions of these externally-guided countries have varied. Among them East Germany was unique. It was actually annexed by West Germany and is deeply influenced by the West German pattern, resulting in the relatively easy reestablishment of civil society and the rule of law. The challenge for political society, as Stephen Szabo explained, is to balance the needs of the East and West and to prevent any influences from the East from destabilizing Germany's democracy. The other countries can be divided into two sub-types: Those where the Communist party has lost power via election and those where it gave up the privilege of permanent, monopoly power but remains in power by election.

Poland, Hungary, and Czechoslovakia are cases where, having lost its power once free elections were granted, the Communist party has been greatly weakened. Andrzej Korbonski's chapter treated these three countries in detail, so we briefly refer to the Polish experience as an illustration of this path of transition. After Solidarity was elected to power, it quickly made the decision to move rapidly and uncompromisingly to democracy and the market system. In the last quarter of 1989, it began the transition to a market system and toward a stable macroeconomy. In 1990, the government lifted restrictions on most prices and canceled all subsidies. In the middle of 1990, it adopted many measures to encourage market competition and began the privatization of small enterprises first, with larger enterprises to follow. These reforms were backed by the working class, members of which were willing to accept the low wages brought by the market and to minimize strikes. Like Poland, the Communist party in Hungary gave up monopoly power in 1989 and the elected ruling party, the Hungary Democratic Forum, introduced comprehensive reforms including marketization, privatization, and democratization. In Czechoslovakia, the end of the Communist party's power was evident in plans to promote privatization through a voucher system.

These three countries are also similar in having shared a history of Western legal tradition, as Alice Tay notes. Where they differ, according to Andrew Arato, is in the path taken to reestablish civil society and the extent to which it has been maintained.

Romania, Bulgaria, Albania and Mongolia belong to the type of externally-guided Leninist states where the Communist party did not immediately lose power even after granting free elections. In Bulgaria, the former Communist party was finally defeated in the 1991 election. The case of Romania illustrates that the popularly chosen perpetuation of Communist rule may stymie the progress towards democratic and economic reform. After the overthrow of the Ceausescu regime in the midst of a crackdown against proponents of reforms, the National Salvation Front (NSF) was elected to power. At first, the NSF included some genuine non-Communist dissenters, but these later left the party because of its empty verbiage. The consequence is that Romania remains essentially governed by Communists with no clear plans for reform. The economy is still centrally planned and has fallen into chaos. Many key governmental positions are held by former Communist leaders who hope to block the transition to democracy and a market economy.[28] And, as Robert Byrnes suggested, the foundations for civil society are bleak.

Yet, the 1989 revolution has irrevocably altered the political climate in Romania, making the return to a 1947-1987 Leninist system impossible. Both Nicholae Ceausescu's attempted crackdown and the former Communists' efforts to halt reform raise the ultimate question about transitions from Leninism to democracy and market-oriented economies: Can such reforms be stopped?

Resisting the Transition from Leninism to Freedom

Because of their common characteristics as internally-directed Leninist states, the Communist party in the People's Republic of China and in the USSR long resisted the transition to democracy and market-oriented economies, although both attempted limited reforms to various degrees. The fact that the USSR succumbed to the force of democracy after the failed coup attempt in August, 1991 is due in part to the consequences of that attempt itself and in part to the differences between the two countries.

First, in China, the leaders in power are from the first generation of the revolution, whereas in the USSR, Gorbachev was from the third generation. Thus, his commitment towards Marxist ideology was different than that of the "eight old men" in the PRC.

Second, the experiences of these countries with economic and political reform differed. The control of the economy in China is less centralized than the USSR was, making economic reforms easier to implement. In rural areas of China, the basic work unit has always been the household. This fact, coupled with other economic reforms that benefitted some sectors of the economy, generates support for the CCP from many individuals. In addition, the relative stability of the Chinese economy compared to that of the Soviet Union decreases the intensity of calls from below for reform. In the USSR, hesitation in economic reforms worsened the failing economy and intensified the crisis, leading to a critical strike by coal miners in 1991. Furthermore, the influence of political reforms such as *glastnost* only worsened the situation in the USSR because they loosened the control of the party over society. Because China retrenched on political reforms while engaging in some economic decentralization and privatization, the CCP retained its power to stabilize the political situation through repression even in the face of democratizing trends throughout Eastern Europe and the Soviet Union.

Third, the fragmented nature of the Soviet Union, attempting to blend republics with very distinct nationalities, facilitated the emergence of competing parties and political actors. In contrast, more than ninety percent of the Chinese population is Han, with the Han peoples being the majority even in the so-called "minority areas," except for Tibet. Though ethnic tension exists in some areas, the centrifugal force of nationalist sentiments that contributed to the disintegration of the USSR and threaten the stability of the Commonwealth of Independent States is absent.

Fourth, the citizens of the PRC, especially the peasants, are less educated than those in the former Soviet Union. In addition, their political culture is further removed from Western experiences than in Russia. Rather than fostering democratic urges, the Confucian culture of East Asia reinforces fatalism and passivity.

Finally, even though events in the spring of 1989 show that the Chinese people are able to rise above these influences and to push for democracy, the military crackdown of the Chinese in June of 1989 has successfully driven the proponents of democracy underground once again.[29]

In the fall of 1989, as Communist regimes in the externally-guided Leninist countries toppled one by one, it still seemed that the Communist parties in the USSR and China might be powerful enough to implement limited reforms but to resist the full transformation from Leninism to freedom. Two years later, evolving political and economic conditions undermined the ability of even a conservative coup in Russia to block the transition there, while the situation in China remains relatively stable in the short term, although not in the long term.

The attempted coup in the Soviet Union in August, 1991 (curiously headed by eight men, the same number as the leadership in the PRC!)

failed for many reasons, some of which we can touch upon simply to illustrate the difficulty of resisting the transformation of the Leninist state once it has begun. By the time the coup was attempted, there were deep internal rifts within the Communist party and within the military on which the party needed to rely to enforce its will. The party had already surrendered its position of monopoly power, and political pluralism was well under way. Communist ideology was no longer persuasive for much of the public, and public opinion was with the forces of democracy, as was demonstrated in Moscow in the days following the coup. Ironically, by sky-rocketing Boris Yeltsin to prominence as the leader of the resistance while Mikhail Gorbachev was in isolation, the junta drastically hastened the process of democratization in the Soviet Union, leading to its *de facto* dissolution within a matter of weeks and the establishment of the Commonwealth of Independent States by the end of the year. Gorbachev's attempts at compromise and moderation were no longer adequate.

In China, the political and economic situation appears to be relatively stable, although it has its vulnerabilities and must necessarily be influenced by the demise of the Soviet Union as a Communist power. Despite the apparent success of the crackdown of June 4, 1989, the ensuing rectification campaign has not been totally successful in restoring the supremacy of Communist ideology even within the party itself. Events abroad clearly indicate that the progress of socialism is not an historical necessity; rather, it is reversible. Furthermore, there are indications that, though not as extreme as the Soviet nationalist disintegration, the central government in China is losing control of the provinces and personnel at lower levels. And to the extent that the Chinese economy is productive, the bulk of its productivity is in those sectors that are more market-oriented, reinforcing support for economic reforms.[30]

The attempt to block further economic and political reforms in the PRC will ultimately fail. The first reason is that the decentralizing reforms that have occurred resulted in serious problems that require further reforms. For example, provincial and other local governments which have gained power from the central government remain influenced by the experience of centralization. They often act at the local level in ways that undermine the efficiency of the economy. In addition, the coexistence of command and market economies, with two pricing systems, increases corruption among the privileged officials and dissatisfaction among the masses. Such corruption is a leading cause of social discontent and instability.

The second reason why reform cannot be resisted in the long run is that previous reforms have created an environment and experiences that run counter to the reassertion of totalitarian control. As Peter Toumanoff argues, in a decentralizing economy, more people dare to think and act independently of the direct control of the party/state. The coexistence of command and market economies breaks the state monopoly of the economy and fosters conditions for the autonomy and self-government of individuals as well as enterprises. It requires some transformation from arbitrary administration to the rule of law.[31] The mixed economy also undermines the legitimacy of the monopolistic bureaucratic system and provides a foothold for the emergence of civil society. Finally, those who have experienced the benefits of decentralization and a privatized economy will not want to give them up. Yet, without further reform, the economy will stagnate and not be able to provide further improvement in the standard of living of the masses, another point with which we agree with Toumanoff.

The experience of the failed Soviet coup, the collapse of the USSR, and the accompanying chaos in the region have clearly alarmed the Chinese leadership and further complicated the situation in the PRC. Although pleased by the removal of the potential security threat from Moscow, the Chinese leaders are very concerned about the destabilizing spillover effects of changes in the USSR and wish to limit the impact of these trends on China as much as possible. Thus, they predict a sullen and miserable future for the East European countries and the former USSR, claiming, "the results of the drastic changes are political instability, economic recession, the downfall of the standard of living, and lost hope for the future. They enter into a stage of darkness, both economic and political."[32] Even though the PRC has expressed interest in normal relations with the Commonwealth of Independent States and all the countries of the former Soviet Union, internally, Gorbachev and Yeltsin have been seriously criticized, even accused as hidden traitors of the CPSU and renegades of the International Communist Movement. The drastic changes in the USSR appear to have reinforced the Beijing leaders' convictions that China should give priority to economic reform and exercise great caution in considering political reform. Political conservatism is favored, with suggestions that great caution be used in selecting successors in the leadership to continue the struggle against "peaceful evolution." Finally, the control of politics and ideology seem more severe than before. In fact, after the failed coup attempt in the USSR, the Chinese leadership responded with renewed repression, including a purge of the army and government.

At the grassroots, especially the Chinese intellectuals believe that the disintegration of the CPSU and the USSR demonstrates the further loss of legitimacy for Marxism-Leninism and is a tremendous blow to the Communist party even where it is still in power. They hope that the winds of change can have a profound effect, pushing the regime to reform. If the conservative leaders instead try to turn the clock back by fundamentally reversing the reform process, they might provoke a hurricane comparable to that now sweeping the former USSR. However, frightened by the uncertainty and instability in the former Soviet Union, including the danger of starvation, riots, and a reimposition of totalitarianism, the Chinese people remain more in favor of a gradual, peaceful evolution than a violent revolution.

Generally speaking, in the short term, the remaining Leninist regimes such as China may persist if their economies and their leadership remain relatively stable. This is especially true where there is no extensive civil society to generate alternative structures of authority - no Solidarity, no Boris Yeltsin, no coal miners' union. Although Kjeld Erik Brødsgaard's contribution makes the case for a repressed but nascent civil society in China following Tiananmen Square, compared to the level of civil society Arato describes in Poland and Hungary in the 1980s, the Chinese democracy movement remains only the seed of what will be required to transform the PRC.

In the long term, the advanced age of the gerontocratic rulers in China suggests that the next challenge to Leninism there cannot be far away. Just as Arendt argued about Hungary after 1954, a succession crisis could result in factional struggles for power that might reopen the door for democratic forces as leaders vie for the legitimacy of mass support.[33] If moderates gain power, further economic reform might facilitate the development of civil society and the emergence of a middle class, moving the PRC further in the evolution toward democracy. If hard-liners retain or even tighten control, however, rebellion might be provoked, with a new democracy movement risking severe bloodshed in order to hasten the transition to democracy. As J. Burkherdt claims, "The more relentlessly an institution combats the spirit of renewal, the more inevitable perhaps is its final collapse."[34] In either case, the people of China must overcome what Kamenka has argued is the temptation to replace one form of highly centralized government with another. They will also need to build a foundation for democracy through civil society and the rule of law.

The lesson of recent experiences in Eastern Europe and the former Soviet Union is that if the party/state does not resist current historical trends, Leninist societies can transition to democracy with minimum losses. If the party stubbornly clings to monopoly power, violent repression is likely to end in the party's own demise, perhaps accompanied by heavy loss of life.[35] A final outcome may also be "simply confusion, that is, the rotation in power of successive governments which fail to provide any enduring or predictable solution to the problem of institutionalizing political power."[36]

As we look to the future of those Leninist states that remain, the unanswered questions concern the duration of their totalitarian and authoritarian periods, the paths of their transitions to democracy and market-oriented economies, and the risk they face of political chaos or renewed authoritarianism. These last two risks also face the newly emerging democracies of Eastern Europe and the Commonwealth of

Independent States. On the whole, however, it appears that history has turned Marx on his head. The inherent contradictions of capitalism have not irreversibly given rise to the superior socialist state. Rather, the inherent weaknesses of the Leninist state seem to push inevitably back toward democracy and some level of a market-oriented economy. As the 20th century nears its close, how astonishing are these journeys from Leninism to freedom!

Notes

1. Stanislaw Gomulka, "Leninists to Reform: Definitions and Questions" (manuscript), 2 (quoted with permission).

2. See Ernst Kux, "Revolution in Eastern Europe -- Revolution in the West?" *Problems of Communism*, May-June, 1991, 9.

3. Carl Friedrich, "Totalitarianism," in Tom Bottomor, ed., *A Dictionary of Marxist Thought*, (London: Blackwell 1983), 478-479.

4. Karl Popper argued that "it is more difficult to pass over from totalitarianism to democracy than from democracy to totalitarianism. . . . Totalitarianism, especially in the absence of private property, completely stifles democracy." Cited from an interview in *Moscow news* No. 46, Nov. 25 - Dec. 2, 1990.

5. See Juan J. Linz. "Totalitarian and Authoritarian Regimes," in *The Handbook of Political Science*, edited by Fred I. Greenstein and Nelson W. Polsby (Reading, MA: Addison-Wesley, 1975), Vol. 3, 264.

6. I prefer the term "Leninist" to "Communist" or "socialist" because these countries are based upon the Leninist party leadership system and are far from what Marx expounded about socialism.

7. Cited in Ernst Kux. "Revolution in Eastern Europe", 3.

8. Paul Hollander. "Communism and Its Discontents," in *Problems of Communism*, May-June 1991, 116.

9. Ernst Kux, "Revolution in Eastern Europe," 2.

10. Samuel Huntington. "Will More Countries Become Democratic?" *Political Science Quarterly* (Summer, 1984), 217.

11. Juan Linz, Seymour Martin Lipset, and Larry Diamond. *Democracy in Developing Countries: Asia* (Boulder, CO: Lynne Reiner, 1989), xix.

12. Hollander, "Communism and Its Discontents," 116.

13. Adam Przeworski. *Democracy and the Market: Political and Economic Reforms in Eastern Europe and Latin America* (Cambridge: Cambridge University Press, 1991), 1.

14. Hannah Arendt, "Epilogue: Reflections on the Hungarian Revolution," in *Totalitarianism*, cited in Edward Friedman, "Alternatives to Leninist Democratization," manuscript, 2.

15. *Complete Works of Lenin* (English Edition) (Moscow: Progress Publishers, 1965), Vol. 29, 535.

16. *The Selected Works of Lenin* (Moscow: Foreign Languages Publishing House, 1952) (English Edition), Vol. 2, 480-481.

17. Moshe Lewin. *The Gorbachev Phenomenon* (London: Radius, 1988), 113.

18. Michel Reiman. *The Birth of Stalinism*, (Bloomington: Indiana University Press, 1987), 120.

19. Cited from Jean Elleistein, *Historic au "Phenomena Stalinism"* (Paris: Bernare Gresset, 1975), Chinese version (Hangzhou: Current Affairs Press, 1986), 128.

20. See Barrington Moore, Jr. *Social Origins of Dictatorship and Democracy* (Boston: Beacon Press, 1966), xvi.

21. Jan S. Prybyla, "The Road from Socialism: Why, Where, What and How?", *Problems of Communism*, (Jan-April, 1991), 1.

22. Samuel Huntington. "Huntington on Authoritarianism," quoted from Liu Jun and Li Lin, eds. *Neo-authoritarianism* (Beijing College of Economics Press, April 1989), 313-314.

23. S. Gomulka, "Leninists to Reform," 8.

24. See Jan S. Prybyla, "The Road From Socialism," 1.

25. See Gilbert Rozman, "Stages in the Reform and the Dismantling of Socialism in China and the Soviet Union," (manuscript), 2-3 quoted with permission.

26. Su Shaozhi. "The Formation and Characteristics of China's Existing System," (in "Understanding Democratic Reform in China," a Bradley Institute for Democracy *Papers on Democracy*, 1990), 5.

27. Ernst Kux, "Revolution in Eastern Europe," 1.

28. See Matei Calinescu and Vladimir Tismaneau, "The 1989 Revolution and Romania's Future," *Problems of Communism*, January-April, 1991, 42-59.

29. See A. Doak Barnett, *After Deng, What? Will China Follow the USSR?* (Washington: The Johns Hopkins Foreign Policy Institute, 1991), 4-5.

30. This analysis is based upon remarks by Barrett McCormick, Assistant Professor of Political Science at Marquette University, in a roundtable discussion sponsored by the Bradley Institute for Democracy in May, 1991.

31. Recall that Alice Tay sees some favorable developments among Chinese lawyers and the judiciary in this respect.

32. Ren Miu Re Bao, in Commentary, *People's Daily*, December 29, 1991.

33. Hannah Arendt. "Epilogue: Reflections on the Hungarian Revolution," in *Totalitarianism*, cited in Edward Friedman, "Alternatives to Leninist Democratization," manuscript, 2.

34. Jacob Burkherdt. *On the Study of History*, Peter Gauz, ed. (Munich, Beck, 1984), 213.

35. Su Shaozhi. "Democratic Reform and the Future of China," (in "Understanding Democratic Reform in China," a Bradley Institute for Democracy *Papers on Democracy*, 1990), 40-41.

36. Guillermo O'Donnell, Philip C. Schmitter, and Laurence Whitehead. *Transition from Authoritarian Rule* (Baltimore: The Johns Hopkins University Press, 1986), 3.

About the Contributors

Editor: **Dr. Margaret Latus Nugent**, Assistant Director of the Bradley Institute for Democracy and Public Values at Marquette University since 1988, received her M.A. and Ph.D. from the Politics Department of Princeton. She has taught political science at the College of the Holy Cross and at Marquette. In addition to organizing the Bradley Institute's interdisciplinary conference on democratization in Eastern Europe, the Soviet Union, and China, she also helps arrange the Institutes annual seminar series on democratic issues, organized a previous conference on campaign finance reform, and edited the volume that stemmed from that conference.

Dr. Andrew Arato, Professor of Sociology at the New School for Social Research, obtained his M.A. in history from the University and conducted research at the J.W. Goethe University in Frankfurt and the Institute for Sociological Research of the Hungarian Academy of Science before completing his Ph.D. in history from the University of Chicago. His recent scholarship includes co-editing *Gorbachev: The Debate* (1989) and *Transition: The Dilemmas of System Change in Hungary* (1991), co-authoring *Civil Society and Political Theory* (1991), and authoring *From Neo-Marxism to Civil Society: Studies in the Critical Sociology of Soviet Type Societies* (1991) and *Civil Society in the Transition: A Comparative Study of the Hungarian Case* (forthcoming).

Dr. Kjeld Erik Brødsgaard is an Associate Professor in Modern and Contemporary East Asian History at the East Asian Institute, the University of Copenhagen. He has authored ten books or monographs about East Asian affairs, including *Readjustment and Reform in the Chinese Economy, 1953-1986* (1989) and *The Chinese Reforms: Progress and Issues* (1990). He holds a cand.mag. degree and a Ph.D. degree from the University of Copenhagen, has been a member of the Board of the Center for East and Southeast Asian Studies of the University of Copenhagen since 1986, and was its Director from 1987-1991.

Dr. Robert F. Byrnes, Distinguished Professor of History at Indiana University, is a specialist in Russian and East European history who was director of Indiana University's Russian and East European Institute from 1959-1963 and from 1971-1975. In addition to his M.A. and Ph.D. from Harvard University, he has received honorary doctoral degrees and prestigious awards from five colleges and universities. General editor of a seven-volume study of "East Central Europe Under the Communists,"

Dr. Byrnes has authored 14 other books on French, Russian, and East European history, lectured throughout the world, and travelled extensively within the USSR and Eastern Europe.

Dr. Elizabeth Clayton is Professor of Economics and Associate Vice Chancellor for Research at the University of Missouri in St. Louis. She received a doctorate in economics at the University of Washington in Seattle and has been a fellow at Harvard University Law School and at the Kennan Institute for Advanced Russian Studies of the Woodrow Wilson International Center for Scholars in Washington, D.C. She is a former president of the Midwest Economics Association and President of the Association for Comparative Economic Studies. She has written many articles on Soviet economic problems and appeared on the television series "Comrades" sponsored by Station WGBH-Boston. She has been a Visiting Professor of Law and Economics at Moscow State University in the Soviet Union.

Dr. Edward Friedman, a Professor of Political Science and Director of the Center for East Asian Studies at the University of Wisconsin, Madison, was awarded his M.A. and Ph.D. from Harvard. His edited volume, *Democratization: Generalizing the East Asian Experience*, the result of a major international conference, is forthcoming, as is *Chinese Village, Socialist State*. In the summer of 1990, Professor Friedman, who has lived and worked in diverse Leninist or once Leninist states such as Cuba, Cambodia, East Germany, the Soviet Union, and China, was selected by the National Endowment for Humanities to direct a seminar for college faculty on Democratizing Leninist Systems.

Dr. Marshall I. Goldman is the Kathryn W. Davis Professor of Soviet Economics at Wellesley College and the Associate Director of the Russian Research Center at Harvard University. He earned an M.A. and Ph.D. from Harvard University, as well as an honorary Doctor of Laws Degree from the University of Massachusetts, Amherst in 1985. A frequent visitor to the Soviet Union, he enjoys international recognition as an authority on its economy, environmental concerns, and foreign relations. His publications include: *Gorbachev's Challenge: Economic Reform in the Age of High Technology* (1987), *The USSR in Crisis: The Failure of an Economic Model* (1983), and *What Went Wrong With Perestroika* (1991).

Dr. Merle Goldman is Professor of History at Boston University and a research associate at the John K. Fairbank Center for East Asian Research of Harvard University. Having received an M.S. from Radcliffe and a Ph.D. in History and Far Eastern Languages from Harvard University, among the many books she has authored or edited are *China's Intellectuals: Advise and Dissent* (1981), *China's Intellectuals and the State: In Search of a New Relationship in the People's Republic of China* (1987), and *Science and Technology in Post-Mao China* (1989).

Dr. Barbara Jelavich is another Distinguished Professor of History from the University of Indiana. Having received her M.A., and Ph.D. in history from the University of California, Berkeley, she has written over 15 books and many articles focusing primarily on the history of Russia and the Balkans. Her most recent monographs include *History of the Balkans: Eighteenth and Nineteenth Centuries* (1983), *History of the Balkans: Twentieth Century* (1983), and *Russia and the Formation of the Romanian National State* (1984).

Dr. Eugene Kamenka, an internationally known expert on Marxism, received his Ph.D. at the Australian National University. He is Professor of the History of Ideas in the Institute of Advanced Studies of the Australian National University in Canberra, a Fellow of the Academy of the Social Sciences in Australia, and a Fellow of the Australian Academy of the Humanities. His many publications include *The Ethical Foundations of Marxism*, *Marxism and Ethics*, *The Portable Karl Marx*, and *Bureaucracy*. He has edited the series *Ideas and Ideologies*, including volumes on *Intellectuals* and *Revolution and Community as a Social Ideal*, as well as those volumes co-edited with his wife, Dr. Alice Tay.

Dr. Andrzej Korbonski, is Professor of Political Science and Director of the Center for Russian and East European Studies at the University of California, Los Angeles. Born in Poland, he received his M.A. in economics from Columbia University, and his Ph.D. in public law and government from Columbia. He has been a consultant to Radio Free Europe, the RAND Corporation, and the U.S. Department of State, has received numerous honors and fellowships, and has written extensively on various aspects of Soviet and East European politics and economics in *Comparative Politics*, *Current History*, *Slavic Review*, *World Politics*, and *Studies in Comparative Politics*, and many other journals and books.

Professor Su Shaozhi is one of the leading Chinese intellectuals calling for democratic reform in the Peoples' Republic of China and an internationally known expert on Marxism. Prior to his departure from China following the events of June, 1989, Professor Su served as Professor in the Graduate School of the Chinese Academy of Social Sciences and Research Professor in the Institute of Marxism, Leninism, and Mao Zedong Thought from 1982-1989, and as Director of that Institute from 1982-1987. Having received his B.A. from Chongquing University in 1945 and his M.A. from Nankai Institute of Economics in 1949, he also taught at Fudan University, and served as editor of the Theoretical Department of the *People's Daily* from 1963-1979. A Visiting Professor at the Bradley Institute for Democracy and Public Values from 1989-1991, his books in English include *Democratization and Reform* (1989), *Marxism in China* (1983), and *Democracy and Socialism in China* (1982). He has also published nine books in Chinese, and more than 30 articles in different languages beyond the more than 250 articles he has published in Chinese.

Dr. Stephen F. Szabo is Associate Dean for Academic Affairs, the Paul H. Nitze School of Advanced International Studies, Johns Hopkins University, a position he has held since September 1990. Prior to that he was Associate Dean and Professor of National Security Affairs, the National War College, Washington, D.C., from 1982 to 1990 and Professorial Lecturer in European Studies for the School of Advanced International Studies, Johns Hopkins University. He has served as Chairman of West European Studies of the Foreign Service Institute, U.S. Department of State and has been an adjunct professor at George Washington University, the University of Virginia, and Georgetown University, the school from which he received his Ph.D. His publications include *The Successor Generation: International Perspectives of Postwar Europeans, The Bundeswehr and Western Security*, and *The Changing Politics of German Security.*

Dr. Alice Ehr-Soon Tay, Barrister-at-Law of Lincoln's Inn (London), Ph.D. (Australian National University), and LL.D., honoris causa (Edinburgh), is Challis Professor of Jurisprudence in the University of Sydney, a Fellow of the Academy of the Social Sciences in Australia, and Academicien titulaire of the International Academy of Comparative Law in Paris. Dr. Tay has published extensively in areas of common law, comparative law, jurisprudence, human rights, and socialist law and legal systems, including *Law in China -- Imperial, Republic, Communist*, and *Introducing Chinese Law for Foreign Businessmen and Investors*. With her husband, Eugene Kamenka, she has edited, among others, the volumes *Law and Society, Human Rights, Justice*, and *Law and Social Control*. President of the International Association for Philosophy of Law and Social Philosophy, she is also an Honorary Professor of Law in the South Central Institute of Political Science and Law (Wuhan, People's Republic of China) -- a function she has chosen not to exercise since the tragic events which took place in China in May/June 1989.

Dr. Peter Toumanoff received an M.A. and Ph.D. in economics from the University of Washington. His 1977-78 fellowship from the International Research and Exchanges Board resulted in articles in the *Journal of Economic History* and *Economic Development and Cultural Change*. His interest in economic reforms extends to the many attempts to reform Soviet industry from 1957 to the present, with publications appearing in *Soviet Union/Union Sovietique* and *Comparative Economic Studies*. In 1990, he received support from the Council on Economic Priorities to join a team of Soviet and American researchers to investigate the problems and possibilities of converting the defense industries of both nations to civilian production. He has also been the recipient of several grants from the Bradley Institute for Democracy and Public Values.

Dr. Jeff Weintraub, a Monnet Fellow at the European University Institute in Florence, Italy for 1991-92 and a Visiting Associate Professor of Political Science at Williams College for 1992-93, received his M.Sc. from the London School of Economics and Political Science and his Ph.D. in sociology from the University of California, Berkeley. His publications include: *Freedom and Community: The Republican Virtue Tradition and the Sociology of Liberty*, and the edited volumes *Democratization in Central/Eastern Europe and Latin America: Civil Society, Political Society, and the State*, and *The Theory and Politics of the Public/Private Distinction*.

About the Bradley Institute for Democracy and Public Values

On July 1, 1986, the Bradley Institute for Democracy and Public Values began operations at Marquette University. Funded originally by grants from the Bradley Foundation, the mission of the Institute is to promote the study, understanding, and functioning of democratic politics and democratic values. To this end, we support research, teaching, and public outreach that helps leaders and individuals to comprehend democracy and public values.

Selected Bibliography

Adam, Jan. 1991. *Economic Reforms and the Welfare System in the USSR, Poland and Hungary: Social Contract in Transformation.* London: Macmillan.

Amsden, Alice H. 1991. "Diffusion of Development: The Late-Industrializing Model and Greater East Asia." *The American Economic Review* 81: 282-286.

Barzel, Y. 1989. *Economic Analysis of Property Rights.* Cambridge: Cambridge University Press.

Becker, Carl L. 1984. *How New Will the Better World Be. A Discussion of Post-War Reconstruction.* New York: Knopf.

Berdyaev, Nicholas A. 1961. *The Origin of Russian Communism.* Ann Arbor: Michigan.

Berliner, Joseph. 1976. *The Innovation Decision in Soviet Industry.* Cambridge: The MIT Press.

Black, Cyril E. 1986. *Understanding Soviet Politics. The Perspective of Russian History.* Boulder: Westview.

Brinkerhoff, D.W. and A.A. Goldsmith. 1990. *Institutional Sustainability in Agriculture and Rural Develoment: A Global Perspective.* New York: Praeger.

Brødsgaard, Kjeld Erik. 1991. "China's Political Economy in the Nineties," *China Report*, Vol. 27, No. 3: 177-196.

_____. 1981. "The Democracy Movement in China, 1978-79: Opposition Movements, Wall Poster Campaigns, and Underground Journals," *Asian Survey*, Vol. XXI, No. 7 (July).

_____. 1987. "Economic and Political Reform in Post-Mao China," *Copenhagen Papers in East and Southeast Asian Studies*, 1: 31-56.

Bunce, Valerie. 1990. "The Struggle for Liberal Democracy in Eastern Europe," *World Policy Journal*, Vol. 7, No. 3, Summer, 395-430.

Butterfield, Jim. 1990. "Devolution in Decisionmaking and Organizational Change in Soviet Agriculture." in William Moskoff, ed., *Perestroika in the Countryside: Agricultural Reform in the Gorbachev Era*, 19-46. New York: M.E. Sharpe.

Conquest, Robert. 1980. *We and They.* London: Temple Smith.

Crummey, Robert O. 1987. *The Formation of Muscovy, 1304-1613.* London: Longmans.

Custine, Marquis Astolphe de. 1951. *Journey for Our Time*. Translated and edited by P. P. Kohler. Chicago: Regnery.

Daniels, Robert V. 1988. *Is Russia Reformable? Change and Resistance from Stalin to Gorbachev*. Boulder: Westview.

di Palma, Guiseppe. 1991. "Legitimation from the Top to Civil Society: Politico-Cultural Change in Eastern Europe," *World Politics*, Vol. 44, No. 1, October, 49-80.

Dvornik, Francis. 1962. *The Slavs in European History and Civilization*. New Brunswick: Rutgers.

Dyker, David. 1985. *The Future of the Soviet Economic Planning System*, Armonk, New York: M.E. Sharpe Inc.

Ekiert, Grzegorz. 1991. "Democratization Processes in East Central Europe: A Theoretical Reconsideration," *British Journal of Political Science*, Vol. 21, Part 3, July, 285-313.

Fedotov, George P. 1960. *The Russian Religious Mind*. Two volumes. Cambridge: Harvard.

Friedman, Edward. 1989. "Theorizing the Democratization of China's Leninist State," in Arif Dirlik and Maurice Meisner, eds., *Marxism and the Chinese Experience*, 171-189. Armonk, New York: M.E. Sharpe.

Gati, Charles. 1990. *The Bloc That Failed: East European Relations in Transition*. Bloomington: Indiana.

Gray, Cheryl. 1991. "Economic Transformation: Issues, Progress, and Prospects," in *Transition* 5: 7-9.

Guroff, Gregory, and Fred V. Carstensen, eds. 1983. *Entrepreneurship in Imperial Russia and the Soviet Union*. Princeton: Princeton University Press.

Halpern, Nina P. 1991. "Economic Reform and Democratization," in Richard Baum, ed., *Reform and Reaction in Post-Mao China*, 38-59. London: Routledge.

Hammer, Darrell P. 1990. *The USSR: The Politics of Oligarchy*. Third edition. Boulder: Westview.

Hanson, Philip. 1990. "Property Rights in the New Phase of Reforms." *Soviet Economy* 6: 95-124.

Harding, Harry. 1986. "Political Development in Post-Mao China," in Doak Barnett and Ralph N. Clough, eds., *Modernizing China: Post Mao Reform and Development*, 13-37. Boulder and London: Westview Press.

Held, David. 1986. Liberalism, Marxism and the Future Direction of Public Policy," in Peter Nolan and Suzanne Paine, *Rethinking Socialist Economics*, 13-34. Oxford: Polity Press.

Heller, Mikhail, and Aleksandr Nekrich. 1986. *Utopia in Power: The History of the Soviet Union from 1917 to the Present*. New York: Summit Books.

Kaminski, Bartlomiej. 1991. *The Collapse of State Socialism: The Case of Poland*. Princeton, N.J.: Princeton University Press, 1991.

Keane, John. 1988. *Civil Society and the State*. London: Verso.

Keenan, Edward R. 1986. "Muscovite Political Folkways." *Russian Review* 40: 115-181.

Kennedy, Michael D. 1990. "The Intelligentsia in the Constitution of Civil Societies and Post-Communist Regimes in Hungary and Poland," The University of Michigan, *CSST Working Papers*, No. 45, July.

Kligman, Gail. 1990. "Reclaiming the Public: A Reflexion on Recreating Civil Society in Romania," *East European Politics and Society*, Vol. 4, No. 3, Fall, 393-438.

Kolakowski, Leszek. 1991. "The Postrevolutionary Hangover," *Journal of Democracy*, Vol. 2, No. 3, Summer, 70-74.

Korbonski, Andrzej. 1991. "Reform In Poland," In Ilpyong J. Kim and Jane S. Zacek, eds. *Reform and Transformation in Communist Systems: Comparative Perspectives, 241-259*. New York: Paragon House.

_____. 1975. "Liberalization Processes," in Carmelo Mesa-Lago and Carl Beck, eds. *Comparative Socialist Systems: Essays on Politics and Economics*, 192-214. Pittsburgh: University of Pittsburgh Center for International Studies.

_____. 1972. "Comparing Liberalization Processes in Eastern Europe," *Comparative Politics*, Vol. 4, No. 2, January, 231-249.

Lavigne, M. 1990. *Financing the Transition in the USSR: The Shatalin Plan and the Soviet Economy*. New York: Institute for East-West Security Studies.

Lewin, Moshe. 1988. *The Gorbachev Phenomenon*. Berkeley: University of California Press.

Linz, Susan, and William Moskoff, eds. 1988. *Reorganization and Reform in the Soviet Economy*. Armonk, NY: M.E. Sharpe Inc.

Manoharan, T. 1988. "Current Rural Organizational Structure in the PRC: An Overview", *Copenhagen Discussion Papers*, No. 2, December.

Moskoff, William, ed. 1990. *Perestroika in the Countryside: Agricultural Reform in the Gorbachev Era*. New York: M.E. Sharpe.

Nove, Alec. 1969. *An Economic History of the USSR*, Baltimore: Penguin Books Inc.

O'Donnell, Guillermo, and Philippe C. Schmitter. 1989. *Transitions from Authoritarian Rule: Tentative Conclusions*. Baltimore and London: The Johns Hopkins Press.

Olson, Mancur. 1971. *The Logic of Collective Action*. Cambridge: Harvard University Press.

_____. 1982. *The Rise and Decline of Nations*, New Haven: Yale University Press.

Pelczynski, Z.A. 1988. "Solidarity and the 'Rebirth of Civil Society' in Poland," in John Keane, ed. *Civil Society and the State*, 361-380. London and New York: Verso.

Pipes, Richard. 1990. *The Russian Revolution, 1899-1919*. London: Collins Harvill.

_____. 1974. *Russia under the Old Regime*. New York: Scribner's.

_____. 1984. "Can the Soviet Union Reform?" *Foreign Affairs* 63: 47-61.

Przeworski, Adam. 1991. *Democracy and the Market*. Cambridge and New York: Cambridge University Press.

Pye, Lucian W. 1991. "The State and the Individual: An Overview Interpretation," *The China Quarterly*, No. 127, September, 443-466.

Raeff, Marc. 1984. *Understanding Imperial Russia. State and Society in the Old Regime*. New York: Columbia.

Rowe, William T. 1990. "The Public Sphere in Modern China, *Modern China*, July, 309-329.

Tony Saich, ed. 1990. *The Chinese People's Movement*. New York: M.E: Sharpe.

Schelting, Alexander von. 1948. *Russland und Europa in russischen Geschichtsdenken*. Bern: Francke.

Schiller, R., M. Boycko, and V. Korobov. 1991. "Popular Attitudes toward Free Markets." *The American Economic Review* 81:385-400.

Schmitter, Philippe C. and Terry Lynn Karl. 1991. " What Democracy Is . . . and Is Not," *Journal of Democracy*, Vol. 2, No.3, Summer, 75-87.

Schopflin, George. 1990. "The End of Communism in Eastern Europe," *International Affairs* (London), Vol. 66, No.1, 3-16.

Seymour, James D. 1980. *The Fifth Modernization: China's Human Rights Movement, 1978-1979*. New York: Earl M. Coleman Enterprises.

Sobell, Vlad. 1988. "Czechoslovakia: The Legacy of Normalization," *East European Politics and Society*, Vol. 2, No.1, Winter, 36-68.

Strand, David. 1989. *Rickshaw Beijing: City People and Politics in the 1920s*. Berkeley: University of California Press.

_____. 1990. "Protest in Beijing: Civil Society and Public Sphere in Beijing," *Problems of Communism*, Vol. 39, No. 3, May-June, 1-19.

Tatu, Michele. 1970. *Power in the Kremlin: From Khrushchev to Kosygin*. New York: Viking.

Tocqueville, Alexis de. 1964. *L'Ancien Regime et la Revolution*. Paris: Gallimard.

Tucker, Robert C. 1987. *Political Culture and Leadership in Soviet Russia: From Lenin to Gorbachev*. New York: Norton.

Walder, Andrew. 1991. "Social Structure and Political Authority: China's Evolving Polity," in Ramon, H. Myers, ed. *Two Societies in Opposition: The Republic of China and the People's Republic of China after Forty Years*, 341-361. Stanford, California: Hoover Institution Press.

Wigmore, J.H. 1990. "Economic Transformation: Issues, Progress, and Prospects." *Transition* 2:7.

Index